THE MEMOIRS OF
JAMES STEPHEN

Memoirs of James Stephen written by himself for the use of his children commenced June 6th 1819 ætat: 60

"Thou O God hast taught me from my youth up untill now; therefore will I tell of thy wondrous works "

O what great troubles & adversities hast thou shewed me, and yet didst thou turn and refresh me; yea & broughtest me from the deep of the earth again .

Facsimile of MS. title-page in James Stephen's
handwriting

THE MEMOIRS OF JAMES STEPHEN

Written by Himself for the Use of His Children

Edited with an Introduction by
MERLE M. BEVINGTON

With a Foreword by
CANON CHARLES SMYTH

1954
THE HOGARTH PRESS
LONDON

Published by
THE HOGARTH PRESS LTD
LONDON
*
CLARKE, IRWIN AND CO. LTD
TORONTO

CONTENTS

CONTENTS

ILLUSTRATIONS

Foreword

THERE is a remarkable passage in Fitzjames Stephen's *Essays by a Barrister* (1862) in which he writes: 'The *Great Eastern*, or some of her successors, will perhaps defy the roll of the Atlantic, and cross the seas without allowing their passengers to feel that they had left the firm land. The voyage from the cradle to the gave may come to be performed with similar facility. Progress and science may, perhaps, enable untold millions to live and die without a care, without a pang, without an anxiety. They will have a pleasant passage, and plenty of brilliant conversation. They will wonder that men ever believed at all in clanging fights, and blazing towns, and sinking ships, and praying hands; and, when they come to the end of their course, they will go their way, and the place thereof will know them no more. But it seems unlikely that they will have such a knowledge of the great ocean on which they sail, with its storms and wrecks, its currents and icebergs, its huge waves and mighty winds, as those who battled with it for years together in the little craft, which, if they had few other merits, brought those who navigated them full into the presence of time and eternity, their Maker and themselves, and forced them to have some definite views of their relations to them and to each other.'

It would be difficult to suggest a better introduction to the private *Memoirs* of the author's grandfather, hitherto unpublished, but now, by the initiative and the generosity of Miss Dorothea Stephen, made available, and skilfully edited by a distinguished American scholar, Professor Merle M. Bevington, of Duke University, North Carolina. James Stephen was one of the giants of the Clapham 'Sect' whose multifarious achievements in the service of God and of their fellow men have lately been recorded in Dr. Ernest Marshall Howse's *Saints in Politics*. His assiduous industry, his indomitable resolution, and the relentless logic of his legal mind, made him a formidable controversialist in the Anti-

Slavery camp. He was a man of volcanic personality: as Zachary Macaulay once remarked to George Stephen, 'In anger, your father is terrific.'' His unfinished autobiography is distinguished by the same "terrific" quality, and has the makings of a minor classic. It is a document of primary importance for the social historian of the period: but in it the general reader will discover descriptive passages which, for their literary power and intensity, are comparable only with James Hogg's *The Private Memoirs and Confessions of a Justified Sinner* (1824). One word of caution may be necessary. That Stephen had a powerful and an active conscience is self-evident; but sometimes men who are deeply and acutely conscientious have strange blind spots. Nobody who has read the *Confessions* of St. Augustine will lightly bring the charge of hypocrisy against the author of these *Memoirs*.

CHARLES SMYTH

Introduction

WHEN James Stephen sat down on June 6, 1819, to begin the writing of these *Memoirs*, he could look back upon sixty-one years of a life that, although it had been difficult in its beginnings, was a successful one. He was a Master in Chancery with a competence earned from his profession which had enabled him to give his children the comforts and the kind of education which had been denied him. He was the friend, neighbour, and brother-in-law of William Wilberforce, the man whom he called "the greatest friend of God and man that modern ages have produced." His daughters were happily married: Sibella to W. A. Garrett, who had been second wrangler and first Smith's prizeman at Cambridge in 1804 and was to become a successful barrister and a forceful writer in defence of Evangelical principles; Anne Mary to Thomas Edward Dicey, who had been senior wrangler at Cambridge in 1811 and was now the proprietor of the *Northampton Mercury*, one of the oldest and most respected of provincial newspapers in England. Stephen's sons were on the way to success in their professions: William was a quiet, hard-working country clergyman at Bledlow, Bucks, carrying on the Evangelical tradition; Henry John was a barrister working on the *Treatise on Pleading* which was to be the standard work on the subject for a hundred years; James was already successful in the private practice of law and as counsel to the colonial department of government was preparing to be the most energetic and effective permanent under-secretary that the colonial office has ever known; George, after a brief and undistinguished stay at Cambridge, had settled down and was apprenticed to the solicitor to the Bank of England.

Stephen could not, of course, know that he had yet thirteen years to live, only one year short of the time when final success would come to the cause to which he had given the major effort of his life, the abolition of slavery in British possessions throughout the world. Nor could he know of the

numerous direct descendants in the four generations following him who would add lustre to the name of Stephen: in
public service, in the legal profession, in scholarship, in literature and the arts. I shall not here name them but refer the
reader to the genealogical table which is appended to the
Memoirs. Certainly there are few families which, in the last
century and a half, have contributed so much and so
variously as have the Stephens to the intellectual life of
England.

What Stephen intended in the *Memoirs* was a complete
autobiography, at least as far as the time of his retirement
from the House of Commons in 1815, but a host of memories
and a natural tendency to prolixity made him linger over his
early years. Other labours, particularly in behalf of the negro
slaves, kept him for weeks and months at a time from writing
in this book meant for his children and his children's children,
and the result is a fragment—though a long one, indeed—
which tells the story of only his first twenty-five years, to the
time of his marriage in June, 1783. I shall not spoil a good
story by recounting the events of those years, but a brief
sketch of the remaining two-thirds of James Stephen's life is
in order.

Late in October, 1783, four months after his marriage,
James Stephen, a briefless barrister dependent upon his
brother for financial support, sailed for St. Christopher's in
the West Indies, leaving his wife behind in England. On the
way out the ship touched at Barbados, and Stephen, through
a letter of introduction given him by a London merchant,
met and was entertained at dinner by a local trader. A principal subject of dinner conversation was the approaching
trial of four negro slaves accused of murdering a white man.
From the talk it was apparent that Stephen's dinner companions doubted the guilt of the accused; it was apparent
also that they had little expectation that the court would
acquit the unlucky negroes. Out of curiosity Stephen
attended the trial. He was shocked by what he saw and by
the contrast between the orderly procedure of an English
criminal court, with its scrupulous care for the rights of an
accused person, and the summary proceedings in this Barbados court. The filthily-clad, frightened negroes sat in the

dock with their wrists painfully bound together; there was no arraignment, no formal charge, and no jury; they were bullied by a judge who assumed their guilt and convicted them on the unsupported evidence of an hysterical girl who was threatened with horrible punishment if she held back anything that made against the prisoners, though "no caution whatever was given as to any sin or danger on the opposite side." Stephen left the courtroom "overpowered by disgust and indignation" at what he had seen and heard. The lawyer and the humanitarian in him were equally revolted. When he learned later that two of the negroes had been spared by proof of an unquestionable alibi, yet that the other two, convicted on the same evidence, which had named all four, had had executed upon them the sentence of "exemplary death" by being burnt alive, and when he saw how callous and unmoved by the incident were the otherwise decent and kindly people who owned slaves, he made a solemn resolution never to be the owner of a slave. This experience in Barbados Stephen always considered the turning point in his life, and probably rightly so, for without it he might never have met William Wilberforce. The course of his life and its meaning to him would have been greatly different.

At St. Christopher's Stephen practised at the bar. He was soon able to send for his wife, and prospered enough that he could return with his family to spend the winter of 1788–89 in England, where his third son, James, was born. At this time he made himself known personally to Wilberforce, with whom he had already corresponded about the condition of negro slaves in the West Indies. He continued to be a voluminous reporter, though he prudently kept his activities secret from his island friends. In the five years from 1789 to 1794 Stephen prospered, chiefly from his being employed by American shipowners whose cargoes had been brought as prizes into the harbour at St. Christopher's, and he returned permanently with his growing family to England. Because of his recent experience, he easily found employment in the Prize Appeal Court of the Privy Council, commonly known as the "Cockpit," where he had a leading share of the business until he was appointed a Master in Chancery in 1811.

Shortly after his return to England, Stephen, with his family, occupied a house on Clapham Common, where he might live as a neighbour to William Wilberforce and Zachary Macaulay and the three of them might work together for the abolition of the slave trade. When Stephen's wife died in 1796, he turned to Wilberforce for consolation in his sorrow. What had been a working arrangement became an affectionate relationship. The intimacy of their friendship deepened, and by 1800, when Stephen married Wilberforce's sister, the widow of the Rev. Dr. Clarke of Hull, he had been carried by the persuasiveness of his urbane and saintly friend into wholehearted participation in the Evangelical zeal of his friends. Stephen took his place in one of the most remarkable groups of influential laymen in the history of the Church of England. The illustrious company is memorialised by a tablet built into the south wall of Clapham Parish Church in 1919:

LET US PRAISE GOD

for the memory and example of all the faithful departed who have worshipped in this Church, and especially for the undernamed Servants of Christ sometime called

"THE CLAPHAM SECT"

who in the latter part of the XVIIIth and the early part of the XIXth centuries laboured so abundantly for the increase of National Righteousness and the Conversion of the Heathen and rested not until the curse of slavery was swept away from all parts of the British Dominions—

CHARLES GRANT	HENRY THORNTON
ZACHARY MACAULAY	JOHN THORNTON
GRANVILLE SHARP	HENRY VENN
	(Curate of Clapham)
JOHN SHORE	JOHN VENN
(Lord Teignmouth)	(Rector of Clapham)
JAMES STEPHEN	WILLIAM WILBERFORCE

"O God, we have heard with our ears, and our fathers have declared unto us, the noble works that thou didst in their days, and in the old time before them."

It might be said of Wilberforce and Macaulay that they were led into the anti-slavery cause by their Evangelical zeal and Christian humanitarianism. The obverse is true of Stephen: he began with a passionate devotion to the cause of the slaves and through the influence of his Clapham surroundings proceeded to a wholehearted acceptance of Evangelical doctrine. When a colonial opponent in pamphlet warfare sneered at him as a fanatical "saint" and urged readers to dismiss anti-slavery agitation as a by-product of religious "enthusiasm," Stephen was quick to set him right. In the Preface to the second volume of his *Slavery Delineated* (1830) he wrote:

> There is one imputation, indeed, which, though not ill calculated, I fear, to enlist strong prejudices against any advocate of a cause like this, with no small part of the community, I cannot desire to contradict; but rather wish, that when fairly interpreted, it were true to a greater extent than it really is. I mean the charge, mixed up with almost every invective of my colonial enemies, that I am actuated by such a zeal for Christian doctrines and principles, as they call enthusiasm and fanaticism; or that I am a character, their familiar name for which I will not quote, because it is a most irreverent, not to say impious use, for derisive purposes, of a scriptural term, appropriate to the venerated first founders of our faith.
>
> Far be it from me to disclaim, as motives of my zeal in this great cause, the fear of God and a sense of Christian duty; but I will not needlessly leave to my opponents the benefit of those prejudices to which they appeal; and, therefore, will not scruple to say, that if my hostility to West Indies slavery were truly imputable to zeal for the peculiar doctrines of the gospel, the effect must have preceded its cause.
>
> When I first knew the West Indies, I was a very young man, and not less ignorant and regardless of Christianity, or of all, at least, that exclusively belongs to it, than young men of my own sphere of life then too generally were. I had early imbibed such theological opinions as are commonly called liberal; and though religion was not wholly left out of my scheme, either in theory or practice, it was a religion in which not only Christians of the lowest standard, but enlightened heathens, might have con-

curred; nor can any man be more disposed than I then was to despise, as narrowmindedness and bigotry, those views which I am now supposed, whether justly or not, to entertain. Yet I can truly say, and appeal to my known conduct in proof of it, that I no sooner personally knew what negro slavery is, in its odious practice and effects, than I conceived and avowed for it all the detestation that I at this moment feel, regarded it as the greatest evil that ever afflicted suffering humanity, and the most opprobrious crime of my country, and devoted my future life, as far as was immediately possible, to that great African cause, in which I have continued to labour for no less than forty-seven years.

It is not true, then, that zeal for Christianity, or what my opponents call enthusiasm in religion, made me an enemy of slavery. It would be much nearer the truth, for certain reasons, to say that this enmity made me a Christian. But I know of no scheme of religion or morals, Christian or Pagan, in which the slavery of the sugar colonies, when truly delineated, can admit of justification or excuse.

Stephen could rightly insist that his hatred of slavery preceded his religious convictions, but he nevertheless made the religious argument an important part of his case for the abolition of slavery. The Evangelical doctrine of supreme importance to Stephen was, as readers of the *Memoirs* will see, his belief in a superintending Providence watching over all the affairs of men and of nations, preserving and sustaining those that follow the way of the Divine will, dealing a just retribution, to individuals and nations alike, for persistent sin. Through numerous books and pamphlets, from *The Crisis of the Sugar Colonies* (1802) to *The Slavery of the British West Indies Delineated* (1st volume 1824, 2nd volume 1830), written to arouse the national conscience, runs the repeated theme that revolutions and civil wars in Europe were "indications of Divine wrath, and forerunners of approaching chastisements on the nations of Europe, for their grievous and impious oppression of the African race." The concluding forty-seven pages of *The Danger of the Country* (1807) are given to an eloquent argument that Britain has sinned greatly and that public calamities are only a part of the chastisements that God owes to the United Kingdom.

Yet Stephen—though Henry Adams may have been justified in calling him, in another connection, a "high-minded fanatic"—was no crank writer. The two stout volumes of *Slavery Delineated* are closely argued, showing that he had studied all the law on slavery and the actions under it and that he knew how to document his illustrations of the practice of slavery so that they would be convincing; the exposition, though inspired throughout by hatred of a brutalizing system, is dispassionate and addressed to reasonable minds. Stephen's writing against slavery was effective and widely read. His colonial opponents once paid him the compliment of addressing a fifteen-page pamphlet denouncing him to every clergyman and dissenting minister in the United Kingdom. Without question the great work of his life was the part he had, second only to Wilberforce, in putting an end to human slavery in British possessions.

It was, however, another activity which brought Stephen into national prominence and into a seat in Parliament. In his legal practice at St. Christopher's he had learned much of how ships flying a neutral flag could evade the restrictions on trade which Britain was attempting to apply against continental enemies. In October, 1805, Stephen published a long pamphlet, *War in Disguise: or, the Fraud of the Neutral Flags*. He pointed to the current situation in which ships, chiefly American, flying a neutral flag, would sail from the French West Indies to an American port, then, without reloading, proceed to France or Spain with their cargoes, and claim their rights as neutrals to carry on such trade. Historically, Stephen argued, England had, in the Seven Years War, maintained what he called the rule of the war 1756—"that a neutral has no right to deliver a belligerent from the pressure of his enemy's hostilities, by trading with his colonies in time of war in a way that was prohibited in time of peace." England, he admitted, had receded in practice from strict application of the rule but had never, either theoretically or practically, abandoned the principle. Prior to the war France had never allowed American vessels any share in the colonial trade; therefore England had every legal and moral right to forbid the trade. Without some such measure England had little hope of defeating Napoleon, or even of withstanding him. And Stephen was optimistic enough to believe that America would not be so unreasonable as to go to war for a trade to which she had no right. One passage of Stephen's fervent argument has an ironically anachronistic sound in the 1950's.

It cannot be supposed, that the present body of the American people are at this period . . . inimically disposed to Great Britain. If they are insensible to the ties of a common extraction, and if the various sympathies of religion, language and manners, that ought to incline them favourably towards us, have lost their natural influence, they still cannot be regardless of the interesting fact, that we alone, of all the nations in the old world, now sustain the sinking cause of civil liberty, to which they are so fondly attached. They see that the iron yoke of a military despotism is now rivetted on the neck of that powerful people, which aspires to universal domination, and which has already deprived its defenceless neighbours of the freedom they formerly enjoyed; nor do they doubt that the subjugation of England would be fatal to the last hope of liberty in America.

Is the Atlantic thought a sufficient rampart for themselves, against the same despotic system? The people of America are neither so ungenerous, nor so unwise, as to act on that mistaken confidence.

War in Disguise had a second and a third edition in 1806; it was reprinted in New York; there was an American *Answer to War in Disguise*, generally attributed to Gouverneur Morris. Although Stephen had written anonymously, his authorship soon became known. The policy he advocated was adopted by the Government and implemented by Orders in Council, the first in January and a second more severe one in November, 1807, the latter drafted by Spencer Perceval, the new Chancellor of the Exchequer and soon to be Prime Minister. Perceval was an Evangelical and an opponent of slavery, and Stephen was soon one of his most trusted friends and advisers. A seat in Parliament was found for Stephen as member for Tralee in 1808, and in 1812 as member for East Grinstead.

In Parliament Stephen spoke often and effectively in support of the Orders in Council, which were generally acknowledged to be of his devising. Brougham, who led the opposition to them in 1812, called Stephen "the father of the system." As it became increasingly clear that restrictions on American trade were leading to war with the United States, sentiment in Parliament, and even in Perceval's cabinet, was for revoking the Orders; but Perceval, even to the day of his assassination, stood loyally by Stephen's policy.

The Orders in Council for suppressing the neutral trade were rescinded June 25, 1812, but too late, for a week earlier the United States had declared war, though the news did not reach England until July. The two points of irritation which had led the American Congress to war were the impressment of American seamen by the British Navy and the restrictions on American commerce by the Orders in Council. Impressment alone, though galling to American pride, would not have been a sufficient reason for war. Had Stephen been able to admit that he was wrong in his predictions about American reaction, or had he been unable to keep the support of the Cabinet for his policy, there would, in all probability, have been no war. One cannot escape the conclusion that the War of 1812 which many Americans derisively called "Mr. Madison's War" might more justly have been called "Mr. Stephen's War."

Brought into Parliament by Tory leaders, Stephen was a fairly consistent party man, partly because, after a radical youth, he had come to general agreement with conservative principles, but even more because he knew that only by party regularity could he hope to have Tory support for anti-slavery legislation. Outraged by a letter from a professed liberal who refused to support him on a slave question, he wrote to Wilberforce:

This instance added to others confirms my antipathy to liberty boys and democrats. In all human character I know of nothing so detestable and contemptible as a democrat slave-master or defender of private slavery. I once was fool enough to think Whigs and Jacobins our sure friends, and therefore should have been a Whig or Jacobin myself, if their private vices had not repelled me from their society.

More than once Stephen served notice on his party leaders that he could not support them unless they were right on slavery. Speaking in favour of a Motion Respecting the African Slave Trade in 1810 he declared: "I would as soon affiance myself in the bonds of friendship with a man who had strangled my infant child, as lend my feeble support to an administration disposed to violate the sacred duty of adhering to and enforcing the abolition of the Slave Trade." When Sir Samuel Romilly taunted him in debate with "guilty silence" because of party obligation to Lord Castlereagh, Stephen retorted that he had the pledge of Castlereagh to do everything possible at the Congress to prevent the French from reintroducing the slave trade in the West Indies: "If the noble lord fails to redeem this pledge, may God not spare me if I spare the noble lord or his colleagues!"

The test came in 1815 when Lord Liverpool's government would not support the elaborate scheme of registration which Stephen thought necessary to prevent the surreptitious reintroduction of the slave trade in the West Indies. With Wilberforce's help he wrestled with his conscience and decided he must resign his seat. He wrote to Lord Liverpool:

Master's Office Southampton Buildings Mar. 2. 1815
My Lord
I find myself placed in a situation which calls on me, with your Lordship's permission, to resign that seat in Parliament which through your obliging recommendation I had the honor to obtain.

I do so with unfeigned sentiments of respect towards your Lordship, and of gratitude for the very handsome, liberal and condescending treatment I have always received from you, both in the manner of conferring that favor, and upon every other occasion on which I have had the honor to correspond with or approach you. The same acknowledgments are justly due to every Member of the Administration with whom I have had the honor of intercourse. My motives therefore for retiring cannot be of a personal kind. Nor do they proceed from any change in my views or feeling with relation to political Parties. In ceasing to act with one, I shall form no connection with the other. I have done with political life.

A clear explanation of the circumstances and reasons

which have determined me to retire from Parliament, might justify the resolution even in the eyes of those who may differ from me on the important subject which has more immediately led to it, that on which I had yesterday the honour to converse with your Lordship. But to explain those circumstances and reasons fully, would be to enter into statements of considerable length, as well as much delicacy, with which I have no right to trespass on your Lordship's patience; and they might savour perhaps of self conceit as attaching an importance to the measure itself that certainly does not belong to it.

I will therefore only trouble your Lordship with the motives of my conduct in the most compendious form, by saying that there is a public cause, that of justice and mercy towards the much injured African race, to which I have long felt myself bound by the most sacred considerations chiefly to devote the voluntary labours of my life; and that I am now convinced I can serve that cause more effectively by retiring from, than by remaining in, Parliament.

I have the honor to be, with the greatest respect
  My Lord
   your Lordship's obliged and most obdt. Servt.
      James Stephen

In the letters which he wrote to friends who tried to dissuade him, he was more explicit about his reasons. A paragraph from a sixteen-page letter to Nicholas Vansittart, March 14, 1815, puts his position succinctly:

". . . the man is not hardly dealt with who is tried by his own moral maxims and I have repeatedly declared *mine* to be that the interests of this cause are paramount to every other motive of political attachment, and that I would never contribute to the support of any government at the expense of those interests. I was a stranger and an enemy to Mr. Pitt, because he was wanting in his duty to that cause. I kept at a distance from Mr. Fox, tho' true to it, because I would not spoil my chance of usefulness to it by incurring the imputation of revolutionary views; yet I walked after his remains to the grave, and wept at it, because, however wrong in his general politics, he had been a true and zealous abolitionist. I might go further; but will only add that in no one instance of my life have I subordinated this sacred principle to any other; and by God's grace I never will.

Stephen's direct participation in political life ended when he accepted the Chiltern Hundreds, April 14, 1815. He retained his place as a Master in Chancery until 1831, when his health began to fail. Out of Parliament he redoubled his efforts on behalf of the slaves. He published numerous pamphlets and the two volumes of his *Slavery Delineated*; he addressed the African Institution and worked tirelessly for that and similar bodies; he urged the cause of the slaves on all his political friends. When, in 1822, after the suicide of Castlereagh, he heard a rumour that either Peel or Canning was to be the new Prime Minister, he wrote a "private and confidential" letter to Peel urging him to accept the office if it came his way, on the ground that Peel was a friend to "the cause of the poor Colonial Slaves" and Canning was not.

His later years were, in the main, happy ones. The death of his second wife in 1816 temporarily overwhelmed him with a sense of his great loss, for he was a deeply affectionate man, dependent on those who loved him. A letter of Wilberforce's, written at the time, reports of him: " . . . in the very extreme bitterness of his grief, which was as great as that of any one I have ever witnessed, though he is now able to control his feelings before company, he said to me while enlarging on the various particulars of my dear sister's extraordinary character, 'O, she was a friend of my soul! She told me frankly all my faults.' " But the companionship of his children and grandchildren and of Wilberforce recalled him to happiness. He retained his vigour and delight in activity to a late age. Leslie Stephen reports a family tradition that on the morning of his seventieth birthday he walked the twenty-five miles from his country house in Missenden, Bucks, to Hampstead, where he had breakfast, then walked on to his office in Southampton Buildings, Holborn, and, after a day's work, across London to his house in Kensington Gore. He had only one year of retirement after resigning his Mastership in Chancery, and died at Bath, October 10, 1832.

Any claim to literary fame that James Stephen had in his own lifetime rested upon his *War in Disguise*, his *Slavery*

Delineated, and his numerous pamphlets and printed speeches on slavery. They are a respectable achievement, vigorous, fervent, logical, and convincing, in a style that was formed in the good eighteenth-century days of controversial prose. Yet his best book, without question I think, is this auto-biography which he wrote for his children and their descendants, that they might know the kind of man he was and might, as he thought, read in the vicissitudes of his life the lesson of Divine Providence. It came from his heart; it could have been written only by an emotionally sensitive man who had grown up in a time which inherited two strong influences, one represented by Wesley, the other by Rousseau.

Stephen wrote the *Memoirs* into two stoutly bound quarto volumes of 225 blank leaves each, fitted with brass hasps and locks so that he might keep them secret until after his death. Beginning on June 6, 1819, he wrote legibly—I have not had to leave a word undeciphered—and almost without erasure on one side of the leaf, and arrived at the last leaf of the first volume (p. 225) on October 28, 1821. Then he turned the volume and wrote to p. 450 on the reverse sides of the pages he had already written. The remaining 162 pages, to p. 612 of the MS., are in the second volume. There are several other indications of date of writing along the way: June 2, 1822, at p. 282; June 30, 1822, at p. 294; October 13, 1822, at p. 312; April 4, 1824, at p. 332; December 8, 1825, at p. 450. There is no way of telling when or why Stephen left off. Whether, looking at the length at which he had written of his youth, he despaired of telling the rest of the story on the same scale, or whether failing memory and strength stopped him in his latest years, we can only guess. One day, some time between 1826 and 1832, he put down the account of his impending departure from England in 1783 and, quite contrary to his practice, left the final sentence without a full stop.

The *Memoirs* have been read by many members of the Stephen family in the four generations that came after James Stephen, and several of them have emulated their ancestor by writing similar documents, though not with the same central principle of illustrating the ways of Providence. Leslie Stephen, in his *Life of Sir James Fitzjames Stephen*, used the

Memoirs for the first chapter, admittedly with omissions.
Until 1947, when the manuscript was deposited in the
British Museum by Miss Dorothea Stephen, it was in the
possession of the family.

Working from a photographic copy of the manuscript, I
have tried to give a faithful edition of the *Memoirs*. A few
passages have been omitted, but only because they were
repetitious. I have arbitrarily broken the book into chapters
and have inserted running heads of dates. In the fashion of
his day Stephen used many capital letters for nouns and
punctuated copiously. I have reduced many of his capital
letters but have left enough to give the feeling of his habit.
Without attempting to conform completely with twentieth-
century conventions, I have simplified the punctuation for
ease of reading. Except for what seemed to be slips, I have
generally preserved Stephen's idiosyncrasies of spelling. The
words are his as he used them.

I have incurred many debts for kindnesses shown me while
I have been editing these *Memoirs*. The officers and staff of
the British Museum Reading Room and Manuscript Room
and of the Duke University Library have been unfailingly
helpful. Generous grants of financial aid from the Duke
University Research Council and the Carnegie Foundation
for the Advancement of Teaching helped to make possible
a year's residence in England, where I might pursue studies
of which James Stephen's history is a part. Most particularly
I wish to express my gratitude to Miss Dorothea Stephen,
without whose unflagging interest these *Memoirs* of her great-
grandfather might never have been published.

MERLE M. BEVINGTON
Duke University,
Durham, North Carolina.
October, 1953.

Introductory Reflections

AUTO-BIOGRAPHY WOULD, if executed on right principles and in a proper manner, be a most instructive and valuable species of composition. As the history of Nations is the best study for a Statesman, so for the prudential conduct of private life would be the history of individuals, if written with equal intelligence and fidelity. But events worthy of a place in the annals of a Nation cannot easily be concealed, at least from contemporary eyes; nor are their causes in general difficult to be traced; whereas occurrences of the first importance in the life of a private person, and such as are the most illustrative of his character, as well as the most influential on his happiness or misery, are often unknown to all but his confidential friends, or locked up, even from them, in the recesses of his own heart. The biographer, therefore, is commonly worse informed than the civil historian of facts the most essential to the justice of his views and the usefulness of his labours. A writer of his own memoirs has in this respect a most important advantage. His work might be rendered by it more instructive in its kind than those of Xenophon or Caesar or Clarendon or Sully, or any other warrior or Statesman who has been the historian of his own campaigns, or of his own Times and Country; because his knowledge of his subject is far more comprehensive and entire. The Statesman may be deceived as to the motives of the Cabinet in which he sat, for he can be sure only of those which swayed his own advice. The General may give a false account of the incidents of a battle which he fought, for he was only in one part of the field. But the auto-biographer knows or may know with certainty the secret springs of actions flowing from his will alone, what those actions were in which he was himself the agent, and what those events which necessarily belong to his work, since they can do so in general no further than as they respected himself, and fell within his own experience. Fidelity, however, is a quality not less essential to the good and useful historian than accuracy of information; and in this point a writer is more likely to fail when he is relating facts connected with his own conduct in life, and which must tend either to raise or depress his own character in the estimation of his readers. This consideration may not unreasonably be thought to counterpoise the former; and even to make it desirable that the life of a private individual, if worthy of narration, should employ any other pen rather than his own.

The object of the history which I propose to write furnishes perhaps a sufficient answer to this objection. If any feeling is powerful enough to guard us against the seductions of self-love, it is parental affection. I write for the sake of my children. I wish to inform them faithfully of the events of my own life, because I think it may be useful to them in the conduct of theirs. They may learn wisdom from what has been wrong in it, as well as from what has been right; and unless I record my follies and my faults, together with those parts of my conduct that I can remember without regret, I shall give them false or at least defective views of the causes of many events the most important and instructive perhaps of any in my eventful life and the lessons of experience which I wish to impart will be imperfect, if not delusive. The sacred nature of that instruction which I chiefly wish to convey will, I trust, be another pledge for my sincerity. The great truth to be learnt from the following narrative, and in almost every event recorded in it is the superintendance of a wise and just, tho' most merciful and gracious Providence, in all the concerns of human life. This truth, the most precious to me of all sublunary things, I most anxiously wish to hand down to my children, and to our posterity, as a matter not of my belief merely, but *knowledge*; as a truth deeply impressed upon me not only by reason and revelation, but by the clearest and fullest experience. A most inestimable and peculiar fruit of auto-biography if practised by a great number of individuals, with strict and undoubted fidelity, would be an irresistible demonstration of that religious truth. I mean supposing those individuals to have been observant during a considerable portion of their lives not only of their own temporal but also of their spiritual concerns, and to write a history of their hearts as well as their external fortunes. Whether it is necessary also that they should have long been in the habit of prayer I am not prepared to say; but if this qualification be added, I have no doubt that their concurrent testimony would put the reality of an all-directing, universally particular, providence, on as high ground in point of evidence as many physical truths which we all regard as certain, and which it would be thought a preposterous scepticism to doubt. This, however, may require some explanation.

There are two ways in which the agency of Divine Providence in the events of a man's life may be proved to him by experience: the one by their providential character; the other by their correspondency to his prayers. Their providential character may be determined, with more or less probability, by indications of various kinds; by their suitableness, for instance, to the Divine attributes; as when vice is punished or virtue rewarded, in a remarkable manner, without the design and perhaps contrary to the foresight and endeavours of the human agents; or when beneficent ends are accomplished by means, singular in their nature or combination, without any human contrivance; or when innocence is rescued from false accusation, or life preserved from impending destruction by extraordinary and unexpected means at a time when deliverance was despaired of or the danger fearful and extreme. The striking aptitude of particular events, good or evil, to reward or chastise actions of which they may be supposed to be retribution, may also sometimes indicate to the reflecting and pious mind a providential direction. It is not however from a single case, or from a few cases of these kinds, that the truth in question can be reasonably inferred. They may have been accidental. If during a given time of observation they become very numerous, the inference will be probable in the direct ratio of the number and the inverse ratio of the time; and a man may have observed so many cases of events indicatory in their nature and circumstance, of a providential contrivance, as to have a rational persuasion that they cannot all have occurred by chance. I think that every man of observant and reflecting habits who is not strongly prepossessed against the doctrine of a particular providence will find in the experience of many years such evidence of its truth. Nor is the evidence always overlooked, even by those who most obstinately reject the right conclusion. On the contrary it is common to hear such persons remark—"How providential was that escape"; "How just and striking that retribution"; "Surely the hand of God is visible in the detection of that murder"; "His fate is a judgment upon him for his oppression, for his unnatural conduct to his parents"; and the like. But such acknowledgments, however sincere, rarely imply any general persuasion of the superintending and disposing providence of God in the ordinary concerns of human life. Sometimes, as in an article in the *Edinburgh Review* of last year,[1] a distinction not less unphilosophical than unscriptural, is taken between what are called "great and extraordinary occasions, worthy of the special interposition of Heaven", and common affairs; and that distinction is too often tacitly admitted even by those who have too much respect for the authority of the Gospel expressly to assert it. To confess the occasional agency of Divine providence in directing or controuling human affairs without a miraculous disturbance of second causes, and at the same time to deny that the same hand regulates all events is to encounter all the difficulties which to our feeble faculties oppose the notion of a Providence universally particular, and to add to them other difficulties which even those faculties can shew to be of a less superable kind. But I must not here enter into the refutation of other men's opinions. My object is to explain my own. It must be admitted that the evidence of a providential government arising from particular cases, however plain and numerous, cannot fully prove the universality of that government in all the concerns of human life. We must rely for the truth of that doctrine, in its whole delightful extent, on the authority of Him who has assured us that "the hairs of our heads are all numbered." But in proportion to the number, and variety, and particularity, of the instances in which we discover the actings of Divine Providence towards ourselves or others,

---

[1] I have been unable to find any article in the *Edinburgh Review* for 1818 where this point is made, and am inclined to believe that Stephen was mistaken in his reference.

will be the presumption that the same unseen agency is universal; and if a number of individuals are able to attest that they have experienced the care and government of an invisible, intelligent, benignant Power, with whom they have held communion by prayer, during the whole course of their lives, and in all their conduct, we cannot well believe them without supposing that the same care and the same government are extended with equal particularity to the whole human race.

I have said that to furnish such testimony it is necessary that the individuals who record their own experience on the subject should have been long observant of their spiritual, as well as their temporal, interests. The man whose views extend no further than the range of natural good and evil, may indeed discern in many cases the hand of Almighty providence in its dealings with himself and others; but he will not, even in the events of his own life, uniformly recognize the same disposing power. He will on the contrary, in a great number, perhaps a majority, of cases, be tempted to say that the event is not to be regarded as an appointment of providence consistent with the Divine attributes. Nor is this at all strange, for how can he who leaves out of his contemplation the chief end in view, judge rightly of the means employed? If the improvement of our moral natures be the grand interest of human life, then all the dealings of a beneficent Providence towards us may reasonably be expected to have a reference to their grand interest; and to judge of them independently of their effects on our moral character is just as rational as it would be to judge of the discipline of a school without regard to its influence on education, or the treatment of a Patient, independently of its tendency to cure. The man therefore who reviews his own life with a wish to discover in the events of it the disposing hand of a wise and gracious providence should much and chiefly consider how by the natural good or evil he has met with, or by occurrences in that respect neutral, his moral, or in other words his spiritual and eternal, interests, or those of others, have been affected. He will thus find the proofs of a presiding Providence within the field of his own experience multiply upon him, and unless from past heedlessness he is unable to trace back the history of his own heart with sufficient particularity will find the accumulation of evidence so strong as not to be easily withstood.

But if to spiritual watchfulness the habit of private prayer has long been added, the result of such enquiry will be more certain, and the demonstration produced by it, to the mind of the man himself at least, perfectly conclusive.

The indications of a providential appointment in the texture of an event itself, or in its known relations, may be very apparent to the pious observer; and the number and variety of such cases may be so great as to preclude any rational doubt of the reality of that unseen agency, to which they are ascribed. But still the discovery is not so clear, and so obvious to every capacity, as when the same events, or even ordinary events which have no providential features in their apparent character, are in an equal number and variety closely correspondent to our prayers. To illustrate this, let us suppose the case of a man perfectly deaf and blind, and that he is attended with great tenderness and assiduity by relatives to whom he was attached by mutual affection and intimacy before he fell into that unhappy situation. He finds himself regularly fed, and conducted to and from his bed and chair at proper intervals, and food always presented to his mouth in due time to prevent any frequent inconvenience from hunger or thirst. It may not always arrive so soon as he wishes, nor of a kind that is agreeable to his palate at the time; but on the whole he has enough, and finds much more of gratification than is strictly necessary to his well being in these respects, while his other physical necessities are also duly provided for by the same or other invisible hands. From the long experience of such treatment he might with certainty infer that he was under the charge of some person or persons who either from their own benignity, or their obedience to some superior power, took care of him in his helpless state. Such is the evidence we have of Providence in its general course. But the unfortunate individual whose case we have supposed could not be sure upon these facts that he was dealt with by any but general rules, and in a prescribed course of treatment. He might be in an hospital, where all the inmates were equally attended to on the same general principles, or in the hands of servants who merely obeyed their Master's commands without any voluntary regard to his comfort or preservation. Such are our sceptical views as to the action of second causes.

Let us, however, next suppose that he finds particular viands such as his domestic friends knew him to be fond of provided most frequently for his meals, and this with accompaniments of an unusual kind, but such as were known to be conformable to his own peculiar taste, and let us add that the instances of the adaptation of treatment in such matters to his own peculiar case are extremely numerous, and various at different seasons, and are to be traced in his cloathing, air, exercise, and every other species of treatment that can be recognized by his remaining senses. He might confidently conclude from these additional facts that the benignity of which he was the object acted by more than general rules, and that his own individual case was watched over and treated by persons to whom it was intimately known, and affectionately, as well as intelligently, regarded. Such is our evidence of a particular providence as derived from the character and exterior relations of events.

Lastly let it be imagined that the same blind and deaf person had been taught by a Father or Wife or some other Friend to whom he may now with probability ascribe the tender treatment he receives certain tangible signs by which he can denote the letters of the alphabet, and so form words and carry on conversation. He finds a hand in contact with his own, impresses on it these signs, and combines them in the way proper to communicate some particular want, as for instance to be taken into the air, or to be conducted to his bed, or to have his dinner; and the want is immediately supplied. It has happened once or twice; but this may have been by a casual coincidence, or his meaning may have been conjectured by a stranger. He therefore repeats the experiment numerous times, and the event is always correspondent, or it is so nearly consentaneous to his wishes in all cases, that when disappointed he commonly soon discovers a sufficient and kind reason for the non-compliance. He perceives, for instance, from the sudden coolness and moisture of the atmosphere that it was raining when he desired to be led into the open air. He goes still further. He communicates by touch to the same unseen hand his wish for something very specific, a rose or a head of lavender, a peach or a nectarine, and it is speedily placed in his hand. The demonstration now is compleat. Repeated experience at least of such specific answers to his requests puts an end to all possible doubt. Nor can it shake his conviction that he does not always succeed. It is enough that the event has corresponded with his requests in such a great number and variety of instances as to convince him that their coincidence cannot have arisen from chance. Such is the evidence of a particular providence that may be found in effectual prayer.

The case of the unfortunate individual here supposed is in truth closely analogous to that of every pious and enquiring mind. We have no faculties, such as angels and all spiritual Beings probably possess, by which the agency of the Divine Providence can be perceived in a direct and immediate way. If we had, the Great Agent, or his intelligent Instruments, and their modes of action, might be as plainly discerned perhaps as the benignant Friend or his servants would be by the blind and deaf man, if his sight and hearing were suddenly restored, while they were in attendance upon him, and presenting the food to his mouth. Such a sudden, astonishing, and delightful discovery, is probably the lot of a happy spirit when released from its bodily prison by death. But in the meantime it is the pleasure of the Most High that what our bodily senses cannot directly perceive in this respect our reason should be able to infer, if, like the blind and deaf man here supposed, we employ carefully the faculties we possess, and reflect upon the facts they furnish. He has also given us in the appointed means of prayer the power of putting his particular providential government to the test of an experiment as satisfactory and decisive as that of the tactile communication in the case supposed. But our prayers are answered only by their effects. The unseen Benefactor might by using the same signs have signified to the touch of his unfortunate friend that his requests were understood, and would be complied with; but to make the illustration perfect I have supposed no such reply. God might answer our prayers if he thought fit in an audible voice; but the course chosen by his infinite wisdom is different. In this, as in all other cases, it seems to be his plan to discover himself and his operations to his rational creatures by means only of their reasoning powers. Truly says the Scripture, "Thou art a God who hidest thyself."[1] But it is nevertheless his holy will that the creatures whom he has endued with reason should search for and discover him in his works of creation and providence "that they should seek the Lord if haply they might feel after him, and find him,"[2] and the neglect of such enquiries, even by those who had only the light of nature to guide them, is treated in Scripture as the cause of men's ignorance of the Divine nature, and a great aggravation of their sins.

Having thus far noticed the two general ways in which the particular government of Divine Providence may be a subject of our experience and be proved to our own conviction, I repeat that the reality of this government might be proved by the copious concurrent testimony of many individuals, each recording his own experience on as high ground as many physical truths which we all regard as certain, and which it would be thought a preposterous scepticism to doubt.

I believe that there is such a Planet as the Georgian sidus;[3] and should be laughed at if I professed the contrary. For what reason? since I never saw the star. The answer can only be because it has been observed numberless times, not only by Mr. Herschel, who first discovered it, but by other Astronomers in different parts of Europe whom we cannot rationally suspect of having combined to deceive us, and who have published their respective observations all confirmatory of each other. Now all this and more may be truly said in support of the great and most interesting facts, that there is a particular providence watching over and disposing the

---

[1] *Isaiah* 45 : 15. The Authorized Version reads : "Verily thou art a God that hidest thyself, O God of Israel, the Saviour."

[2] *Acts*, 17 : 27.

[3] Sir William Herschel (1738–1822), Hanoverian born English astronomer, in 1781 discovered a new planet, to which he assigned the name "Georgium Sidus," now known as Uranus. For this discovery he was awarded the Copley medal of the Royal Society and made private astronomer to George III. The name was early objected to by continental astronomers, but it persisted in English usage as late as 1850.

concerns of human life, and that this providence is responsive to prayer. Hundreds and thousands of pious men in different ages and countries have given their concurrent testimony to their observation and experience of these truths; and of many or most of them it would be preposterous to suspect that their statements were insincere. David, and the other authors of the Psalms, have had numberless successors in every age including our own who have recorded the efficacy of their prayers, and the impressive discoveries they have made of the hand of Providence in the incidents of their own lives.

Why then, possessing as we do a host of witnesses on the subject between whom there is no disagreement, should it be desired to add to their number? How can auto-biography make the precious truths in question clearer than they already are?

Certainly there is evidence enough to convince a candid enquirer; and there are limits perhaps beyond which a proof, though in its nature cumulative, cannot be advantageously enlarged. But we have in this case strong natural prejudices to combat; and the object is not merely to establish a fact, or class of facts, by a competent number of witnesses, but from a multitude and vast variety of facts, all indicatory of an intelligent cause, to exclude the solution of chance. Besides there is in Biography written for the public, a necessary reserve which often detracts much from the force of the evidence it might furnish on this interesting subject. If the author were perfectly informed of all those secret motives of an action, or circumstances of an event, which might be necessary to explain the plan of Providence, and might most clearly indicate its hand, in some incidents of the life, they might be facts of which delicacy or prudence would forbid the publication. There is also a peculiar difficulty in submitting to the public eye a multitude of occurrences and combinations in the life of the same individual the number and coincidence of which may have rationally fixed his own convictions on this subject; especially when the providential character has been chiefly impressed upon them by their correspondence with his private prayers, or their influence on his spiritual interests;

because when taken separately and independently of their effects on his own mind, they will appear for the most part of a mean and trivial kind, and be more likely to excite ridicule with the generality of readers, than to remove prejudices against, or win a serious assent to the opinions they are adduced to support. The Journals of pious Missionaries or private Christians eminent for devotion may illustrate these remarks; for when given to the Public they are generally found to contain many notices of occurrences regarded by the Journalist himself as providential, which seem of too ordinary and trivial a kind to deserve any mention in that view; and they are scoffed at by unbelievers, as the offspring of vanity and superstition. Yet the unfavorable impression may in such cases arise from our not being sufficiently informed of what went before, and followed, in the mind of the writer; and perhaps if we peruse with a candid spirit the whole of the Journal in which such questionable passages occur, we may change our opinion. We may find at least in many instances that the seemingly insignificant occurrences had important results in the life or heart of the Journalist; or was a link in the chain of consequences the concatenation of which was probably in his thoughts, tho' he did not enable us to trace it in his account of the particular case. When such explanations cannot be found, it is still profitable that a reserve proceeding from delicacy or prudence may have concealed from us some material circumstance that gave in his own mind a providential aspect to the rest.

I mean not, however, to dispute that many fanciful and superstitious notions have found place in the Journals alluded to, or that vanity and self love may have magnified trifles into matters of importance, and imagined traits of a providential contrivance in events of an ordinary kind merely from the egotism which was flattered by such a view of them. But it is easier for a Writer to avoid errors of this kind, than to escape the imputation of them in recording for public use his own experience of the ways of providence in a history of his own life. Without numerous and minute details of circumstances of no substantive interest except to the writer himself, he cannot possibly do justice to his

argument, and yet such details will almost infallibly expose
him to the imputation of egotism and conceit. In shewing
the efficacy of his prayers especially, he will incur this
prejudice with most men who have not themselves had a
like experience. They will fancy that there is something
arrogant even, in the belief that his prayers have had an
influence in producing events beneficial to himself, through
the interposition of Divine Providence for his sake; especially
as such events can rarely affect him alone. Their prepossessions and their want of reflection on the subject prevent
their perceiving that an omniscient and all-disposing director
of human affairs can make the same event which is accorded
to the prayers of one individual, fall in at the same time with
the beneficent and righteous designs of his providence
towards all whom it may directly or indirectly affect. For
these and other reasons, the testimony of experience to the
reality of a particular providence, and to the efficacy of
prayer, falls short of that effect which it ought to produce,
and tho' the evidence that has been given to the public is
stronger perhaps in its collective force than that which has
gained general reception for most of the best established
physical truths, further corroboration cannot be regarded as
useless. It is desirable at least that the attestation of a
Parent's experience in a private way should not be withheld
from his children.

Such are the views upon which I shall proceed if God
grants me life and leisure enough to record in the following
pages the chief occurrences of a life in the course of which
His wise and gracious providence has been more than
commonly conspicuous.

MEMOIRS OF JAMES STEPHEN

Written by himself for the
use of his children

Commenced June 6th 1819 aetat: 60

"Thou O God hast taught me from my youth up untill now ; therefore will I tell of thy wondrous works." [1]

O what great troubles & adversities hast thou shewed me! and yet didst thou turn and refresh me ; yea and broughtest me from the deep of the earth again.

[1] The Biblical quotation on Stephen's title-page is from *Psalms* 71 : 17. Here, or elsewhere when he is quoting the *Psalms*, Stephen quotes the Great Bible Version from the Book of Common Prayer. For other parts of the Bible he quotes, usually accurately, from the Authorised Version. The second passage is not Biblical, but seemingly Stephen's invention.

Introductory Reflections

Auto-biography would, if executed on right principles & in a proper manner, be a most instructive
& valuable species of composition. As the history of
Nations is the best study for a Statesman so for the
prudential conduct of private life, would be the history
of individuals, if written with equal intelligence &
fidelity. But events worthy of a place in the annals
of a Nation cannot easily be concealed, or hidden from
cotemporary eyes; nor are their causes in general
difficult to be traced; whereas occurrences of the first
importance in the life of a private person, & such
as are the most illustrative of his character, as well
as the most influential on his happiness or mis-
-ery, are often unknown to all but his confidential
friends, or locked up even from them, in the recesses of
his own heart. The biographer therefore is commonly
worse informed than the civil historian of facts

Facsimile of first page of MS. in
James Stephen's handwriting

Chapter One

[1758–1768]

MY Father was the third son of James Stephen and Mary Stephen, whose maiden name was Brown. They were both natives, I believe, of Aberdeenshire, and resided in that County or in the skirts of the Shire of Buchan, which is contiguous to it, all their lives. Her Mother lived near Slaines Castle and attained to a great age. I visited her there in 1775, when she was reputed to be 105, yet retained all her faculties and moved with agility. I have since heard that her age was overrated by five or six years. She died I think in 1777, after having been shaken by, but having perfectly recovered from, a severe fever, in the preceding year. Dr. Livingstone, then the most eminent Physician in the North of Scotland, declared it was a regular inflammatory fever, of as marked a character as ever he saw in the youngest patient. She had been a widow from the age of 35 or thereabouts, and five daughters, of whom my Grandmother was one, survived her. The women of my Father's family, and of my Mother's too, with the exception of herself, have all attained to old age, while the men have in general died young. My Father was one of nine children, seven of them sons, who I have heard were distinguished as the finest young men of one family in all that Country. He measured six foot, three inches, and some of his brothers were nearly or quite as tall; but they are all long since in their graves and all died in their prime, with the exception of the eldest, who lived, I think, to be near 70. One of the two Sisters on the other hand, is still living, at an age considerably exceeding that; and the other died two years ago aged 88.

My Grandfather's situation in life was not affluent, and was, I apprehend, barely such as by the courtesy of a poor but literate country might be deemed not degrading to the character of a man who claimed to be considered as a gentleman, or boasted of a liberal extraction. He had a Farm, I think, which he held under Lord Errol, a nobleman to whom my Grandmother told me we were related; but he was also a merchant, and I fear dealt a good deal in contraband importations. To say, however, that he was a smuggler would be giving too harsh an idea of his character. The fact is that at the time, and to a much later period, no importer of dutiable articles in that part of the kingdom did or could abstain from contraband adventures. I have reason to believe he was well esteemed and respected in the circle of society he moved in. As a Father he had the merit of giving a liberal education to his numerous children, and sending them into the world with the manners and feelings of gentlemen. My Grandmother, whom I knew well in her old age, was a very worthy, amiable, and sensible woman. She was a zealous episcopalian of the nonjuring communion, and apparently religious, as far as might be inferred from her attendance on public worship, the only evidence of religious feeling that I was likely then to observe, or which I can recollect seeing any specimen of in Scotland, except among the Seceders. Neither there, nor here I believe at that time, had religion begun to shew itself in family life, except among Sectaries despised as fanatics. It is too probable that her character in early life, and that of my Grandfather also, were deficient in this most important point; for I fear that not one of their sons quitted the paternal roof with any serious religious impressions; and some of them alas were in after life profane in their conversation, and apparently destitute of Christian faith. It is a subject on which I write with pain, and with feelings of moral embarrassment. I will therefore only add that their conduct in other respects and their fortunes in life were not such as to encourage the neglect of early piety. "The fear of the Lord is the beginning of wisdom," of that true wisdom "in whose right hand is length of days, and in her left hand, riches and honor."[1] The eldest son, Alexander, was the only one who settled in his native country. His first employment was in the manufacturing line, in or near Glasgow, in some branch of the weaving business. He married a Miss Bruce, a young lady of antient and respectable family and good connections in Clarkmannonshire and that neighbourhood, but with little if any fortune, who lived till they had both long passed the

[1] *Psalms*, 111: 10; *Proverbs*, 3: 16.

prime of life, and was a very worthy sensible woman, and
much regarded and esteemed by all his relations. But the
union was not happy. My Uncle, whose company was in
general request in a large circle of acquaintance on account
of his powers of understanding and companionable qualities,
rarely spent his afternoons or evenings at home, and these
habits grew I fear into intemperance. Large dining and
supper parties, with late hours, hard drinking, and cards,
were at that time the reigning modes of social amusement
among the gentry of Scotland; and to have a hard head, as
it was called, or the faculty of drinking to excess without
intoxication, was regarded as matter of emulation and boast.
My Uncle, I remember, was celebrated for this species of
excellence, and was rarely if ever known to expose himself to
ridicule or inconvenience even in the most intemperate
parties. Yet to such habits I presume it was owing that he was
unsuccessful in business, and was at a late period of life
deprived of an office which had become his chief or sole
dependence for support, that of Treasurer to the Grand
Canal Company in Glasgow. His wife was by that time dead,
and at the age of 70 or near it, he became dependent on a
Sister for subsistence. For years before his death he was in a
helpless state, and would have felt the consequences of his
imprudence in extreme destitution and misery but for her
kindness, and that of my Sister Morison, which was very
great. William, the second son, was bred to surgery and
physic. He went abroad when a young man to the West
Indies, but returned for a few years, and was engaged in
some commercial speculations, but whether as a dormant
Partner with my Father, then a merchant, I do not distinctly
remember. I only know that on my Father's first failure in
business, of which I shall have hereafter to speak, he was
seriously involved in the misfortune, and that a quarrel
between them was the consequence, which made them
strangers to each other, and enemies too alas, till the end of
life. My Uncle William returning to the West Indies, settled
as a medical practitioner in St. Christopher and continued
there till his death, which happened I think in 1781 about the
50th year of his age. He was very successful in his profession,
which there unites together all the branches of physic,

2*

surgery, and pharmacy; and living a batchelor, would probably have amassed a very large fortune, if he had not, like most professional men in that country, been tempted to engage in the planting lottery, and bought an Estate in Dominica. In that speculation he sunk great part of the fortune he had made and probably would have persisted in the losing game till he had lost the whole if he had lived a few years longer. One way in which as I have heard he made considerable gains, was purchasing what are called "refuse negroes" at the Guinea Yard Sales in the Island he lived in, and curing them (for it is on account of their diseased and debilitated state that they are refused in the public market) and then reselling them in their healthy state at prices greatly advanced. Of course, therefore, he felt no great dislike either to slavery or to the horrible commerce which then supplied it in our colonies. I think, even, I have heard that his first professional outset was as Surgeon to a Guineaman. Certain it is he did not in this respect resemble a nephew whom Providence afterwards made his fortune the means of raising from early difficulties into his present prosperity in life, tho' without, and even *against* what had been the deceased owner's intention. He was what the world calls a very prudent man; but how blind is human prudence! He was also a very sensible man; but how foolish is human wisdom, when its views are bounded by this world! In a few years all the fruits of his long and painful industry perished, without any remaining benefit to his relatives or friends, except one to whom in extreme need he had refused a helping hand. This is anticipation of my future narrative; but having gone so far, I must explain that I never asked his aid. It was my dear departed Brother, his adopted child, who being with him and hearing of my distress in England, beg'd of him the means of easing his own affectionate feelings by sending me a small remittance, and was refused. To that brother a year or two after, all his property was on his death-bed bequeathed, and the first use of it was that which he had denied. It gave me the means of entering into a profession in which Providence has abundantly blessed my feeble endeavours, and enabled me to be a resource in time of need to the same kind brother, whose prosperity my poor Uncle had vainly thought to secure.

Having said so much of two of my paternal Uncles, I will
notice, but more briefly, the characters and fortunes of the
rest. Robert, the fourth son, was a brave young man, of a
generous but violent and impetuous temper, who perished
(through the effects of those faults perhaps) at an early period
of life. The profession chosen by, or designed for him, was
that of commerce; and as an introduction to it he went on a
voyage to the West Indies in the character, I think, of
Supercargo, in a fine new Ship then belonging to my Father
and a maternal uncle of mine with whom he was in partnership, and called after my Mother the *Sibella*. They were
armed, it being in time of War with France (I believe in or
about the year 1760), and in their outward passage fell in
with a French Privateer against which, tho' of greatly
superior force, they made a gallant defence. The Captain
was obliged at last to strike his colours; but my Uncle, who
was acting as chief officer in the cabin, where some of the
principal guns were, not knowing that the colours had been
struck upon deck, fired another broadside just as the French-
men were preparing to take possession of their prize. The
consequence was that the Captors on boarding singled him
out for vengeance and gave him numerous wounds, either
of which but for the great vigour of his constitution might
have been fatal. But such was his strength of habit that during
the space of time which elapsed between the capture and
arrival of the Privateer with her prize at Martinique, he had
advanced far towards recovery. Unhappily, he could not
subdue his resentment at what he deemed barbarous treatment contrary to the law of war, or restrain the expression
of it while in the hands of his enemies. On the contrary he
vehemently reproached them, and threatened them with
complaints, not only to his Government, but their own, as
soon as he should get into port. According to the opinion of
the Captain and officers who returned from captivity, these
threats cost him his life. On their arrival at Martinique the
Privateer hoisted out two boats, and most suspiciously put
my Uncle alone of all the prisoners in one of them, the Captain and his officers in the other, and rowed towards the
shore, which was at the distance of some miles, in different
directions; so that the people in one boat could not see what

passed in the other. When they met on the beach the French-men showed to the Captain and officers of the *Sibella* my Uncle's dead body, and asserted tht he had died suddenly in the boat from the effect of his wounds, tho' he had been seen by his fellow Prisoners to step over the ship's side with much apparent strength. My Father represented the case to the French Government, and I think the commission of the Privateer was taken away, for her cruel and illegal con-duct. Of course the murder could not be proved.

My Mother was a great favorite with this warm-hearted young man; as indeed she always was with all her husband's brothers. He told her at parting "Well, if we are obliged to strike to an enemy, I will give him one more broadside for the honor of the *Sibella*," and I have heard her express fears lest this promise should have led him to the act which proved fatal to him; but he would hardly have acted so unwarrant-able a part as to fire after he knew of the surrender; and his subsequent conduct, as well as the opinion of the Captain and Officers, seems to prove the contrary.

The Brothers next in age were Thomas and John, both of whom I well remember tho' they both died young men. My Father, who seems to have had it at heart to provide for all his younger brothers, sent for them to introduce them into business in this country. He engaged the former, first as a clerk, and afterwards as a partner, in some commercial under-takings of his own, and as I shall hereafter have occasion per-haps to notice, the event was not satisfactory to either. My Uncle Thomas some time about the year 1768 married a Miss Coker of Winborn Dorset, a Lady of great personal attractions, and as I believe of good family connections, but without fortune; and this in its consequences, as I at the time was led to believe, produced a quarrel between my Father and him, the Lady's family having looked to the partnership as an adequate support for a family, and having interpreted my Father's candid assurances to the contrary as a self-interested opposition to the marriage, and having afterwards on a like misconception, pushed my Uncle into disputes with his brother respecting the partnership accounts.

I desire, however, to be understood in everything I may say respecting family differences, as giving merely the impres-

sions made on my own young mind at the time by the statements I heard, which of course were my Father's chiefly, and
therefore liable to distrust from a cause the effects of which I
did not then know how to estimate and allow for. I mean the
unavoidable influence of self love. I did not hear the other
side.

The Partnership being dissolved, and my Uncle with the
prospect of a young family at a loss for other means of support, he was glad to obtain through the interest of his wife's
family the place of Collector of the Customs at Perth
Amboy[1] in the then Colony of New York. He went there,
and after a few years of trouble and danger consequent on
the quarrel between the Colonies and Mother Country, was
cut off by one of the diseases of the climate while yet in the
prime of life. His widow with two children returned to this
Country, sometime as I remember in 1777 or 1778, and she
afterwards married Mr. Lyte, Treasurer of the Household to
the Prince of Wales, whom she also survived, and ended her
days at Bath sometime in or about 1815. She was a sensible,
well-bred woman, and *I hope* something better, tho' her
religious advantages were small. Her son, I think, died a boy.
Her daughter, an amiable and, I believe, worthy young
woman, married Mr. Wilkinson, now of Springfield Bath, a
gentleman of landed property in that neighbourhood, but
with no very large estate, tho' enough to sustain him gen-
teelly out of business. I wish I had seen more of this first
cousin of mine in her later years. She was long taught in the
School of affliction. Sickness, loss of children, etc., long preceded and I hope prepared her for her dissolution. She died
within a year or two at most of her Mother; but whether
before or shortly after I cannot now recollect. She left several
children, I forget the number. The eldest is now a cadet on
the Royal Establishment at Woolwich, a promising young
man. Her husband has married again. My Uncle John went,
through my Father's assistance, into the Sea service of the

[1] Perth Amboy, in the colony of New Jersey, not New York, was founded in
1683, first called Amboy from the original Indian name, then in 1684 named
Perth for one of the proprietors, the Earl of Perth, and a little later known by the
combined name. It alternated with Burlington as the meeting place for the
general assembly and supreme court during the period of royal government,
1702–1775.

East India Company, and made, I think, two voyages. The service was then very lucrative, and he might soon have risen to a command and made his fortune, if my Father's second failure in business, of which I shall have hereafter to speak, had not involved him in the same ruin, or at least cut him off from the means of further advancement and success. The Captains and Mates of East Indiamen, to which latter station only my Uncle had attained, obtained their then great commercial advantages by loans of capital on respondentia bonds. In some of these to a large amount my Father had been his Surety, and had the matter rested there my Father's failure of course could not have been injurious to him; but they had dealings together the result of which was a dispute which was the creditor, and who ought to take up the respondentia Bonds.[1] I pretend not to say which was right; but it led to another unhappy family quarrel. My Uncle John quitted the East India Service, and went to his Brother William at St. Christopher, who sent him to manage his Estate at Dominica, and there he died. He had not, I suppose, attained his thirtieth year, but was a victim to the diseases of the climate.

I remember him well. He was a handsome young man and good natured, but I grieve to recollect was profane in his conversation, as sailors too commonly are.

The youngest of my paternal Uncles was David, whom I faintly remember. He was a tall, handsome young man, but was cut off before any of the rest, Robert excepted, by a rapid consumption, without attaining, I believe, his twenty-first year.

Of my Father's two Sisters the eldest married Mr. Nuccoll of Alloa, N. Britain, or as he was commonly called Capt. Nuccoll, because he had been in the East India Co. sea service, and I suppose commanded a vessel on the Coast. In their regular service he had advanced only to the rank of Chief Mate, tho' he was on the point of going out Captain when ill health obliged him to retire. He afterwards carried on business as a Merchant, trading to the Baltic chiefly, first from Alloa, and later in life from Leith. He was a worthy

---

[1] A respondentia bond is a loan upon the cargo of a vessel, to be repaid, with maritime interest, only if the goods arrive safe at their destination.

man and kind connection whose memory I hold in respect.
They never had any family. He died sometime about 1785
or 1786, and my Aunt surviving him lived to a great age, as
I have already noticed. She died in or about 1816.

The youngest Sister is still living. She is the wife of Mr.
Calder, a Merchant in Aberdeen, and they have had a
pretty numerous family, four of whom remain, and all in
proportion as they are known to me possess my regard and
esteem. It would be difficult perhaps to find a more united
family, or one of greater sobriety and prudence. Mr. Calder
is in several respects, and most of them of a laudable kind, a
very extraordinary man. For a union of a severe, self-denying prudence, with liberality, kindness, and charity, I have
perhaps hardly known his equal. Certainly none for steadiness, equality, and consistency of character; or I may add
for moderation and content. His virtues, I must admit, are
more those of the Stoic Philosopher than the Christian. I
suspect he has not indulgence enough for the frailties and
follies of others, and that without being actively vindictive,
he is not ready enough to forgive. I think, too, he indulges
the pride of opinion, and values himself upon an unbending
stability of resolution such as, when moral principle does
not require it, ill becomes a shortsighted erring creature in a
changeful world. But after all, I repeat, he is an extraordinary
man, and I will add an estimable and respectable one. I trust
he is a sincere believer in Xtianity, and if not yet sufficiently
impressed with the importance of what is peculiar to it, at
least open to such impressions. If so, what is wrong will I
hope be corrected, and what is wanting supplied. True
Xtian *humility* would go far towards both. My Aunt is a good
wife, and a good woman; a sensible woman too; and they
have lived forty years, I think, very happily together.

One of their daughters is married to Mr. Elmslie,
a Merchant in London. They are pleasing, respectable friends,
for whom I have much esteem and regard.

This account of my Father's family has been extended far
beyond my purpose. I now proceed to speak of that Parent
himself, and of the extraordinary circumstances by which he
became my Parent, through his union with my beloved
Mother.

He was originally designed, I believe, by my Grandfather for the legal profession in Scotland. But if so, the purpose was soon changed; for at an early age—so early, if I remember right, as eighteen—he was sent first to Holland, and then to France, on mercantile business, or to finish his education as a merchant.

After residing some time at Bordeaux he sailed from that port, sometime I believe in the year 1752, on board a ship laden with wine, under his own charge I think as supercargo, bound for some port in Scotland. His plan was then to settle in his native country as a merchant. But Providence ordered otherwise. Had it not I should in all probability never have come into being. Not at least if it was necessary to my identity that I should be born of the same Parents whom God actually gave me.

The Ship had proceeded up the Channel nearly as far as the Race of Portland when she encountered a terrible storm, and being on a lee shore was at length by the violence of the wind and sea cast at midnight on the rocks, under the high and nearly perpendicular cliffs of the Isle of Purbeck.

My Father, the only passenger on board, was at the moment the ship struck taking some refreshment with the Captain in the Cabin. They rushed together up the companion staircase to the deck; but the Captain, who was foremost had barely put his foot from the ladder, when they were parted to meet no more. A tremendous surge which at that moment broke over the ship swept him into the sea. At the same time it threw my Father down again and floated him back into the cabin where he soon found himself immersed in deep water and in great danger of being drowned. Much of the briny fluid was actually forced down his throat, and I have heard him describe in a lively manner the pain it gave him; but when near suffocation, his hand came in contact with a candlestick attached to the upper part of the Cabin wainscoat, by a convulsive grasp of which he got his mouth above water; and after some time he with great difficulty made his way upon deck. He there found that four only of the Crew survived, three foremastmen and a cabin boy, all the rest having shared the Captain's fate.

But he found on the other hand that the same surges which swept them off had thrown the wreck further in upon the rocks, so that they were nearly in contact with the cliff that rose to a fearful height above them. The only chance that appeared of saving their lives was their being able to wade from the wreck to the nearest projecting rock and from thence perhaps to find some means of ascending the cliff. Accordingly my Father and his four companions in distress resolved to make the trial, and in order that they might mutually help each other, or perish together, they passed a rope round each man's waist, and thus tied themselves to each other at convenient distances in file, my Father, as the strongest and tallest, going first, and the boy last. They expected by this expedient to guard against the fatal effects of a false step on the slippery rock, and found the precaution not unnecessary. When one man slipped, the rest sustained him, and enabled him to recover his footing, and they were enabled to follow each other's footsteps and holds in the steep ascent notwithstanding the darkness of the night. It was not, however, without great peril and extreme fatigue that they made their way to the summit, and when the place of their ascent was afterwards viewed by daylight their escaping destruction in the attempt seemed a wonderful interposition of Providence. The remark was that a cat could hardly have been expected to get up where these men had climbed. I have heard my Father mention a curious incident that contributed much to their preservation. When about halfway up, they found a small ledge or flat on which they were all able to sit down and rest themselves, when one of the sailors an old man, surprised them by producing a small keg of brandy, containing perhaps about a quart, which he had, unperceived by them, brought away under his arm. Happy was it for them now that he had hug'd this darling property at the increased hazard of his life. Without the powerful succour it gave to their strength and spirits they would probably have been unable to finish the laborious and difficult ascent. As it was, they were all so much exhausted when they reached the summit, as to be obliged to lie down on the wet ground a long time, before they could find strength enough to advance into the country in search of shelter from the storm. When able to do so they wandered a great while before they could find any habitation, but at length were guided by a distant light to the cottage of a shepherd, and after convincing him with some difficulty that they were not thieves but shipwrecked mariners, were received hospitably for the night. They now learned that the rocks they had been cast upon were those of the Isle of Purbeck, and the place of their asylum a wild unpeopled part of that Island, distant from any Town or Village in which they might find the further relief their situation required. The next day, however, they found all such difficulties pleasingly removed. Mr. Milner, my maternal grandfather, was at that time Collector of the Customs at Poole; and Purbeck being within his official province, he no sooner heard that a Ship with French wines was cast away there than he hastened to the spot, feeling it to be his duty to see that if any part of the cargo could be saved, it should not be smuggled on shore but landed under the inspection, and placed in the custody, of the Officers in his department. On finding that four mariners and a gentleman Passenger had escaped, he treated them with the greatest kindness and generosity, supplying all their wants, and pressing my Father to go home with him and reside at his house until he should proceed to Scotland. The invitation was accepted, and thus began that acquaintance between my Parents without which according to our notions of personal identity I could never have come into being. The acquaintance, however, would probably have ended forever without ripening into intimacy, much less into mutual attachment, if my Father had not felt that he had duties to perform to the family of the deceased Captain and the Owners of the Cargo, duties which detained him long on the spot. The Ship had been driven up so high among the rocks that she had stuck fast there through the gale, and a considerable part of the cargo was found capable of being saved, the wreck being left dry at low water. But the barbarous practice of plundering wrecked vessels had not been then reformed in that part of England, and to restrain the people of the coast from laying hands on such tempting plunder as wine and brandy was a work of no ordinary difficulty and danger. It was necessary to reinforce the revenue officers by all the strength of the local police and by volunteer assistance, which my Father was of course the first to render with great energy and zeal. Putting himself in the place of the Owners and deceased Master, he took the leading part in landing and securing their property and defending it by arms against the greedy bands of depredators by which the wreck was surrounded. In spite of his utmost vigilance many thefts were committed; but I have heard him more than once relate a singular occurrence which brought superstition at length to the aid of the police and materially tended to preserve the remainder of the cargo. He had a dream one night during this anxious employment that the Captain appeared to him and pointed out a place in which were papers of great importance to his widow and children. He described a Sea chest which my Father recollected to have seen on board, and a scarlet waistcoat in it which he remembered to have seen him wear, and said, in the pocket of that waistcoat he would find a pocket book in which the papers were contained. My Father in the morning mentioned the dream and declared he would go on board the wreck at the proper time of tide to satisfy himself whether any such papers were to be found. He accordingly went and actually found the chest, the waistcoat, and the papers, exactly as imagined in the dream. I forget what the papers were; but they were highly important to the family of the deceased. The strange coincidence immediately got abroad, and with it a rumour that the Captain's ghost appeared to his young friend the Passenger and told him of whatever was stolen from the wreck. Some later discoveries, I think, of goods found and seized in the cottages favored this notion, and the effect was unusual security in landing goods from the wreck during the remainder of that process.

Before these friendly offices could be compleated by disposing of the property saved, my Father had naturally to wait returns of letters both from Bordeaux and Scotland. He therefore availed himself pretty long of my Grandfather's hospitality; and I presume by the time of his departure from Poole that attachment between him and my

Mother was formed which not long afterwards led to their
union.

This attachment, I am sorry to say, was kept a secret from
both her parents, and the subsequent marriage was without
their consent or knowledge. It is painful to record the faults
of those to whom I owe my birth, and especially those of the
best of Mothers; but these acts of filial misconduct were, I
verily believe, the only serious sins she ever committed; and
deep was her penitence for them during the whole remainder
of her life. Often I have heard her pious self reproaches on
this account, and she regarded all the heavy afflictions she
met with as chastisements of Divine providence for this great
violation of duty towards her parents. I believe the inter-
pretation was right. There is no species of sin against which
I have so strikingly and uniformly seen the displeasure of
God manifested in his temporal retributions. Yet in my dear
Mother's case there was some extenuation of the offence.
She was very young, only fifteen years of age when the
attachment began, and she had not attained sixteen at the
time of the marriage. An elder Sister was the single confidant, and she not only approved of but persuaded her into
the fault. They well knew that their Father would not consent to such a choice. Tho' pleased with the young stranger,
whose strong natural talents and energy of character were
probably, at his then early age even, conspicuous, he could
not be expected to approve of him as a son-in-law, as he had
neither property nor any certain means of support for a
family, and his intended commercial establishment in a
remote part of the Kingdom was yet wholly unformed. My
Grandfather, it is true, was not wealthy and had little
beyond his official income, while he had six children, of
whom my Mother was the youngest, to provide for; but he
was rather a proud man, and looked higher for his children
than his circumstances would well warrant. He valued himself on his family extraction and perhaps too on his literature
and talents, which had given him friends, I believe, of distinction and rank. Besides, my Mother was very handsome,
had a fine voice, and had been carefully educated according
to the fashion of the day. From these and other circumstances it was foreseen by the two Sisters and my father that

the discovery of the attachment would certainly lead to his prohibition and the prevention of future intercourse. My Mother, however, was far from designing to marry without first obtaining the consent of her parents. All that she agreed to was a correspondence, in the hope that my Father's establishment and success in business would soon remove the main ground of objection. I do not recollect on what errand or pretence he continued to visit her in Dorsetshire again; but he was there at the time when the Marriage Act[1] was depending in Parliament, and it was this circumstance that gave him a success which he otherwise perhaps might never have attained. The expectation naturally was that the Act would be made effectual to its purpose, and that no way would afterwards remain open for marrying without the consent of parents. This consideration was so strongly pressed on my dear Mother, not only by him but [by] her Sister Hannah, that she was alarmed and hurried into a step to which her sense of filial duty made her yield with great reluctance; and they were privately married just before the Act took place. The secret was kept for some time; but at length her Sister, I think, insisted on its being communicated to her Mother, being alarmed at the responsibility she had herself incurred. A reconciliation soon took place, and my Father seems to have easily conciliated the confidence and good will of the family, for he not long after settled at Poole as a Merchant in partnership with Mr. William Milner, the second son of my Grandfather. There my elder brother and I were born; he in 1756, and I on the 30th of June 1758, and my dear Mother found herself for two or three years compleatly happy, her Parents being so much delighted with their grandchildren that she seemed not only to have atoned for her disconduct but added by it to their comfort and

---

[1] Because of the scandal of Fleet marriages, the Chancellor, Lord Hardwicke, proposed and in 1753 succeeded in getting passed a Marriage Act (26 George II, c. 33) which provided that, with the exception of Jewish and Quaker marriages, no marriage should be valid in England that was not celebrated by a priest in orders, according to the Anglican liturgy, and that the service could not be performed unless the banns had been published for three successive Sundays in the Parish Church, or unless a licence had been procured. Licences, which could be obtained only from the Archbishop, were made very costly. See W. E. H. Lecky, *A History of England in the Eighteenth Century* (New York, 1883), I, 533.

happiness. But Heaven had not yet ratified their forgiveness. I speak her own penitent and pious language when I say so. Her afflictions were soon to arrive, and to end only with her life. They began in the ruin of that mercantile establishment in which her Husband and Brother were engaged. Whether they had ventured too boldly upon extensive dealings I do not know. From my Father's disposition it is not unlikely. Certain it is that in a few years they became insolvent, and I think, but am not sure, that a bankruptcy ensued. The consequence most painful to my dear Mother was family discontent and discord, and it was not only between my Father and her own relations. His brother, William Stephen, was involved in their failure, not I think as a partner, but as surety; and a quarrel was produced by it between my Father and him which made them strangers, if not enemies, from that time to the end of their lives. In vain did she who was a great favorite with my Uncle (as indeed she ever was with all her husband's brothers) interpose her conciliatory efforts. With her own family they were equally fruitless; nor was my Father of a disposition to yield in such cases, or to admit himself to have been prudentially or otherwise in the wrong. Her affectionate and delicate mind therefore was doomed to lament in vain discord among those she most loved, in addition to alarming prospects of indigence and distress. So deeply was her sensibility wounded by these and similar occurrences in after life, that she felt a horror at all partnerships or joint concerns in matters of pecuniary interest between Members of the same family, at least after they have acquired by marriage connections that are not mutual. "My dear boys (she would say to my elder Brother and me) you will, I hope, hardly feel a separation in your interests in life till you marry; but after that, the more distinct they are kept, the better for your comfort and peace. You will still, I hope, love and be ready to assist each other; but you will avoid if you are wise all associations in matters of business." My experience and observation have certainly not tended to impeach the wisdom of this advice. My Father had too much energy of character and too much confidence in his own powers to be cast down by these early misfortunes. He did not doubt of forming some new commercial establishment with better success. But while in quest of that object it was necessary to relieve himself as much as possible from the immediate expense of a family. He therefore took my Mother with her two children to the North of Scotland, and placed us for a while under the wing of his Parents, returning soon to London himself to look out for some mercantile settlement there. He was not long in finding one that seemed to promise favorably enough. He found means to buy what proved a very beneficial lease of a wharf and extensive warehouses in the center of the City, comprising a comfortable dwelling House, and there he soon engaged in different branches of commerce. How he supplied the want of capital I do not know, but believe it was partly by the aid of friends, and partly by the resources of a partner, a Mr. Ross, with whom I can remember his being for some time connected.

Finding himself no longer at a loss for the expences of family life, he soon brought my Mother to London, but at the earnest request of his Father and Mother suffered my brother and me to remain with them near two years. He insisted, however, that we should not be taught to read, a judicious precaution against our being inextricably fixed in the Scotch pronunciation and idiom.

The earliest occurrences and scenes of my childhood, of which some faint images remain in my memory were of this period, when I was about three years old. I can recollect something of my Grandfather's person, and of a remarkable stream of water or "burn" near his house; but more distinctly my sea passage from Aberdeen to London with my brother, and our Uncle John Stephen, my Father's youngest brother, whom he had sent for us. My brother was then, I think, between six and seven, and I between four and five years old; and we had gained such a hold on the hearts of our Grand Parents that it was not without great reluctance, and almost by absolute compulsion that they could be brought to part with us. The old man even took offence at my Father for insisting on the separation, and declared he never wished to see another grandchild, that he might not have again to suffer the same affliction. My Mother, who had by this time brought into the world two other children, was of course overjoyed to see again her two elder boys

after so long an absence and at our then interesting times
of life. But there was a slight drawback upon her satisfaction
in her inability to understand us; for we both spoke such
broad Scotch, in true Buchan tone and dialect, that she was
obliged to call in my Father to interpret; and he found it
sometimes no easy task. I can remember one specimen of
this which I heard her relate. Hearing a noise in the nursery,
where we were with my Sister Mary (who afterwards died
at an early age) she went to listen, and heard me loudly
exclaiming "Wully, Wully, the lassy's tint the buekie! Fat
a ye deen wie the buekie, lassy?" "What do you say brother
Jemmy?" was the child's reply; but I could only repeat the
same unintelligible jargon. My Mother at length discovered
that a little gilt book which had been given to me to learn
my letters from had been lost by my Sister; and the translation is "William, William, the little girl has lost the
book! What have you done with the book, child?" yet
such was the effect of my Father's precaution, that being
put to a day school, and taught to read with the English
pronunciation, we in a very few months wholly got rid of
the Scotch dialect and idiom, so that it could not be discovered that we had ever been infected with them. We
also so soon overtook in reading and spelling boys of the
same age in school, that my Mother doubted much whether
the pains taken to teach children to read before they are
six years old might not well be spared. My Father, finding
the air of the City unfriendly to the health of his family,
or induced by the love of long daily walks which I have
inherited from him, took a house at South Lambeth where
my brother William and I constantly resided for two or
three years, going to a day school at Vauxhall that was
kept by the well known Peter Annett.[1] He was, I believe,
a man of considerable erudition, and of good moral character

[1] Peter Annet (1693–1769), called by Leslie Stephen "the last of the deists,"
was a miscellaneous writer and schoolmaster who lost his employment through
bitter attacks on Bishop Sherlock and others, c. 1744; he attacked the credibility
of the Old Testament in his paper, the *Free Inquirer*, which ran for only nine
numbers in 1761; for this he was tried on a charge of blasphemous libel, and
was condemned to imprisonment, pillory, and hard labour in 1763; after
imprisonment he went back to schoolteaching. James Stephen was probably in
his school from 1764 to 1767, at a somewhat later age than ascribed to him by
Leslie Stephen, *Life of Sir James Fitzjames Steshen* (London, 1895), p. 8.

but of a sceptical turn, and he had published a dissertation impeaching the truth of the Mosaical Scripture, for which he had been prosecuted by the Government, and convicted and punished as a blasphemer. My Father regarded him as a well-meaning persecuted man, and I suppose concluded that we were too young to be in any danger from his religious errors. I fear, however, that he did not regard these with sufficient firmness of dislike. He had himself spent much time in France, and was partial to the *literati* of that Country. Annett probably gained some esteem as well as sympathy by the steadiness and courage with which he maintained his opinions; for his school, as I recollect, was large; but he soon after became too infirm to conduct it, and in the last stage of his life laboured under poverty and external distress as well as long-continued sickness. Archbishop Secker[1] heard of his situation, and sent him a sum of money for his relief with offers of further assistance; but the old man's feelings would not allow him to accept it. He had always regarded the Archbishop as the Author of the prosecution against him, and therefore sent back the money, saying he could not think of accepting favours from his persecutor. The Prelate acted in a far more Christian spirit. He wrote a kind and condescending letter, assuring him that he was under a mistake, for that he, the Archbishop, had no share whatever in the proceedings against him, and expressing a hope therefore that he would not deny him the pleasure of contributing to his relief.

I well remember all the interesting occurrences of this period of my early life. The daily walks with my dear brother from South Lambeth to Vauxhall, with our satchels containing our books and our dinner, which we were allowed to eat at the house of a kind old woman, a humble friend of my Mother, near the school; our returns in the evening; our plays at cricket &c, with which we ended the day; the

---

[1] Thomas Secker (1693-1768) was Archbishop of Canterbury from 1758 to the time of his death. As a prelate he deprecated the progress of Methodism but did not persecute its adherents. His pamphlet advocating an American episcopate, the *Answer to Dr. Mayhew's Observations on the Charter and Conduct of the Society for the Propagation of the Gospel in Foreign Parts* (London, 1764), aroused opposition both in England and in America.

faces of all the people we were familiar with; the figures of the houses and trees we daily passed, are all in my recollection, with greater freshness and particularity than the objects of yesterday's attention. This has been frequently during the last five and twenty years a source of pleasure to me the nature of which I cannot well describe. In my walks through South Lambeth to Clapham, local recollections connect themselves with a train of ideas that bring back to me as it were the mind of my childhood, a mind vivid, romantic, and susceptible of the keenest sensations of pleasure as well as pain. I can recall the happiness that I experienced from the possession of a trap ball and a miniature pack of playing cards, from catching the large yellow cucumbers that floated from the gardener's grounds down the creek towards Vauxhall, scooping them into boats and rigging them with a wooden rudder and paper sail &c; also the exquisite pain I suffered from the sting of a hornet, and other trifling accidents. I have reason to believe that few human bodies or minds were ever endued with a keener sensibility than mine were at that period, and indeed have continued to be till age has blunted its edge. My imagination also was extremely active and wild. It gave an interest to every flower and leaf and insect. I followed a butterfly with more eagerness than a Naturalist would a nondescript to enrich his museum. At every holiday hour the garden, the orchard, and field, were theatres to me of inexhaustible curiosity and interest. I can remember even preserving the fallen leaves of Autumn, sticking them on broken panes of glass to observe better their variegated tints and fibers. I was then, as I have ever continued to be, an enthusiastic admirer of the works of nature; and that I have nevertheless remained profoundly ignorant of natural history in all its branches, may seem strange, till the story shall be told of my much neglected education. At the same period, and till mature manhood, I had a strong belief (shall I not say an intuitive consciousness) of spiritual beings, with which I was surrounded. I mean chiefly the apprehension of ghosts. I would rather have encountered a lion, than been left alone in a dark room; and even at night with my brother for my bedfellow, I used to cover my face with the bed cloathes, enduring the difficulty of respiration, lest I should see some terrible apparition; and actually persisted in this practice so long as to have acquired by it, and still to retain, a power of enduring in that way, what to another man would seem a semi-suffocation, without inconvenience. My Brother and the servants used to play upon this weakness; and if I was intractable at any time the threat of leaving me alone soon brought me to reason. In winter we were generally left there five days in the week to the care of a servant, my Father being confined by business to his house at Brooks Wharf, which I suppose prevented my dear Mother's effectual interposition to prevent my being confirmed in these terrors of imagination by improper treatment. The house at South Lambeth which my fancy thus peopled with invisible guests, still remains. It is the white house opposite the path which crosses the end of Lark Hall Lane, and leads to the Wandsworth road. No part so near London is less altered. The very field opposite our door has yet escaped the Builders. My local recollections, and the pleasures that attend them, are so much the stronger. A curious and pleasing occurrence once marked to me and others the accuracy of these recollections. I was walking by that residence of my childhood about twenty-four years ago with my dear Nancy and two other friends, when I stop'd before a cottage, the next house but one beyond my Father's in the way to Stockwell, and said, "Here lived Brock the Potter, with his Son, who was notwithstanding his inferior station in life a playground companion of mine. I wonder whether I can learn there what is become of the family." I step'd across the road, knocked at the door of the cottage, and out came a little boy, the identical Tom Brock, as my surprised imagination immediately told me. In size, in features, in his timid respectful air, he was precisely the same humble companion of my childhood. "Is not your name Tom Brock?" exclaimed I. "Yes Sir," replied the boy, startled at the question. I found on further enquiry that he was the son of Thomas Brock, my quondam playfellow, who had long before been removed to another, I hope a happier, world.

Here let me open a view on which I have often meditated, and which concurs with everything else around me, and within me, to confirm my full conviction of a future state, in which we shall revisit, perhaps consciously, the scenes of our human existence, or at least know again (if among the blessed) its companions, connections, and friends. It seems to be a maxim of the Divine œconomy in what we call the works of Nature not only to satisfy, but [to] exceed, all that we can fancy in the varieties of creation, and especially to leave no innocent desire, and no capacity for enjoyment, in this sublunary state, without its proper objects and means of gratification. We may not attain those objects, or possess those means; for privation and disappointment are parts of the discipline necessary for us in this our state of trial; but it is nevertheless true of the species, tho' not of the individual, that every capacity for enjoyment has its potential gratification. There is no waste in the bounty of the Creator. He has not given to his sensitive and rational creatures an aptitude for any enjoyment that he has totally and universally withheld from them. Our purest and best desire indeed are very sparingly gratified in the present scene—

How starved on earth, our Angel appetites!

It is a truth that forms no mean argument for a future life. Philanthropy, the love of justice, the desire of knowledge, above all the love of God, can find their full satisfaction only beyond the grave. We therefore justly reason that there they will be found. The Almighty has not given us such desires, and such capacities for happiness in the fruition of them, without providing for their full indulgence.

With less certainty I admit, but by the same train of reasoning, I am led to conclude, that the desire we feel to recall the faded impressions of our early years, the nameless pleasures that we feel in their clear revival, when no consciousness of sin poisons the recollection, especially the joy that arises from renewing our intercourse, after a long separation, with the objects of our virtuous affections, or the intimate companions of our youth, indicate a much fuller attainment of such gratifications in a future state. If we are not to revisit the scenes of our human life, if we are not to know again our beloved relatives, companions and friends, then we have here a class of enjoyments, and those too of an innocent and amiable kind, which God certainly might, and yet does not confer. We have capacities for happiness of a species which we are but scantily indulged with in this life, and not at all in the next. It is true that blessed Spirits must have infinitely nobler and more delightful subjects of contemplation than the most interesting scenes and fondest attachments of their human state can furnish; but the Creator, as I have premised, seems to delight in bestowing every possible or conceivable variety of good. He does not in the works of Nature withhold the less, because he has provided the greater, means of enjoyment, when both are adapted to the capacities with which he has endued his sensitive and rational creatures.

It is not, however, from the loss of potential happiness alone, that our ignorance of human scenes and our human friends and relatives after death, seems to me incongruous with what we know and experience of the ways of the Most High. There would be also in that case a loss of lessons, which blessed Spirits, if their knowledge and felicity is progressive, may well desire to learn. What can we suppose more instructive to them, or more fruitful of holy admiration and love, than their witnessing the development of the plans of Divine Providence on earth, in the sequels and consequences of actions and events in which they once took part, the progress of religion and virtue in hearts that were dear to their own, and the vindication of God's justice against the sins which they could not reform by their pious admonitions, in the evils and mischiefs which ensue? Almost every retrospect which memory affords to pious contemplation in the present life presents to us new views of God's mercy and justice in the course of his temporal providence; but they become clearer, as well as more numerous, in proportion as the horizon widens by the length of our experience and observation. Surely the progress of this highly interesting and elevated species of knowledge, honorable as it is to the Divine Governor, and useful to his creatures, will neither cease, nor lose its interest, in death.

It is a leading object of these self memorials to record my observations of the ways of Providence. Subordinate only to this, and forming indeed the most important branch of it, is the tracing back the history of my own moral sense or conscience. I will therefore here mention the earliest instance I can recollect of my consciousness of sin, which was during this residence at South Lambeth. I had learnt from some of my companions a practice which we called "transporting frogs". A flattened piece of stick or slip about a foot long or more was poised on a rail and the frog put on one end, the weight of which was counterbalanced by a longer arm of the lever on the hither side of the rail. To the extremity of this a smart downward blow was given by a bat or cudgel; and the poor animal in consequence was projected to a considerable hight in the air, from which it came down dead, or was killed by the fall. The boys who shewed me the cruel trick sometimes previously blew up the unfortunate reptile to a great size by means of a straw inserted into its body; but I have no recollection of taking part in that aggravation of the crime. I remember only my conscience having reproached me for joining in the transportations. It was perhaps my first feeling of remorse, and I hope led me to desist from the practice. A rail which was the instrument of it (often no doubt renovated during the half century and more that has since elapsed) still remains, bounding the field opposite to my then abode, and generally as I pass freshens the recollection of my boyish sin and repentance.

During this residence at South Lambeth, I had a very narrow escape of my life, from a sore throat and fever, combined with that most common aggravation of all such dangers, mistreatment by the Faculty. It was a disease of the putrid, now called the typhus kind; but they treated it as inflammatory, and the consequence was my being confined to my bed above a month, and reduced to the last extremity. At length Dr. Grant,[1] then a very eminent Physician, was brought from London, who quite reversed the treatment,

---

[1] William Grant, M.D., (d. 1786) physician to Misericordia Hospital, Goodman's Fields; published treatises on the London Fevers of 1771 and the following years, and one on *Observations on the Influenza of* 1775 *and* 1782.

and among other antiseptics made them squeeze plentifully
the juice of grapes tho' not then quite ripe, into my mouth,
the capacity of drinking being gone, and my throat in a
dreadful state of ulceration. This new regimen operated as
a charm and speedily restored me to health. I have often
heard my dear Mother speak of the case as the most desperate
disease and most wonderful recovery she had known in her
family. I recollect as well its commencement as if it had
happened a Month ago. I had been at Vauxhall and seeing
some damsons in a shop when I had some halfpence in my
pocket, bought a pint measure of them and devoured them
with a greediness of appetite and keenness of relish such as I
have rarely felt for any food. I was taken down the same day
but am strongly persuaded that the partial antidote thus
obtained by the direction of nature at the onset of the
disease contributed much to the saving of my life. I have
never felt such a keen appetite for fruit since, except once in
the beginning of convalescence after my keen India seasoning fever, when the free and extreme indulgence of it probably saved me from a relapse, and certainly hastened my
recovery. It is a common opinion, and I believe a gross error,
that eating plumbs is unwholesome. The source of the
notion is that fevers, fluxes, cholera morbus, and other
diseases of the bilious and putrescent kind are peculiarly
common in Autumn, and therefore likely to come on soon
after eating Autumnal fruits. But if I am sure of any medical
fact it is this: "Experience & observation have taught me
that whenever in a morbid state of the body the appetite
strongly directs us to any particular food, that food is
medicinal in a high degree." The Author of our frames knew
their exigencies better than physicians do. He has therefore
provided a thousand curative expedients in the propensities
of disordered nature which work uniformly and mechani-
cally in a right direction when purblind art does not check
and controul them, and he has wonderfully adapted the
œconomy of the vegetable world in this respect to the
ordinary local and periodical necessities of the human
frame. I have seen in numberless instances plain traces of
this bounteous contrivance. Hot climates, and hot seasons
of the year in temperate climates, strongly predispose our

bodies to putrescent diseases; but the same climates and seasons produce rich flavoured fruits of a highly antiseptic quality, and our palates dispose us to indulge in them exactly in the same proportion as they are necessary to save us from the morbific effects of the atmosphere. I might add also of the *place*, for it is a curious concurrent fact that the same low and moist situations which concur with the heat to produce putrescent diseases are the most favorable to the growth of fruit trees, especially of those which bear the most powerful antiseptic fruits. I have observed this even in the West Indies. These facts being admitted, it is easy to see how the prejudice against plumbs has arisen. The remedy to which nature directs us is not in the artificial state of society that we live in always within our reach. If it were, it might effectively prevent any visible disease by correcting the morbid tendency at its first stages. But when this tendency has advanced too far to be entirely controuled and just before the disease itself appears, the remedial provision of nature meets the eye or the imagination of the patient. He obtains the fruit and eats it with an eagerness that seems to lead him to excess. The coming mischief is mitigated, and to a degree decisive perhaps on the side of life; but the disease nevertheless soon after shews itself; it is remembered that the patient had last fed upon plumbs or some other fruit, and they bear the blame of the malady which in fact they tended to prevent. If the patient were still left at freedom to consult his appetite he would resort again to the same remedy, and be cured; but medical science, that erring, fickle, and notoriously inconsistent, yet ever specious, and positive science, interposes, lays her arbitrary veto on the wise suggestions of nature, and if the patient at last recovers, art, which had only endangered and long retarded the cure, obtains all the credit of it. Sometimes, as in my case at South Lambeth, the Physician is obliged to recur to the very remedies which nature indicated from the first, but still art has the praise. Even my anxiously affectionate and very sensible Mother, I dare say, did not reflect that if unripe grapes saved my life in the last instance, damsons could hardly have been bad for me at the first, tho' these were prescribed by nature, and those by Dr. Grant. I will not advise my children always to trust to and follow the propensities of nature when they are sick; but this I will confidently tell them as the result of near 50 years recollection of the history of my own feeble frame in different climates, and of much observation and thought, that I verily believe if there were no physicians or other medical professors much fewer disorders would prove fatal. Unfortunately most men suppose that tho' they naturally fall sick, they never naturally recover, and that something must be done to make them well, or else they shall certainly die, or incur some terrible mischief; wheras nothing is more certain than that these bodily machines of ours "fearfully and wonderfully made" are so contrived as to contain remedial means within themselves for almost every accident and disordered movement (not fatal to the moving power itself) to which they are liable. The *vis medicatrix naturæ* can do almost every thing without the aid of the Faculty, but the Faculty nothing without it; and nothing but mischief can ensue when its action is artificially controuled. Yet in all internal diseases the true line of this action may be mistaken, and has often been so for ages, in diseases even the most common and conspicuous, and by all, even the best Physicians, witness the old method of treating the small pox, now proved and universally admitted to have been fatally wrong, and by which during the many generations subjected to it, millions of men must have perished.

Sometime in or about the year 1767, as I can best fix the time, my elder Brother and I were taken by my Father to our native place Poole in Dorsetshire and placed at the boarding school of the Rev. Mr. Howell, a Dissenting clergyman. I well remember the journey as well as the change of situation. My Uncle, Mr. George Milner, my Mother's younger brother, lived in the Town, and his only son, my long beloved and affectionate friend, and now my brother-in-law, Mr. Milner of Comberton, was a day scholar at Mr. Howell's school. Whether it was through this connection that the school was recommended to my Father, or he had previously known Mr. Howell, I do not recollect; but can remember that both he and my Uncle thought highly of Mr. Howell as a pious clergyman, a scholar, and kind-hearted liberal man; the latter of which characters at least I believe he deserved. He had a Meeting House, respectable I think for such a Town as to the congregation, and was an Independent of the Sect of the old Dissenters now commonly distinguished by their having been Dr. Doddridge's[1] School. He had probably, however, fallen off, as most of that school have done, from the doctrines which that excellent man taught and which are usually called orthodox. I am not sure of this; but from the connections he had as I have since learnt I should suppose that his theological opinions probably resembled those of Dr. Price.[2] I do not think they were Socinian. Indeed am pretty sure they were not, for I remember that he used Dr. Watts's[3] Psalms and Hymns. My impressions of him are favorable to his piety, as well as his benignity of temper and manners. In the pulpit, and in our family devotions, he was solemn and impressive, but I recollect nothing of the particular doctrines he inculcated, and suppose his sermons exclusively practical, for had he expressly taught any of those doctrines which are now called evangelical or had he on the other hand taught any of an opposite kind, I should probably have remembered them wheras my mind was an absolute blank on all such subjects till long after I attained to manhood. I can indeed remember that there was another Meeting House in the Town in which a Mr. Ashburner preached, and that I understood he differed from Mr. Howell in holding that men might be saved by Faith alone without good works; but this was the full measure of my ideas as to the differences in point of doctrine

---

[1] Philip Doddridge (1702–1751), nonconformist divine; tolerant of Arminianism though rejecting its claims; a celebrated hymn writer, e.g., of "Awake my soul, stretch every nerve, but press with vigour on"; author of *The Rise and Progress of Religion in the Soul* (1745) and *The Family Expositor*. (6 vols., 1739–1756).

[2] Richard Price (1723–1791), nonconformist minister and writer on morals, politics, and economics; friendly opponent of Priestley within the nonconformist connection, upholding the Arian position and doctrine of the freedom of the will against Priestley's Socinianism and materialism; friend of the American and French Revolutions; denounced by Burke in *Reflections on the French Revolution* for his sermon approving the French Revolution; author of *A Review of the Principal Questions in Morals* (1756).

[3] Isaac Watts (1674–1748), hymn-writer; nonconformist minister in London; composed six hundred hymns; published doctrinal treatises of Arian tendency.

The Customs House at Poole

that divided one sect of protestant dissenters from another (the question of infant baptism excepted); and as to Calvinists I supposed that the term meant only such Christians as followed Calvin in rejecting episcopal government; consequently that my Mother and Mr. Ashburner were equally of that description. Mr. Howell, however, was a warm Whig politician, a great admirer of Mr. Wilkes,[1] the then reigning demagogue, and he afterwards as I have heard entered violently, or at least very zealously, into the democratical spirit which alarmingly prevailed in this Country after the revolution in France. Tho' then a very old man, he came from the West of England to London to keep the anniversary of that event when celebrated by the revolutionary Party here with a grand public dinner. I fear therefore that my old Master was by this period at least become more ardent in political controversy than became a Minister of the Gospel of peace.

Such was the Clergyman in whose boarding school I was placed when first sent from home for education.

My Brother and I like all newcomers to a large school had to undergo some persecution from our companions. I can remember a ludicrous species of it to which we were subjected in consequence of our speaking better English than our companions; for besides the boarders who were mostly from the Western Counties Mr. Howell had a great number of day scholars who all spoke the peculiar dialect of Dorsetshire, or at least of Poole. When our Metropolitan English differed from their provincial corruptions we were of course supposed by them to be wrong and ridiculed for it; e.g., in Poole they scarcely ever used the accusative cases of the pronoun *I*, especially in the plural, or indeed, any case but the nominative. "Will you fight *I* or *we*?" "Will you play with *we*?" were the substitutes for "*me* and *us*". My Brother and I were

---

[1] John Wilkes (1727–1797), the most flamboyant radical politician of his age; one of the rakes of Medmenham Abbey; M.P. for Aylesbury, 1757, 1761; founded *North Briton*, 1762; arrested for libel, 1763; expelled from House of Commons and outlawed for publishing #45 of the *North Briton* and the obscene *Essay on Woman*, 1764; reinstated in Parliament and outlawry reversed, 1768; expelled again, 1769; Sheriff of London and Middlesex, 1771; returned to Parliament 1774–1790; lord mayor of London, 1774; city chamberlain, 1779–1797.

therefore thought very incorrect for our use of the latter; and actually on this account got the nickname of *"utch two"*, (for so they imitated the novel sound "us"): We were hooted after in the play ground, and even as we passed in the Street, with "there goes *'utch two'*." This and the other petty persecutions we met with as newcomers sat lightly on my dear Brother, whose temper was always gentle. But I, alas! was, on the contrary irascible beyond the ordinary standard, and did not patiently endure these boyish insults. The consequence was my getting into quarrels and battles, and as my courage in moments of irritation was beyond my strength, I had nothing to boast of in the event. I remember having formally challenged a boy who in the language of schools was much above my match, and going, attended by all our play fellows, to a neighbouring ground to fight him, but it was soon evident that I had no chance in the contest. I had too much pride, however, to submit and therefore endured a severe beating till our companions at length, seeing it was no match, interposed and forcibly parted us. On this my mortification was so great that I burst into tears, ran away without my cloaths, and never stop'd till I arrived at a distant sand pit, where I concealed myself to hide my shame, still crying from the rage and indignation till some of the older boys who had followed me with my cloaths, found me and brought me home. This was afterwards the subject of conversation at the dinner table; and powerful is the effect of censure or praise at that early time of life, for I can recollect to this hour the lively sensations with which I heard the remarks of Mrs. and Mr. Howell. She, who was a coarse tho' goodnatured woman, said, "Why Jem it was like a coward, was it not, to cry and hide yourself?" but Mr. Howell with more discernment as well as kindness, said, "No, by no means; it was rather a proof of his spirit. He cried and hid himself because he could not bear to be conquered and he had fought while he could." I was sinking with shame at the reproof, till relieved by this, which I felt to be a just defence. Censure for my petulance and passion would certainly have been more proper, but I believe that neither for these nor for the practice of fighting did I receive any admonition. Mr. H. perhaps thought as many do that such contests between boys ought not to be discouraged. Soon after this, finding or supposing myself and two other boys about my own size to be oppressed by our seniors in school, I proposed to and formed with them a league offensive and defensive, by which we mutually engaged that if any boy above our match injured either of us, we should assist each other in beating him. This compact was also extended to, and cemented by a communion of property, all our own pocket money and play things being brought into a common stock. This alliance also came to Mr. Howell's ears, and his remarks upon it, while he laughed at my contrivance, were not of a nature to discourage me, or repress my natural vanity. In fact I was always a favourite with him, and perhaps for these very qualities that were most dangerous to myself in after life, and required the most controul. I remained at this school about two years and have no reason to believe that my progress in education was great. Mr. Howell's qualifications and habits as a teacher were probably not above par. Such I know is the opinion of Milner, who was longer at the school and left it at a riper age. But I had an imagination that always disposed me to be idle; and the discipline was very lax. I remember once, and once only, being punished by Mr. H. for neglect of my school duties. I was improved a good deal in reading, to which a laudable attention was paid, Mr. H. himself hearing us read select pieces in verse and prose including some of the dramatic kind, and taking pains to give us not only correct pronunciation, but proper emphases and tones and adaptation of voice and manner to the sense. In writing and cyphering of course I was also somewhat advanced. But as to Latin my progress must have been very small except I allow much for the effects of a subsequent and long interruption in that branch of education; for when it was resumed I knew nothing beyond the declensions, conjugations, and a few of the more general rules of grammar; not even these very well. I can recollect, however, tho' indistinctly, having read Corderius, Erasmus, and Cæsar[1] or

[1] These were the three standard textbooks for introducing schoolboys to Latin for three hundred years. The *Colloquia Scholastica* (1564) was the best known of a long series of grammatical works of Mathurin Cordier (1478–1564), who first taught at Paris, where he had John Calvin as a pupil, and after he became a Protestant settled in Geneva, where he was famous as a skilful teacher

some parts of those Books. My mind during the latter part of my stay there was occupied with a subject far more interesting than my studies, and that was my Master's eldest daughter, with whom, tho' I was scarcely more than ten years old, I fell desperately in love. She was I think about fifteen, and I suppose rather a handsome girl; but she appeared to me a perfect Venus and I conceived an affection for her so romantically strong that it made me follow her with my eyes whenever she could be seen and think of her continually when absent, at the expence not only of my lessons but my peace. The attachment was too ebulient not to be soon perceived, and it soon became a subject of merriment not only in the school but in the parlour. Mr. H. himself used to jest with me about my love for his daughter. As to the young Lady herself, tho' she doubtless joined in the laugh and could feel nothing reciprocal towards a boy of ten years old, my folly perhaps gained me her good will, for she was very kind to me, and once at least set my heart a leaping and inflamed my passion to the highest degree by casting her arms round my neck when we met on the staircase and giving me a kiss. She once also condescended to flatter me by praising the dimples in my cheeks. But neither such encouragements nor the strength of my feelings ever emboldened me to tell her (except with my eyes and my blushes when they encountered hers) of my presumptuous attachment. I was conscious that such a declaration could only be received with ridicule, and that my wishes were

---

of youth. Selections from the *Colloquia* were popular textbooks throughout Europe, particularly in Protestant countries, and in America, until well into the nineteenth century. The latest school edition in the British Museum is dated 1851. Equally long-lived and popular was the *Colloquia Familiara* of Desiderius Erasmus (1467–1535), first published in a collected edition in 1524, containing seventy-nine conversations intended to introduce young pupils to the leading principles of poetry, rhetoric, physical science, and ethics as propounded by the great humanist, but also to furnish them with a model of the most eloquent colloquial Latin of the time. The statement is made in the *Encyclopedia Britannica* (11th edition) that no book ever appeared that received such large immediate circulation: one Paris publisher sold 24,000 copies as fast as he could furnish them. The Duke University Library has an American school edition dated 1815. By the end of the nineteenth century only one of Stephen's schoolbooks, the *Commentaries on the Gallic Wars* of Julius Caesar, remained in general use, much to the loss—in the opinion of this annotator—of the schoolboys who were left to struggle with a dead instead of a living Latin language.

hopeless unless I should when arrived at manhood have the happiness to find her disengaged. Nor was my imagination sanguine enough to present this to me as a probable event. On the contrary I concluded that so lovely a creature could not but have a multitude of offers. Every time she was going from home I feared my hopes would be cut off before her return, and every young man who came to visit in the family appeared to me a dangerous rival. Often did I feel in such cases the severest pangs of jealousy, and wish that I was of an age to defy the assassin of my peace to mortal combat, and take his life or yield to him my own. Such are the foolish miseries of this vain and anxious life. Thus early are our desires and our destinies irreconcilably opposed to each other; and thus in every stage of life, even in the bright morning of our days, do the storms of unseasonable or un-gratified passions darken our human prospects and disturb our peace.

It will be a frequent object in these memoirs to record the preservations to which I have been indebted to a gracious Providence, and I have more than one such subject of grateful recollection during the time of my residence at Poole. I was attacked there with a fever so violent that it was thought necessary to send to London for my Father, who came down to see me. My recovery was owing as I have heard him say (and my experience in later life assures me of the fact) to the use of that noble medicine in the infancy of its reputation, Dr. James's Powders.[1] The localities of Poole are in respect of lowness and moisture of situation, like South Lambeth, with the addition of a muddy sea beach. In such a situation my constitution always strongly exposes me to fevers and other maladies of the nervous and bilious kind, and to such as used to be called putrid, but now typhus fevers. I should probably therefore have had another and perhaps fatal attack of fever at Poole, but for an accident of a serious kind. In running violently round the play ground I

[1] Robert James, M.D. (1705–1776), educated at Lichfield and St. John's College, Oxford (B.A. 1726); M.D. of Cambridge, 1728; L.R.C.P. 1745; life-long friend of Dr. Johnson, who contributed to his *Medical Dictionary* (1743); published a *Dissertation on Fevers* (1748), in which he recommended a powder and a pill which he had patented in 1746 and on which he made a considerable fortune.

fell headlong and struck my temple against a sharp flint stone by which so serious a wound was made that they thought my skull was fractured, and sent for a Surgeon. I lost much blood, and shall carry the scar (which was once a very large one) to my grave. But this wound proved a vent for such an accumulation of sharp and morbid humours as perfectly astonished the Surgeon and led him to say that he doubted not it had saved me from a very dangerous fever. It is a part of the body in which wounds usually heal very soon; but for a month or more there was a perpetual flow of a sharp watery humour so acrimonious that what escaped from the dressings blistered and excoriated my cheek all the way to the chin. I remember to this hour the discomfort which it caused me, and the wonder expressed by the Surgeon and others at the virulence and quantity of the humours discharged from such a part of my frame. I shall have occasion to notice a similar preservation in the West Indies, tho' my knowledge of my own constitution makes these cases much more impressive on my mind than I can probably make them to others.

I had also while at Poole a preservation of a different kind. I was at play with some school fellows at the sand pit before noticed and we were cutting our letters and figures on the side of the excavation with a sandy cliff rising above us to the hight I suppose of twenty feet or more. Suddenly a large part of the cliff over my head gave way and falling upon me buried me as I fell, all but the head and neck, which happily fell outward from the cliff (for had I fell with my head towards it I must have been smothered). My companions immediately came to my rescue and after some delay got enough of the sandy earth removed from me to enable them to drag me out with the loss only of my shoes and buckles. But they had barely time to do so before another huge fragment of the cliff fell down and covered to a considerable depth the place where my head a minute before had lain. I had therefore a very narrow escape from being suffocated and buried alive. Boys tho' we were, we all stood aghast at the sight of the huge mass by which I had been so nearly entombed. Whether gratitude to Providence for the deliverance formed any part of my own feelings on the occasion I cannot recol-

lect and therefore it is most probable I had at that time no
such sentiment. Indeed I am not clear that religious sentiments of any kind had yet any place in my heart, or even in
my thoughts when alone.

Chapter Two

[1768–1770]

I WAS still with my brother William at Mr. Howell's school when a new plan of life which my Father unfortunately adopted induced him to come with my Mother and her younger children into Dorsetshire and establish his family home within a mile of Poole.

Whether his commercial affairs in London continued up to this time to be prosperous, I doubt; tho' I never heard to the contrary. Most probably his business, if successful, was not adequate to the permanent supply of such an income as his rapidly increasing family and stile of living demanded. But however this might be, a prospect seemed to open to him of greatly improving his situation in a way more to his mind than the monotonous and dull pursuits of ordinary commerce. Sir John Webb, a Roman Catholic Baronet of large fortune, had long been acquainted with my Father, and was an admirer of those great natural talents which he conspicuously possessed. He therefore consulted him on plans he had formed for the improvement of his estates in Dorsetshire, particularly an extensive but sterile one situated at Ham, or Hamworthy, near Poole. It had by its situation on the sea coast facilities of maritime carriage, and was supposed to contain under its barren soil not only excellent brick earth and tobacco pipe clay, but coal and other mineral treasures. My Father on visiting the estate with its Proprietor confirmed him in his sanguine expectations. Indeed I believe it was by his suggestion that the opinion of there being coal under the surface was entertained. Extensive projects were in consequence adopted. A Town or maritime village was to be built, a trade with London opened, and ships constructed on the spot for which Sir John Webb's woods at Canford, a part of the country not far distant, were to furnish the materials. Brick kilns, lime kilns, &c., were to be formed, clay pits sunk, and a colliery opened if upon the usual methods being tried the hope of finding a good coal vein should be confirmed. But the essential means of all these improvements in Sir John's opinion was my Father's intelligent and energetic conduct of them on the spot. He therefore made to him very tempting offers to induce him to give up his business in London, to come as a resident to Ham, and there devote himself to the prosecution of these projects, on the footing of a mutual participation in the profits that might attend their success. My Father, who was at least as sanguine as the Baronet himself, entered into written contracts with him on this basis; and their general stipulations naturally were that each party should contribute what he could best supply, Sir John the pecuniary means, and my Father the personal conduct of the joint concern. There was not at the time any house on or near the estate fit for a gentleman's residence; but it was agreed that till this want could be supplied a farm house not far from the seat of the intended improvement should be fitted up as well as speedily might be for my Father's reception, and he chose also from motives of family convenience to have the farm to which it was attached. These arrangements being made, the affairs of the house in London were wound up as speedily as possible, Brooks Wharf with the extensive warehouses &c., belonging to it, as well as the House at South Lambeth, let or given up, and my dear Mother with her nursery removed from a social circle in which she was highly admired and beloved to the coarse and solitary residence provided for her at Ham. Sir John was profuse in his expressions of concern for her bad accomodations, and of impatience to see her settled in a better habitation to be built on his estate for her use. On her part she was far from murmuring at the change. Her mind was always too much elevated to care much about external circumstances, and tho' highly delicate in her person and manners she could endure hardships with as much chearfulness and indifference as if she had been born and brought up in a cottage. As to Society she never desired any but that of her husband and children, and others who were dear to her heart. Such was her maternal tenderness that reunion with my elder brother and me was, I dare say, an ample compensation for all she had left in London.

If I remember right the only change at first made in

regard to him and me upon fixing the new family home so near us was the having us there on Sundays and holidays, tho' I am not sure that we were not afterwards converted from boarders into day scholars or halfboarders going home every night. What I remember with more certainty is that during this residence at Ham I was seized with an ague which preyed upon me with great severity for above six months, and led perhaps to my being taken from school, as I have no recollection of going again to Mr. Howell's after this disease had fastened upon me, or of my Brother being with me at the time. To this hour I can recall distinctly and circumstantially my unfailing attacks upon alternate days, first with the rigours of the shivering fit and afterwards the hot fit, attended with a high degree of fever, sometimes delirium, and going off with a most profuse and exhausting perspiration. The intermission was sudden and perfect; the next day I went out to play and exercise as usual, and a keen appetite helped in some measure to recruit my strength before the next paroxysm arrived. When the shivering fit came on I used to run to the kitchen fire side, there being no fire, I presume, in any other room, and there was indulged with a close arm chair and blankets, which experience long failed to convince me were of no use. A hundred furs or down beds would not at all allay that morbid sense of cold, which is in truth wholly uninfluenced by the external temperament. In some degree it always precedes fevers, as much experience of those diseases of every type and name almost, enables me to say. But in the ague, at least in so regular and well defined a one as mine, the convulsive kind of shivering is peculiarly severe, and totally disables the patient while it lasts. I remember having gone one day on some errand to Poole expecting to return before the hour of the day at which the fit usually came on, but it was so much earlier than common that I was seized with the shivering at about a quarter of a mile's distance from home. I found it quite impossible to proceed under the convulsive motion, and was obliged to lie down in a dry ditch by the road side, which furnished some little cover, till the cold fit was gone.

From the first all the known remedies for this disease were successively tried on me in vain tho' well seconded by the assiduous care of my dear Mother. The bark especially was administered unsparingly, but without any effect, and I was become at length so emaciated and weak as to excite some alarm about the consequences, when a friend of my Mother's, Mrs. Hiley, who lived less than a mile from us, but on a small eminence, called Upton, kindly proposed to her to take me home with her to try the effect of a change of air. I went, and a cure was the immediate consequence. From the moment of that change of place the fit never once returned. I record this as another instance of the many proofs I have had from observation and experience of the high importance to health and life of avoiding a bad air, especially that morbific atmosphere which belongs to marshy situations. The farm at Ham was a place of that description. I can well remember the fields being flooded and that just beyond them was a swamp where the gnats were very annoying in the Autumn. That troublesome insect, called in hot climates the musquito, is bred from stagnant water, under the same circumstances and probably in the same degree, in which marsh miasmata are produced. Perhaps, therefore, one Providential design of the association is to repel the human species from a noxious atmosphere. In some parts of the world where the morbific influence is at particular seasons peculiarly great and fatal, the conservatory provision is raised to such a power as to give it an irresistable force and effect. Bruce[1] in his *Abyssinian Travels* describes a Country which in the rainy season of the year is always inundated till its soil becomes a kind of quagmire, and the subsequent evaporation in that hot climate produces such a morbific atmosphere as no human constitution can endure; but myriads of large musquitoes, which he calls flies, are given birth to by the same rank and stagnant moisture and their sting, or to speak more correctly, the inflammation produced by the insertion and suction of their probosces, is quite intolerable; so that all the inhabitants of the pestilential region are actually compelled to migrate to the upper Country at this which is called the "Season of the

[1] James Bruce (1730–1794), Scottish explorer of Africa; author of *Travels to Discover the Source of the Nile in the Years 1768 to 1773* (5 vols., 1790; 3rd edition corrected and enlarged, 8 vols., 1813). Stephen may have known the original work or one of the many abridgements frequently published from 1790 on.

Fly" and do not return till the compleat exsiccation of the soil has removed at once the lethiferous nuisance, and the tormenting, tho' benificent invaders. I do not recollect whether Bruce points out the wise contrivance of Divine Providence in this instance for the preservation of human life. He is not a writer, I think, by whom we are often expressly invited to such reflections; but who can doubt that this conservatory effect of the Fly is one which the all-wise Creator intended, among the many remedial and compensatory expedients by which the evil tendency of natural causes is by his general providence controuled, and actual evil counterbalanced by consequential good? I have often thought that some of the natural sciences, and particularly that of Medicine, might be usefully advanced if the observers of Nature always regarded her with a religious eye. They would be led to search more carefully for the final causes of the phenomena before them by the light which the Divine attributes afford; and having clearly discovered any such cause, or to speak less technically, such a desired effect, they would be guided by it to the explanation of other phenomena in which the chain of consequences, tho' less obvious, might be found to have been contrived on the same principles, and to lead to like results. Thus, for example, in this account of Mr. Bruce we are forcibly struck with the wisdom of Divine Providence and its benignant care of human life, in making the same natural cause which would be fatal to a whole population if they continued stationary, produce the effectual remedy for their danger, by giving birth to an inconvenience that compels them to migrate till the lethiferous cause subsides. The evil and the remedy are both in such prominent extremes that the action of each and the connection between them cannot be overlooked or mistaken. To the pious mind the providential design is equally apparent; but the Atheist or the Sceptic in religion might regard the case as no more than a fortuitous tho' happy coincidence; and therefore I maintain he might lose important consequential discoveries to which the other would be naturally led. The Atheist (and what is disregard of Divine Providence but practical Atheism?) would see no reason to suspect, as the Christian observer would, from the wonderful simplicity and uniformity of design which characterize the works of creative wisdom amidst all their infinite varieties, and from the benignity that pervades them all, the existence of a similar conservatory purpose wherever the same local inconveniences, tho' in a far slighter degree, are found. The former therefore might overlook a very important physical truth (such from much experience and observation I can affirm it to be) that annoyance from gnats or flies always indicates a situation unfriendly to health; and the degree of danger, I believe, will be generally found proportionate to the degree of sensible annoyance. In the West Indies this is remarkably the case. Wherever there is a neighbouring marsh or stagnant pond the musquitoes are peculiarly large and numerous, and I have witnessed the salutary effect when dining in a situation of that kind notoriously sickly and fatal. The surviving residents had become seasoned to the malaria and at the same time callous to the bites of the swarming insects; but all the guests were so tormented tho' accustomed to the same annoyance in its ordinary degree that we were effectually prevented from prolonging or often repeating the visit. We were obliged repeatedly while at table to drive our tormentors away and obtain a temporary relief by filling the room with the smoke of burning straw. Through a like beneficent and wise provision the sensibility of different constitutions to this species of suffering is proportionate to their different degrees of danger from the local influence on their health. A newly arrived European is preeminently exposed to dangerous sickness from marsh air in the West Indies, and he is also annoyed in a preeminent degree by the musquitoes. The young, those who are of a sanguine temperament, and persons with fair complexions and thin skins, are also acted upon in a greater degree than others both by the morbid influence and the repelling stings. I am persuaded that the same distinctions will be found in marshy situations even in this temperate climate; and accordingly I who have been always in a high degree obnoxious to the ill effects of bad air have also been always keenly susceptible of the annoyance in question. I can say the same of the offensive smell which marshes and stagnant moisture in hot seasons produce. I not only distinguish but am nauseously affected by degrees of this nuisance of which others are inconscious. This also seems to me a benignant provision of the Creator connected with and auxiliary to the former. Man, if not sophisticated by his artificial wants and habits, would be driven by his nervous sensibilities from those parts of the region he inhabits that are least friendly to his health and life.

The projects in which Sir John Webb and my Father had engaged were for some time prosecuted with mutual satisfaction. Coals were found; and tho' of too sulphurious a kind for use, it was confidently supposed that this defect would be found only in the seam nearest the surface, and that by sinking a pit to a greater depth a seam of great extent and good quality would be found. Engines were consequently erected and expensive works pursued below the soil. At the same time houses were built, or begun on a considerable scale; a ship was built, and launched which my Father called (in compliment to his particular friend, the late Mr. Albany Wallis) the *Albany*; an export trade in tobacco pipe clay, &c., was opened with London. In short, all the proposed improvements were carried on with great energy and of course at no small expense.

Whether the Baronet began to be alarmed at the extent of the disbursements, or whether as my Father supposed, his mind was poisoned against him by others, I do not know. But he became pretty suddenly cool in his conduct, and diffident as to the success of their projects, and at length proposed to rescind the contracts and abandon the joint undertakings. To this my Father would not consent; and the speedy consequence was an entire and open rupture.

Sir John, who, I apprehend, was a man of narrow and little mind, and under the influence of Priests and a Catholic Steward, who had conceived jealousy and ill will towards my Father, did not act in the quarrel either with liberality or justice. Determined not to execute the contracts, and yet unable to find a legal ground for avoiding them, he formed a plan of compelling his opponent to relinquish them by reducing him to distress. With this view he applied to the chief, I believe the only, considerable creditor of my Father, Sir Robt. Herries, to whom he owed £1500 on bond as security for his brother John, it having been a loan to the latter on his last East India voyage. How the account stood between the Brothers I know not. It became, alas, the subject of a dispute and final break between them. But my Father was at least debtor in that amount to Sir Robt. Herries, and had with his entire consent left it unpaid when he retired from his commercial business. Sir John bought or paid off this debt, taking an assignment of the bond with power to sue for it in Sir Robt's. name. The latter afterwards declared to my father that he thought Sir John acted as his friend in the transaction, and that had he known the oppressive purpose he would not have assigned the debt. Having obtained this hostile weapon the Baronet immediately began the attack. He put the bond in suit, and I think by the mode of an arrest, the better to crush his victim by the destruction of his credit. The action was bailed. But Sir John did not stop here. His next measure was to demand immediate payment of a large sum as rent for the farm and on the non-payment of it to send in a distress, tho' my Mother and her family were still living in the house. On my Father's statement of the case this proceeding was not more unhandsome than unjust, because by the intention of the agreement between them no rent was to be paid for the Farm except as an item in their general account of profit and loss on the mutual undertaking to which its occupation by him was incident. The distress was removed by a replevin; and my Father in his turn brought an Action on the contract which he was afterwards, I think, obliged to abandon, and in its stead file a Bill in Chancery as a better means of redress. These troubles were aggravated by a violent family quarrel that about the same time broke out between my Father on the one side and his Brother Thomas and a family into which the latter had recently married, on the other. The Brothers had been for some years partners together in a Dorchester ale brewery at Winborn and some other business connected with it which my Uncle Thomas managed as the resident partner in Dorsetshire, while my Father was settled in London. The former, without the latter's approbation or knowledge, paid his addresses to Miss Coker, a handsome and accomplished young Lady whose Mother, a widow lady of narrow fortune, resided with her daughters in Winborn and was favorably received; but my Father, when he heard of it, strongly disapproved of the connection, and did all in his power to break it off, first by advice to his brother, and finding that ineffectual, by representing to Mrs. Coker the great imprudence on both sides of a marriage between two young persons both entirely destitute of fortune. Such interference was excusable in one who stood in a parental as well as fraternal connection to the young man; for my Father had brought him when a boy from Scotland, placed him in his own Counting House to learn commercial business, and afterwards put him over this establishment at Winborn which was formed by his own capital or credit alone. My Father alleged (truly enough I dare say) that his Brother's Moiety of the profits would ill suffice for his support as a married man, and that by taking on himself so prematurely the charge of a family he would endanger his own solvency and make the partnership a perilous connection. The young people however were too much in love to listen to advice; and the old lady, who was a clever bustling woman and valued herself on her shrewdness, ascribed my Father's opposition to a self-interested wish to keep his brother in a state of pupillage and to avoid accounting to him for a moiety of the profits of the joint business which she had been taught to regard as very considerable, and as resting in my Father's hands. The event was that the marriage took place, that the Brothers quarrelled upon it, and the partnership was dissolved. Unfortunately the accounts of the joint dealings had not been regularly kept, or were at least unadjusted. My Uncle's claim of a large balance therefore could not be immediately clearly repelled, tho' indignantly denied by my Father, who bore himself, I fear, too haughtily, as towards an ungrateful and rebellious child, and treated the wife's family as his seducers and injurious abettors. The latter, on the other hand, the Mother-in-law at least, entered with so much violence and bitterness into the quarrel that they at length pushed my Uncle on to an extremity which I believe was very opposite to his natural disposition and subjected him to general reproach. He forgot so much what was due to a man who had the united claims of a brother and father upon him as actually to commence an action against my father and arrest him for a large sum which he swore to be due to himself on a balance of the late partnership accounts. To aggravate the proceeding still more, the arrest was made, tho' probably without the intention at the moment, when my Father was setting off from his home to the Dorchester Assizes to try his replevin against Sir John Webb. Bail might no doubt have been easily found, but my Father chose to go in custody of the bailiff to the Assize town, I fear for the sake of exhibiting publickly the ungrateful and un-seasonable persecution of his brother and adopted child, at which of course his indignation was very great. My Uncle, to do him justice, hastened to Dorchester and discharged the writ. I had walked with my father all the way from Ham to Dorchester, for he generally made his journies on foot and thus early initiated my elder brother and me in pedestrian exertions. The journey was, I think, thirty miles, a great one for a boy of ten years old, and I remember dis-tinctly the fatigue and blistering of feet that I felt toward the close of it, but of which I was too proud to complain. An incident that occurred at the Inn serves to mark my temper at that early age in a way not much to my advantage. My Uncle Thomas came to the same Inn, not knowing, I presume, that his Brother was there, and meeting me on the staircase stop'd to shake hands with, or kiss me, as usual; but I returned his kindness with as hard a blow as my little fist could give him, and passed him without speaking. On the report of this to my Father and his party, I was not found fault with, but praised alas, for this act of impotent revenge. That I should enter with ardour into his quarrel when regarding him as the victim of injustice, ingratitude, and oppression was natural enough, and I have not been allowed to forget a sally of mine on his behalf of a different kind, a pasquinade which I produced against Mr. Catton, Sir John Webb's Steward, who was supposed to have poisoned that gentleman's mind against my Father, upon jealous and envious motives. Mr. Catton squinted; and I made *that*, illiberally enough, the theme of the following verses.

Kind Nature, when a man she builds,
For piety designed,
With some sweet grace his features gilds,
By which we read his mind.
And on all knaves, a mark has lain,
Which warns us quick to fly;
God in his forehead, marked Cain;
And Catton, in his eye.

Tho' this, I think, was not a bad epigram from the pen of a boy about ten years old, the spirit of it certainly merited reprehension, and probably my dear Mother might have gently reproved me for it; but my Father praised it beyond bounds, preserved a copy of it, and not rarely read it to others in my presence, who of course joined in his applause. At or before the same time, as well as afterwards, I was much addicted to writing verses, which were generally hymns or other religious compositions, and for many of these I was also rewarded with praise till I began to regard myself as no contemptible poet.

But to return to my Father. He succeeded in his replevin at the Assizes; but this victory went but a very little way towards ending the litigation in which he was involved. It decided only that the distress was illegal on the ground of irregularity in the proceeding, but did not at all involve the general merits of the controversy between them as to the nonexecution of the contracts. The other suits therefore proceeded; and to that on the bond, brought in the name of Sir R. Herries, my Father had no legal defence. Having discovered that it was in fact the suit of Sir Jno. Webb, who had bought an assignment of the bond as an instrument of oppression, he filed a Bill, if I rightly recollect, to connect it with the question between them and bring it into the account under the contracts, but if so, he must have failed to obtain an injunction; for judgment and execution were obtained against him on the bond and he was obliged to surrender himself in discharge of his bail to the Kings Bench Prison.

The feelings of my dear Mother on this occasion may be easily conceived. Hitherto her hopes had been sustained by her husband's too sanguine hopes of obtaining redress for his disappointments and their injurious effects, by law, and thus reestablishing his affairs. But she could now no longer shut her eyes to the real prospects before her. She had just before brought into the world another daughter (now my Sister Milner) which made five surviving children, and found herself with this large family in immediate danger of actual want, or what to her delicate and liberal feelings was hardly less terrible, dependency on the charitable assistance of relatives and friends. I was privy to her sorrows and indeed her only confidant, for my Father in going to the Kings Bench Prison took my elder brother with him and left me at Ham with my Mother. I can well remember some instances of the ordinary effects of such reverses of fortune that were peculiarly trying to her susceptible mind; I mean the mortifying changes of conduct of former intimates and friends, one of them especially marked with great ingratitude and which cost her many tears. Yet all professed to feel deeply for her; even those most inimical to my Father, and who blamed most his imprudence or misconduct. Such in fact had always been her exemplary conduct as a wife, a mother and every other relative character, such was her good sense, her undeviating propriety of manners, her sweetness of temper, and benignity to all around her, that she was respected and beloved in a high degree by all who knew her, and if her feeling heart was shocked in adversity by the neglect or unkindness of some whom she thought her friends, it was only because no degree of acknowledged merit can secure the unfortunate from such mortifications in a selfish world. Soon after it pleased God to visit her with new afflictions. Her Father, who then resided at Wareham in Dorsetshire, was taken dangerously ill, and she went there to comfort and assist my Grandmother, and attend her sick parent, to whom she was tenderly attached, leaving all her family, I think, but the youngest child at home. The disorder proved fatal, but not till after a long time, during which her fatiguing attendance on her dying father impaired her health, and soon after his death before she could return to her home, she herself was attacked by a violent disease of a pleuritic kind, from which after a long confinement she narrowly escaped with life. During the extremity of her danger I was sent for by her desire that she might see me before her death, and I well remember the first interview between us on account of the pain which a misconception on her part cost me. I had no adequate idea of the danger she was, or had been in, or that there was any such idea in her mind as a final separation between us; and seeing nothing to alarm me in her appearance, was enough at my ease after a minute or two of conversation with her, to indulge my curiosity by looking at the pictures in her bed room. My dear Mother' spirits were low, and she bursted into tears at this trait, as she thought it, of indifference on my part to her sufferings and her danger. Dear Woman! she did me injustice. But it was the only time in her life that she ever gave me pain, except in the kind discharge of her parental duties, when faults too real called for her reproof; and her disordered nerves were in this instance the cause of her mistake. No—my beloved Mother, want of affection for you was not among the number of my faults! My filial love and reverence for you were great indeed, and are still deeply engraved upon my heart, though forty-five years have now elapsed since I first wept over your grave.

Hardly had this amiable sufferer recovered her health when she was called to new trials. My Father finding no prospect of an early release from his imprisonment wrote to her a request that she would come to him, and tho' greatly shocked at the idea of having a prison for her home, she was too generous and too observant of her conjugal duties to refuse. To part with any of her beloved infants was a very painful sacrifice, but to shut them up with herself in the Prison was worse, and indeed from the account of matters there was impracticable for want of rooms. She therefore accepted her Mother's offer to take charge of them, and set off with me only in the Stage Coach for London. It was then a wearisome journey of two days, and I well remember the state of fatigue and distress of mind in which my dear Mother arrived at the end of it, at an Inn in Friday Street. It was after the close of daylight, and she had resolved not to go over to the Prison till the next morning but to take a

bed at the house of Mr. W.,[1] one of the more intimate and
kindest of her friends, who resided in Aldermanbury. Her
delicacy, however, suggested that it would not be right to go
there without being assured that it would suit the convenience of the family. She therefore sent a note by a porter to
Mr. W., saying that she was just arrived at the Inn and
requesting to see him there. Mr. W., tho' a Merchant of
eminence, had been so obsequious a friend, that when she
went from London with her children to join my Father in
Dorsetshire, he insisted on taking the journey to escort them.
Yet when the porter returned he brought with him not Mr.
Wharton, but a letter from that gentleman, coldly civil and
apologizing for not being able to wait on her on account of
some slight impediment. My dear Mother after a look of
astonishment, and a blush of ingenuous feeling, felt herself
quite overpowered by this most unlooked for repulse, and
gave way to a flood of tears. She thought for a moment of
resorting to some other of her former friends, but at length
summoning up the resolution of which she was always
Mistress in time of need, "No my dear Jem," said she, "we
will expose ourselves to no more repulses. The distressed,
I see, must not reckon upon friendships—if *Mr. W.* is
capable of treating me thus, from whom can I expect
better? Come, my dear boy; we will go over to the Prison
at once."

   I have the most lively recollection of our arrival at the
Kings Bench and the scene that awaited us there. The
Prison was far less cleanly and commodious then than it has
now become, it since having been burnt down in the riots of
1780, and afterwards rebuilt on a more extensive and better
plan. The rooms at that time were small and dirty; and those
prisoners even who could afford to pay the highest rents,
were unable to obtain more than a single room, which served
them both for eating and sleeping. Into one of these apartments, after passing the surly examinations of the Keeper's
Lodge, was my dear Mother, weary and dispirited and
alarmed as she was, suddenly introduced. She was not
expected that night; and my Father therefore had with him

---

[1] Evidently Stephen intended at first not to name "Mr. W.", but on the next
page he is given the name of "Mr. Wharton".

at supper three fellow Prisoners, gentlemen strangers to her, with whom he had formed an intimacy, and who messed together with him, taking their meals alternately at each other's rooms. A turn-up bedstead was buttoned up against the white-washed wall, to make the better room for a table, around which they were sitting. The smell of the meat and liquor, added to the other disgusting objects of the senses, would have been enough to overpower a woman of such delicate sensibility as my Mother, if her mind had been at ease; but her feeling heart received a shock harder to sustain from finding her unfortunate husband in such a scene, and with a squalid appearance indicatory of his altered state. A loud cry, and a flood of tears, gave vent to her emotions as he clasped her in his arms, and I saw no more; for his companions with a proper delicacy instantly retired, one of them taking me with him to share his bed, as the only lodging that could then be found for me.

I forget how long my dear Mother and I were inmates of this painful abode; but think it must have been several months. My brother William was not there, a mercantile friend having been prevailed on to take him into his Counting House. For my part I was soon pretty well reconciled to the place. All my Father's Friends and acquaintances there treated me with great kindness and flattered my vanity with applause of my poetical and other productions. Among them was a novel, or rather romance, of which I recollect only that it was full of marvellous and miraculous incidents, the general stile and character of which formed a medley of the works I was then best acquainted with, Plutarch's *Lives*, *Don Quixote*, and the *Arabian Nights Entertainments*. It was also, like most alas, of the more recent labours of my pen left unfinished. Tho' these early compositions of mine had, I believe, nothing very extraordinary, even in a boy whose education had been much neglected, they procured me praise enough to turn a sounder head. I was called by every body the Poet, and they did not scruple to predict before me that I should rival Pope and the other great writers of the age then just gone by. Nor do I believe that these praises, however improperly uttered in my hearing, were wholly insincere; for among the fellow Prisoners with whom my Father was acquainted were three or four literary characters, from whom I can remember to have received particular attention, out of his presence, and the loan of books, &c., with a view to the cultivation of my taste. Among them was Christopher Smart[1] the Poet, and the Revd. W. F. Jackson,[2] afterwards too well known as a powerful political writer, who became at last a revolutionary conspirator in Ireland, and escaped, alas, by suicide only, receiving judgment of death as a traitor. Another was Mr. Main,[3] a Scotchman, who had been an eminent Bookseller and publisher, at Boston Massachusetts, and was driven away by an insurrectionary Mob there, on account of his siding zealously with the British Government, and writing powerfully on its side on the question of taxation. He narrowly escaped tarring and feathering, by his courage in firing several pistol shots among the Mob which pursued him, and so keeping his pursuers in check till he got to the beach and threw himself into the boat of a British Ship of War which brought him to England. His House and warehouses, I think, were burnt. His business at least was broken up and ruined. He was consequently unable to pay his debts and was thrown by his creditors into the Kings Bench; but the Government, I believe, supported him there and gave him a pension afterwards, which he enjoyed to the time of his death. He was a man of strong parts and some literature, and, as I have reason to believe, laboured with his pen in political controversies on the side of Government long after this period. I never knew a more ardent Tory; but he was a good-natured man and was at this time warmly attached to my Father and Mr. Jackson, tho' men of very opposite political feelings. A fourth literary friend and fellow Prisoner of my Father who was also very kind to me

[1] Christopher Smart (1722–1771), poet, best known for his remarkable religious poem *Song to David*, first issued in 1763; twice confined to a madhouse, where he was visited by Dr. Johnson, who thought his madness harmless; most of his life caught hopelessly in debt; died in King's Bench Prison in May, 1771, nearly two years after the time when Stephen knew him.

[2] William Jackson (1757?–1795), best known as an Irish revolutionist; popular preacher at Tavistock Chapel, Drury Lane, secretary to the Duchess of Kingston; his later career as a revolutionist led to his being tried for treason; had a sensational death by committing suicide in the dock at his trial.

[3] I have been unable to identify "Mr. Main".

was Mr. Wm. Thompson,[1] a Royal Academician. He was a
tolerable Painter, as may appear from a portrait of my Father
from his pencil, an admirable likeness, which with a print
afterwards taken from it, is still in the possession of the family.
But he was fonder of poetry and general literature than of
his profession, which perhaps was the cause of his misfortunes and his imprisonment.

I could mention several other characters with whom I
became acquainted in the Prison as visitors of my Father,
and might, from a lively recollection of everything I saw at
that age, give some amusing accounts of them, but must not
digress too much from the main subject of this narration. I
have mentioned Smart, and Jackson, and Main and Thompson, because they all took a particular interest in the dawn
of my understanding, if I may judge either by their professions or their conduct; for they were very kind to me, and
the three latter continued to be my friends long after they
ceased to be my Father's. And here I ought to observe that
these gentlemen, tho' two of them, Jackson and Main, were
certainly men of licencious manners, never did or said anything before me tending to corrupt my principles, and on the
contrary shewed on several occasions a desire to promote my
moral as well as intellectual welfare. I particularly remember
one expostulation of Mr. Jackson's with me in private which
made a deep and useful impression on my heart. It was at a
house within the Rules of the Prison at which we afterwards
lodged and where there was a well staircase. I was amusing
myself with dropping a cat from the top of this well to the
bottom, not with any consciousness of its cruelty to the poor
animal, but from mere boyish curiosity to ascertain by
experiment that a cat always falls on her feet. Mr. Jackson,
however, who caught me thus employed, took me aside and
read me such a lecture on the sin of cruelty to animals as
made me deeply ashamed and shocked at my own conduct.
I might say that he effectually reformed me (as I am not

[1] William Thompson (1730?–1800), portrait painter; born in Dublin but
removed to London early in life; between 1760 and 1782 exhibited 43 portraits
at the Society of Artists; married a wealthy lady, squandered her fortune, and
was imprisoned for debt; after death of first wife married another wealthy
woman; author of *An Enquiry into the Elementary Principles of Beauty in the Works
of Nature and Art.*

conscious of having ever again committed a fault of the same nature) if it were not for a belief that I did not need reformation in that line, except by calling my attention to the effect of the act on the poor animal's feelings; for I well remember having long before this period desisted from birds nesting, of which I was very fond, from a sense of cruelty, and that my conscience was always very susceptible as to the duty of humanity towards the inferior ranks of the creation. I nevertheless owe a grateful tribute here to the memory of Mr. Jackson, and it is instructive to reflect that this humane admonition came from a man who afterwards on the spur of a criminal ambition would have deluged his country with blood. In the former case, no selfish passion seduced his judgment, or subdued his moral sense. In the latter, it is possible that he was as blind to the natural consequences of the revolution he aimed at, as I was to the sufferings of the cat. His character, however, was progressively deteriorated, and by means that I could in great measure trace; for I knew much of the history. Perhaps I may recur to it hereafter.

The favourable opinions formed of my capacity procured for me attentions in another quarter and an offer of early patronage. Mr. Clinton, then the Chief of the Jesuits in England, and the man of the first influence among the Catholics of rank and fortune, was a relation of my Father's and like all his family much attached to my Mother; nor did he shun them after their reverse of fortune, but shewed himself a true friend by many substantial acts of kindness. He not only made, but pressed repeatedly on my Father, an offer to take the whole charge of my education and introduction into life, in whatever profession he might choose for me; and finding that the apprehension of my being converted to Popery was an objection, he said all that was possible to remove it, declaring that I should never be solicited for such a change nor even talked to on the points of faith in dispute between Protestants and Papists. My Mother was desirous that the offer should be accepted; for on the one hand Mr. Clinton declared I should have an education the best that Europe could furnish; and on the other hand my poor Father had no means or prospect of giving me any liberal education at all. I had already been long from school, and was living in idleness with them in the prison, forgetting daily the little I had learnt at Mr. Howell's, and giving myself wholly up to the reading of Novels, Poetry, and Plays, with which the prison friends I have mentioned copiously supplied me. My Father, however, resolutely declined Mr. Clinton's friendly offer. I fear he was less led to do so from the danger of my conversion than from that of my being made a Priest, and the hopes he had formed of my rising to eminence in future life being that way defeated, to which was probably added a proud reluctance to accept such an adoption of his Son. Whatever his motives were, I have reason to be thankful for his decision. I believe at least it was very fortunate for me that he refused, for tho' Mr. Clinton no doubt meant fairly, my education would naturally have been at St. Omers[1] or Paris, in one of the schools or colleges of the Jesuits, then in full reputation, and such were the arts of those able men in moulding the minds of youth to their purposes that it would be presumptuous to think I should have escaped them. A conversion and profession that were made to be my own free choice would of course have been held no violation of Mr. Clinton's engagements. My disposition through life has strongly inclined me to pass the middle line of moderation when pushed by any impulse bad or good into any new habit of thought or action. In youth this propensity was peculiarly strong. I think therefore that had I become a Catholic I should also have become a priest; and I am sure that the vows of the Catholic Priesthood would not have been easily kept by me. The utter ruin of my character, moral and religious, would probably therefore have been the result of this friendly adoption, if my Father had not in this instance, perhaps in this only, opposed my dear Mother's wishes properly and wisely. In how many instances has a gracious Providence controuled my own blind choice, and that of Friends who have desired to promote my happiness, when we were choosing evil instead of good! In-

---

[1] A college founded by English Jesuits at St. Omer in 1592 was a popular school for the youth of English Catholic families until the time of the French Revolution. The grounds and buildings of the college are now occupied by the lycée of the city of St. Omer.

stances enough will be seen of this in the course of the events that I have hereafter to narrate.

My Father, stung with the injustice of his imprisonment, was led to enquire into the origin and authority of the law which was made the instrument of his oppression. He read the elementary writers and soon discovered from them that the practice of imprisonment for debt was founded rather on juridical usage than on the antient principles of the common law or positive Statutes. In fact, it seems to have been a progressive extension by the Courts of a process originally given by the accountant act (Westminster 2ᵈ· 13 Edw. 1, c. 11. A.D. 1205)[1] against accountants or stewards of the antient Barons who being found in arrear to their Lords were to be taken and imprisoned *in irons* till they made satisfaction. I write from memory and do not think it worth while to consult the Books in order to state the matter more correctly. But if I rightly recollect the *capias ad satisfaciendum* was afterwards progressively extended, by practice only, to the cases of other debts, by a supposed analogy to those of defaulting accountants; tho' the latter were evidently regarded by the Act as breaches of trust or frauds, which on account of the confidential relation of the Steward to the Lord, and no doubt through the powerful influence of the Barons in those aristocratical times, were punished with a severity contrary to the genius of the Common Law, the confinement *in irons* shewing that the process was penal as well as remedial. I think it clear that the Courts of Westminster in this and many other cases usurped upon the province of the legislature upon the specious principle of what was called "advancing the remedy" and a maxim justly repudiated in our own days *"est boni judicis ampliare juris destionem"* but in fact upon the selfish feeling that their own dignity or importance and emoluments were increased by the increase of their business. The various fictions by which the different Courts progressively obtained the cognizance of suits from which they were originally excluded cannot well be referred to any purer source. Of these fictions, the *ac etiam, latitat, quo minus,* &c.,

---

[1] Stephen left this parenthesis vacant. The citation was supplied by James Fitzjames Stephen, whose note on the margin of the page reads: "Note by J. F. Stephen, the author's grandson .15/3/84."

my Father was naturally led to from that unfavourable judgment when he discovered their origin and use; and as they all tended to multiply the remedies of creditors against the debtor's person, he regarded the whole system as a multiform scheme of oppression, devised by mercenary lawyers to enrich themselves by the spoils of the unfortunate, at the expence of sound legal and constitutional principles.

Impressed strongly with these views, and with those moral and political objections to imprisonment for debt which are of a less disputable kind, he resolved that he would not tamely and silently submit to what he regarded as lawless oppression, but would appeal on behalf of himself and fellow Prisoners both to the Courts of law and the Public. Accordingly he obtained a writ of Habeas Corpus, and on the return of it personally addressed the Court of Kings Bench in an argument wherein he contended that his imprisonment on a *capias ad satisfaciendum* or execution for debt was illegal; and demanded his discharge. The Court, of course, overruled his objections and remanded him into the prison; but Lord Mansfield,[1] the then Chief Justice, was struck with the manly impressive countenance and intellectual energy of the unfortunate man who addressed him, and in saying he must be remanded added, "It is a great pity." I remember the scene; for my Father took me with him and I stood by his side in the Court. In retiring with the Tipstaff he looked firmly at the Bench and exclaimed, "It is tyranny, my Lords—it is oppression—but it is not law." As we passed through the Hall a well dressed gentleman followed us, caught me by the hand, slip'd five shillings into it, and went back too suddenly for me to tell my Father of it before he was out of sight. The next sentiment was naturally that of indignation against the Judges, who without answering his arguments had thus adhered to the illegal and unconstitutional practice of their Court, and the next resort was an appeal to the Public through the medium of the press. My Father not only published numerous essays in the *Public Advertiser*, then the leading opposition Newspaper, but a

---

[1] William Murray, first Earl of Mansfield (1705–1793), chief justice of King's Bench (1756–1788); unpopular because of his severity of judgment in cases of seditious libel; termed by Macaulay "the father of modern Toryism."

pamphlet intitled *Considerations on Imprisonment for Debt*[1] in which he strenuously maintained the illegality as well as inhumanity and impolicy of the practice; and inveighed against the Judges, particularly Lord Mansfield, in no measured terms. I have no copy of the pamphlet, but am told it is still extant in one of the libraries at Cambridge. From what I remember of the stile it was vigorous and well adapted to popular effect, but intemperate and not very regular or elegant in point of composition, much less indicatory of any great extent of legal knowledge, which of course he did not possess. The main hinge of his arguments as to the illegality of the practice was that all customs of juridical usages, however antient, if contrary to *Magna Charta*, and to the Common law as it existed prior to that Charter, are unlawful and void. He had adopted, I think, an opinion which must be admitted to be a constitutional sophism in respect of that boasted code of English privileges, namely that it has such a peculiar and inviolable sanctity as to be unchangeable by Parliament itself. But he argued more speciously that by every successive confirmation of *Magna Charta* all customs and even all Statutes previously abrogating its provisions were virtually abolished and repealed. If so, then as the Charter had often been confirmed subsequently to the extension by practice of the *capias ad satisfaciendum* to cases of ordinary debts, it followed that this practice, if contrary to the Charter and to the antecedent Common Law, was still illegal unless it could be shewn that some Act of Parliament subsequent to the last confirmation of the Charter had given validity to the practice. True it is that many Acts sufficiently modern for that purpose had recognized it as a subsisting practice of the Courts, and without condemnation. Among others the many periodical Acts for the relief of imprisoned debtors had done so, but my Father,

---

[1] I give the full title page of this pamphlet: *Considerations on Imprisonment for Debt; Fully Proving, that the Confining of the Bodies of Debtors Is Contrary to Common Law, Magna Charta, Statute Law, Justice, Humanity, and Policy; and that the Practice is more cruel and oppressive than is used in the most arbitrary kingdoms in Europe. With an account of the various applications to the King and Judges by the Prisoners of the King's Bench, for obtaining Redress; and some Remarkable Cases of Prisoners now confined there.* By James Stephen.

Veritas a quocumque dicitus a Deo est. London: Sold by T. Evans, No. 54, Paternoster-Row; MDCCLXX.

I think, got rid of this objection by a proposition less untenable than the indestructable force of the Charter, maintaining that the liberty of an Englishman's person ought not to be taken away by the side wind of a Statute thus dealing with an existing abuse, contrary to the direct enactment of another Statute made for his protection. The whole of this reasoning rested on the 29th Chapter of *Magna Charta*: "No free man shall be taken or imprisoned &c., but by the judgment of his Peers, or the *law of the land*," which last terms are construed by Lord Coke &c. to mean the Common Law as it stood when the Charter was first promulged.

I will not stop to enquire whether by these words imprisonment for debt was virtually precluded. Enough has been said to make my Father's views intelligible, and their defence or refutation would be matter of little or no importance. The moral and political, not the legal objections to the practice, are those alone on which it ever will, and on these I think it clearly ought to be, reformed.

In those days the Government was very unpopular. It was the time of Wilkes's riots and his well merited prosecution for libel, his expulsion &c., or soon after those events I forget which—certainly during the high tide of his popularity in the City. My Father attempted to induce him to become the champion of the imprisoned debtors. But Wilkes was not disposed to take up a cause to which his City friends, as Creditors, could not be well inclined. My Father therefore next attacked him before the Public as a recreant to his professed principles; and Wilkes in one of his addresses to the citizens complained that Mr. Jas. Stephen among others had been hired by Ministers to write him down or lower him in the esteem of his Constituents.[1]

There was one class of persons, however, among whom my Father naturally found many willing and zealous proselytes. I mean his fellow prisoners. They were easily convinced that their confinement was illegal and warmly shared his indignation at the oppression of which they were the victims.

Backed by their common feelings my Father at length con-

[1] I have not found a direct report of this speech by Wilkes, but something of the same charge is made in a letter signed "J." which appeared in the *Public Advertiser*, November 25, 1771.

ceived a very rash, romantic, and dangerous project. It was nothing less than that they should mutually force the doors of the Prison in the forenoon of a day on which the Courts were sitting, march in a Body to Westminster together, and there demand their discharge from their illegal imprisonment; but that if refused, they should peaceably return to the prison again, after thus shewing their sense of their violated rights, and forcing that attention to them which had been hitherto withheld. When I consider that he was certainly a very sagacious, sensible man, and that others who adopted this wild project (among them the three gentlemen before described) were also men of judgment and experience, I am astonished that such a plan should have been conceived. They actually, however, proceeded far towards its execution. A few of them headed by my Father entered the Lobby and seized the turnkeys. He being a powerful man grasped one of them who held the outward door, in his arms, took the keys from him, set open the door, and called to his fellow Prisoners to come out and accompany him to Westminster. Providentially the greater number of them, I believe all but a few, shrunk at this moment from the dangerous enterprise. After therefore keeping the doors open a considerable time and after he and all who adhered to the purpose had actually gone out and had nothing to obstruct their further progress or escape, they concluded that it would be right to return, and did so, restoring to the affrighted turnkeys their keys and saying that having now shewn their power of delivering themselves from oppression they should go back and submit to it till they found peaceable means of redress.

The Marshall the same day obtained a warrant to remove my Father on a charge of riot and prison-breaking to the New Gaol in the Borough. But this was far from answering the desired purpose of intimidating his fellow prisoners in the Kings Bench and preventing further resistance there. On the contrary it excited general indignation among them, and after ineffectually demanding that their champion should be brought back as the price of their forbearance they proceeded to such riotous conduct with an apparent intention of forcing the doors that the turnkeys and officers who were assembled in force with firearms in the Lobby at

4

length fired several shots at them from the windows, but providentially without any fatal effect. The Prisoners dispersed, but with a resolution only to wait for the night and then to break through the Walls, with the desperate purpose of proceeding to the New Gaol in order to set my Father at large by force. Accordingly at night they tumultuously assembled at the side of the wall which bounds the Prison towards St. George's Fields and began to prick into the wall with such implements as they found. The Marshall and his officers finding it impossible to suppress them by their own force, at least without danger to themselves, sent for a Party of Soldiers, but before these arrived, a hole large enough for the body of a man was worked through the thick wall, and one or two who looked to their own freedom rather than the common cause actually escaped through it. The rest were about to follow and prosecute their desperate enterprise when the Military coming up to the breach compelled them to desist, and happily without bloodshed. The Marshall then proceeded to seize four or five of the leaders, among whom were gentlemen whom I have already mentioned, and sent them also to the New Gaol.[1]

I have for some time been silent as to my dear Mother, tho' it was chiefly for the sake of her sufferings that I entered on my Father's history thus fully. It may be supposed how much her delicate feelings and habits were shocked with the manners of a Prison. Her maternal feelings also were alarmed on my account, lest I should fall into corrupting society, for of course it was not possible to confine me to their own single apartment, or that of Mr. Main, who kindly accomodated me with a lodging. I read a good deal in the Novels and other Books of entertainment with which that gentleman was well supplied, but when tired of this, was allowed to stroll into the Courtyards of the Prison where fives and rackets were plaid by persons of all ages, and soon became expert at those games. I can recollect circumstances which give me cause for gratitude to Providence that I escaped contamination of morals. It is right, however, to

---

[1] A fairly full account of the insurrection of the prisoners is given in the *Annual Register* for 1770 (Chronicle entry for November 19) and 1771 (Chronicle entry for January 31).

add that whatever laxity of moral sentiment may be supposed to belong to the inmates of a Prison there was no attempt to corrupt me. My dear Mother nevertheless was not unreasonably apprehensive; and on my account as well as her own, she prevailed on my Father after we had been there three or four months to let her send for her younger children from Dorsetshire, and take a lodging within the Rules of the Prison. I believe I have already mentioned that a situation had been formed for my elder Brother in a Merchants' Counting House, and he lodged in the House of his Employer in London. From this new family abode my Mother went frequently, I believe almost daily, to see her unfortunate husband and spend part of the day with him. Her Society was always most acceptable not only to him, but the three fellow Prisoners whom I have described, who for the most part messed with him, for they were all gentlemen in their manners, and she was a woman of a cultivated mind and refined taste, whose accomplishments and pleasing conversation adorned her more substantial good qualities and made her a universal favorite. She was an excellent singer; so much so that her voice and execution were often compared with those of the most eminent performers on the Stage, and such was her sweetness of disposition and cheerful resignation that she did not refuse to enliven these Prison parties with her songs. Not that there was wanting the most exquisite sensibility to the distress and disgrace of their situation. Alas I was often witness to those floods of tears which attested in our evening privacy the constraint which she had kindly practiced through the day; but like the son who has never ceased during six and forty years to remember her with love and veneration, she was sustained by a constitutional flow of spirits, as well as religious consolations. Her sorrows were either sun showers or the darkness of a passing storm, not the nocturnal gloom of despondency or dejection. She unbosomed herself freely to me, and to my dear Brother when with us, except when a sense of conjugal duty restrained her tongue, and made her afflictions useful to us by the wise and pious reflections with which the discovery of them was always accompanied. She employed us often in reading to her not only for amusement but for religious improvement and consolation, talked with us on what we read, and anxiously taught us to read with feeling and propriety. In that important, tho' much neglected, branch of education she was no ordinary Mistress. She also wrote with elegance in the only line she ever attempted, epistolary composition, and laboured to improve our taste in stile as well as to make us speak and write with grammatical correctness. She was fond of poetry in general, but particularly so of Young's *Night Thoughts*, which she engaged me to read to her so often that I could when a young man repeat the greatest part of it by heart. It forms from its lengthened periods, its involutions, and even its frequent obscurity of meaning unless well marked by the voice, a preeminently good exercise for a young reader; and my dear Mother, who was an adept in the work, taught me so carefully to read it with the proper stops and emphases, that I ascribe to this, and her lessons in general, much of the little skill in reading and speaking that I possess; nor do I scruple to say that no other education I ever received from other living teachers has contributed so much to my professional success.

It is needless to say how much this dear woman was agitated by the alarming disturbance in the Prison in which my Father had so large a share, and by his removal to the New Gaol. Thither also she followed him; and there as everywhere else her interesting appearance and manners contributed with that commanding air and imposing conversation that marked my Father to procure for them favour and respect. Instead of placing them among the criminals as the Marshall of the Kings Bench desired, the Keeper Mr. Strange and his wife, both people far above their station in feelings and manners, gave up to my Father and his companions their own best apartments, and treated them in the most respectful manner, while Mrs. Strange behaved towards my Mother on her visits to the Prison with a courtesy and kindness not to be surpassed.

I remember well this new scene. How vivid are the impressions on the youthful mind when of an interesting kind! If I were a Painter I could draw the pictures of the Keeper and his wife and the whole Party assembled in their principal room, tho' it is half a century ago. Well also do I remember the being sent repeatedly to the Kings Bench Prison with communications between my Father and his Friends in that place, and the rudeness with which I was treated and examined in the Lobby. Strikingly has it recurred to my thoughts of late years since I have been in the habit of frequently going there in my official character as Master in Chancery to take the Answers, &c., of Prisoners. What a contrast in the profound respect with which I am now ushered by the turnkeys into their best room while the Prisoners are sent for to attend me! I am neither elated nor abashed by such recollections and contrasts, of which many instances will occur in the course of these memoirs; but they have often made a pleasing, and I trust proper, impression on my mind, as marking in a lively manner the bounties of a gracious Providence. "He taketh up the simple out of the dust, and liftest the Poor out of the Mire; that he may set him with the Princes; even with the Princes *of his People.*"[1]

The confinement in the New Gaol was not of long duration. How it ended I forget; but believe that upon my Father and his friends giving bail to answer to an Indictment for a riot and prison breach at Sessions, they were sent back to the Kings Bench. The ultimate event of the prosecution was either a compromise between them and the Marshall, or their being discharged after conviction on a nominal fine by his consent. They had on their part indicted him for firing upon the Prisoners, and the temper of the times perhaps with the unpopularity of Lord Mansfield his Patron, made him glad of a mutual amnesty.

What I with more certainty recollect is that soon after this period my Father was discharged from his imprisonment and his debts. He had continued to prosecute his suit in equity against Sir John Webb by the aid of his old friend Mr. Albany Wallis; but at length through the mediation of the Baronet's confessor, and I presume also through the good offices of Mr. Clinton, a compromise was effected. The terms of it were that Sir John paid all the costs, gave my Father a full release from the assigned debt for which he

[1] *Psalms,* 113: 6-7, Book of Common Prayer.

held him in execution, with a sum of money, I think £500, and settled an annuity of £40 on my Mother for her life. I think he also paid his debts to other persons, which I believe were not large.

My Father had now to explore some new means of providing for his family's support; and the plan of life he fixed upon was rather an extraordinary one for a man of his past habits, and who had now I think reached the age of thirty-five. It was to enter himself in one of the Inns of Court and make his way to the bar as a profession. During an imprisonment of twenty months he had been reading law, chiefly indeed for the sake of maintaining the controversy he had engaged in; but his Friends gave him credit for having acquired much general knowledge of law and he had confidence in his talents that he might by perseverance rise to eminence at the bar. He certainly possessed much colloquial eloquence, and had as I have before remarked an imposing and commanding manner, aided by a manly expressive countenance and figure, that naturally favoured this opinion; and he was not of a character to be kept down by any want of confidence in himself. His general education had certainly not been such as to qualify him well for a learned profession. On the contrary he was, I believe, worse furnished, at least in respect of the learned languages, than Scotchmen usually are who have been brought up to commerce, from his having left school and entered into business or preparation for it in a French Counting House at a very early age; for tho' I remember to have heard that he was originally intended for the Scotch profession of a Writer or Solicitor, that plan must have been very soon abandoned. A novitiate of five years was also a very formidable objection to a man who had already as many children and no present means of support. But it was thought that he might obtain profitable employment, even while a student, as a conveyancer and chamber counsel, especially in mercantile affairs of which his knowledge was, or was supposed to be, very extensive. After all, the grand considerations were the necessity of attempting something, and the want of any better choice. Accordingly he entered himself as a Student in the Middle Temple, began to keep his terms, and engaged professedly in the study of the law. Whether this plan if unobstructed would have been ultimately successful may be reasonably doubted, tho' regular education and literary attainments were at that time not held so indispensable in a Barrister as they now are; and some men then of great eminence had found the want of them no insuperable disadvantage. But my Father still persevered in his public hostility to the practice of imprisonment for debt, and in his efforts to excite a popular spirit of indignation against it by means of the periodical press; and as a natural consequence he incurred so much ill will among the Heads of the legal profession and the Benchers of the Inns of Court, that it was soon resolved among them to stop his progress to the bar. He certainly provoked their enmity much more than his cause required, for in numerous newspaper essays under his own name[1] he arranged the Judges of venality and oppression for upholding the practice contrary to law, because it was productive to them of great official emoluments which would be lost by its reformation. Lord Mansfield especially was an object of his frequent attacks, and he did not fail to avail himself of the popular hatred in which the Chief Justice was then involved by his political character while the tide of democratical feeling ran high against the Court on the question of general warrants and the first angry disputes with the North American Colonies, now the United States. The Benchers of the Middle Temple, however, were too politic to avow that they were actuated in the measure that ensued by complaisance to the Judges or by resentment against a man who had intemperately arraigned the practice of the Courts. They intimated to him that he would not be allowed to make his way through their Society to the bar, and as I believe but am not sure, made an order for his expulsion, and assigned as their reasons for it quaintly, harshly, and certainly in one point injuriously, "want of birth, want of fortune, want of education, and want of temper." In point of birth he certainly was not inferior to many of those who have attained the first honors of the profession; nor was it, I believe, ever before or since held

---

[1] See particularly Stephen's letters in the *Public Advertiser*, November 26 and 28, 1771, and in the *Gazetteer* and *New Daily Advertiser*, November 26 ,1771.

that a man's pedigree was of any consequence in a learned profession in this Country; still less that the humblest extraction was any impediment to the being called to the bar. This part of the charge therefore secured only to shew the personal ill will that actuated the proceeding, more especially as he had not been called upon to give any account of his parentage of which they could have had none but loose and malicious information. The want of fortune was certainly no groundless imputation, but a strange reason for shutting against a man the door of a profession in which it is proverbial that few men without the stimulus arising from the necessity of gaining a subsistance by it ever succeed. That his education was defective I cannot deny; but neither on admission to the Inns of Court nor on a call to the bar is any enquiry made how the law student has been educated. A man wholly illiterate might easily become a barrister; nor is it in this, as in other professions, a matter of public mischief or inconvenience, because the qualifications of the practitioner can alone procure him any degree of employment from which his ignorance could be injurious to others. Without as much literature at least as is requisite for general practice, a counsel could hardly rise into notice, or obtain business of a kind in which the benefit of a learned education may be felt. But however this may be, certain it is that the Inns of Court have never required this qualification in their Members, and even the regulation which now encourages, without prescribing, a previous academical course, by making a degree at the University a title to an earlier admission to the bar, or a substitute for two out of the five years standing in the Society, was at the time I am speaking of and for many years after unknown. The law Student who had never been within the walls of any College was on an equal footing at all the Inns of Court with a Master of Arts from Oxford or Cambridge. It may even, I think, be inferred from what Sir W. Blackstone says on the subject that the necessity or utility of a good classical education for a practising Counsel then was or recently had been matter of dispute in the profession.

Whatever weight might have been in this objection in point of justice, it probably had little or none in the minds of

the Benchers. It was doubtless brought forward, like the rest,
to cover their real motive, which seems more than half to
discover itself in their last imputation; for the "want of
temper" of which my Father was accused had been exhibited
only to their knowledge in his opposition to imprisonment
for debt. In this, his conduct and his writings had certainly
been intemperate enough, especially in his attacks upon
Lord Mansfield and the Courts of law in general, the true
subject of offence.

Finding himself thus stop'd in his progress to the bar he
still resolved to persevere in the new path he had chosen.
Indeed it was difficult to find another. As a Conveyancer or
Chamber Counsel admission to the bar was not strictly
necessary, and it was possible also to practise as an Attorney
and Solicitor in the name of some person in that walk of the
profession, who for a share of the emoluments or other consideration would allow his name to be used. This though no
creditable mode of practising, was not at that time regarded
as subjecting the attorney or Solicitor lending his name to the
censures of the Court. My Father therefore found no difficulty
in obtaining from a practitioner whose business was but
scanty the sanction that he wanted, and the sensible conduct
besides of the business he found when the personal appearance of an Attorney or Solicitor was necessary. It may seem
to have been less likely that he should find Clients who would
place a confidence in him, notwithstanding his want of any
regular professional education or character. But he possessed
as I have already remarked a very imposing appearance, and
conversational powers such as gave him great advantages in
the ordinary business of life, and gave strangers a high
opinion of his general information and talents. He had also
a very extensive circle of acquaintances, especially in the
commercial world, and among them some who had friendship enough for him to employ them for his own sake in any
business that they thought him capable of conducting and to
recommend him to others. His want of a regular title to
practise of course subjected him to be regarded as a legal
empiric by regular practitioners, but few were bold enough
to treat him with disrespect; and the supposed victim of Lord
Mansfield's hatred and revenge found with many that his

4*

want of a Barrister's gown was rather a recommendation than the reverse. After all, his business was not very extensive, nor often of a profitable kind, and at times he found scarcely any employment at all: so that this his only source of income was precarious as well as scanty at the best. He was often in consequence reduced to great difficulties or actual distress, and but for a frugality and self denial of the severest kind on the part of my dear Mother, he would not have been able to keep his large family from want, or himself from returning to a prison. It was on her that the most painful effects of his inadequate and precarious income and frequent difficulties fell. He, unavoidably perhaps, lived much from home. It was necessary to the obtaining practise that he should cultivate and extend his acquaintance in London and throw himself in the way of those among whom Clients might be found. But he could not afford to keep company at home or to have a home at which a professional man could be seen in a creditable way. His morning and afternoon hours therefore were almost always spent abroad except on a Sunday, and his parties were generally at a tavern or Coffee House or at one of those more accomodating dining houses in the City where men of business were used to meet. Merchants of some eminence were accustomed at that time to dine and spend their evenings at such places. I do not mean, however, to say that such were his only associates. He was obliged to stoop to society of a meaner kind for the sake of business; and concessions of that kind are commonly progressive. But I am imperceptibly touching on subjects that I think it allowable and right to avoid. I will only add that as his slender finances were often hardly adequate to his necessary personal expences abroad, my dear Mother was obliged to sustain very hard privations at home, to deny herself not only the luxuries of life, and alas sometimes to be content with too small a share of its necessaries, as well as to employ her delicate frame in servile domestic drudgery, in order that her beloved children might not want cloaths and food. I could enter into details that would be very affecting, and honorable also to her memory; but think it better to abstain. It is right, however, to say that all was borne with chearful patience; and that tho' a woman uncommonly refined and delicate in her taste and manners she accomodated herself to the painful duties of her situation with as much propriety and effect as if she had been born and brought up in a labourer's cottage. Sustained by a pious reliance on the care of Divine Providence, and the hope of a blessed immortality, she was anxious only to fulfill well her arduous duties, and especially to train up her children in the fear of God and obedience to his commandments, and to cultivate their understandings by all such means as she possessed. There was no human object about which she was so solicitous as the care of my education, and the neglect of those branches of it which a School only could supply was matter of deep regret with her and frequent expostulation with my Father. As to my brother William he continued in a Merchant's counting house, and the design being that he should follow the mercantile profession he wanted no more school education. He lived with the gentleman to whom he was clerk, and was supposed likely in due time to be taken by him into the business as a partner; but I, from the time of my leaving Mr. Howell's at Poole had been left without a school or a teacher, and lived in perfect idleness at home, except that I was very fond of reading, and spent, I think, a very adequate, if not an excessive portion of the day, book in hand. But what were the books I read? Chiefly, or almost exclusively, the English Poets, Dramatists, Novelists, and Romance Writers, of which I was quite insatiable. Poor as we were, a subscription to a circulating library was not beyond my reach; and never perhaps had such an establishment a more troublesome Subscriber. Upon an average I believe I read two volumes every day, except when Folio Romances of the *Great Cyrus*, *Clelia*, &c., stop'd my way a little longer.[1] It may seem strange that my dear Mother did not direct my reading into a better channel. She tried much to do so, and succeeded so far as to engage me to read history now and then. I laid aside my beloved Novels and Plays often enough at her

---

[1] Madelène de Scudéry (1607–1701) published under the name of her brother, George de Scudéry these two (among others) prose French romances: *Artamène, ou le grand Cyrus* (10 vols., 1648–1655) and *Clélie* (10 vols., 1654–1661). Both were widely popular throughout the eighteenth century in 5-volume folio English translations, *Le Grand Cyrus* from 1653–1655, and *Clélie* from 1656–1661.

request to read the *History of England* by Rapin,[1] some Roman and Grecian Histories, and a great deal even of the *Antient Universal History* of Rollin.[2] As to Plutarch's *Lives*,[3] I had long been conversant with, and fond of them. But I was not, alas, so tractable by my dear Mother in this point as I ought to have been. She did not indeed absolutely prescribe to me what I should or should not read at any given time. If she had, I hope and believe that her commands would not have been directly disobeyed. But she was always indulgent; and seeing me so delighted with the Novels, &c., could not find in her kind heart to do more than intreat me in general to give a portion of my time to reading of a more useful kind. As to the Poetry and Plays and indeed works of imagination in general, I suspect she thot it would be an advantage to me to indulge my fondness for them. I continued from time to time to produce verses which to her partial eyes were extraordinary for my years; and I have reason to believe that both she and my Father seriously expected I should become an eminent Poet. Then she was always hoping that I should soon go to a classical school where I should find no time for such reading. Nor was this dear woman wholly disinterested in the question. One recreation, and only one, did she enjoy. It was that of hearing me read after the children were put to bed till my Father's return, which was generally late in the evening. While she was busily plying her needle, not with embroidery or fancywork, but with humble family makings and mendings, her mind was relieved by a little light reading of the kind I was so fond of, tho' her taste, which was elegant and correct, made a good selection from it, and the Novels I read to her were the best

[1] Paul de Rapin, Sieur de Thoyras (1661–1725), whose *Histoire d'Angleterre* (13 vols. 1724–1736) and particularly the translation into English by Nicholas Tindal (15 vols. 1725–1731) and several later editions was the most widely read History of England in the eighteenth century.

[2] Charles Rollin (1661–1741), French historian and educationist; rector of the University of Paris (1694–1696) and from 1699 principal of the College de Beauvais. His *Ancient History* (Paris, 1730–1748), a popular compilation rather than a scholarly work, was widely read in translation in England.

[3] Stephen could have been reading the translation by John Langhorne (6 vols. 1770), but equally likely the translation by John Dryden (5 vols. 1683–1687), of which there was a 6-volume edition in 1763. North's translation of 1579 was reprinted as late as 1676.

of the day. As to the Poets, she knew them all well, and directed me to the best pieces of those which are called our classics. But Young's *Night Thoughts*[1] had charms for her far beyond their poetic merits. Her fervent piety, her sorrows, her glowing hopes of immortality, enlisted her strongest sympathies in favour of that wonderful work, for such I still esteem it. She was never tired of hearing me read the *Night Thoughts*. I continued frequently to do so, even while she lay on her death bed, and I believe till the very day before she died. From that period my admiration of the book was increased by my affectionate and reverential partiality for her opinions. It was much in my hands, therefore, in my hours of religious meditation, and without attempting to commit it to memory I became so familiar with it that scarcely a line could be quoted to which I could not add the whole of the connected passages. Let me add that there are few books, if any, to which I have been more indebted. The two Parts called "The Infidel Reclaimed" are particularly valuable. They contain nearly all the arguments for a future retributory state of existence that are derivable from the light of Nature. Many of them are just with irresistable force of reasoning, and the effect of the whole taken together must be felt, I think, by every unprejudiced mind as amounting to full demonstration. The poetic embellishments of the argument are also in my judgment very great, tho' not uniformly in good taste, the standard of which was not so well settled in Young's time as it has since been by the labours of judicious critics. His great faults are the mixing incongruous metaphors, the extending his similies into allegories, or pushing them into various points of resemblance, and occasional obscurity of stile. But with all its defects the *Night Thoughts* will charm as a Poem all who are capable of entering into its spirit, and who laying aside fastidious criticism will suffer it to work its natural impression on their understandings, their imaginations, and their hearts. It was a most favorite work with most pious persons of education in my early years, and the generation next before my

---

[1] Edward Young (1683-1765) published, anonymously, *The Complaint, or Night Thoughts on Life, Death, and Immortality* in four instalments, 1742, 1743, 1744, and 1745.

own, and I have been frequently struck with the mention of it in the memoirs of eminent Divines to whom the revival of religion in our own times, and the latter part of the last Century, was chiefly owing, as a work which contributed much to excite or confirm their serious and devout impressions. It is also said to be much admired by learned and pious men on the Continent, who know it only through the medium of a French translation. I make these remarks the rather because the *Night Thoughts* have fallen of late into neglect by many pious readers. It is partly, I suspect, through the rivalship of Cowper, as a more modern poetic advocate for the same sacred cause, and certainly a more popular writer. My dear Wilberforce, than whom a man of more various reading or better taste will not readily be found, said to me above twenty years ago in commending Cowper, "He is the only religious poet I know." When I mentioned Young he admitted the exception, but not so cordially as I thought due to the Author of the *Night Thoughts*. The fact is he is very little acquainted with this Poem, while Cowper is his constant companion. We have a standing amicable and jocose controversy on the subject, and he says I am angry with Cowper because he prefers him to Young. I on the other hand maintain that Young has a sublimity to which Cowper never rose, and that he prefers the latter not because he is more religious, but because he is more doctrinal. This beloved Friend however is not, to speak seriously, attached to any doctrines respecting which Christians differ, more than he ought to be. He values them chiefly as they conduce to what he himself gives so bright an example of, a pure and holy life; and he is not what Cowper certainly was, a Calvinist. I mean he does not agree with him as to Predestination and other points in which Calvin was opposed to the tenets of Arminius, and Whitefield to Wesley. He dislikes all such controversies; and in an intimate acquaintance of above thirty years I have rarely if ever known him to mention them either with his pen or tongue.

Ill chosen tho' my reading in general was, it was not wholly useless to me in after life. I acquired from the quantity and variety of it a *copia verborum* in my native tongue which has been useful to me as a public speaker and writer, and a facility in English composition in which many a man of learned education is very deficient. By the aid also of my dear Mother's fine ear and taste I learned to read with propriety, and with a right management of the breath and voice. The long periods of Young's blank verse, with his frequently involved and difficult construction, made the *Night Thoughts* in this respect a peculiarly useful exercise; and I do not scruple to say that all the regular education I ever received has contributed less to my success in life than the advantages I thus derived from the circulating library and my dear Mother's domestic teaching.

Chapter Three

[*1771–1775*]

IT was not, I think, till two years or more after I left Mr.
Howell's that I entered the door of a school of any kind or
read a line of Latin. I was then first put to a day school in the
Borough to a man who professed indeed to teach that language along with writing and arithmetic, and who put the
Latin Grammar in my hands, the first rudiments of which I
had nearly forgotten. But before I had attended his school
long enough to make any progress even under a competent
Teacher, my Father being released from his confinement,
took a house in Walnut-tree Walk, in the road from Westminster Bridge to Kennington, and I was soon after put to
another day school of a like character kept by a Mr. Lloyd
by the side of Kennington Green, at which I remained, I
think, about a year. Here I was turned into a New Latin
Grammar, and put to read Corderius I think, and Erasmus,
and afterwards Cæsar's Commentaries; but the Master might
perhaps with equal modesty have professed to teach Arabic
and Sanscrit. I am sure I learned nothing of Latin correctly,
nothing that was not afterwards to be unlearned, not even
the pronunciation or proper quantities of words. In fact it
was what is commonly called a commercial school. Writing,
Arithmetic, and Bookkeeping were much more attended to
than the Latin, or French, which Mr. Lloyd also professed
to teach; and an hour or two at most every day was all that
was allotted to those languages. He had been, as I afterwards
heard, a Cheesemonger who having failed or not succeeded
in that business put on a clerical wig and black coat, and by
dint of a specious gravity passed himself with the unlearned
as a competent schoolmaster, and taking a large house in
what was deemed a very healthy situation, contrived to get
a good number of boarders, as well as day scholars from the
neighbourhood. My Father being no good judge of his
qualifications, and seeing that he had a large school within
two or three furlongs of our house, thought no doubt he

could not do better for me at the time than send me to him
as a day scholar.

While at this School I formed an acquaintance that had
no small influence on the events of my future life. Among the
day scholars was Thomas Stent, a fine handsome boy about
a year or a little more younger than myself whose Father
was a Stock Broker and had a house in Walnut-tree Walk
exactly opposite to that which my Father had recently taken.
We therefore frequently walked to and from school together,
and played together in our holiday and evening hours.
Hitherto I had no companion whatever near my own age.
Such society therefore had all the charms of a novelty; and I
soon began to feel for him those emotions of friendship which
are so natural to the human mind, especially in the ardent
season of youth, and to prefer Tom's company even to my
favorite reading. The feeling became warmly reciprocal on
his part, and not the less so perhaps because his Parents, his
Mother at least, took some pains at first to check the growing
familiarity between us. They had heard no doubt of my
Father's misfortunes, and thought that a boy who had lately
been an inmate of a Prison was not unlikely to be a dangerous
friend for their son. Tom therefore was in general forbid to
play with me, and when seen from the windows in my company was frequently called in and kept at home for the rest
of the Evening. They could not, however, prevent our intercourse at the School and our daily walks twice a day to and
from that place. Indeed I believe the prohibition did not
expressly extend to this; for Tom was of so mild and tractable
a temper and stood so much in awe of his Mother that he
would probably not have disobeyed. His regard for me and
my ascendancy over him were soon increased by the protection he found in me in the quarrels that school boys so often
engage in. He was of a stronger make than mine but not
near so tall; and tho' not deficient in courage had not the
same ardour and impetuosity of spirit that enabled me often
to check the aggressions of boys more powerful than myself.
A stout lad that worked in a garden in our way to school once
assaulted us with stones, and not content with this sent me
afterwards a challenge to fight him. Tom and others would
have had me decline it, not only because they said he was

above my match, but because he was a tradesman's apprentice and therefore below me as an antagonist. But my resentment and pride got the better of their remonstrances, and of
my own fears also as to the event, which were not small. I
accepted his challenge. A crowd of our schoolfellows went to
see the combat, the field of which was the garden he worked
in, and the men who were at work with him gladly made a
clear stage for us. The lad might certainly have beat me
with ease had his courage been equal to my own; but after
several rounds in which we were both in the boxing phraze
severely punished, he gave in, and all the encouragement and
reproaches of the gardeners could not prevail on him to fight
any more. I was so covered with his blood and my own that I
was afraid to appear in my Mother's presence lest I should
alarm her and incur her anger and that of my Father if at
home, but Tom and some of the rest went with me to make
my excuse by attesting the provocation, and what more
effectually reconciled my Father to the condition I was in,
my having beat a boy stronger than myself. But I was seen
also by Mr. Stent's family, and the spectacle perhaps did not
diminish their apprehensions that my company would do
Tom no good. The latter, of course, however, was not the
less attached to me for this exploit. His Mother, a very
handsome woman, but of a strong and violent temper and
who governed imperiously the whole family, was the great
opponent of our holiday meetings, for the Father was very
little at home; but I had another enemy, as I found, or Tom
another restraint, in his Sister, a young lady a few months
older than myself, who had recently returned home from
finishing her education at a Country Boarding School: not
that she directly thwarted her brother between whom and
her there was great mutual affection, but that she was obliged
to second her Mother's purpose by admonishing him when
in the absence of the latter he was desirous of complying
with my invitation to ramble or play together. This of course
predisposed me not to like the young Lady very much, and
one day when before a companion of our own age of the
name of Graham whose Parents were also near neighbours,
my friend opposed to some plan of mine that his Sister
objected to it, I said with levity something reflecting upon

her. Tom, who knew I was in jest, was not offended; but
Graham went and reported it to his Mother, a meddling
malicious woman, and she, with whom I was no favourite,
thought it worth her while to go over and report my words
with aggravation to Mrs. Stent. The consequence was a
positive interdict to Tom of all future intercourse between us.
He was obliged sorrowfully to obey, and it was some time
before he could find an opportunity to tell me the cause of
his conduct. When I heard it, my first step was to chastise
Graham by pulling his nose. My next was to go over to Mrs.
Stent, whom I had never spoken to before, to beg her
pardon, and that of her daughter for my levity, and to
assure them that it was not from any disrespectful feeling
that I had spoken the words really used, but on a sudden
emotion on hearing that Miss Stent opposed her brother's
going with me to play. Mrs. S. was a shrewd clever woman,
as well as a very pleasing one in her person and manners.
She saw perhaps in my language and conduct on this
occasion something that attracted her liking and esteem, or
that raised me above the wild and mischievous boy of
whom she before thought unfavorably. So it was, however,
that from this moment she not only did not oppose my
intimacy with her son, but treated me with much kindness
and allowed him to bring me over to the house to drink tea
and partake of their evening's amusements. I was able to
improve those opportunities so as to become soon a great
favourite with the Mother and Daughter as well as the Son.
They found in me qualifications that they did not expect,
and such as contributed to their entertainment in the long
winter evenings that ensued soon after this acquaintance
began, for tho' they often were on visits abroad, at the house
as I understood of a relation, they saw very little company
at home, and their ordinary evening amusements were reading, and embroidering with the tambour frame, then considered as an elegant branch of female education, varied now
and then with a tune from Miss S. on her Pianoforte, on
which she was then supposed to be a tolerable performer, and
with an occasional game at cards, drafts, or backgammon.
In all these I was found a useful associate. I was not unskilful
at Quadrille and Picquett, then the reigning games, and at

drafts and backgammon I was, or soon became, an adept. By imitation of my dear Mother I had also become a tolerable singer, so as to accompany Miss S. at the Pianoforte; but above all they found me a valuable evening companion as a reader. My taste in that respect and my information too, was found, to their surprise no doubt, much above their own, especially in poetry and plays; and the ladies were particularly fond of hearing me read while they employed themselves at the tambour frame and other work at the fire side. Nor was I less fond of being so employed. It gratified my vanity while it indulged my favourite habits. My poor friend Tom was the only one of the four not quite satisfied. He loved our boyish play better than hearing novels and poetry, and would rather have been with me alone than with his Mother and Sister. The case was reversed hardly enough upon him. Instead of being grieved that they disliked me, he repined perhaps that they liked me too well. Tom however made good natural allowances; for by this time I had fallen in love with his Sister, and did not long omit to make him my confidant. I believe also he soon suspected or learned from her that the feeling was reciprocal.

Here let me give a slight sketch of my beloved Nancy, afterwards my faithful companion for many years, and the Mother of my children.[1] She was at this time like myself about fourteen years old, or a little more, for she was four months my senior, and I had just attained that age. We were both tall for our years. Indeed I do not believe that either increased in stature after this time, and she, who in person was rather below than above the middle size, was quite the woman in appearance, and in understanding and manners. Her features in general were not pretty, but her eyes were very good, and so at this time was her complexion, and her hair was auburn, or rather at that time more inclining to red. Her person was pleasing, her manners lively, and she possessed what to me has always been chiefly

[1] Stephen's first wife, Anna Stent, was, by his account, born in February, 1758; at the time of their meeting in 1772 they were fourteen years of age; eleven years later, in June 1783, they were married at the age of twenty-five; she died in December, 1796, before she had completed her thirty-ninth year. In the twelve years of the marriage she bore Stephen seven children, two of whom died in infancy, and five survived their father.

attractive, a great share of sensibility, with a more than
ordinary share of good sense. Her heart was warm and
affectionate in a high degree. As a Sister, a daughter, a Wife,
and a Mother, I never knew in that respect her superior.
Had she been less attractive, it still would not have been
strange that she should captivate a heart so susceptible and
romantic as mine then was, when we were brought into such
familiar intercourse with each other, and with such a
common bond of attachment as my friend Tom, between
whom and her there was the fondest fraternal affection. I
soon became as ardent a lover as a man of any age could be,
and after discovering it no doubt very plainly with my eyes,
and by my obsequious attentions, at length I mustered confidence enough expressly to declare my feelings. We were
both too well read in plays and novels not to know how
such things should be managed, but my dear Nancy had
great frankness and cordiality. She therefore after receiving
it at first as badinage, and for some time rallying me upon
my early gallantry, did not long leave me in suspence, but
gave me the delight of knowing that the attachment was
mutual. We both, however, had far too much sense to suppose
that such an attachment would be sanctioned by our
Parents. We knew that from our ages, mine especially, it
would be deemed not only imprudent but preposterous, and
that her Parents particularly would be alarmed at it, since I
had not even the prospect of a profession before me, nor
education enough to prepare me for one. On her side there
was no fortune, but her Father was then in a prosperous way
of business, and his children only three in number had considerable expectations from a rich maternal relative, in
which from painful events that I shall have to notice they
were ultimately disappointed. But we were sanguine enough
to hope that all obstacles would one day vanish; meantime
we resolved to be faithful to each other, and to keep the
precious secret inviolable except from our faithful Tom. He,
poor fellow, was alarmed with the fear of his Mother's and
Father's resentment, but we easily engaged him to secrecy,
and as to the sin of filial undutifulness in the matter, we
thought, alas, but slightly of it. Here our novels had furnished us with too many seducing examples. We had pro-

ceeded for some time, for some months perhaps, in this course of conduct with mutual delight and ever growing fondness for each other, when an old family servant who had observed my frequent visits to her young Mistress in Mrs. S's absence, and seen or overheard enough to clearly detect our secret engagement, became alarmed for the consequences, and felt herself bound to disclose the matter to Mamma. The latter certainly ought to have foreseen the consequences of such an intimacy as she had encouraged, but had strangely conceived no suspicion of it, and was now greatly alarmed and incensed at the discovery. She questioned my poor Nancy on the subject, and having obtained from her candour an admission of the truth, was violent and severe in her resentment. She consulted with Mr. Stent, and the consequence was that my poor dear Nancy was for some time forbidden their presence, as well as prohibited from ever seeing me again. Tom was involved in their displeasure, and also told that he must never speak to me more, but was allowed, I believe, to bring or send to me the heart-breaking news.

My feelings upon it may be easily imagined. I did not, however, despair. I grieved for my dear Nancy's sufferings, but relied on her constancy and flattered myself I should find expedients for keeping up an intercourse with her by person or letter in spite of the harsh prohibition. So far was I from feeling the sinfulness of this that I was ready to conceive myself the injured party, to think myself contumeliously and cruelly treated, and to think it besides due to the dear sufferer to find means of relieving her feelings, which I doubted not were as painful as my own. My first expedient for this purpose was a clandestine correspondence. I contrived to convey letters to her and to receive them in return without the knowledge of her Parents. Her maid servant and her brother also, if I remember right, were auxiliaries in this intercourse; and it went on undiscovered for a considerable time during which a great many plaintive, consolatory, and passionate epistles were interchanged with vows of mutual fidelity. The hero and heroine of an amatory play or novel were never, I suppose, more ardent or romantic in their stile. Of course, we were not content with this but wished to find some means of private interviews with each other. This, however, was found extremely difficult or rather quite impracticable, for Mrs. Stent never suffered her daughter to go out beyond the limit of a small garden behind the house but in her own company. Even into this garden she could not go without being under her Mother's eyes in the day time, and in the evening when at home they were always engaged together. I nevertheless did contrive to appoint one meeting with my dear Nancy at the bottom of her garden, to which I made my way after dark by climbing over the high boarded fence from a nursery ground adjoining, but while waiting for her there in breathless impatience under cover of a small shrubbery, and when the approach of a quick female step set my heart in palpitation, the Mother, not the daughter, suddenly presented herself before me. Perceiving my poor Nancy's flurried and restless deportment, I presume, as the appointed time arrived, and seeing her steal towards the garden, she suspected the truth, ordered her to return to her seat at the parlour fireside, and sallying into the garden, surprised me at my post. Her expostulations were not sharper than the occasion demanded. She could, in fact, hardly finish them with gravity; for she was distracted with my surprise and disappointment. She reasoned with me, however, on the impropriety and imprudence of my conduct, and the ill consequences that must ensue from it to her daughter, professing that she should not oppose our mutual attachment if we were of an age and in circumstances to indulge it without ruin to both, but that at present it was impossible to permit any further intercourse between her daughter and me. In short she treated me with a kindness that had its effect on my feelings, but not enough to make me desist from my pursuit or enter into any promise to do so.

I cannot recollect whether it was before or after this adventure that Mrs. Stent, suspecting our correspondence, demanded of her daughter the keys of her scrutoire where she had imprudently preserved many of my amorous epistles. My poor Nancy, after much fruitless intreaty, was obliged to comply, and a discovery ensued which gave both the Mother and Father more serious views of the case than they had before entertained. They now thought it necessary to make a formal complaint to my Parents, and lay the letters before them.

My dear Mother did not learn for the first time of my attachment to Miss Stent. She had observed or heard of it before, but probably did not regard it in a very serious light, or know of the uneasiness it had given to the young lady's parents, for she had not laid her very influential commands on me not to indulge it; she had not gone further than gently to suggest to me that I was too young yet to form such attachments, and that I ought first to be in a situation to marry without imprudence, or at least to have some means of subsistence. I have reason to think that my dear Mother did not go further at that time because she saw enough of the dangerous side of my character to think a virtuous attachment a safeguard I was likely to want; and that, however premature, it was not more so than the perils which it might lessen or prevent. She had also a very good opinion both of the understanding and disposition of my dear Nancy, who, before our mutual attachment was known to her Parents or avowed by us to each other, had cultivated my dear Mother's acquaintance sufficiently to admire and love her and gain her esteem in return. The complaint to my Father took the case in a manner out of my Mother's hands. She did, however, express to me my sense of the duty of desisting from attempting to see or write to Miss S. contrary to the commands of her Parents. She said, I doubt not, all that her own excellent principles suggested on the duty of filial obedience; for she thought most reverently of that important obligation and has often said to me that she regarded all the afflictions of her life as just providential chastisements for her filial disobedience in marrying without parental consent. But I do not recollect that she interposed any injunction of her own against the further prosecution of my courtship, and strongly believe she did not; because tho' I might have disobeyed, it would have been with a pain to my feelings of love and reverence for her that would have printed the sin deeply in my mind. Certain it is she did not injoin me to give up the attachment itself. On the contrary I have recollected a thousand times with pleasure her saying to me, "My dear Jem, you shall have my free consent to take Miss Stent for your wife as soon as you are able to marry; for I think well of her & like her much." *This* no doubt was accompanied with remarks on the imprudence of a premature engagement and the sinfulness of inducing her to see or correspond with me after her Parents had forbidden it. But it was in the way of observation and advice and not, I am confident, of command. Perhaps this judicious, as well as tender parent did not think it wise or right to put my filial feelings towards herself to too severe a trial; or perhaps knowing that my heart was very sore on the subject, she thought it harsh to call on my sense of filial duty for a final renunciation of an intercourse which would most probably be cut off on the other side without my will.

As to my Father he neither commanded nor condescended to reason with me on the subject. In telling me of Mr. Stent's complaint he said something sternly, I think more in the way of sarcasm on my folly than grave reprehension, and sent me as his custom was when angry out of the room. There the matter ended between him and me; but I heard afterwards from my brother, or a servant, that he made a jest of the matter before some friends at dinner, adding that he had told Mr. Stent he must take care of his daughter, and not rely on him. My letters as I further heard were produced, much to the amusement of Mr. Jackson and his Wife, the latter of whom, a witty lady, exclaimed "Dear me! *Where was the Nurse?*"

All this did not improve my disposition to give way to the interdict of Mr. and Mrs. Stent. So far, alas, was I from being actuated by right principles, and so little did I think of our Savior's golden rule, that I actually thought myself the injured Party. The complaint which had exposed me to my Father's anger, and the ridicule of others, seemed to me an indignity and insult; and I was vindictive enough to think of punishing it by beating or personally affronting Mr. Stent, till I recollected that this would be disrespectful and revolting to my dear Nancy, and would be visited on her. The fancied wrong, however, was a new stimulus to me, tho' my heart did not want one, to prosecute my courtship to the utmost, and to see and correspond with the daughter if I could, in despite of the Father and Mother.

This I found was now no easy task. My poor Nancy was a close prisoner, shut up by day as well as night in her bed room, not allowed to see her Parents or Brothers, and waited upon only by a trusty servant on whom they could depend.

These difficulties however did not dishearten me. They rather whetted my invention, while compassion for the dear girl's sufferings augmented my desire to learn the state of her mind and send her consolation if I could. I had the advantage of being able to reconnoitre their House and garden from a window of my own bed room. Here therefore I spent hours, I might say almost entire days when at home, in watching whether the poor prisoner was ever allowed to take the air, and whether anybody had access to her, and in the more interesting hope of seeing her and catching a glance from her eyes at the window of her prison. I contrived also by management of shutters or otherwise to do this without much observation from the sitting rooms of their house, tho' these were in front. But the strictness of my dear Nancy's confinement would have continued to frustrate all these efforts, she being shut up in a back room and not suffered to leave it, if Mrs. Stent's ultra caution had not at length defeated itself. Fearful of my stratagems in the garden and at night she took her daughter to lodge and sleep in her own bedroom which was in front towards the Street. My eyes were now soon gratified with the sight of that beloved object for which they had ached so long, and by watching opportunities we were able by signs and talking on the fingers, at which we were both expert, to devise a new mode of correspondence. At the dining hour the windows of the room below were shut and she was left upstairs alone. At this time therefore she gently opened her window and threw a letter over a slight railing below into the street. With the aid of a line of small twine also thrown from her window, my own letters were drawn up. I was there, of course, to receive the one and dispatch the other; except when the better to avoid observation I employed in this service a servant of my Mother's who was as willing as women usually are to serve me and a distressed damsel in that way. It was not long before the vigilance of the Parents, aided by an accident, discovered this new correspondence. While sitting in their

dining room in the evening they had left the upper part of
one of the window shutters open, probably from suspicion;
and my dear Nancy, not aware of this, threw down a letter
which was carried by the wind within the garden pales. I
saw the accident and sent over my confidant, the maid
servant, to walk by the house and reach the letter through
the open rails in her way; for I had seen Mr. S. come to the
window and knew that if I went out myself I should be
observed. But Mr. S. was watching the event; and no sooner
had the servant attempted to execute her commission, than
he rushed out and with angry exclamations drove her away,
at the same time taking up the unfortunate letter and returning with it to the house. Of course its contents were such
as to bring down upon the poor writer additional anger tho'
it was not easy to find for her increased severity of treatment.
If I rightly recollect, this new detection led to wiser and more
healing measures, better adapted both to my dear Nancy's
disposition and mine. An appeal was made to her filial
affections and sense of duty. She was forgiven, received into
her Father's favor again and promised in return to correspond with me no more without their consent. My dear
Mother also, being informed of my new fault, expostulated
with me in her gentle, sensible, affectionate manner upon it,
and convinced me that it was sinful and inconsistent with a
generous attachment to the young lady herself thus to involve
her in the guilt and the painful consequences of disobedience
to her Parents.

These recollections have still a lively interest, tho' not
unmixed I trust with penitential pain. I have therefore been
led to dwell upon them too minutely. This youthful passion,
however, had important consequences in my future life. And
alas! my poor dear Nancy!—But I will not anticipate the
painful reasons I have for fearing that this trespass against
filial duty on her part, renewed at a more mature age at my
sinful instigation, was visited upon her, as such offences with
a wonderful uniformity are, in the present world.

It is high time to return to the subject of my much
neglected education. Tho' my Father by this time had
destined me for the profession of the bar he was content to
keep me still as a day scholar at Mr. Lloyd's, where I was

literally throwing away my time. My attendance perhaps was not very irregular, but except writing and cyphering it would, I believe, have been difficult or impossible for me to learn anything properly there if my industry had been ever so great. My poor Father, however, was inconscious of this. He never examined me as to the progress I was making in Latin, probably because he had forgot whatever he once knew of that language, and feared to expose his own deficiencies. But if he had known that the School was bad, it would not have been easy for him to place and keep me at a good one.

In the Spring of 1773 an opportunity occurred which promised to rescue me from this ruinous disadvantage. My Uncle George Milner, my Mother's youngest and then only surviving Brother, who had acquired a handsome fortune in right of his Wife, resided at Winchester for the benefit of his only Son, now my affectionate friend and brother-in-law, who had been for some years at Winchester School, but boarded at home, for the sake of avoiding the very bad company out of school hours of the boys and young men on the foundation; for the school was then not less low in moral than high in literary reputation. Besides him, my Uncle and Aunt had only one child, a daughter then about fourteen who was generally admired and beloved for her amicable disposition and manners and was the idol of her Father's heart; but it had pleased God a little before this period suddenly to deprive him of her by death; and the unexpected blow had plunged both him and my Aunt in deep distress, to soften which they left their now melancholly home and spent some time in London. Mr. Milner, who was a man of warm and liberal tho' inconstant feelings, had always been much attached to my Mother, and feeling for her sake an interest in her children, was much concerned to find how compleatly I was wasting my time, and desirous to assist in the cultivation of talents of which he, like my Parents, thought very favorably. This kind disposition was no doubt much improved by his finding that I had written an elegy on the beloved object of his grief. The verses, of which I have no recollection, were, I dare say, poor enough; but I had written them from the heart, having shared in the

general grief for the death of my amiable cousin; and therefore the tribute to her memory could not but recommend me
to my Uncle. In short, he formed the design of taking me to
Winchester or receiving me into his family there on their
return and placing me at the school on the same plan that
he had adopted for his Son. My Mother was overjoyed at the
proposal, and my Father's consent was obtained. For my
part I was not much charmed with the plan when I considered from whom it would divide me. Tho' restrained from
seeing and as I believe at that time from writing to my
beloved Miss S., still it was something to be near her and to
hope that I should now and then see her perhaps in the
Streets tho' under her Mother's arm; but Winchester was a
frightful distance for a lover, especially as I could not hope
to hear from or of her. She might forget me; or she might
transfer her affections to another. Already my busy imagination had figured to itself a rival in a Captn. MacWilliams, a
fine looking young man, a friend of her Father, who had
been observed to be frequently visiting there since my
rupture with the family. My dear Mother indeed had rather
injudiciously conjured up this fiend in my mind with a view
of showing me how imprudent it was to indulge an attachment so unlikely to be gratified. With such feelings I shrunk
from the prospect of speedily turning my back for six months
upon Walnut-tree Walk; but I had another and I believe
equally strong repugnance to such a seperation from my
beloved Mother. I had the feelings of the man and boy together. I was at once love-sick and home-sick.

I had too much sense, however, and too much ambition
to have declined, if I could, a plan so much for my advantage.
Preparations therefore were made for my departure; the
sad hour arrived! I quitted with mutual tears the arms of my
dear Mother; I passed with a heart-rending sigh the
windows of that house which contained my beloved Nancy,
and tasted in their full bitterness for the first time, those
sorrows with which my life has since abounded, seperations
from those I love. If my Uncle had not well known the uncommon disadvantages under which I laboured, and kindly
provided against their consequences, my entrance at Winchester would have been very mortifying, and my situation

in the school intolerable. While in stature fit for the highest forms, I must have been put into one of the lowest, as I hardly knew so much of the Latin as the youngest boys who go there. But Mr. Milner very properly told the Masters, with whom he was well acquainted, the true nature of the case, and they judiciously adopted for it a peculiar treatment. To save my feelings they put me in the senior part of the Fourth form, where, though the boys were younger than myself, the disparity was not quite disgraceful; but as it was impossible for me at the outset to do all the business of a class which was reading Virgil and the Greek Testament, while I did not know even the Greek Alphabet and was miserably deficient even in the Latin Grammar, Dr. Collins, who had the charge of that class, took the course of never calling on me to read and construe and parse with the rest until I should have time by private application to retrieve my defects. Had this arrangement been made known to me it would have saved me much discomfort and anxiety, but I was not aware of it and consequently never stood up with the Class to go through our readings and examinations without the fear of a detection and disgrace. It was thought, no doubt, that this fear would be a useful stimulus, and it was easy to hide the plan from my observation and that of my class fellows, because the practice was not to call on us in any regular order, but to *dodge* us as the phraze was, and therefore my being always passed by appeared to be accident rather than design till my long repeated escapes from the disgrace I dreaded, at length opened my own eyes to the distinction with which I was treated. A previous candid explanation to me would, I am convinced, have been much better, if coupled with notice that I must not expect such a cover for my ignorance beyond a limited time. I should then have set myself anxiously to avoid the future and evitable evil by extraordinary private industry, whereas expecting as I did detection from day to day, there was no hope of ultimate escape to animate my exertions. I wrote the exercises in the Latin Syntax, which were our evening's tasks, by my cousin Milner's help, and got by heart the prescribed number of Latin verses, because I had to give in the former, and repeat the latter, with the rest; but as to the

Greek Testament and our other work, I lost, in the vain attempt of preparing myself in some sort for examination, time that might have been employed in laying those sound foundations of which I stood in need.

I did not altogether escape that ill treatment from my schoolfellows to which newcomers at a public school are usually subjected. By living at my Uncle's I was indeed exempt from it in the play ground and in the dining hall and sleeping rooms, the ordinary scenes of such annoyance, for I mixed with them only in the Public School. But there they made themselves amends. I sat in a part of that large room remote from the chairs of the different Masters, and as each boy had a chest of his own called a Scob to contain his books, &c., the cover of which was prop'd up, leaving a desk board on which we read and wrote below, we were as we sat at work screened a good deal from observation, except by those who sat in the same cross line or were passing down the avenues between the rows of seats and scobs, to whom we were exposed sidewise. This arrangement presented means of persecution, especially about the close of day, of which I soon found myself the unlucky object. While anxiously intent on my lesson I was saluted by a violent blow on the head from some book thrown at me across the room. Presently after a boy would come for the book claiming it was his own, and alleging that somebody, he knew not whom, had snatched it from him and thrown it. I had hardly settled at my work again when the same process was repeated, and again at short intervals till the school broke up, when half stunned and with bumps on my head from the contusions, I went away without being able to discover one of my tormentors. This persecution was continued many evenings till at length my Uncle suggested a remedy that had not occurred to myself. The next time I put every book that was flung at me into my Scob; and whenever a boy came to demand it as his own, my answer was, "Find me the boy that threw it, and you shall have it when I have given him as good a beating as I can, or if you choose to turn out in the Meads (the play ground) and fight me you shall have your book; but if not, I will keep it." This expedient was soon effectual, but not till I had literally filled my Scob with a collection of the Latin and Greek Classics, Dictionaries, Lexicons, &c., of which I became the undisputed owner, and ultimately carried them from the School. Among the many bad customs there, most boys, or all, had an unlimited power of taking up school books from the College Booksellers, so that they gave themselves little concern about the loss or destruction of their books. I do not recollect that these spoils, or any quarrel I had in the school, cost me a single battle, but it was probably because they saw I had no disinclination to fight. Such is man! that kindly, equitable, well disposed being, as unchristened philosophers would paint him; such is he even from his childhood!

My stay at Winchester was very short—only as I best remember, from the Midsummer to the Christmas Vacation. When the holidays arrived, I was naturally very eager to go home. My Uncle, I can remember, made some faint objection to it, but easily gave way; and well can I recall at this hour the strong emotion of joy with which I set out in the Stage to return to my dear Mother, my brother, and as I fondly hoped also, to some new intercourse with my beloved Miss Stent. I was nevertheless boy enough to quit the Stage with some of my schoolfellows, and spend the money we had in hiring hack horses, which we galloped through thick and thin for a stage or two, preceding or overtaking the Coach. Strange had been the revolutions in all that was most interesting to me that a few Months had produced. Our Family residence was removed from Walnut-tree Walk, that place endeared to me by the most lively and tender recollections, into the City. My poor Father, pinched in his income by the slender and precarious returns of his irregular business, thought, I suppose, that he could improve it, or lessen family expences by removing to Town; and I found him living in a dark uncomfortable House in a Street near Queen Street Cheapside, called St. Thomas Apostles. Here, however, were my dear Mother, my three Sisters and younger Brother, all dear to me, tho' yet mere children, and the latter a child in arms; and here also I found living again at home, my dear Brother William, the companion of my childhood; for the Merchant with whom he had been placed had failed in trade, and my Father having no better plan for him meant to bring him up to the law as an Attorney, and had articled him, I think, with the Attorney in whose name he practised. With such Society I could not but feel the family home delightful after the confinement of the School: but I soon found my satisfaction damped and my mind disturbed by two painful discoveries. The one was that my dear Mother had a severe fixed cough and other symptoms that were supposed to be consumptive. The complaint, I think, had begun some months before; but not so as to excite alarm or much attention. It was supposed to have been superinduced by her persisting in suckling her youngest child, my brother John, for near twice the usual period, tho' I fear alas that her too abstemious and laborious habits, both the fruit of her self denying spirit and devotedness to her arduous maternal and conjugal duties, were concurrent causes of the diseases. It certainly was not hereditary, nor had her constitution originally any tendency that way. She had been strong enough to suckle nine children without assistance and had arrived at an age (thirty) when the danger of consumption, even under a predisposition to it, is generally supposed to be past. It was now, however, too apparent that her complaints were of that dangerous kind, and tho' her undiminished chearfulness, activity, and strength inspired good hopes that her constitution would triumph over them, it was impossible not to feel anxiety about her as well as painful simpathy with her sufferings from the distressing cough.

The other painful discovery that I about the same time made was a great surprise as well as mortification and concern. A calamity astonishing to all who heard of it and knew the parties, had overwhelmed and broken up the family of Mr. Stent. He had detected his wife in an adulterous intercourse of long standing with a man once his particular friend, and had in consequence sent her away, broken up his family establishment, and placed his daughter under the care of Mrs. Thomas, a respectable lady with whom and her husband he had long been on very intimate terms. Of all the cases of conjugal infidelity that I have ever heard of this was in some respects the most remarkable. Mrs. Stent, as I have observed, was not only a very handsome, but a very sensible

5

woman, and apparently of the correctest manners. She had
no taste for gaiety or dissipation, was strictly attentive to her
domestic duties, and seemed a pattern for Mothers, being
never seen out of her children's company. I observed that
she generally went to Town once a week after dinner and
returned in the evening, but her daughter and two sons always went with her, and I understood they went to visit a
sister or some near relation of hers whose name or residence,
however, I never heard them mention. But this was conjecture of mine, for I had never asked Miss S. whom they
visited, and Tom on my asking him once, frankly told me he
was forbid to tell; from which I suspected it was a near
relation in some poor situation in life whom they were
ashamed to produce and avow. Strange to tell, this woman
had for several years carried on a criminal intercourse with
a Mr. Machell, a man who had been on terms of friendship
or intimacy with her husband, and took her children with
her when she visited him, in order by their company to
prevent suspicion, thus making them inconscious instruments
of their Father's wrongs and dishonor. That they should
visit with her for years at his house every week at least or
oftener, knowing that it was a secret which they were intimidated from mentioning to anybody, even their Father, and
yet never suspect the truth may seem very extraordinary;
yet such was the fact. She had habituated them to this course
of conduct from their childhood long before they had a
capacity to form suspicions on the subject, and the habit was
so formed with my poor Nancy and Tom of considering
both the visits and the secrecy as matters of course, that they
no more thought of enquiring into the reasons for them than
a Catholic into the secrets of the Confessional or the Mysteries
of the Church. All they knew was that a Mother of whom
they stood in extreme awe made it her imperious will. The
knowledge I had of Mrs. Stent's character lessens my surprise that she should have been able so to govern the minds
of her children. She was not generally harsh to them, rather
on the contrary kind and indulgent; but she seemed born
to give the law to all around her, and to subdue their understandings too. She was able even after her disgrace to
maintain an influence of the strongest kind over all her own

relations, and persuade them of her innocence to the last. It must be observed, however, that her children never saw in her anything but the most perfect correctness of behaviour towards Mr. M.; nor any thing in his carriage towards her that could give birth to suspicion. They were taught to regard him with respect, and supposed him, I apprehend, to be an old family friend whose House, he being a batcheller, his Mother occasionally assisted him in superintending, and from whom she might have expectations, he being engaged in a lucrative Manufactory, and reputed a very wealthy man. She may have given them reasons for secrecy towards their Father which I never heard, or may have forgot, if secrecy towards *him* was expressly injoined. This I think must have been the case, and yet it is possible that she may have relied on the general injunction, and on the rarity of their intercourse with him out of her presence. I think too that there was some connection in business between Machell and a Brother-in-law of hers who lived near him, such as might have been made a blind for some intercourse with the former had Mr. S. heard of it. But in fact he saw little of her or his children, generally dining in town and returning at a late hour.

I never probed so deeply into this painful subject as to learn very clearly the whole of the artifices by which this extraordinary woman deceived my dear Nancy, and my poor friend Tom, as well as her injured husband; but certain it is that the detection of her criminal conduct was a great surprise to them all, and I believe to every other connection and friend. The discovery was made, through what means I never heard, by a gentleman with whom Mr. Stent had long been in the most intimate habits of friendship, and was communicated to Mr. S., then at a distance from home, with irresistible proof of the fact. Mr. S. in consequence wrote a letter to his Wife commanding her to quit the house before his return, and to see his face no more. She obeyed, and there his vindictive measures ended. He sought for no divorce, nor brought any action against the Adulterer, but quitted the residence where his disgrace was incurred, and removed with his younger son, a boy about eight years old, to a private abode near his business in the City, placing my dear

Nancy as I have already mentioned under the care of Mrs. Thomas, a married Lady who lived near Vauxhall, with whom and her husband he had long lived on terms of family intimacy and friendship. As to my friend Tom, he was about the same period by his own choice put into the Navy as a Midshipman under Capt. Lancelot, afterwards Admiral, Brown.

It was not long after my return to London that I went over to Walnut-tree Walk, the spot endeared to me by so many pleasing and tender recollections, but only to meet "the ghosts of my departed joys." The Home to which, and its garden, my young and fervid imagination had attached a thousand interesting ideas, and my dear Nancy's home which possessed perhaps a still more lively interest in my mind, the parlour in which I had spent with her so many happy evenings, were in the hands of strangers. I had the sensations of a poor bird who in early spring returns to his new formed nest built amidst the fragrant buds and blossoms but finds the bough cut down, and his mate no longer there. I learned, however, by enquiries on the spot, the new residence of my dear Nancy, and resolved to make an early attempt to see her, to assure her of my fidelity and my simpathy with her filial sorrows. That purpose was soon to the best of my power performed. I wrote a letter to her, which I doubt not was sufficiently delicate and tenderly expressive of the warm feelings of my heart, and sent it to her at the house of Mrs. Thomas. I received an early answer, and at the sight of her well known hand opened it with trembling eagerness, but only to receive a death blow to my hopes. Instead of the artless, open, endearing stile to which I had been used from a heart not less warm, confiding, and empassioned than my own, I found nothing but cool expostulations on the impropriety of my attempting to correspond with her and a peremptory prohibition ever again to renew that attempt. I read the letter again and again before I could be thoroughly persuaded that such language could really proceed from her pen and that she was in earnest, but at length saw too clearly that her heart was changed, and all my fond hopes for ever at an end. I felt it bitterly; but pride and resentment came to my aid and diverted the current of my grief. I thought it would be mean and degrading to pine for one who could so coolly renounce my affection; and resolving to subdue my weakness was able ee'r long to do so, or at least to persuade myself that the victory was gained.

The School vacation was drawing to a close, and it was time I should prepare for returning to Winchester. But in this, more to my dear Mother's concern than mine, we found financial difficulties of a mortifying kind; for such was my Father's poverty that he could not immediately raise the money wanted to pay the school bills that I had brought home with me, with the expences of my journey, and to provide me with a proper stock of cloaths, in which I was before deficient. It is probable that if my Uncle Milner had been apprised of this difficulty he would have removed it. I am persuaded at least that had my Father or Mother applied to him he would not have refused to supply the means of compleating the work he had kindly undertaken, and he most probably intended from the first to be at all the charge of my education, as my Mother certainly understood when he proposed my going to Winchester. But if so, he ought to have paid my school bills, without giving them to me, or telling me their amount, so as to put the impression on my mind that I was to bring money to pay them. He was very far from an ungenerous man, or unsusceptible of delicate feelings. But unfortunately he was dissatisfied with my poor Father's character and conduct, and suspected him at this period of spending in Taverns and other places of that kind, money which ought to have been reserved for the education of his children and the better support of his family in general. I will not undertake to say whether there was in this and other cases reasonable cause of blame in the conduct of that unfortunate Parent. If I were conscious of demerit in him, however great, it would be my duty to draw a veil over it. Let me not therefore in what relates to *him* in these family memoirs be understood to pledge myself for more than the truth of what I expressly assert in his favour. But the fact was that had he lived more with his family he would not in all probability have been able to provide even in the scanty way that he did for us. He was obliged to find his Clients and his business abroad, and at that period gentlemen, at least in the mercantile world, did more of their business at Coffee Houses and Taverns than is customary or would be thought creditable now. He had, as I have before remarked, great conversational powers and a strength of natural talent that had a very imposing influence in the social circle. He owed to this almost all his employment, and he could not afford to keep his large family in any stile that would have enabled him to cultivate useful connections in a private way. Mr. Milner nevertheless might have apparent grounds for thinking as he did; and it was perhaps therefore his design to put it to my Father in the first instance to supply my expences if he could, concluding that our bad family prospects would leave but too much room for his future assistance in another way. But unfortunately this line of conduct did not comport well with my Father's pride or mine, nor with my dear Mother's delicate and liberal feelings. Well, alas, do I remember her anxiety and distress on this occasion. Yet she did not condemn my extreme unwillingness to return to Winchester without the means of paying the bills in question. On the contrary I think she fully acquiesced in it. She always cherished in her children liberal and independent feelings. She solicited my Father, however, most earnestly to find some means of supplying the money wanted, and he kept us in daily expectation of his doing so; but he was so much disappointed at Mr. Milner's conduct as not much to relish incurring further with him the obligation of boarding me in his family. So it was, however, that the School had recommenced, and the money was still unfound, and after some time it was to my Mother's grief resolved that I shod. return to Winchester no more. The cause I dare say was not concealed by her, and I have some recollection of Mr. M. having then expressed a willingness to take the charge on himself, but not in such a way as induced even my Mother to think that the resolution ought to be recalled. I suspect after all that Mr. M. had by that time begun to regret having given me as a companion to his son. After the loss of his daughter, he had contracted a morbid and extreme anxiety about my cousin's health, and conceived that the only way of preserving him from fatal maladies was to keep him from night air and all exposure to the weather except in the most favorable circumstances. My cousin therefore was subjected to very strict and painful restraints, such as though a most dutiful son he could not always very patiently endure. But I of course was left to follow my inclinations in a different course, which to my Uncle's apprehension, as he more than once discovered to me, tended to excite discontent in George, and sometimes made it necessary to consent that he should follow my example. Once for instance when the boys were acting plays in the college I naturally chose to be an auditor, and George was so desirous of going with me that it was thought too harsh to restrain him tho' in a bad winter night. Unfortunately he fell in running home after the play, and cut his head so as to return covered with blood. My Uncle was agitated to the last degree, and shewed to me on that occasion plainly that if he lost his son, he would regard my company and example as the fatal cause of it.

From whatever known or unknown causes this unexpected frustration of my best early prospects arose, its influence on subsequent events of my life was very important, and not more important as I can now clearly see, than beneficent. In this, as in many other cases, the hand of a gracious Providence has defeated my own plans, or the plans of those who wished my welfare, sometimes contrary to all probability, and sometimes by the most critical and unlooked-for event, and to my great apparent prejudice at the time, and yet these counteractions have afterwards proved the sources of my preservation, my prosperity, and welfare. I therefore love to develope their secret springs, their effects, relations, and dependencies. In their number and coincidence they will be found extremely strange by those who are not used to contemplate the ways of Providence in human life, and very edifying by those who are, at least if I live to finish these too lengthy memoirs.

If I had returned to Winchester and gone through the upper classes there, means would probably have been found through my Uncle's assistance of finishing my education at Cambridge, where he afterwards placed his son; and I might possibly have turned out no contemptible scholar; but when I look back on my own moral character at that period, and consider the temptations to which I should have been exposed at the University, I find abundant reason to conclude that my immortal interests would not have been promoted by such a prosecution of the path on which I had entered. Nor is it likely that my temporal welfare would have been found in that path so copiously as by a beneficent guidance of Providence it has been in the very peculiar and unpromising one upon which I was cast. A thousand difficulties would have opposed my entering advantageously into either of the learned professions; and even had my Uncle been liberal enough to introduce me properly into that to which I was destined, my prospects in it, from the want of any useful connections and other causes, would have been uncommonly bad. It is far from probable that I should have been able to gain the means of subsistence during any term of years for which I could hope or consent to be sustained by the purse of a collateral relation who had not a great redundancy of income for his own and his Son's support. I should at best have long had to endure the discomforts of dependancy, for which my spirit was ill framed, and probably to struggle against the current of adversity for life, instead of being very early enabled not only to provide for myself and a family of my own, but to be a staff of support to my dear Mother's children, and attaining before the evening of life professional honors and affluence in my Native land.

A more important difference would have been that I should have lost in great measure, by returning to Winchester, the benefit of my dear Mother's impressive example and precepts during the long and deeply interesting period of those protracted sufferings which closed her exemplary life. I should have been learning Latin and Greek, while instead of them I was by God's gracious appointment, learning moral and religious lessons of inestimable value, and of which no human heart perhaps had ever greater need.

From the Xmas of 1773, to March 1775, when I was deprived of this excellent parent I lived constantly with her. I was placed at no other School after leaving Winchester, and believe that the plan of my receiving a liberal education was abandoned by my Father, and regarded by my Mother as hopeless; nor would I during the latter part of that period have consented to be removed from her, for any prospects that learning or fortune could have opened to me. I was allowed to recur to my former habits of pleasurable reading, ransacking daily the catalogue of a circulating library for new food to my imagination in the poetry, plays, and novels unread before, which at length were not easy to find. It perhaps may be worth remarking, for I do not recollect having noticed it before, that among the trash of this kind I preferred the old romances, and even beyond these tales of the Genii, Fairies, and other Stories of Beings influencing human events in a supernatural way. Nothing of that kind that I ever heard of escaped my cormorant appetite; and I derived from such works so high a pleasure of a peculiar and nameless species, that I have sometimes in the recollection of it been inclined to think we have an instinctive notion of the existence of such unseen agents and their importance to our human destiny, and that the pleasure proceeds from the lively tho' indistinct revification of ideas with which our spirits, or spirits from which our own have descended, were once most deeply impressed. It resembles perhaps in its nature and sources another mysterious pleasure which I have often felt very keenly, arising from the survey of natural scenery and other inanimate objects familiar to me in my childhood and boyish years. Ideas beyond the reach of distinct recollection so far revive in the mind that without being able to catch their fleeting forms or trace their associations, we taste again part of the interest and pleasure they once imparted. They recall, tho' faintly and confusedly, the sensations of a distant stage of my existence, in which I was happier, or at least more exquisitely alive to every feeling than I am, or have since been.

My Mother as before often chided me in her own gentle way, for wasting my time in such unprofitable [reading] and to gratify her I often mixed with it history, travels, and other subjects not of a fictitious kind, but these were tasks of duty, while the others were my hourly amusement and delight. Sometimes, however, she engaged me in reading religious and devotional works, especially Young's *Night Thoughts* and others to which I think I have before adverted, such as Sherlock,[1] and Drelincourt[2] on Death, Secker,[3] and other Divines, the favorites of the pious in that day. When her arduous domestic duties permitted her to sit with and hear me read, such books were usually her choice, tho' often while working with her needle in the evening she partook of those works of entertainment of the better sort of which I was so fond.

I have spoken of her arduous domestic duties. It may be judged how laborious they were when I state that with six children at home, four of them under eight years old and the youngest a child in arms, she kept but two maid servants, including a nursery maid, and yet did all the business of the Laundry, as well as that of the Seampstress, at home. Never was woman more actively patient and humbly industrious and through her own personal exertions chiefly, all the disgusting features of poverty were avoided upon such narrow means as could often barely afford the mere necessaries of life. Her children could not have been kept cleaner or neater in their dress and person, nor delicacy in her own personal appearance and at her table &c. have been better preserved, if she had possessed an easy income. Our fare was frugal enough, and did not on the whole perhaps exceed that of cottagers, but she never neglected nor suffered her children to neglect, those habits of cleanliness and delicacy, which mark the gentlewoman and her family far more than all other distinctions of an exterior kind.

Had this dear woman been cast in a vulgar bodily and intellectual mould, these virtues might have been less extraordinary. They would have cost at least less effort and

[1] This may have been either William Sherlock (c. 1641–1707), in his last years Dean of St. Paul's, whose *Practical Discourse Concerning Death* (1690) was widely popular; or it may have been his son, Thomas Sherlock (1678–1761), successively Bishop of Bangor, of Salisbury, and of London. The latter's *Tryal of the Witnesses of the Resurrection of Jesus* (1729), a treatise on Prophecy written against the deists, ran to fourteen editions; and his *Pastoral Letter* (1750) on "the late earthquakes" was widely read.

[2] Charles Drelincourt (1595–1669) French Protestant divine, from 1620 minister of the Reformed Church at Charenton. His *Consolationes de l'ame fidèle contre les frayeurs de la mort* (1651) was translated into English and frequently re-printed as *The Christian's Defense Against the Fears of Death*. Defoe's *A True Relation of the Apparition of one Mrs. Veal* first appeared as an appendix to the fourth edition of Drelincourt (1706).

[3] See above, p. 57 *n*.

self denial. But her person was delicate even before her
wasting malady began to reduce it; and her taste and
manners were refined. I know not whether I have noticed
before that she had a voice of the first order for power and
sweetness and sang with great taste and execution. She had
an elegant little person, a fair delicate complexion, and
lovely expressive features. A lock of her fine pale brown hair
preserved in a locket which I wear next my heart is the
only visible memorial of her personal attractions that we
retain, for unfortunately her portrait never was painted.
But the charms of her conversation were still greater than
those of her exterior. It was an unfailing spring of amusement to my Brother and me whenever she had leisure to
converse with us and was equally gratifying to the Friends
who at different periods of her life enjoyed her Society and
confidence. She aimed not at brilliancy of wit, or display of
knowledge or judgment, but was always animated and
lively, and never at a loss for a variety of topics of the lighter
kind, chosen with propriety to keep up the intercourse of
thought in the social circle. She had in common with all her
family a naturally colloquial eloquence but was always
unobtrusive, and more willing to listen than to speak when
with those who had information to impart. Above all, her
language was always inoffensive and kind, and so strictly
governed by the law of charity that I believe her tongue
never made a foe or disobliged a friend. To my Brother
William and me she was not only the most affectionate of
Mothers but the most amiable and endearing of companions.
There being the wide interval of seven years between me and
the eldest of my Sisters, her other children were too young to
join in our family conversations; but to her dear boys, as she
called us, she loved to pour out her heart as to her best and
most confidential friends, relating to us the events of her
varied and anxious life, informing us of the history of our
family in both branches, with a variety of interesting family
anecdotes, and of the situations and characters of our
relations and friends. Her opinions of them were given to us
without any reserve, except such as charity suggested, and I
do not recollect a single instance in which I ever found occasion in after life to deem her judgments of character

erroneous or to alter the impressions I had thus early received from them.

Her favorite topics however were of a higher kind—high as the immortal destinies of Christians. She loved to talk of God, of the joys of Heaven, of the probable employments and delights of blessed disembodied spirits, and the infinite importance of the things which are unseen and eternal. The temporal providence of God was also with her a subject of frequent conversation, as it always was of her careful observation, comfort, and support. She had seen as I have done, and as all who observe will do, very numerous and decisive proofs in the events of private life that the course of this world is neither left to necessity nor chance, but is under the particular, as well as general, government of infinite wisdom and goodness.

It pleased God that this excellent woman should have far more than ordinary opportunities of illustrating her faith in the way of patience and resignation. Her trials became daily more severe, and her human prospects darker and darker.

I will not enter into further details of her sufferings from external causes. I will only say that independently of poverty and of the precariousness as well as scantiness of her means of providing even common necessaries for her family, and of the many painful mortifications to which her feeling and delicate mind was subjected by the expedients to which for avoiding present want she was frequently driven, such as the obtaining small pecuniary supplies from a few kind friends who still adhered to her, and of the hardships and fatigues which the duties of a severe domestic œconomy imposed on her now sickly and feeble frame, she had other trials from without, which she found it still harder to sustain. But a cruel cough now progressively increased in its frequency and violence, with an expectoration that too plainly marked its fatal character; a hectic fever also preyed upon her, she wasted gradually into an emaciated state, and it became too certain to herself and others that the termination, however long protracted, must be fatal. She always, however, maintained her accustomed chearfulness. Her melancholly at least was a sunshower, or a passing cloud. The parental anxieties which alone gave to Death in her view a dreary aspect were soon allayed by her pious confidence and her trust in the effect of prayer. Her tenderness also to my feelings, and my Brother's, led her to repress, for the sake of better concealing from us, anticipations which she saw we could not bear to hear of. Yet she judiciously and kindly prepared us in some degree for the affliction she knew to be impending over us by occasionally suggesting what she felt as to the nature and progress of her disease. Meantime she used all such means as were well recommended as likely to promote her recovery. She had the advice of Dr. Arbuthnot,[1] then an eminent Physician, and one of the friends of her better days, who kindly insisted on giving it gratuitously, but the case was beyond the reach of medical art. It was probably in pursuance of such advice as well as for other reasons that my Father changed our family residence from the City to Stoke Newington, to which place we removed, I think early in the Spring of 1774. I know not how he found means to obtain so good a house as he found there; but it was a very pleasant and a genteel residence situated in a garden, on the North side of Church Street, and may still be known by the description of the first respectable looking house on the right as you pass down that main Street from the North Road having an iron open work gate or wicker through which you see it at about a pistol shot from the Street. The end of the House only there meets the eye, with a Green house projecting beyond the front, which faces East towards the Garden. You see only a single window, I think, on the ground floor, and one on the upper story, belonging to the chamber from which my dear Mother's spirit took its flight to Heaven.

I can remember feeling a keen tho' but short lived pleasure from this change of abode. I always dearly loved the country, and the transition from the thickest smoke of London to a pleasant garden in the Spring of the year was naturally very exhilarating. But my dear Mother's cruel disease was too far advanced to receive much mitigation from this change; and I had soon to submit to a seperation

---

[1] Not to be confused with Pope's friend, Dr. John Arbuthnot, who died in 1735. I have not been able to identify this Dr. Arbuthnot.

from her which in such circumstances was peculiarly painful while it suspended all my social comforts. I was resolved that she should accept an invitation from her Brother Milner to try what effect her native air in the West of England would have, coupled with his kind attentions. To assist her spirits a little my Brother William went with her and I was left with my Father and the younger children, or rather with them, for he was very little at home. I remember well during this period my dear Mother's tender and frequent letters to me, full of anxiety about the children, and with too little notice of herself.

She returned within a Month or two no wise improved in health, but overjoyed to be again surrounded with her beloved children, tho' convinced that she was soon to bid us a final adieu, final on this side of the grave. Indeed it was then, or soon after became, plain that she was sinking irrecoverably. E'er long she was too much debilitated even to take the air in the garden, was next confined to her bedroom, and last, for a long, very long period, to her bed. She nevertheless survived the winter of 1774–5. Never perhaps did consumption produce sharper and more protracted sufferings. Never did nature maintain a more obstinate struggle with disease. Her constitution was naturally excellent, and the disorder, as I have already intimated, was not native, but superinduced by extraordinary causes. Hence, as I suppose, the severity of her ultimate sufferings. Very long before her death it was difficult to turn her in bed because the bones had literally come through the skin, and she was found at last mortified in several parts. The state of the lungs also was such that nothing but the strength of my filial affection could have enabled me to endure being long at her bedside; yet to her latest breath she was shaken by a convulsive cough, the paroxysms of which tore her feeble frame in an agonizing manner, and gave her numberless times the expectation of immediate death. To these bodily sufferings were added all that the tenderest of Mothers could feel from the bad prospects of her children. It is a subject on which I must avoid many details; but generally speaking nothing in a human view could be more alarming or more hopeless. My Brother and I just rising into manhood, without having even entered the avenues of any profession, and without education qualifying us to do so, or in any other way to provide for our own subsistence. Three girls, the eldest only nine years old, and a boy under three; and all depending on the precarious, scanty means of support of my Father's irregular business, which was plainly declining, and likely very soon entirely to fail. Total ruin and return to a Prison were much more probable than that he should long be able even to keep us from a Parish workhouse. His health, too, and his powers of mind were evidently declining.

My dear Mother had sensibility as acute to all these subjects of anxiety as ever woman was endued with. A hundred times did she talk of and weep over them. But never did she weep long. Never I believe did she for any considerable time, not perhaps even for an evening or an hour, indulge any despondent feelings. Prayer to God and trust in his benignant Providence were her speedy and sure resource, and her confidence in Him became stronger and stronger as she drew nearer to her end. Sustained by this, her triumph over all her complicated trials was glorious and compleat. Patience had with her its perfect work. She was not only serene but chearful, and gave utterance to a hope full of immortality, and full also of unshaken assurance that God would provide for and bless her helpless children. I wish I could remember the very terms she used on this latter subject. When compared with the event, yet to be traced in these sheets, they would appear like revelation. Her trust in God was doubtless acceptable in his sight, and graciously and wonderfully has he shewn that it was not unfounded. To these pious feelings she added unaffected and lively gratitude for every alleviation of her sufferings and every remaining comfort. Well do I remember one affecting instance of it. A few weeks before her death we had a fine mild day, with brilliant sunshine, and feeling herself about noon a little more at ease than usual, she said smilingly to my Brother and me: "My dear boys, do you think you could carry me into the garden? I should like once more to breathe the free air and feel the sunbeams." We accordingly placed her upon pillows, and crossing our hands under them while she put her dear wasted arms round our necks, we carried her down stairs and into the garden. She could not above a minute or two sustain the posture, and desired us to take her back to that bed from which she rose no more, but previously lifted up her expressive blue eyes to Heaven, with an angelic smile of grateful joy, and blessed God that she had lived to be carried in the arms of her dear boys.

To the latest period of her illness, and as I best remember, till within a few days of her dissolution if not to the last day but one, she used occasionally to desire us to read to her the religious books she was fond of, especially her constant favorite, Young's *Night Thoughts* as she was now become too weak to read for herself. I can well recollect sitting by her bedside at this employment when from the overpowering effluvia that at last attended her expectoration I found it very difficult to continue in the room. She was happily inconscious of this; or such was ever her tenderness and delicacy that it would have been difficult to prevail on her to suffer us to perform these filial duties.

I know not whether I have mentioned it before, but my dear Mother often told us that this lingering and suffering passage to the grave was one that she had been used in her earlier life to pray for, in order that she might be better prepared for death. Few persons, I believe, had ever less need of such an opportunity of preparation; but she improved it to the last, and her faculties were continued unimpaired to her last sigh, as if to exhibit to all around her the invincible strength of her faith and patience, her chearful resignation, and her hope full of immortality. During the last few weeks of her life her sufferings were dreadful. Fits of coughing many times a day shook her pained and nearly exhausted frame in a cruel manner, and ended in an apparent struggle of which immediate death was the likely issue. Yet such is the delusive effect of that slowly progressive malady that we were at last surprised by its natural termination, as an event which we still thought at some distance. I should not otherwise have been absent when it happened.

It was on the 21st. of March 1775, a day ever memorable to me, that I heard the last kind words of this tender and beloved Parent on my going in the morning to her bedside to learn how she had passed the night. She seemed much in the same state that she had been in for weeks before; and I walked to town after breakfast to get some books that I wanted at Bell's circulating library in the Strand.[1] I was returning with them and had made no stop in Town, but had been desired to call in expectation of some errand from my Father at the Flowerpot in Bishopsgate Street where the Stoke Newington Stages stop and where he usually called in his way. On my asking for him at the Bar, the Landlady looked hard in my face, and said, "When Sir did you come from home?" and on my reply as to the time, "Then Sir I suppose you have not heard of your Mother's death," was her inconsiderate, tho' well meant remark. A burst of thunder and a thunderbolt falling at my feet would not have agitated me more. I sprang from the house into the Street, and they ran in vain to detain me. I rushed down the mid street to avoid the obstruction of the crowded foot path, and fast as my breath would allow made my way to Shoreditch and from thence to Stoke Newington, as if my speed could yet intercept and detain my dear Mother's spirit. When I came to the Garden Gate, it confirmed the mournful news. It was fast, and the shutter, as at night, closed its open iron work, to hide the House of mourning from the gaze of passers-by. I did not stop to ring, but got over the gate, rushed down to the House, and in a minute was in the room that contained the lifeless frame of my beloved Mother. No words can do justice to the emotions that I then felt. My dear Brother's tears and those of the elder girls burst out afresh on my arrival; but my heart was not yet prepared for such relief. My anguish was of a deeper and sterner kind and led me to some excesses which I still remember with penitence and grief. Soon however the recollection of my dear Mother's example and precepts, and the fear of offending that God who alone could restore her to me, brought down my rebellious spirit, and softened my sorrow into its proper character, tho' not into a moderated degree. Copious floods

---

[1] Stephen, it will be seen, managed to become remarkably well read because of the existence, in the second half of the eighteenth century, of the commercial circulating library. His father was certainly not able to buy many books in these years.

of tears succeeded, and exhausted spirits at length gave me for a while the repose, if not the peace, of resignation.

I learned from my Brother and the Servant who attended my dear Mother in her room that the last struggle took place soon after I left home. It was a severe one, and at or about the close of it, as she regained the power of utterance, she said raising her eyes upwards, "O my God; send some Angel to deliver me!" The prayer was instantly accorded to. She looked earnestly in the face of my Brother who held her hand, said with a fainting emphasis, "My dear Boy!" and immediately expired.

It seemed to me an aggravation of the blow that I was absent at the sad event. I remember asking the servant anxiously "Are you sure that she said 'my dear boy!' Was it not *boys*?" I wished to suppose that I, as well as my Brother, occupied her last tender thought. The servant to soothe me said she was not sure which it was she said. Of course as my Brother was in her eye at the moment, the words were addressed to him.

I will not dwell on the sad days that followed till we laid her in the earth. It was a period of peculiar sensations such as I know not how to describe, tho' I have three times since in my eventful life experienced the same, or nearly the same, feelings. It was not dejection, but rather a gloomy exaltation of spirits. Poor Romilly.[1] Often have I thought that had I been unfortunate enough to disbelieve or doubt of a future retributory state, I should on this, or other occasions, have taken his course to relieve myself from the exquisite misery I felt. Nor am I sure that I should not have had the same excuse that I hope he had, that of a disordered understanding. It is extremely difficult to determine in such cases where reason drops the reins wilfully, or where she is jostled from her seat, but in one of the more recent instances alluded to my mind was for near a week in a state of sleepless agitation on which I still look back with a doubt whether it did not amount to insanity.

Religious impressions however may have a salutary in-

---

[1] Sir Samuel Romilly (1757–1818), law reformer; M.P. 1806–1818; solicitor-general to cabinet of "all the talents" in 1806; effected great reforms in code of criminal punishment; committed suicide on the death of his wife.

fluence even in actual madness, and I have ever had too much fear of God and too firm an expectation of the life to come to incur the guilt of suicide.

It is some time since I have said anything of my own moral and religious character, to trace the progress of, and change in, which is by far the most important object of these memoirs. The period at which my narrative has now arrived was in this respect a very critical one. It is proper therefore here to pause a while in my story and give some account of what I will take leave to call "my spiritual state" up to the death of my Mother, that the effects of that event upon it may be the better understood.

I believe I have already mentioned my earliest recollections of conscience or the moral sense, the self reproaches and uneasiness which I felt in my childhood for having joined some companions in an act of cruelty to reptiles. Whether my apprehension of God as the witness and judge of my actions was equally early, I do not certainly remember, but think it was. Neither can I recollect how that apprehension was first acquired. I should almost suppose it was innate, if my dear Mother's piety did not make it highly improbable that she had omitted, even in my earliest infancy, to instruct me in such religious truths as my mind was capable of receiving. The same is the case as to my habits of private prayer. I cannot remember their having been injoined or taught, nor when they began; but am pretty confident that by the age of ten and perhaps much earlier, I was conscious of the continual presence and government of God, and prayed to him occasionally, if not at stated periods, when alone. I believe also that from a time as early, our infinitely gracious and condescending Father which is in Heaven kindly encouraged and confirmed me in a practice on which all my human and superhuman happiness was dependent, by shewing me in the events of things interesting to my childish hopes and anxieties, when made the subjects of prayer, that my petitions were not fruitless. Why should this be doubted? The cases indeed were trivial; but so are the concerns of Kingdoms and Empires, when compared with the infinite eternal purposes of Him who governs the whole Universe. In his benignant eye, however, the fate of every immortal soul is precious, and to encourage an Infant's prayer may be to form a future Angel. Our blessed Saviour seems to have intimated a like reason for his condescension when he said, "Suffer little children to come unto me and forbid them not; for of such are the Kingdom of Heaven."

Would to God that habits of prayer at that or even at more advanced periods of my life when they became more regular and copious, had saved me from offences against the pure and holy Being to whom I prayed! This, alas, was far from the case; and no wonder, for sin was not the evil against which I earnestly prayed to be preserved, nor holiness the blessing I fervently desired to obtain. My prayers in general, and my most sincere ones, had far lower objects. Yet God graciously encouraged the habit by giving it success in things not wrong or hurtful just as an earthly Parent gives the toy that is asked for to win the child's affection and confidence with a view to their future good effects in things of greater moment to its true and lasting welfare.

But tho' prayer did not save me from sin, nor from sins of a heinous kind when the temptations to them assailed me, it kept me from being at ease under a sense of them. I could neither suspend such intercourse with God without remorse and alarm, nor resume it without contrition. My penitence indeed did not prevent my offending again in the same way innumerable times. It was not, therefore, true repentance; but prayer still brought me back with real sorrow and sincere resolutions of amendment. It prevented my heart becoming hardened and alienated from God, which but for such temporary reconciliations would most probably have been the ultimate event.

I speak here chiefly in reference to the latter part of the period now under review, and when my sinful passions had attained to their full growth and strength, as I think they had done before my dear Mother's death.

It will not be expected, nor would it be right, that I should be more particular and distinct upon such subjects. It is enough to say that I was a very great offender in the sight of God, sinning against his known laws, against the clear dictates of my own conscience, and contrary to solemn resolutions and vows, many times renewed at seasons of penitence and devotion. God's forbearance and mercy towards me were wonderfully great. But my case required strong and bitter medicine, which he was graciously pleased to provide for me, in the feelings excited by the loss of my beloved Mother, and by that of my own health which followed.

Whether doubts had been early impressed on my mind as to the extremity and eternity of the punishment to which sin exposes us in the life to come I cannot recollect. I believe the case only was that those from whom I derived my religious views were not fond of that topic and instead of alarming by the terrors of God's law appealed chiefly to what they regarded as more liberal and ingenuous feelings. So it was, however, that my fears of the righteous indignation of God respected rather his temporal vengeance against sin in the ordinary and extraordinary appointments of his providence in this life, than "the worm that dieth not & the fire which is not quenched."[1] What may seem, too, a little singular in such a character, I was chiefly uneasy under a sense of God's displeasure because with a busy imagination prone to torment itself with the prospect of approaching evils, often created or greatly magnified by its own delusive power, I could no otherwise tranquillize my mind but through a reliance on the protection of Divine Providence; and this I could not feel while under the sense of unrepented sin.

During the latter stages of my Mother's disease, the dread of losing her and the apprehension of her daily aggravated sufferings were main subjects of such anxieties and tended a good deal, I believe, to lessen the fervency to my penitential prayers. But when the long dreaded blow at length fell upon my heart, my fear of God's displeasure was not lessened. On the contrary it was much increased, but with other and better views. I now formed to myself the apprehension of a consequence to which sin would subject me in the life to come more fearful by far than any ideas of punishment after death that had ever before appalled me. *It would seperate me from my beloved Mother for ever.* That her pure and gentle

---

[1] Stephen is adapting a pair of metaphors which appears in *Isaiah* 66: 24 and is echoed in *St. Mark* 10: 44, 46, 48. In the latter place it is a refrain: "Where their worm dieth not, and the fire is not quenched."

and holy Spirit had ascended to the realms of bliss, I could not doubt. My only hope, therefore, of reuniting with her would be cut off if I continued to offend God by my sins, or did not conciliate his favor in this life by true penitence and effectual reformation. These alarming views were at the same critical conjuncture rendered more impressive and awful by the decline of my health and the apprehension of being an early victim to the same disease that had proved fatal to my Mother. About two months before her death I met with a very serious accident. A tree having been cut down in the garden I took up the axe it had been felled with, and planting my left foot on the trunk levelled the axe with all my force to cut off a small branch that was left on it. From my unskilfulness the edge glanced from the knot I aimed at, and came with such force against my leg below the calf as to pass nearly half through the bone. I was less alarmed by the wound and the effusion of blood that followed than by the fear of fatally shocking my dear, tender Parent. I therefore injoined silence to the servants and binding up the wound with a handkerchief walked or rather hop'd away to a neighbouring Surgeon. He was not at home, and his apprentice was not skillful enough to know that a wound which had so compleatly divided the fibres as to make them recede above and below in that part of the frame was not likely to heal by the first intention, and would demand much confinement and care. He therefore, after dressing it, fell in with my earnest desire of concealing from my Mother that any thing serious had happened, and instead of desiring his Master to call and see me, left me to my own management. The consequence was that in a few days the wound got into a dangerous state, and when at length intolerable pain obliged me to send for the Surgeon, he was frightened at its appearance, and with difficulty saved me from a mortification. For several weeks I was confined to a chair, and had not well recovered from the debilitating effects, when my health and spirits were still more harshly assailed by grief for the loss of my beloved Parent. The seperation from my Brother and two Sisters which I shall have presently to notice soon increased my depression. But it was supposed, and I think rightly, that a more direct cause of the disease that followed was infection; for pulmonary consumption is, I believe, infectious in its latest stages, and I had been much at my Mother's bedside when the effluvia from her decayed lungs and expectoration could hardly be sustained. So it was, that she had hardly been laid in her grave when I became so ill that every Friend supposed I was destined soon to follow her. An obstinate cough, spitting of blood, night sweats, and every other ordinary consumptive symptom, came upon me; and my flesh wasted so fast that in two or three months I was reduced almost to a skeleton. I had seen enough of the disease to be fully conscious of my danger, and my alarm was much aggravated by certain reasons that I had for apprehending that it was in great measure the natural effect, as well as the just punishment, of my sins. It pleased God by these concurrent means to lead me to repentance more sincere and reformation more lasting than I had ever before attained. My prayers became more fervent than ever, and tho' the principal object of them was less the averting the eternal than the temporal judgments of God, he was graciously pleased to accept them, and at length to restore my mind to peace through a strong assurance of his pardon and reconciled favour.

To return to the sad period beyond which I have carried on this account of my spiritual state, one of the melancholy duties that fell on my elder Brother and me was the filling up of my dear Mother's coffin pursuant to her request, with letters from the friends she most loved which she had preserved, and burning what it would not contain. My Father chose that all her six children with himself should attend her funeral. It was a humble one. We walked after the coffin to Stoke Newington Church Yard; and there it was deposited by the margin of the path which leads from the Street to the more Easterly door on the South side of the Church, opening near the Chancel.[1] Well did I mark the spot: and my memory

---

[1] Stephen's directions are clear enough that I had no difficulty in finding the tomb in January, 1950. Stoke Newington was badly hit in the air raids of the second World War. The interior of the new (nineteenth-century) church was burned out; but the old church escaped serious damage, so that in 1950 services were again being held in the church that Stephen knew as a boy. Many of the monuments and markers in the churchyard had been shattered into debris, but Stephen's tomb, a tremendous rectangular stone box, was untouched. By the

was a more lasting designation of it than the turf with which
alone her dear remains were covered. Often indeed did I
afterwards go to weep over it. I was therefore at no loss one
and twenty years afterwards, when I deposited the remains
of my first dear wife in the same hallowed spot, to identify
it with precision. And here let me stop to adore that bounteous Providence by which one of the six hapless orphans
who had no other inheritance than the prayers of that saint-
like Parent, has been enabled to secure to her humble grave
an honour of which the proudest Mausoleum might be
envious. That exalted character, my beloved Second Wife,
the Sister of Wilberforce, will rise at the resurrection from
the same spot, because the remains of that kindred Saint,
my dear Mother lay there; and what is more, Wilberforce
himself, the most distinguished Friend of God and Man that
modern ages has produced, has given me his faithful promise,
confirmed by her who is nearest to him on Earth, that the
same grave shall be his own. I have built a Vault and Tomb
there, but without an inscription, and mean it to remain a
blank till this consummation of its honors can be recorded
on it. Perishable will be that memorial; but not so the name
of Wilberforce. Distant posterity will ask where his dust was

kindness of the rector I was allowed to scrape away enough of the moss that I
might copy the inscription from the flat top. It reads:

HERE LIES

JAMES STEPHEN

BORN JUNE 30, 1758.   DIED OCT^R 10, 1832

IN HIS 75TH YEAR

IN CONNECTION WITH HIS BROTHER IN LAW

WILLIAM WILBERFORCE

HE TOOK A LEADING PART IN THE

PROCEEDINGS WHICH LED TO THE

ABOLITION OF THE SLAVE TRADE

AND OF COLONIAL SLAVERY

HIS MOTHER, HIS FIRST WIFE,

HIS SECOND WIFE AND TWO OF HIS

CHILDREN ARE BURIED WITH HIM IN

A VAULT UNDER THIS STONE

HERE LIE ALSO THE REMAINS OF

JAMES STEPHEN

THE FATHER OF THE ABOVE NAMED

JAMES STEPHEN

WHO WAS BORN IN ABERDEENSHIRE

AND DIED AT STOKE NEWINGTON

IN SEPTEMBER 1779 AGED 46 YEARS

laid; and may the answer be: "in Stoke Newington Church Yard, in the Tomb which one of his fondest and best loved friends built over the best of Mothers, of Wives, of Sisters, and of Women."[1]

Deep were the groans, and copious were the tears, with which alone on that memorable day the 25th of March 1775, my dear Mother's memory was honored. To me, it was like my own living heart's inhumation. But I held my poor little fellow orphans by the hand. I remembered the charge she gave me of them; and said, "With God's help I will live for *them*."

[1] Wilberforce's promise that his ashes would mingle in the tomb with those of his brother-in-law was no doubt given in good faith, but it could not be kept. Stephen died October 10, 1832; Wilberforce, nine months later, July 29, 1833. The Wilberforce family decided that the superior claim of the nation for a tomb in Westminster Abbey superseded the promise to Stephen. The prominence given to Stephen's association with Wilberforce in the inscription on Stephen's tomb (see the preceding note) indicates his children's desire to honor his wishes as far as possible.

Chapter Four

[1775]

ONE of the most striking, and also the most useful, observations, that all who have contemplated the ways of Divine Providence in human affairs are agreed in, is that events seemingly the most adverse to our welfare and to the objects of our prayers, are often made to produce to us the most happy consequences.

> *Behind a frowning providence,*
> *He hides a smiling face.*[1]

To human eyes the death of my dear Mother was an event pregnant with calamities to all her children. It was an extinction, rather, of every rational hope that could be formed of their temporal or spiritual welfare. But God made it a source to us of all the advantages and blessings we have since enjoyed; and I hope of far better things than these. I shall have occasion hereafter perhaps to record an observation of the Revd. Mr. Ramsay,[2] my precursor in the cause of the oppressed West India Slaves; but as I may forget it in its proper place, I will quote it now: "Every happy occurrence of my life" said he, "has had its origin in some deep affliction." My Brother William at this period was above 18, and I very near 17 years old. We had long been living at home in idleness. We had no means of gaining our bread either in possession or prospect. Tho' taught to look forward to liberal professions, we had received no education to qualify us for them, not even that preparative commonly deemed indispensably necessary, a moderate acquaintance

---

[1] William Cowper, "Light Shining Out of Darkness." Stephen's memory amends Cowper's "shining" to "smiling."

[2] James Ramsay (1733–1789), divine and philanthropist; educated for medicine and was surgeon in Navy, but later took holy orders; settled in West Indies, where he interested himself in the condition of the slaves; returned to England in 1781 and worked to arouse sentiment for abolition of slavery; worked almost alone until joined by Wilberforce and others; author of numerous anti-slavery writings.

with the learned languages. We could both read and write
our Mother tongue, and that was all. For my part, my
handwriting even had been neglected so much that I could
not hope for employment even as a copying clerk. Our
Father whose long supineness under these alarming circumstances our Mother's anxious and frequent solicitations
had failed to correct, was not likely to change his conduct
now when there was no longer any Monitor who could
venture to tell him that his parental duties were neglected.
In fact, poor Man, little or nothing was in his power to do for
us. He had neither money, nor interest, nor any remaining
Friends, and found it hard with his scanty and precarious
means to provide for the daily wants of his family. The
annuity of £40 a year, part of the reparation granted by Sir
John Webb, died with my Mother; and what was more
important, the occasional aid which friendship and respect
for her procured for him through her means, without
offence to his pride (because without his interposition or
previous knowledge), ceased to be a relief to him on those
distressing emergencies to which his narrow and un-
certain income often exposed him. What then had his
children to expect, but want and idleness, and disgrace, and
vice, and ruin? To my Sisters, the prospect was no better
and was rendered still more deplorable by their sex. They
were about the ages of 10 and 8 and 6, and my brother John,
I think, was under 4. To be left to the care of common
servants, except during the very few hours per week that their
Father could be at home to see anything of them, seemed
now their hapless destiny until his death or final ruin should
transfer them perhaps to a Parish Workhouse. Such were
the prospects which the tenderest of Mothers, with great
sensibility of feeling, and a most delicate and liberal mind,
could behold without dismay on her deathbed, because she
trusted in the gracious Providence of God. She relied upon
her prayers for her poor orphans. And what has been the
result? During 46 years that have since elapsed not one of
those six orphans has felt any of those evils to which they
were so imminently exposed. They were all wonderfully
rescued from want, and most of them raised to very early
independence and affluence. Instead of descending in the

social scale, they have advanced in it. Instead of infamy or contempt their portion has been found not in the kitchen or the workhouse, not among the low or the worthless, but among the elevated, the learned, the liberal and the excellent of the Earth. They have been uncommonly favoured in their temporal lot. Health and ease and peace and comfort and kind friends, and estimable connections and relations, have with few exceptions, been theirs in a more than usual portion. To crown all, the means of grace have been bestowed in preeminent abundance upon them, destined tho' they apparently were to a hapless destitution of religious culture and example, and to scenes of dangerous temptation. How far the rich bounty of Providence in this grand respect has been improved by them is an awful question for themselves. He who writes can only answer it by striking on his breast, and saying, "God be merciful to me a Sinner." But as far as we can judge of each other, the moral and religious characters of all my three dear Sisters, who I bless God still survive, illustrate more impressively than all the rest the gracious care of Providence and the efficacy of their Mother's prayers. It was for *them* no doubt, it was for their spiritual and immortal interests, that she felt, as she reasonably might, till prayer and faith relieved her, the most painful apprehensions and concern. Yet I can look back and trace clearly to the death of that excellent Mother the source of all that is right in their characters, and happy in their temporal lots.

Before I proceed to shew how it pleased Providence to order for them after that mournful event, the chronological order of these memoirs leads me to speak of a new affliction I was soon after subjected to, seperation from my dear elder Brother.

I have noticed the unhappy family feud that had long subsisted between my Father and his Brother, Doctor William Stephen, who resided in the Island of Saint Christopher, and was understood to have acquired during his long practice there a considerable fortune. I believe I have also mentioned that tho' irreconcilably at variance with my Father, he, like all the rest of the family, always retained great regard and respect for my Mother; but all correspondence had naturally ceased between them. During the last few months of her life she had more than once suggested to my Brother, who was his Godson, that if he could go out to his Uncle she thought it probable he would receive him kindly and put him in some way of providing for himself. She knew nothing of the sad state of morals and manners in that part of the world; for if she had been well informed on that subject her virtuous and pious feelings would have shrunk from such a recourse tho' want had been the known and sure alternative. It was not probable that our Father's consent to the measure would be given, and she would not have counsel'd the taking it if prohibited by him; but she probably foresaw that what his pride and resentment would have revolted at if considered as a measure of his own, might not be forbidden by him, not in his heart disapproved, if resolved upon in the first instance by my Brother without previously consulting him. It was too plain that he would not, and indeed could not put us in any way of getting our bread in England, and therefore she rather encouraged both my brother and me in the wish we both felt to seek our fortune abroad. We all in our conversations on the subject suppressed the painful condition which all our hearts tacitly prescribed, viz, that our plans of migration should be suspended till after that event the near approach of which was manifest; but both my Brother and I were secretly determined that whenever our dear Mother should be taken from us, we would embrace that only remaining hope of ever raising ourselves to independency, or maintaining that station in life to which we thought ourselves intitled. My own favorite scheme was to go to America,[1] and inlist myself as a soldier of fortune in that cause which I admired as the cause of liberty, and which it was now pretty clear must be finally decided by the sword. I shall find a more proper place hereafter for the origin, progress, and changes of my political notions and principles. At this time they

---

[1] The date here is late spring or early summer, 1775. Stephen did not finally give up the thought of going out to serve as a volunteer in Washington's army until late in 1779. See below, pp. 259-263. It is an interesting commentary on the times and on the circles young Stephen moved in that he, a respectable though penniless young man, should have had no qualms of conscience about taking up arms against an English army and fighting on the side of the rebellious colonists, even after three years of open hostilities.

were mere prejudices, naturally and unavoidably imbibed from the concurrent opinions of all with whom I had any conversation or connection. Immediately or soon after our Mother's funeral my Brother announced to our Father his plan of going to St. Christopher, and as I best remember it was not opposed in any such way that the prosecution of it was an act of filial disobedience. The means of executing it, however, were not and probably could not be furnished by him. Mr. Clinton, I think, supplied all that was absolutely necessary in the way of outfit; and Capt. Oliver, who commanded one of the regular Ships of the Island and was a friend of our Uncle, was prevailed on to take my Brother as a Passenger, trusting to the former for payment. The Ship sailed, I think, early in May 1775.

The seperation between my dear Bill and me was exquisitely painful on both sides. We had, with short and few intervals, been constant companions from my birth to that melancholly hour. Our mutual misfortunes had been causes of additional endearment to each other. Our reciprocal confidence was without reserve; and neither of us had any other friend on earth to share it, our Sisters being too young for that purpose. When I add, what all who knew my dear Brother at any period of his life would attest, that his disposition and temper were uncommonly benignant and amiable, it may be imagined that my heart, still smarting from a deep and recent wound, was agonized by his departure. I was chiefly sustained by the hope that I might e'er long be enabled to follow him to the same part of the world. He suggested that if his Uncle should receive him kindly he might be able to explore some settlement in St. Kitts or a neighbouring Island for me, through the help of the same friend, and beg'd me not to think of going to America or elsewhere till I heard from him. The advice was not hard to enforce. In fact I had no present means of migration, nor could I well reconcile myself to the thought of leaving our elder Sisters in their then situation under the care of common servants, especially as a plan for their benefit had just been started to the adoption of which I might hope to contribute.

My Father's elder Sister, Mary, had married Mr. Nuccoll,

an officer in the Sea Service of the East India Company, who from the decline of his health was obliged to quit that Service just as he was attaining the summit of his ambition, the command of one of their regular Ships, a situation in which at that period a large fortune was usually made. He had in consequence settled in his native country, at Alloa in Clarkmannonshire N.B.; where he carried on some business as a Ship Owner and Merchant in the Baltic trade.

My Aunt was a woman of very singular character. She had a strong masculine understanding, with a mind far from destitute of kindly affections and generosity; but her temper was uncommonly violent and bad, yet with this peculiarity, that towards *men* with rare exceptions her behaviour was uncommonly courteous and kind, while to her own sex it was capricious at best, and often harsh and malignant to excess. She might have been said to be a woman hater; for tho' she could occasionally be very liberal and kind to female friends and connections, especially when they were in distress, it was impossible for them by the utmost caution, or by the meekest and most respectful demeanour, long to retain her favor, or not to become objects of her virulent abuse, and persecution. Neither her Mother nor Sister nor any other female relative could keep on decent terms with her except by avoiding her Society.

Even my dear Mother with all her gentleness and amiable manners, with all her self command and good sense, had found it impossible to maintain harmony and peace with this extraordinary woman. They were for some years indeed on terms of mutual good will and even of grateful attachment, for she had behaved with great kindness to my Mother when my Father's first misfortunes obliged them to take shelter for a while in my Grandfather's family in Scotland. My Mother in return had invited her, then a single woman, to come to her in London as soon as she was again Mistress of a House to receive her in, and made it so agreeable to her that she occupied part of our house at South Lambeth while the question of Mr. Nuccoll's return to India was undecided. But my Aunt had not long changed her situation before she gave vent to her splenetic temper against her Sister-in-law; and instead of being softened by her forbearance and gentleness, proceeded to treat her with such persevering and studied disrespect and insult that my Father at length interposed and declared it should be tolerated no longer. An instance which I recollect may furnish the best general idea of her conduct. My Mother had brought a servant from Scotland with her, whom she had borne with for that reason under much misbehaviour; but the woman at length added to her other faults such saucy language that my Mother could not consistently with decorum or without a bad effect on the minds of other servants put up with it. The woman therefore was discharged; but not before Mrs. Nuccoll had heard of the case and had expressed her clear opinion that the measure was necessary. Yet the next day she hired her as her own maid and brought her back under the same roof, with her late insulted Mistress.

By treatment like this Mrs. N. at length succeeded in her object of fastening a quarrel upon her kind and patient Sister-in-law, yet as usual with her in all such cases talked and acted as if she herself had been the wronged and insulted party, and broke off all intercourse and correspondence with our family till a few months before my Mother's death. It pleased Providence that business at that time calling Mr. Nuccoll from Alloa to London she came with him, and hearing that my Mother was in a dying state, her heart so far relented that she came to Stoke Newington to see her. The spectacle of her emaciated frame to one who had seen her last in her full health and beauty, could not but be deeply impressive. Mrs. N. was much moved; a cordial reconciliation was the consequence.

Whether my Mother took that occasion to recommend her children to their Aunt's protection I do not know. She no doubt spoke at least of her own approaching dissolution and of those maternal anxieties for which she had too much cause. The sight of the family must at the same time have awakened in my Aunt's mind those kindred feelings and that compassion of which she was by no means unsusceptible; and on the whole this visit was Providentially directed to prepare for the orphan family of my dear Mother a needful resource.

Mrs. Nuccoll's influence over the mind and conduct of her husband was unlimited. He was a man of a good plain understanding, and by no means generally deficient in that firmness of mind that leads to independency of character and action. But he had a great respect for his Wife's capacity, which in fact was much superior to his own. When her passions did not disturb her judgment it was uncommonly vigorous and clear; and she had a restless energy that would have made it extremely difficult to oppose her will. But she took care never to provoke such opposition when it could consistently with her purpose be avoided. She was the kindest and most obsequious of wives, and governed him chiefly by infusing into his mind with great address, and endless assiduity, her own opinions and principles, her own attachments and dislikes. She had consequently been able to induce him to take part in her quarrel with my Mother and Father so far as to estrange himself from them; but she found it much easier now to make him simpathise with her altered feelings, for he was a very kind hearted man. With his entire approbation she wrote to my Father pressing him to entrust her with the education of his two elder daughters, and without waiting for his answer she induced Mr. Nuccoll to go in one of his own Vessels to London that he might second her request in person, and if complied with bring the girls with him to Scotland on his return. The better to overcome a reluctance which from the knowledge of her Brother's temper she foresaw, she sent the concurrent request of his Mother, who also, I think, charged herself with the care of one of the girls, if he would consent to it, in the then expected event of her settling in the North of Scotland. If I remember right, my Grandmother's plan of life was then undetermined. She very soon after fixed her residence at Peterhead, but had with her younger Daughter, then unmarried, resided for a long time with Mrs. Nuccoll, or near her in the South, till the violent and persecuting spirit of the latter had directed itself with so much perseverance towards her Sister as to make a seperation unavoidable. Yet at the same time this singular woman was acting with the greatest generosity in money matters both towards her Mother and Sister; so that it seemed doubtful whether she laboured most to improve their comforts with her purse, or to make them miserable with her temper. My Grandmother's only other resource

for her own and her younger daughter's support was an
annual remittance which my Uncle William had sent her
from St. Kitts from the time of my Grandfather's death, and
had promised to continue till her own. It was a small one,
only, I think, £40 pr. annum; but in that cheap country and
with her frugal habits it was thought sufficient. At all events
she preferred living upon that with peace, to the residing
longer with or near her elder daughter, and subjecting the
younger daily to all the excesses of her Sister's malevolent
temper. But I think that at the time to which my narrative
has arrived the removal to Peterhead had not yet taken
place.

Whatever influence I had with my Father was employed
zealously to second Mrs. Nuccoll's kind request, and at
length on Mr. N.'s arrival his consent was obtained. What he
well knew of his Sister's vile temper was, I believe, his chief
objection; but this was materially palliated by the consideration that the girls were yet too young to be the objects of her
malignant feelings; for toward children, tho' of her own
hated sex, she was kind and indulgent enough. It was only
when they attained or approached to womanhood, that her
dislike and her persecutions began. These strange feelings
had, I believe, their root in envy. She had lived single till she
despaired perhaps of an offer. She married rather late in
life at last and was childless. She therefore envied those
perhaps who had been or were likely to be more fortunate.
At least I never could guess any other source of an antipathy
which She certainly felt and hardly attempted to conceal or
deny. Indeed, if I remember right, she sometimes expressly
avowed her dislike of women in general. Sure I am that to
them her conduct was as uniformly bad almost as to all her
male relatives and friends it was kind, liberal, and obliging.
Mr. Nuccoll, having obtained my Father's consent that the
two girls should be sent to the joint care of his Mother and
Sister, hastened to avail himself of it. Indeed his Vessel had
not long to stay in London. I had therefore, before the two
recent wounds in my heart were healed, to sustain a third,
by a seperation, not unlikely to be final, from my interesting
fellow orphans, Sibella and Hannah. Well do I remember

the pangs I felt when I went with them on board the Vessel, gave them there what I thought was probably a last embrace, mingled my tears with theirs, and bade these dear girls, the precious charges committed to me by my beloved, lamented Mother, a long and sad adieu. As I passed in a boat under the stern of the Vessel now falling with them down the tide, my eyes met theirs again as they ran to catch a last glance of me from a window of the Cabin. They waved their hands, while I raised my streaming eyes to Heaven and prayed earnestly that God would protect them and give me yet to see them again and promote their happiness in life.

I now returned to my sad and solitary home. Sad and cheerless indeed it was to me. My Father, poor man, was rarely at home, and when there we rather avoided than sought conversation with each other. It was *then* more my fault than his. He saw and pitied my sufferings and was more than usually affable and kind to me; but I felt uncomfortable in his presence, and among other reasons, because I had for the first time expressly thrown off as it were his paternal government, by telling him of my resolution to follow my brother to the West Indies as soon as I could find the means of doing so. He had received the declaration without anger, and said little to dissuade, tho' enough to shew his disapprobation, and I, being resolved to persevere, thought it best to leave the matter there.

It was now that the consumptive symptoms of which I have spoken, rapidly increased upon me. They were of the worst kind and such as are usually thot. to be fatal. A violent cough shook me night and day. I expectorated copiously a purulent matter mixed with blood; a hectic fever, followed with profuse night sweats, turned my rest into weakness; and my flesh wasted so fast that I soon had scarcely more to lose. I have rarely seen any other man so much reduced even in the latest stages of a decline. My Friends, as I could discover at the time, but have since learnt more expressly, thought me irrecoverably lost.

My own apprehensions of the danger now became great. Conscience performed its office with more than former fidelity, and I justly dreaded death, because I felt myself to be, as I was, a heinous sinner and utterly unfit to die. It was not the fear of Hell that dismayed me, for I hardly, if at all, believed that there was such a place of torment. Annihilation rather was the punishment I feared and the consequent dreadful loss of all the felicity, including a reunion with my dear Mother, that I might have enjoyed in Heaven. Nor was the painful passage to the tomb with which I was threatened a slighter subject of alarm. I had seen its distressing nature and felt my inability to sustain it as my Mother, by her piety and Christian fortitude, had been enabled patiently to do. To my sorrows then, and my bodily discomforts, were added anxiety and terror. But all these sufferings were salutary; and less than such a measure and combination of them would probably have failed to produce the effect which a gracious Providence had in view. I was driven by them not only to fervent prayer, but real penitence and reformation. I speak here solely or chiefly in reference to those sins that then most easily beset me. Of universal obedience to God's law, or holiness in heart and life, I had no adequate conception; but there were sins of which my own conscience loudly accused me, and over these I was enabled to obtain a conquest of such extreme difficulty at that period of my life that nothing short of the powerful means which Divine Providence was graciously pleased to employ could have sufficed for its accomplishment. It was necessary that my heart should be softened with grief to the utmost, that my purest earthly affections should be inlisted on the spiritual side, that the fear of God, even "that fear which hath torment," should spring up within me, and be sharpened by the apparent near approach of Death. Bounteous, compassionate, long-suffering, Author and Preserver of my being!

Among thy list of blessings infinite,
Stand this the foremost, that my heart has bled.[1]

My situation excited strongly the simpathy of my Aunt and Uncle Webb. They invited me to their House at Gravesend, kept me there for a long time, and employed their care with equal tenderness and judgment for my recovery. My dear Mother herself could not have nursed me with greater

[1] Edward Young, *Night Thoughts*, Night IX, ll. 497–498. Young has "Among *my* list. . . ."

assiduity than Mrs. Webb did, and her cares were the more efficacious because the affection which prompted them soothed and cheered my heart. It may not be useless to mention the medical means which I recollect to have been used. They were not of the kind now so generally and so fruitlessly prescribed in similar cases. Neither bleeding, nor blistering, nor a vegetable regimen was employed; nor can I remember taking any medicine except the vitriolic acid at night to check the nocturnal perspirations, or colloquiative sweats, as they are called, by which I was much weakened; but I was sustained by nutritious food, especially shell fish, drank milk from the cow at rising, with a little brandy or rum in it, and had my breast covered with a shield of flannel hung round my neck with a ribband and worn next the skin. It was summer, and I was encouraged to take as much air and exercise as I wished, especially riding on horseback. My Uncle, who rode every day, kindly hired a horse for me and took me with him; but this was not long continued; for then, as now, I liked walking better, and found it at least equally beneficial. I think my visits to Gravesend must have been intermitted and renewed; for I remember being at Stoke Newington when cherries were ripe, of which we had great quantities in our garden, and that I had an almost insatiable appetite for them which I indulged to great excess at all times of the day, so as almost to live upon them. I notice it because I have always thought they contributed more than all other means to bring my disease to a favorable crisis. The quantities I eat were so great, probably many pounds a day, that if they had not been salutary the effect must have been perceptibly bad, but it was precisely at this time that my cough and spitting of blood and the other bad symptoms ceased.

Meantime my ill health did not alter my resolution to go to the West Indies. On the contrary I was confirmed in it, and all my friends approved the plan from the known influence of a hot climate in removing pulmonary consumptions. My Father, I believe, was led by the same consideration not to attempt to turn me from my purpose, tho' he never expressed his assent to it. But it was not from him that I could expect the means of its execution. I applied to my

Mother's friend, Mr. Clinton, and he kindly expressed his disposition to assist me to the utmost of his power. He soon found what we thought a happy opportunity of doing so. Among the Roman Catholic Gentry of whom he was the the favorite Confesser, was a Mr. Nisbet, an eminent Jamaica Planter, and if I remember right a West India Merchant also, then resident in London. To this gentleman he applied in my favor and easily obtained from him a promise of sending me out in the capacity of *Bookkeeper* to one of his Estates, paying for my passage and giving me a competent Salary for my subsistence from the time of my arrival. Little did I or Mr. Clinton know what the name of Bookkeeper on a Jamaica Plantation meant. We naturally supposed it to be a confidential sedentary occupation, in which I might learn the business of conducting one of those imaginary diamond mines, a Sugar Estate, and soon arrive at a share of that opulence which such a business could not fail to scatter on all its agents. Far, indeed, was I at least from suspecting that my duties would be to superintend the work of two or three hundred wretched human beings driven to their labour by a Driver's lash, to be with them in the sultry field by day and in the steaming boiling house by night, to be the subadministrator of a system from which my heart would recoil with abhorrence, and to sustain for a mere comfortless subsistence, physical hardships and dangers under which the coarsest nerves and the strongest muscles usually sink in a few years. Of negro slavery, I had never thought and never enquired but had imbibed the common ideas carefully propagated by West Indians here, and fatally believed, that the system was bad rather in theory than practice, except under cruel Masters. I was not in a greater error in supposing that because Jamaica was in the West Indies, I should by going there be near to and often see my dear Brother, whereas he would have been more out of my reach from that Island than from Europe.

Under such ignorance of the wretched and degrading situation offered to me by Mr. Nisbet, I went with a letter of introduction to that gentleman, gratefully accepted his offer and settled with him that I was to sail for Jamaica in a Ship of his, or his friends, which was to leave the river, I think, in September. I can recollect that he said some things tending a little to damp the ardor of my expectations of early wealth and to prepare me for some discomforts, but by no means in a way to open my eyes at all to the true nature of the employments to which I was destined, and for which he ought to have seen from my appearance and manners I was utterly unfit. What he said, therefore, was probably no more than a salve for his own conscience or his future credit with Mr. Clinton. It certainly rather gave me a favorable opinion of his candour, and further confidence in his patronage and kindness, than any discouragement in my purpose. He told me what cloaths and other necessaries it would be proper to provide myself with; and these by the pecuniary assistance of Mr. Clinton and Mr. Webb I was enabled to obtain. I proceeded therefore to prepare for my outfit, which I soon accomplished, and waited with impatience for the appointed time that was to open to me the path of independence and place me in the same part of the globe with my beloved brother. I had already received letters from him apprizing me of his arrival at St. Kitts, and that he had been very kindly received by his Uncle, but giving me no information about the Country, or none that could tend at all to correct my erroneous notions.

When I told my Father of the appointment I had obtained and my prospect of an early departure from England he told me briefly the little he knew of the situation I was going to, and said he was sure I should repent my choice; but he had no alternative to offer, except the disheartening one of my continuing unemployed, and without a prospect of providing in any manner for my own subsistence. He knew nothing of the West Indies beyond a general notion of the oppressive slavery that prevails there, which he always spoke of with aversion. What he said of it on this occasion I set down to his disinclination to part with me, and on the whole was not at all turned from my purpose, but glad that he did not expressly forbid it, so as to make my perseverance a direct act of filial disobedience.

When the appointed period of my voyage was near at hand my heart strongly suggested that there was one object of yet unextinguished attachment whom I could wish to see and take leave of before I quitted my native country to return to it perhaps no more. It is long since I have mentioned my dear Nancy. From the time of her refusing to see me on my return from Winchester in a way so mortifying to my pride I had made no attempt to renew my acquaintance with her, and fancied that I had vanquished an attachment which it would have been humiliating still to avow; yet there were times at which my heart suggested that the tender feelings she had for me were probably not yet extinguished, and that the letter which gave me so much offence had perhaps been dictated to her by her Father and her Guardian, Mrs. Thomas, in a way she could not resist. I more than once with a view of ascertaining this point endeavoured to find out my old friend, her Brother, but in vain. He was serving his time as a Midshipman in the Navy, but in what ship, or in what part of the world, I could not learn. I now conceived the purpose of addressing a letter to her openly under cover to Mrs. Thomas, telling her that I was going immediately to the West Indies, probably to return no more, and requesting to be allowed an interview with her, if only for a few minutes, before my departure. After some hesitation I took this step; but the only fruit of it was the deep mortification of finding my letter returned through the hands of her Father to mine, who gave it to me with a few words importing, both in relation to that and my plan of migration that it was useless to give me advice which he saw I was determined to resist.

The indignation that I felt both against Father and daughter for this contemptuous, and as it seemed to me, most unfeeling conduct, was extreme. I was almost tempted personally to chastise the former for thus daring to treat me like a boy by making his complaint to my Father; and tho' a little reflection made me desist from such violence, I wrote a bitter letter calculated to mortify and offend both my poor Nancy and her Father to the utmost of my power, and as to make any future reconciliation impossible on either side.

This incident of course did not diminish my desire to hasten from a country where poverty and consequent contempt were likely to be my only portion, and fly to one where I hoped soon to raise myself above them. Sadly indeed

should I have been disappointed. I have since seen enough
of the West Indies, and enough of that miserable situation
there into which I was about to plunge, to know that a fearful
extreme of human wretchedness would have been the immediate, and premature death the speedy fruit, of my intended
migration. The Overseers, as the subaltern white agents of
the Sugar Planter are called in the Leeward Islands, or
Bookkeepers as they are preposterously named in Jamaica, are,
I think, of all human beings in point of employment the
most to be compassionated or despised; compassionated if
they cannot, and despised if they do not desire to abandon
their odious situation. They are in the middle rank among
the administrators of that cruel private despotism under
which the poor negroes groan, being placed immediately
above the black drivers, and below the Managers, called in
Jamaica the Overseers. Over the former, they have the same
unlimited power, practically at least unlimited, as the
Managers, or the Proprietor himself, when present, and of
course also over the poor human herd who are driven to
their labours: but they are servilely subordinate to the
Managers; men whose minds for the most part are steeled
against every humane and liberal feeling. There doubtless
are soft hearted Managers, for there are benevolent Gaolers;
but the turnkey of a gaol has functions less odious to perform
than the Overseer or Bookkeeper of a West Indian Plantation; for the authority he assists in administering is limited by
equitable laws, and the subjects of it are men who have
become such in consequence of their crimes; whereas the
Overseer or bookkeeper has to execute the arbitrary man-
dates of a Manager however unfeeling or merciless, as well
as unjust, he may perceive them to be. The Drivers indeed
are the executioners, but the Overseer or Bookkeeper is the
immediate superintendant of the excessive labour they are
often directed to exact, and the unmerited and shocking
punishments they are not rarely commanded to inflict. He
may indeed restrain the excesses and needless severities of the
Drivers when they abuse the authority they possess. But even
this power would make the situation to a just and liberal
mind the more distressing; for such are the effects of this
unnatural and opprobrious system that it is for the most

6*

part absolutely impossible to exercise such a power without danger of committing injustice, as well as exciting insubordination and producing disorder and mischief. It is only in extreme cases, or upon accidental discoveries of improper motives in the Drivers, that the Overseer can certainly distinguish between partiality and impartiality in the coercion of labour from the individuals who compose the gang; or between the necessary and superfluous infliction of the lash. Such, in a moral view, were the odious and sordid functions on which I was inconsciously going to enter. Ill as they would have suited the constitution of my mind, my body would have been still less fitted if possible for the physical hardships which the Overseer or Bookkeeper is destined to sustain. He must endure the noontide blaze of a tropical sun while surveying the labours of the field, and the steam of the boiling house by night. He must expose himself to the morning and evening dews; must visit the nauseous sick-house, when dysentery and other infectious diseases add their pestilent effluvia to other offensive smells in a room so hot and close that the negro slaves alone could endure even its temperature without annoyance; and he must be content for the most part with such animal food as aggravates instead of lessening the general dangers of the climate. Salt beef, salt pork, and salt fish, are in most places the only allowances, flour excepted, allotted to the Overseers; and their Salaries are too low to afford the purchase of more salutary food. Without enumerating the other hardships and privations to which these unfortunate men are doomed, it will be plain that their situation is one that a constitution of the strongest kind only can sustain. It is commonly filled by hardy young men from Scotland and Ireland taken from the ranks of life not much above the lowest, and who are prepared by early habit to sustain well every physical hardship. Yet even among these, the proportion that perishes in the seasoning, or in a few years of service on the Plantations, is frightfully large; and I doubt not that for one European Overseer or Bookkeeper who lives long enough and is successful enough to emerge from that wretched situation and revisit his native land, at least twenty pass to an untimely grave.

For my part I am as sure as it is possible to be of what

consequences would have ensued from any supposed event
that the situation into which I was eagerly rushing would
have been fatal to me in a few months at most. Both to my
mind and body it would have been quite intolerable, for to
both a West India residence afterwards proved in a high
degree unfriendly, when instead of administering a detestable system under all the hardships here adverted to as a
friendless stranger in Jamaica, I had to encounter only such
inconveniences of the Climate as independent and easy
circumstances could not obviate, in a profession that imposed upon me nothing distressing to my moral feelings,
except the knowledge of oppression and cruelty which I
could not effectually redress, and no exposure to the main
physical danger of Europeans in that Country, the rays of a
vertical sun in the open air. I had also from the moment of
my landing in St. Christopher a most affectionate Brother
for my Physician, well acquainted at once with the diseases
of the climate and the particular constitution of his patient;
and yet, as will be seen hereafter, I very narrowly escaped
with my life from more than one disease, the ordinary fruit
of migration from a temperate to the torrid zone. I repeat
therefore that the plan I was on the point of carrying into
execution would infallibly have conducted me to an early
grave.

Here as in many other incidents of my eventful life a kind
Providence strikingly interposed for my preservation. Every
preparation for my voyage was made, and the time of sailing
very near at hand, when an event the least expected suddenly
arrested my purpose and reversed all the powerful motives
on which it had been formed. My dear Brother returned
from the West Indies just in time to prevent my departure.

Our Uncle in St. Christopher had received him very
kindly. His regard for our Mother had been revived by the
news of her death, and as my Brother's casting himself uninvited upon his protection was *her* act in great measure, and
not at all our *Father's*, there were no feelings of pride or
resentment to oppose the natural emotions that disposed him
favorably towards an interesting, unfortunate youth, his
nephew, namesake and godson. He therefore did not long
hesitate in resolving to adopt my Brother so far as might be

necessary to enable him to provide for himself in some liberal profession. This he soon determined might best be done by educating him as a Surgeon and Physician, and making him when duly qualified his own assistant in practice and ultimate Successor. The want of classical knowledge at the age of nineteen might have seemed a bar to this plan; but my Uncle, who had himself been educated in Scotland, and was perhaps scantily furnished with all but professional science, thought the objection not insuperable. He resolved to send his Nephew to Aberdeen, to recommend him to the special care of his own old friends, Doctors Livingstone and Robertson of that place, the most eminent Physicians and Surgeons there, who had the sole charge of the Aberdeen Infirmary and had no rivals in Medical reputation in the whole North of Scotland. As a pupil to them for the usual term of three years, finishing afterwards at Edinburgh and taking his degree at its University, he knew my brother would have the best means of qualifying himself for practice in the West Indies, where, as in the North of Scotland, Physic, Surgery, Pharmacy, and all the other branches of the healing art are united in the same practitioner; and he relied on his private industry under some competent Tutor for his acquiring during his course at Aberdeen a sufficient knowledge of Latin and Greek. As my Brother of course implicitly adopted his views, no time was lost in putting the plan into effect. He was sent back to England by the return of the same Ship that carried him to the West Indies and arrived in the River Thames just as I was preparing to sail from it.

My joy at this sudden and most unexpected reunion with my dear Bill, the companion of my childhood, the confidant of all my thoughts, the sharer of all my joys and sorrows, my only friend, may more easily be conceived than expressed. But it was not long the subject of unmixed emotions. We must soon part again. I must go to the West Indies, and my dear Brother was no longer there. We must be divided for many years at least. He in return was not less uneasy, and still more alarmed to find me on the point of embarking as a Plantation Bookkeeper for Jamaica. He had seen enough of the situation of an Oversee (as the subordinate Plantation

Agents are more properly called in the Leeward Islands) to know that it was one which I should find highly disgusting, and which my constitution would ill sustain: and he had learnt that the only roads to independency and fortune in the West Indies are the learned professions, or that success in the planting line is at least very difficult and rare, and of slow growth to men who do not set out either with capital or credit. Happily the facts and reasonings upon which his Uncle's determination for himself had been founded were all applicable to my own case, so far at least as they checked the hope of success in the path I was about to enter on. He had seen little during his short stay of the treatment of Plantation slaves, but the little I heard from him was not of a kind to increase my liking towards the employment of superintending their labours; and the account he gave of the degree of estimation in which Overseers are held among gentlemen was alarming to my pride. Notwithstanding that kind of peership which belongs to all white faces in the West Indies, Overseers, on account chiefly of their subordinate and dependent situation under the Managers, are not seen at gentlemen's tables. Perhaps it was a circumstance of disappointment not less influential with me to discover that when my dear Brother should return to practice in St. Christopher, I should be as much out of his reach in Jamaica, and he out of mine, from the effects of the trade winds, as if the whole Atlantic rolled between us. Such was the damp cast on all my hopes by these views, that when he earnestly dissuaded me from my purpose my heart was not ill-disposed to listen to his advice; but my pride could ill brook the thought of receding, after having persisted so far in my purpose contrary to my Father's opinion, and having accepted pecuniary assistance from friends for its execution, which having been expended on cloaths and other articles of outfit could not be restored. Besides, there was apparently no alternative, but one against which inclination and prudence equally revolted, that of remaining idle at Stoke Newington without any prospect of being placed in a way of providing in future for my own support, or escaping from indigence and contempt. I should probably therefore still have persevered and cast myself upon destruction, if the

same benignant Providence had not engaged my poor
Father's parental feelings so far in the attempt to change my
purpose at this critical period as to make him devise a rival
plan peculiarly attractive to my fraternal affections and my
ambition too, and to press it upon me both by my dear Bill's
solicitations and his own. It was that I should again set my
face towards that profession for which I had been once
designed, the Bar, that I should be immediately entered at
Lincoln's Inn, and to repair my want of general education
should proceed with my Brother to Aberdeen and place
myself at the University there during the two years of the
five years standing at an Inn of Court, wherein no time is lost
by not keeping the Terms in London, and finally, that being
called to the bar about the time in which my Brother would
finish his medical education, I might go out with him to St.
Christopher, where, according to his and all other accounts,
a successful lawyer was sure of soon acquiring an ample
fortune.

Chapter Five

[1775–1777]

YOUNG tho' I was, and sanguine tho' I have ever been, there were difficulties in this scheme which did not escape my observation. To go to a University while almost entirely ignorant of the learned languages, was, I too reasonably feared, to expose myself to derision and contempt. My Father however gave me a credit my vanity was not slow to take, in ascribing to me powers of mind that would easily surmount this disadvantage by private application, while keeping pace with others in the proper studies of a College. He suggested also that the first year at a Scotch University is allotted to Greek, with which few Students there are previously furnished, and that by a letter to Dr. Skeene, an old friend of his, one of the Professors, he should be able to procure for me such exemptions or facilities as I might at the outset stand in need of to save my credit and obtain time for the advancing myself in classical knowledge by private means. There was another difficulty which I and my brother too clearly foresaw. Giving my poor Father full credit for a sincere and earnest desire to furnish pecuniary means for the execution of this plan, we knew that he might very probably be unable to do so, and that I might therefore find myself when at the University in great embarrassments, and with still greater probability might by his death or the utter failure of his precarious income, be disabled from prosecuting my plan so as to be called to the bar, and have at a more advanced period of life to look out for some other means of subsistence. My dear Brother, however, palliated this objection by the opinion that in case of need our Uncle William would not suffer such a plan to be abandoned for want of means after it had been for some time prosecuted, but would extend his patronage to me, so far as to enable me to enter on my intended profession. In short, an answer was found to every objection specious enough to satisfy a mind which from fraternal affection and

even firm fililal feelings was disposed to be convinced, and
after consulting with the friends who had kindly contributed
to my means of migration, who now freely left me to my
own judgment, I excused myself to Mr. Nisbet for my
change of purpose, gave up all thoughts of going to Jamaica,
and resolved to accompany my Brother to Aberdeen.

Thus did a gracious Providence rescue me from the
destruction into which I was rushing and lead me contrary
to my own precious resolutions to adopt a plan of life the
happy effects of which I have reaped near forty years and
still enjoy and which has been productive also of many
blessings spiritual as well as temporal to my dear Mother's
children in general.

I was entered as a Student at Lincoln's Inn, sometime I
think in September or October 1775. I could ascertain the
date; but it is not worth the time it would cost. It was early
in the latter Month, as I best remember, that my dear Bill
and I took our passage in one of the ordinary Packets, or
Smacks (as they are called) from London to Aberdeen.
The parting from my poor little fellow orphans, Elizabeth
and John, was not without pain, but was softened by the
reflection that at their tender years they could feel no lasting
pain from, and lose little or nothing by my absence.

Nothing remarkable attended our voyage. We had the
usual sufferings of landsmen, and the usual exhilarations on
finding ourselves again at the end of about a week on shore
except that the revulsion on my part was greatly diminished
in pleasure by the dreary aspect of the country in which I
was to remain at least two years. The Town itself had nothing
inviting to the eye. It has been since greatly improved in its
avenues streets and buildings, but was then very unsightly
and mean to an eye accustomed to London and its handsome
suburban villages. It was the circumjacent country, however,
that chiefly tended to dishearten me. Always enthusiastically
fond of the beauties of Nature, I could not behold without
disgust and alarm a place of residence in which it was in
vain to look around for trees or hedges or verdant fields, but
which presented to the eye on every side either rough stone
dykes, inclosing patches of tinted vegetation, or black
heaths encumbered with bare rocks so thickly sprinkled .

that it seemed doubtful whether the heather or the stone occupied the greater part of the surface. The immediate environs of the Town, indeed, contained some garden ground in which kale and turnips covered the barren soil enough a little to relieve the eye, and there was a strip of land by the sea shore where a meagre green sward was formed interspersed with sandy hillocks, or, in the language of the country, "*bents*"; but beyond these on every side the landscape presented to the English eye features alone of dreariness and sterility and desolation. I am credibly informed that much has been effected since in the way of improvement, and the Earl of Leven told me of his own knowledge that garden ground now lets around Aberdeen for rents that would be thought high in the environs of London. I think he mentioned as much as £10 per acre. Great in such cases are the powers of industry and wealth when employed by local interests and attachments; but a new creation, I think, would be wanted to make the country in general within twenty miles or thirty north or south of Aberdeen other than repulsive in a high degree to an English eye, and disheartening to an imagination that had been formed and indulged amid the rural beauties of England.

We found, however, nothing sterile there in the hearts of the few friends we were introduced to by letters from our Father and from other relatives and friends. Their hospitality and kindness were beyond our expectation. By their advice and assistance we were soon comfortably settled in a Boarding House, such as the more respectable of the College Students and Medical Pupils took their meals in, and where we also were provided with lodgings. Such was, and I believe still is, the system there; and it was then so cheap that the whole charge for our board, lodging, and washing coats, and candles, &c., was only £20 a year each; tho' if I remember right there was only one other Boarding House in the Town where the terms were higher.

I now entered upon that which perhaps, all things considered, was the most anxious and painful period of my life. During the two years that I spent in Aberdeen ill health was my almost constant companion and with it, what is far worse, incessant disquietude of mind, or painful anxieties at least, the remissions of which were short.

The chief cause of my bodily maladies was the humid and ungenial atmosphere of the place. Aberdeen stands in a low situation at the Mouth of the river Dee on the East coast of Scotland exposed to all the asperities of the Northern Ocean. The broad estuary of the river contributes with the sea to load its atmosphere with fogs and vapours; and the filthiness of the town, at that time destitute of sewers and cesspools, and every other means of cleanliness and exsiccation, added much, no doubt, to the insalubrious effect.

There was, however, a powerful concurrent cause of the ill health I was prey to in the period of my residence at Aberdeen; anxiety of mind, to which may be added much more of sedentary labour and less of bodily exercise than I had been accustomed to before. I soon found how just my apprehensions were of extreme difficulties at College from my want of Latin and total want of Greek, and how inadequate that expedient of private application was to which my Father had referred me. Nothing but dexterity of management above my years combined with singular good fortune could have saved me from disgrace; and they did not save me from the daily apprehension of it, which continually preyed upon my spirits. It would have been better if I had used perfect openness with Dr. Skeene;[1] but my Father having in his letter of introduction either not spoken of my want of classical education at all, or only in very extenuating terms, I was ashamed to be explicit with him on the subject; and as he did not think fit to examine me or make any enquiries as to my past education, I confined myself to the acknowledgement of my deficiency in Greek, saying nothing of my want of Latin, which I felt would be the more disgraceful because most even of the younger boys who go to College in Scotland are pretty good Latinists. The consequence was that Dr. Skeene would have advised me to go into the Greek Class like other Students of the first

[1] George Skeene (1741–1803), physician in Aberdeen; professor of natural philosophy in Marischal College, Aberdeen 1760–1775; succeeded his father, Francis Skeene, as professor of civil and natural history, 1775–1788. The Skeene family had a long connection with Marischal College.

year, but this I had anticipated, and knew it would not suit
my case; because as the Greek was taught through the
medium of the Latin my ignorance of the latter would in
that Class be inevitably exposed, and would besides be an
insurmountable bar to my improvement. But my plan was
limited to a two year's course, and this my Father's letter
had mentioned, and from the regulations of the Greek Class
those who belonged to it could learn nothing else in their
first year, having no time to attend the lectures of the other
Professors. It was happily, therefore, not difficult to get Dr.
Skeene to agree with me that, limited as I was in point of
time, it would be unwise to allot one of my two years to the
Greek Class, and that I had better make the best use of my
time by attending the Classes of the two last years, in which
Mathematics, Natural Philosophy, and Moral Philosophy or
the Belles Lettres are taught, and those Students who have
made progress in Greek during the first year have an opportunity of being further advanced in it, for the Professor
of the second class lectures on the higher Greek Classics,
Dr. Skeene, who himself then filled that chair, was reputed
the best Grecian of his day in Scotland, and he naturally
advised me to attend his own Greek lectures, tho' apprised
that I was ill prepared for them, thinking that I might glean
something from them by the aid of private application. I
entered myself, however, with his concurrence in the
Natural Philosophy Class of Professor Coupland,[1] with the
Students of the third year, and in the Mathematical class
under Doctor Trail[2] with the Students of the second year, in
which by the course of that University, the study of Mathematics begins. I am speaking of the University of *New*
Aberdeen or the Marischal's College, at which I was placed.
Old Aberdeen, within a mile of the former, also has its
College or University; but they are quite disconnected with

[1] This is Patrick Copland (1749–1822), professor of natural philosophy at
Aberdeen 1775–1779 and 1817–1822, and of mathematics 1779–1817, the
founder of a museum of natural philosophy at Aberdeen.

[2] William Trail, LL.D., was professor of mathematics at Marischal College,
Aberdeen, and author of a widely-used textbook, *Elements of Algebra*, which had
three editions in 1779, 1789, and 1808. He also wrote an *Account of the Life and
Writings of Robert Simson, M.D., Late Professor of Mathematics at the University of
Glasgow* (1812).

each other and proceed on very different systems,[1] and New
Aberdeen was at this time by far in the greater repute having
besides the eminent Professors I have mentioned, the celebrated Dr. Campbell[2] for its Principal and Theological
Professor and the more widely celebrated Doctor Beattie,[3]
the Author of *The Minstrel*, &c., and of the essay on the
Immutability of Truth, for its Professor of Moral Philosophy
or the Belles Lettres.

By the plan which I adopted my time would have been
pretty fully employed without my deficiencies to retrieve in
private. I had daily four or five lectures to attend, and of the
three of them, those in the Natural Philosophy Class, I had
to make notes, which were sent periodically, every week
as I best remember, to the Professor for his perusal. When to
these duties were added my endeavours at evening hours to
retrieve my classical deficiencies, my labours were sufficiently
arduous for a youth who up to that period was almost a
stranger to all application of a serious or useful kind. I had
always read much, but hitherto only for pleasure. I had now
no time for works of entertainment. I read from necessity, not
from choice, and my studies were embittered by anxiety and
by difficulties which I could not always surmount. I had no
guide or assistant whatever. The system of tutorage, public
or private, has no place at a Scotch University. The Professor is the only Teacher, and his public lectures his only
mode of instruction. If the singularity of having a private classical Tutor had been within the reach of my purse, my pride
would have revolted from the implication that I was so
much worse furnished than my class fellows as to stand in
need of such assistance. My books therefore, and my own
sagacity in the use of them, were my only resource.

[1] Aberdeen University consists of King's College in Old Aberdeen, founded
by Bishop Elphinstone in 1494, and Marischal College, in Broad Street,
founded in 1593 by George Keith. In general, arts and divinity are taught at
King's; law, medicine, and science at Marischal. Since Stephen's time Marischal College has been rebuilt and extended.

[2] George Campbell (1719–1796) was principal of Marischal College, Aberdeen, 1759–1792, professor of divinity there 1771–1792, and author of *A
Dissertation on Miracles* (1762).

[3] James Beattie (1735–1803), Scottish poet; professor of moral philosophy
and logic at Marischal College, Aberdeen, from 1760; published *Original Poems
and Translations* (1761), *Essay on Truth* (1770), and *The Minstrel* (1771).

Among the various disadvantages that I have since found
from this very defective and very scanty plan of education
the most embarrassing and insurmountable has been my
ignorance of prosody. I have always had a good poetic ear for
English verse, but this goes a very little way towards enabling
a man to read the Latin Poets with propriety, the Horation
measures especially. Their distinctions between long and
short syllables are for the most part unintelligible to an
English ear, and my endeavours to understand and apply
the rules of scanning as laid down in the Grammars were so
unsuccessful from the want of a living guide and auditor,
that I soon gave up the attempt in despair. I have therefore
always been afraid to quote Latin, or to read it in the presence of well-educated men, knowing that false quantities
would probably subject me to ridicule and make my want
of education appear far greater than it really was. Amidst all
my difficulties and terrors as a Student, I found however
some encouragements. I was far better informed on all
ordinary topics of conversation than any of my fellow
students or any companions I met; and the stile both of my
tongue and pen was still more beyond them, not only from
the correctness of my English idiom and pronunciation,
which scholars in that Country thought the most desirable
and most difficult of attainments, but also from the effects of
that idle reading in which I had so long indulged myself. I
had the gratification, therefore, of finding myself a consequential man at the Boarding House and in the College
Circles, and that notwithstanding the deficiencies of which
I was conscious I stood high in general estimation for knowledge as well as talents among those who were my daily
companions. In the common dining room of our boarding
House where we were generally above twenty in number,
comprising several gentlemen who had already entered into
the learned professions, and three at least of the most distinguished scholars of the University, we generally discussed at
and after dinner the politics of the day and not rarely subjects
of taste or morals such as every man supposes himself in
some degree to understand, and other general topics of a
superficial kind; and in such discussions I commonly was
allowed to take a prominent part, and was or fancied myself

to be an overmatch in argument for those who impugned
my opinions, surpassing them in volubility at least if not in
my reasoning powers, and perhaps in point of intelligence
also. The great interesting political subject of the time was
the American quarrel, and I was enthusiastically attached to
the cause of the Colonies, while in Scotland it was so hard to
find an opinion on that side, that with one exception they
had no other advocate in our numerous circle ; and such was
the loyal zeal with which the Rebels, as the Americans were
then termed, were reviled, that it required some courage
to take their part; but in such courage I was not deficient,
and when assailed with violence and rudeness of manner,
which argumentative warmth in the loyal cause not rarely
gave birth to, I generally retorted in a way that brought
the assailants to reason. The other champion of the Colonies
was a sensible and very amiable man some years my Senior.
Mr. James Gillies,[1] brother of the Historian and afterwards
a Minister of the Scotch Church, who was then finishing his
Theological studies at Aberdeen under Principal Campbell.
Before I became his fellow boarder at Mrs. Stewart's, he
had suffered so much persecution at her table for his
rebellious opinions and his religious fanaticism, as they
thought his preeminent piety to be, that they could rarely
provoke him into argument or dissent by their abuse of his
Party; but I became so zealous and so pugnacious an Ally
that he no longer shrunk from the wordy war, and almost
every new Gazette produced a warm debate, in which he and
I sustained the American cause against many warm and
sometimes angry opponents. This alliance and other sympathies begot considerable intimacy, and at length a very
cordial friendship between Gillies and me. He was what
may be properly perhaps called an enthusiast and an
eccentric character, but all his enthusiasm and all his singu-
larities were of a generous and benevolent cast; and he had
a resolute decision and firmness of mind which contributed
much to place him high in my esteem. For instance, he
thought it unjustifiable to kill animals for our food, unless
indeed it were clearly necessary for our support or health

---

[1] James Gillies is not listed in the *Dictionary of National Biography*, though two
of his brothers are.

(for I think he made that exception) and having ascertained as he thought that he could well dispense with animal food, and even be more healthy without it, he resolutely and perseveringly gave it up, disregarding all the inconveniences and all the ridicule to which in so public a boarding house the singularity naturally exposed him. I laughed sometimes like the others, at his Gentoo[1] creed, but in my heart respected the amiable principle of his abstinent rule and the resolution with which he adhered to it. My simpathies with and interest in his character were also increased by finding that he was a lover, and that the object of his affection was a pleasing, handsome young Lady of a pious disposition like his own, to whom he introduced me. He was received in her family as an accepted Suitor, and their union was only postponed till he should be ordained and presented to a living, which had been promised to him, I think, through the interest of Lord Hopetown. Gillies had originally been destined to the legal profession, and when his religious feelings decided him on going into the Scotch Church, he was arrived at an age that made the established course of theological studies at the University a path to ordination unpleasantly and inconveniently long, especially with such an interesting prospect as he had at the end of it. To shorten it, therefore, he went, about a year after our acquaintance commenced, to the North of England and obtained ordination, or what is equivalent to it in the Scotch Church, from an assembly or Synod of Clergymen of its communion, dissenters in this Country. Upon this qualification he was presented to a Church in or near Brechin, his native place, the Presbytery of which allowed it. But though such qualifications had been in several former instances admitted as valid some Members of the Presbytery appealed against him to the Provincial Synod, and there I think the decision was adverse to his presentation. The cause was ultimately carried by appeal to the General Assembly and was a subject of great public interest and of long and doubtful deliberation by that supreme tribunal, but was at length finally decided in Gillies's favour. The Assembly, however, allowed of the

---

[1] Hindu; specifically Telugu.

ordination in his particular case only on the ground of the practice having for some time prevailed without being questioned and the hardship that would therefore be felt in the particular case by its disallowance, and declared that in future no ordination in England should intitle any man to hold a living in the Scotch established Church. I shall have occasion to mention my friend Gillies again in the account of my last visit to Scotland. For the present I will dismiss him with what is perhaps, or may seem, a boast, that my Friends have been generally found among those who were highest in the moral scale in the circles I have moved in. As I write for my children, it would be false delicacy to suppress a fact of the greatest practical importance in the history of my life; and it is, in a right view, no subject of self-exaltation, but the reverse. The moral taste with which I was early indued ought to have guarded me better against the sins into which my impetuous passions and vicious propensities have plunged me. In my collegiate business I found less difficulty than I reasonably apprehended. I attended, by Dr. Skeene's advice, his own daily lectures on the Greek Classics, which would have been an infallible source of exposure and disgrace if he had called me out for examination on the subject of the preceding lecture as the course was with others of his class, but as he was apprized of my deficiency in respect of Greek, he never did so, and I had the advantage of obtaining some little smattering of that language under him, tho' very little indeed and of which I do not retain enough even to read the characters correctly. I attended with much more satisfaction Dr. Trail's first course of Mathematics. Here I started on equal terms with most of my class fellows, as few of them had acquired any elementary knowledge of that science before they came to the University, and I was soon distinguished by the Professor as the most attentive and intelligent of his mathematical tyros, or at least among the first of them. In fact I liked this subject of study greatly. The novelty of demonstrative reasoning pleased and satisfied my judgment, and I have always thought that if I had gone to Cambridge, or found elsewhere means of plunging deep into mathematical science, I should have gained distinction and fame in it. It will be seen hereafter that of this as well as other branches of knowledge I gained but a mouthful, and a smaller one even than Scotch Universities generally impart; yet the morsel has been of great use to me. It gave me adequate notions of what close reasoning is, and what demonstration as applied to physical science in its full severity requires. Still I venture to disclose the opinion that tho' thus far was necessary and extremely useful, yet had I pursued the study of Mathematics further than I did, i.e., beyond Euclid's Elements, the effect would rather have been adverse than auxiliary to my success in life as a public speaker and writer. Great mathematical scholars (as my dear Wilberforce and I have often remarked to each other, in respect of some of them whom we much esteemed and loved) have not the same tact, and the same quickness, with other men of general capacity in weighing the force of evidence and perceiving the consequences of propositions on subjects beyond the range of physical demonstration. They speak with less effect in public and private than their knowledge and judgment would enable them to do if they had not been used to go by steps when they should vault and fly. The *habits* of the mind, in reasoning as in morals, are of unspeakable importance; and the most important business of education is to form them aright.

In the Natural Philosophy Class I was not less successful, and here I had better means of proving to the Professor Mr. Coupland how well I listened to and understood his lectures. Dr. Trail gave me frequent commendations for clearly going over the demonstration of a theorem or problem when called upon to do so, but Mr. Coupland gave me stronger and more gratifying praise for my notes of his lectures which clearly proved to him that I entered into his meaning and followed him with an entire apprehension of every subject. Here I had a grand advantage in the facility of composition which I possessed, the consequence in part of my copious English reading, while my class fellows in general found nothing so difficult as writing correctly their native language. It is, or at least then was, the last attainment of Scotch scholarship to do so. Nor is this strange considering how widely the colloquial dialect in the North of Scotland differs from the English tongue. A consequence of this difficulty was that the students in general shrunk from the task of writing original notes of the lectures they heard, and yet this was a part of their prescribed duties. Once a week every student sent his notes to the Professor and on the following day he made his remarks upon them in the public class. They therefore fell upon the expedient of making copies of notes made by other students in the same or a preceding year and often took from the lecture book, Helsham[1] for instance, passages in the same words. I, on the other hand, finding no difficulty in putting my own ideas upon paper, gave in original notes, which however erroneous they might be in some particulars, proved to the Professor that I in general understood and digested his lectures. For this I had the gratification of often receiving his public praises, and his private attentions to me proved that I was a particular favorite.

With such encouragements I should have been tolerably happy in my new situation if my health had been unimpaired. But my constitution soon felt the bad effects of my altered habits and of the insalubrious change of air from Stoke Newington to Aberdeen. The unfriendliness of this change to my health from local causes has been already noticed, and beyond doubt my sedentary employments with the anxieties I felt as to my credit at the University, contributed to the complaints that followed. They were chiefly those which are technically called Dyspepsy. My digestive organs became deranged, and performed their functions so weakly and irregularly that I was at length almost in a perpetual state of discomfort or positive pain. I had soon and amply the best medical advice, for Dr. Livingstone on account of my Brother's connection with him as a pupil, and his friendship with some of my Father's family, volunteered his gratuitous assistance. My Brother also progressively learnt the proper or ordinary treatment of such cases and formed friendships with pupils who had nearly finished their course, with whose advice I was frequently favoured. Two

[1] Richard Helsham (1682?–1738), a friend of Swift, was a distinguished teacher at Trinity College, Dublin, where he was lecturer in mathematics 1723–1730, Erasmus Smith professor of natural philosophy 1724–1738, and regius professor of physics in Dublin University 1733–1738. His *Lectures on Natural Philosophy*, edited by Bryan Robinson (1739), was for years a standard textbook.

of them, Drs. Finlay and Fraser, were men of superior attainments. But if I had been attended by all the Physicians there, and if the best of the Faculty I have ever known had been on the spot, I should have had no benefit from them, but the reverse. I was treated quite *secundam artem*, but it was one of the many cases in which nature points one way and established rules of art another. Wine or some other cordial regimen was what, as I have since learnt from experience, the case required. This my circumstances would not have afforded. It was therefore perhaps better tacitly to leave me to the water or miserable small beer of the boarding house. Opium I also believe would have cured me; but there were still stronger reasons perhaps for not leading me to such a resource which unless regulated by inflexible self-denial becomes a remedy worse than disease. But vegetable acids, as I have since found, would have been extremely useful, and yet from the use of these I was by every medical adviser anxiously debarred. My maladies increased upon me from day to day and from week to week. At length I was, every four and twenty hours almost, attacked with a painful cholic, accompanied with an inflation of the intestines and swelling of the abdomen, almost to bursting, and from which I found no relief but by keeping myself in a kneeling or reclining posture for a great length of time, and by an acrimonious diarrhœa that ensued. A whole tribe of nervous and imaginary diseases, the consequences of indigestion, next made me their prey, and I suffered the more from them because I was continually reading in my Brother's books or hearing from himself or his fellow pupils of a hundred frightful disorders, and seeing in the bones and anatomical preparations he brought to our room, as well as in plates and drawings, the images of disease and death. I no sooner was apprized of them than I began to feel them in my own frame, and to add new sufferings of the imagination to the real ones of which I was the victim. In short I became a hypocondriacal wretched creature. My life was almost a burthen to me, and I found it extremely difficult, and at length hardly possible, to keep up to that regularity with which I had hitherto attended the classes, and to prosecute in any degree at the same time my plan of private studies. The going out by daybreak in a severe winter through the cold fog that the place is subject to, and sitting in a chilly lecture room, for an hour or more before breakfast tended much of course to increase my complaints. It is singular, however, that the pulmonary disease from which I had had so narrow an escape during the preceding Spring and Summer returned no more. I have sometimes thought that the morbid influence, whatever it was, had been, from the change of air and the other causes I have mentioned, transferred from my lungs to my stomach and bowels, and that the maladies under which I suffered so much at Aberdeen were perhaps the price I paid at that critical time of life for escaping a fatal return of my former disease.

To my bodily discomforts was added, as the close of the annual college Session approached, a new subject of anxiety. There is a public examination of all the students on the subjects of their respective studies during the session, which is called the Blackstone examination, from the old custom of each student sitting on a large black stone while examined. The custom had always been to have this examination in Latin, and I felt the utter impossibility of my going through it by any preparation I could make, without disgrace. What then was to be done? It may be thought an extraordinary thing that a youth of seventeen should have the boldness to conceive, and the dexterity to accomplish, a plan for covering his own defects, and saving his credit, by innovating on the established practice of an antient University. Yet this I conceived and effected.

Professor Coupland was then at Aberdeen what my dear friend brother-in-law Farrish[1] has since been at Cambridge. He was very expert in mechanical philosophy, strictly so called, and added to the ordinary lectures an exposition illustrated by models and experiments of various engines and machines in use for manufacturing and other purposes. This improvement was introduced in the same session in which I became his pupil, and it formed no small part of the business

[1] William Farrish (1759–1837) was Jacksonian professor of natural and experimental philosophy at Cambridge 1813–1836. He had been professor of chemistry from 1794 and incumbent of St. Giles's, Cambridge, from 1800. He was married to James Stephen's sister Hannah.

of the Class. It became therefore a question among us how we should find Latin for the many technical English terms that were necessary to make this branch of our studies intelligible. It was understood among us that the Professor felt the same difficulty, tho' he did not choose to avow it publickly to the other Professors and Principal of the University, so as to obtain any alteration of the established practice. It was surmised even by some that he was deficient in classical knowledge, tho' I dare say without reason, and perhaps his knowledge of this suspicion made him unwilling to propose an innovation of which, as the event shewed, he felt the expediency. I saw the opportunity which these circumstances afforded, and seized on it with avidity. After sounding many of my class fellows, and finding them as well inclined as myself to my object, I convened a meeting at which we unanimously agreed to a petition, drawn up by myself, to the Heads of the University (the Principal and Professors) praying that we might, on account of the special circumstances, be examined in English. After full deliberation, our request was acceded to, and I had the gratification of hearing that the arguments and stile of the petition had been highly commended.

I was a favorite with the Professor before, and it was plain to me that this achievement did not lessen me in his regard. On my part I was not ungrateful. I employed again my influence in the class, and successfully, to obtain for him an unprecedented and very acceptable compliment. He was much at a loss for adequate philosophical apparatus, which the University was too poor to supply. I thought it therefore would be a good example, and gratifying to him, to present him by means of a subscription with some article of which we had oftenest found the want in his lectures, and which he had mentioned as a desideratum. I think it was a capital Solar Microscope. We got it from London and inscribed on it with all our names a respectful tribute of well merited praise, or rather our grateful sense of his talents and assiduity as a Teacher. I am not sure on recollection whether we did not abstain from this, the gift being to the College, but it was understood and accepted as a testimony of respect and regard to our Professor. This business cost me more trouble than the other. There was much opposition by many in the class to whom (as indeed to myself) the contribution tho' small was not very convenient. The article cost, I think, only sixteen guineas, and our number in the Class was between thirty and forty. But a half guinea was no trifle to the generality of students at a Scotch University, and tho' the opponents did not choose to plead poverty in their own cases, they objected speciously enough that the precedent might lead to a practice very inconvenient to future students, and tending to enhance the cost of education, which was already more than many could well afford. I persevered however, and in a set speech (the first I ever made) at a general meeting so well recommended the measure as to carry it by a great majority, after which the malcontents did not choose to stand out.

Amidst these College employments my time was not wholly devoted to business. I partook sometimes, tho' not very often, of social recreation in the evening, especially cards and dancing, of both which the young people of that day in the North of Scotland were extremely fond. With the latter I was delighted when well enough to enjoy it, not merely from my love of the exercise, and of the lively Scotch airs, which retain all their animating power over me still, but from what was my ruling propensity: amatory feelings, and admiration of female beauty. Aberdeen was famous for its numerous young Belles, and she must have had small pretentions to that name who as a partner at the ball had not attractions enough to be very interesting to my susceptible heart for the evening. As I had now abandoned forever all thoughts of my poor Nancy, it may seem strange that I passed two years at Aberdeen without forming some new love engagements, especially as the young ladies there were sufficiently accessible and were not unjustly thought to spread their nets a little too assiduously. But I had one guard in my own mind, and more than one in theirs. The first was that I had hardly been three days in Aberdeen before I fixed my admiration on a young Lady, the Diana of the throng, whose Endymion I tried in vain to be. My other securities were that I was known to be in point of circumstances and apparent prospects in life not worth catching and had besides a constitution that seemed to menace me with an early grave. No other young Lady of any attractions therefore thot. it worth her while to win those affections which the beautiful Raky (Rachel) Willox did not fix by meeting them with her own. To this young Lady's Father I had been introduced by a letter from my own, with whom he had been intimate in early life. He in consequence invited my Brother and me to his house and made us acquainted with his daughters, the most celebrated beauties of the place, and in whose education the Baillie, as he was called (being a Baillie or Alderman of the Town), had spared no cost, so that they were as much distinguished by their accomplishments as by their beauty. Rachel, the eldest, especially had a fine voice and sang with great power and taste. She had, I think, the finest and most graceful figure I ever saw, and perhaps the best complexion, with a profusion of flaxen hair which she had the policy to display to the best advantage in its native hue tho' powder was then generally worn. Her large blue eyes had great expression and power, and her other features also were good, tho' the general expression of the whole had certainly more of dignity and conscious power than sensibility or sweetness. She had in fact been so much and so generally admired, and her fond Parents had made her so completely her own Mistress, that it would have been strange if pride had not formed so much of her habitual feelings as to be legible in her face. That I should be captivated by such a young lady then in the full prime of her youthful beauty was natural enough. Not so perhaps that I should have the presumption to hope that I could make her the successor of my dear Nancy in a mutual attachment; for apparently the best offers that could be desired courted her acceptance. Among those gentlemen who paid obsequious attentions to her at that time was a Mr. Waller, an English Student at Old Aberdeen said to be a descendant of the Poet and generally supposed (how truly I know not) to be heir to an English Estate of £5000 a year. He was also a fashionable and good looking young man, and not destitute of understanding, tho' an idler and a coxcomb. To suppose that I could possibly rival a man like this was, to be sure, absurd enough; but I

have never been too diffident in such cases; and tho' Waller
was pretty evidently a suitor, I suspected, not erroneously,
that he would not make proposals of marriage; for he was a
kind of male coquette that had flirted with other young
ladies before, and was actuated pretty plainly by vanity
rather than by passion. I was aspiring enough therefore to
make Raky Willox my Dulcinea, to despise all lower game,
and to take at every opportunity the ordinary means of
conveying to her by my eyes and my particular attentions
the admiration I felt for her. She was apparently not dis-
pleased with this homage. She received it at least not in a
way to make me despair of one day gaining her affections,
nor so as to mortify my vanity except when Waller was
present; but her preference for that fortunate coxcomb (at
whom all the young ladies in the Town were with mutual
emulation "setting their caps" (as the phraze is) was conspicuous enough, and he was vain enough to lead her
into an exhibition of it by alternative particularities, and
affectation of neglect, when he met her in public companies. This was carried so far on one occasion at a Ball
when I was her partner for the evening, that I was quite
disgusted, and tho' it cost me some serious pain for a while
I abandoned the hopeless project of making an impression
on the heart of the beautiful, but vain and self interested
Raky Willox. From this time to that of my final departure
from Aberdeen my too susceptible heart was unimpressed,
with any particular attachment. Every young lady that
was tolerably handsome attracted my eyes and my attentions for the evening, but not having any private intercourse with any one of them in family life, I fell in love no
more.

It may be worth while to mention the result of Baillie
Willox's or rather his Wife's speculations on the beauty and
accomplishments of his daughters. Nothing was wanting on
the prudent Mother's part to assist them in finding advantageous settlements in marriage. Every young man of fortune or good expectations in life found easy access to them
under the parental roof; and Mrs. Willox courted Waller in
particular pretty assiduously, in the hope of making him her
son-in-law. But that young man was too prudent or too cool

to take the bait. His ruling passion was vanity, and the
conspicuous partialities of poor Raky and other fine young
women for him ministered to that feeling as powerfully as if
the repute of his rich expectations in life had not been the
source of it; but his vanity itself perhaps secured him from
being intangled in any serious engagement. It was his mean
and unmanly practice to exhibit his power over them by
exciting jealousy and rivalship between them. In short Miss
Willox, disappointed of this rich prize, fell a few years after
to the lot of a Captn. Pringle, an officer in the Army, who
left her a young widow destitute of any provision and I think
with a child or two to return to her Father's house for subsistance. She was still attractive enough to captivate a young
man of good expectations, but who married her against the
will and without the knowledge of his Father, an eminent
Merchant in Aberdeen on whom he was dependent. The
consequence I think was poverty or difficulties and troubles
through the Father's resentment, and she died, a young and
still beautiful woman, after a short union thus improperly
formed. Miss Jenny (called Jefsy Willox), the second Sister,
was also very handsome. Some thought her more so than her
Sister, tho' much inferior to her in understanding. There was
an attachment between her and a friend of mine, the late
Mr. George Gordon, of which I was the confidant. He was a
very handsome young man and Jefsy was evidently very
fond of him. But Gordon had no fortune and had to find his
subsistence as a Writer to the Signet, a walk in the Scotch
law answering to the English attorney and Soliciter, to
which he had been recently admitted. He was not successful
enough to earn even a good Batchellor's income. He therefore was too prudent to marry, and the courtship I presume
was broken off, tho' honorably and tenderly, on his part,
soon after I left Aberdeen. He himself e'er long quitted
Aberdeen, and came to settle as a Scotch Agent for law
business in London. Poor Jefsy was afterwards addressed by
an Army Lieutt. whose name I think was Campbell and
whom she married without the consent of her Parents. The
consequence was her being, like her Sister, left a destitute
widow and as I best remember with several young children.
I am not clear indeed that she survived her husband, for

7

she fell into a rapid decline and died a very young woman. Her young family, if not she herself, also became a new burthen on her Father, who was by no means in easy circumstances.

I do not remember what became of some younger daughters, who were children when I left Aberdeen but afterwards became, like their Sisters, celebrated Beauties and Toasts. The poor old Baillie, however, found so severely the folly of relying on beauty and accomplishments as provision for his daughters, that he used afterwards to say, as I have heard, that if "he had another family of them he would bring them up to milk the cow and muck the bire" (clean out the cow house).

Those who have never felt the difficulty of providing for a family are sometimes too fastidious and severe in their censures of Parents who are anxious to marry their daughters; but that anxiety, unless well concealed, generally frustrates its own purpose, and especially when the means employed are those of fashionable and ornamental education, and such as plainly aim at an elevation in life beyond that of the family circle. The sobriety and moderation of religious principle in this respect as in others lead to a wiser course. "Godliness is profitable unto all things, having the promise of this life as well as that which is to come."

My Brother and I had the recreations occasionally while at Aberdeen of a better kind than those the mention of which has led me thus long to digress. We went at Xmas, and at the other vacations, to visit our relations at Peterhead, a small seaport town about thirty miles north of Aberdeen; and very affectionate relatives they were, of whom it is high time I should speak.

When my two elder Sisters, Sibella and Hannah, went with Mr. Nuccoll to Scotland, a seperation had recently taken place or was on the point of taking place in his family which under the direction of a gracious Providence was productive of happy effects to Hannah at least, and as I believe to both the girls. My Grandmother, as I have already mentioned, ceased about that time to reside with her daughter and son-in-law in the South of Scotland and went with her younger daughter, now my Aunt Calder, to live at

Peterhead, near which she was born and in the neighbourhood of which her Mother and almost all her surviving
relations had always been settled. The most influential tho'
secret reason of the change was that Mrs. Nuccoll's unhappy
violence and acrimony of temper had at length become
intolerable to the good old woman, tho' her own was of the
mildest and most patient kind.

Annie, as my Aunt Calder was called, was the object of
incessant persecution, and the treatment she met with
became daily worse and worse, for no other reason, strange
tho' it may seem, than that she was a handsome pleasing
young woman, much admired by more than one gentleman
who paid their addresses to her, and at the same time a great
favorite with Mr. Nuccoll. Till near that period and still in
every lucid interval of temper Mrs. N., who was old enough
to be Annie's Mother, had treated her with maternal kindness and with great generosity, had taken her to Edinburgh
for the sake of giving her there under good Masters a better
or more ornamental education than she had before received,
engaging Mr. N. to be at the whole expence of it, and was
profuse in presents to her of dress, &c., as if it had been her
main object in life to add to her Sister's natural attractions
and to promote her satisfaction and happiness, and it was at
her earnest request that both her Sister and Mother had
taken up their abode in her family. Fits of ill temper indeed
they always had occasionally to endure from her; but her
conduct was substantially kind, until that case arose which
tho' Mrs. N. herself had probably long wished for in this
instance, she never could patiently endure, the trying
spectacle of a young woman the object of admiration and
courtship, and likely to become the wife of a man she loved.
My poor Father used to account for this, and for her ill
temper in general, from her not having herself had any offer
of marriage till a period of life at which celibacy appeared
to be her destined state, and from their Father having used
her to habits of governing the family imperiously in her early
life. She had, however, and would sometimes confess it, a
dislike to her own sex in general, tho' it seems not to have
acted against them till they arrived at a marriageable age.
The most intolerable part of her conduct in her Sister's case

was her treatment of the gentlemen who with her own approbation were allowed to visit her as suitors. One of these, a
relation and heir to a considerable estate, was favoured by
Mrs. N. up to a certain point; but when she thought there
was danger of his succeeding she took part against him, and
Annie, who had no great predilection for him because he was
rather below par in point of understanding, was easily induced to refuse him. But before he desisted Mr. Calder came
forward and met from Mrs. N. every encouragement he
could desire. He was then, as he has ever been, a man of
extraordinary merit and good sense, and much esteemed by
all who knew him. He had just established a commercial
house in Aberdeen, in connection with his Uncle, an eminent
Merchant at Oporto, and with the support of the House of
Thinloch and Hogg in London, whose important business
he had long superintended as their principal clerk. His
prospects therefore were good; but prudential considerations
made it right that he should not marry for a year or two, as
he frankly explained to Mr. and Mrs. N. when he first asked
their consent to his paying his addresses to their Sister. They
were greatly pleased with him and so in due time was the
object of his attachment; and my Grandmother, a sensible
old woman, was so pleased with his character and manners
that she rejoiced at the prospect of such a settlement for her
unmarried daughter. In short he was accepted as the future
husband of my Aunt to the satisfaction of all the family. But
no sooner were mutual engagements made than this extraordinary woman completely reversed her conduct, treating
him with not only sullen reserve and repulsive coldness, but
actual incivility, railing at him before her Sister and Mother
in the bitterest way, without the shadow of a provocation or
rational cause, and urging her Sister to refuse him and accept
in his stead the Suitor rejected before. Mr. N. for some time
opposed himself to this perverseness; but she soon found
means to bring him over to her side. He was not only a kind
and worthy man, but one of a good understanding, and yet
such was the ascendancy that my Aunt had acquired over
him by her affectionate conduct as a Wife, by the superiority
of her masculine intellect, and by her pertinacity in every
purpose, that her will, soon or late, always gave the law to

his. Even her bad and violent temper aided her influence, tho' he was rarely if ever himself the direct object of it. He was a lover of peace, and knew by painful experience that it was in vain to oppose the storm, the noise and discomfort of which must be his, tho' it blew in another direction. When she quarrelled with her friends or his own, he was sure that until he entered into the quarrel and adopted her opinions, his opposition would only inflame her violence against them and subject himself, not indeed to any thing offensive to his own feelings, in her terms or manner, but to arguments without end. Nor did she fail after some time to make sincere converts of his judgment and feelings; for great were her powers of ingenious perversion, and exaggeration, and dextrous suggestion, when she had good-natured prepossessions to overcome in his mind, and to change his regard and esteem for any person she had quarrelled with, into ill opinion and dislike. It is not without hesitation that I record these characteristics of a woman whose kindness towards myself and my brothers was uniformly great, and who after all was a great Benefactress to our family; but I will do justice to her good qualities too; and without explaining the strange peculiarities of her character I do not know how to make several incidents that I shall soon have to relate intelligible, or to avoid giving them an air injurious to others.

My Grandmother, on the seperation of her family from Mrs. Nuccoll's, insisted upon taking my Sister Hannah to live with her at Peterhead, which Mrs. N. with some difficulty I think agreed to; and Sibella was left with herself at Alloa, where she then resided. The arrangement was productive of happy consequences in the sequel not only to Hannah but to my youngest Sister, and in my judgment ultimately to Sibella also; and therefore it forms one link in the long chain of providential appointments by which my dear Mother's prayers for her children were answered; but this will be best explained in a future part of my narrative.

Hannah, who was a pretty and engaging child, soon deeply engaged the affections both of her Grandmother and Aunt, so that when my Brother and I went to Peterhead we had the satisfaction to find that dear fellow orphan as happy as we could wish. We ourselves also were received with true maternal happiness, and we found at and near Peterhead many other relations who kindly welcomed us to their houses and contributed to make our occasional visits there agreeable. They were in general remote; but the Scotch laudably and amiably extend their regard to consanguinity much beyond the English. Such at least was remarkably the case at that period in the North of Scotland.

That I may not have to recur to the history of family affairs at Peterhead I will mention here that Mr. and Mrs. Nuccoll in the summer of 1776 came to visit my Grandmother whose health was declining, and she soon after died in a lingering disease. While they were with her, poor Mrs. Nuccoll indulged her bitterness of temper against her Sister to such excess as to widen still more the breach between them; and she treated Mr. Calder who still visited there as an accepted lover, so very ill that he could not avoid becoming a Party to the quarrel. On my Grandmother's death, therefore, it was impossible for my Aunt Annie to find an Asylum in Mr. Nuccoll's family; and it was resolved that she should still keep house at Peterhead till Mr. Calder's more established success in business should enable him to marry. My Uncle William, as was expected, continued to her the allowance he had made for her and her Mother's support. But on this new plan a violent controversy arose between the two Sisters as to which of them should have the charge of my Sister Hannah. Mrs. Nuccoll was bent on taking her away to live with herself at Alloa together with my Sister Sibella. Mrs. Calder, on the contrary, then having to live as a single woman alone, remonstrated against the cruelty of depriving her of an adopted child to whom she was strongly attached. My Brother and I were appealed to, and all our wishes were with the latter, as we well knew it was from her our Sister would receive the kindest treatment. But we could do little in the matter except representing the circumstances to our Father. He, however, knew as well as we did poor Mrs. Nuccoll's temper; and therefore on the question being referred to him, he decided it in favour of his younger Sister; and Mrs. Nuccoll acquiesced only when she found it was necessary to do so.

The decision was a happy one for Hannah, whose feelings,

young tho' she was, had declared strongly for her Aunt Annie, and had formed a weight in that scale with us all. It fixed her more strongly in that kind friend's maternal affections; and Mr. Calder became equally attached to her; so that when they afterwards married she found in them both all the feelings of the fondest natural Parents and had a happy asylum in their family till I was able about twelve years after to remove her to my own. A kind Providence also prepared by the same incidents a resource that was wanted about two years after and might not otherwise have been so easily found, for my Sister Betsy and brother John, both of whom on my Father's death were taken by Mr. and Mrs. Nuccoll. I have reason from the circumstances to believe that if both the elder girls had been with them such an addition to their family would have been thought too much; for it was nothing but the necessity of the case and the absolute want of any other Asylum for those little orphans that induced Mr. and Mrs. Nuccoll kindly to submit to the inconvenience of such a charge. On how many coincident and predisposing causes, some of them apparently of an adverse tendency and others seemingly irrelevant, have those events depended, which when produced, we see to have been the work of a beneficent Providence!! But the truth of this remark will be much more forcibly illustrated in the subsequent incidents of the lives of my dear Mother's children if I live to record them.

The recreations which occasional visits to Peterhead afforded were not the only ones to which my Brother and I were indebted to our kind relatives at that place. Mr. Calder from his attachment to them often invited us to his rooms where we spent many a cheerful evening; and some other family connections also were kind to us in the same way, so that few weeks passed over in which our Evening studies in our room were not once or oftener suspended by some cheerful party. These were great, and I believe necessary, alleviations of my bodily sufferings as well as aids to my spirits, the former, from a cause the important action of which on my frame I had not yet discovered, viz., the addition of some wine or punch to the water or wretched small beer with which alone my meals were diluted at home.

My stomachic and bowel complaints nevertheless on the whole gained ground upon me and by their effects greatly impaired my powers of application to College business as well as private study. Daily was I obliged to lay by my pen or book and to throw myself for an hour or more on my knees, pressing my stomach against a chair, or to go to bed for relief. I found it also indispensably necessary to sacrifice an hour or two each day to exercise; for this, among the remedies prescribed for me, was the only one from which I found sensible relief. The more I walked the less in general were my sufferings for the next 24 hours. I therefore was forced to take long solitary walks in those intervals between the lectures in which others were making up their notes or reading on the subjects of them in Helsham and other Guides.   To this chiefly it was owing that tho' I kept my credit in the Natural Philosophy class under Professor Coupland to the last, I felt myself first embarrassed, and soon after quite thrown out, in the Mathematical Class under Dr. Trail. For some time when I had missed a lecture or two I was able to retrieve it by reading at home, and he kindly invited me to come to him in private for assistance in such cases.   He was in fact particularly desirous to carry me forward with the comparatively few students who went on with him beyond Euclid's Elements and the first branches of the Science, for he found me in the beginning far beyond the generality of the lads he had to do with in quick and correct apprehension.   Perhaps I may truly say beyond any one in his first Class, except a man between 20 and 30 of the name of Casey, who had made considerable advances in Mathematics before he came to College, and James Hunter, a youth nearer my own age, of extraordinary talents, whose Father, a clergyman, had taken great pains with him and who eclipsed all his contemporaries in every year of his course. He afterwards went to the East Indies as a Physician and was very eminent there, not only in his profession, but as a general Scholar. Even to these I was scarcely, if at all, inferior in the business of the Class while able regularly to attend it, and obtained at least as much praise from the Professor when called up in our turns to demonstrate the Propositions we were learning. I was particularly fond of the Mathematics as far as I advanced in

them, which was not beyond the three or four first Books of
Euclid's Elements, and am persuaded there is no science
which I could have mastered more easily. I was charmed
with the clearness and certainty of the knowledge it conveyed
and the new kind of exercise which it gave to my reasoning
powers, nor was my vanity uninterested in finding that I
could get forward with ease, when the generality of my fellow
students were at a dead stand, from inability to comprehend
at all the subjects of our lectures. But at length from frequent
non-attendance I lost the clue, and was unable to regain it,
having no private Tutor, and being ashamed to call on the
Professor and give him all the trouble that would have been
necessary for my assistance. Long before the end of the first
year I ceased to attend at all, and did not begin the second
year's course.

In my second year I attended the Moral Philosophy Class,
as it is called, under the celebrated Dr. Beattie; and here I
certainly derived from his Lectures much that has been
useful to me in active life. I had before acquired the knack
of composition, and perhaps imbibed some taste in it, as well
as some copiousness of language, from my extensive English
reading; but I knew little or nothing of critical rules, and
therefore must very often have offended against them. To
logic, and all the other branches of rhetorical science, I was
equally a Stranger. But on all these subjects Beattie was an
excellent Guide. He had great natural taste and judgment,
as his writings sufficiently prove, and he was perhaps the
fitter for his province because his own knowledge of the
English tongue in respect of purity and elegance had been
laboriously acquired by study and reflection, rather than
by limitation and habit. Born and educated in Scotland, at a
time when the intercourse between the literary people of that
Country and this was far less frequent than it has since
become, and ambitious of excelling in English composition,
he had assiduously studied our idiom and the stile of our
best writers, and extracted from them various rules for his
own use, by indefatigable attention to which he had corrected
all his vernacular errors in pronunciation as well as grammar,
and had learnt both to write and speak so much like a well-
educated Englishman, that I do not recollect once detecting

7*

him in a Scotticism, except once or twice in the distinctions between the auxiliary verbs *shall* and *will*, the use of which he himself observed was a nicety in our idiom that no Scotchman could perfectly attain. These rules he anxiously explained to his pupils, to whom they were of great importance, and was careful to make the stile of his Lectures exemplary of the correctness and purity the rules of which he taught. Though I had few or no Scotticisms to unlearn, it was probably no small advantage to me to have my attention thus directed to the careful avoidance of grammatical improprieties and the importance of cultivating correctness and elegance of stile both in writing and conversation. In metaphysics, or rather the theory of the human mind and its faculties, he led us far enough to give us a general view of what belongs to the science, and to excite in me a curiosity and interest which I have not yet lost in regard to it. If the necessary employments of an active life had left me more leisure for studies of a voluntary kind, there is no subject of human knowledge to which I should have allotted a larger share of it. Busy though I have been, I have not wholly neglected metaphysical writings; and let me mention here lest I should afterwards forget it, that Dr. Reid's[1] *Essays on the Human Mind* have of late years been my favorite guides on such subjects, and seem to me to deserve even more celebrity than they have attained. There are few if any works of that kind by which the understanding is more enlightened and the reasoning powers more happily exercised, and none I believe more unexceptionable in point of moral and religious principle. I can satisfactorily recommend it to my children, and *their* children, as a Book well fitted to improve their intellectual faculties, without danger to their hearts. Dr. Beattie had a highly prepossessing countenance. Its expression was full of intelligence and benignity, with a mixture of tender gravity or melancholly, the effect perhaps

---

[1] Thomas Reid (1710–1796), philosopher; became librarian of Marischal College, Aberdeen, in 1733 and professor of philosophy at Marischal College, 1751; published his *Inquiry into the Human Mind*, 1764, as an answer to Hume and was in 1764 appointed professor of moral philosophy at Glasgow; later published his essay on the "Intellectual Powers," 1785, and one on the "Active Powers," 1788; the leading representative in the eighteenth century of the "common sense" school of philosophy.

of his bad health. Sir Joshua Reynolds said that if he had to draw the face of our Saviour he would wish Dr. Beattie to sit for it. His Essay on the Immutability of truth in reply to Hume, had procured for him much credit in England, and he had been very well received at Court and in the higher circles of Society, in London as well as at our Universities. But this had excited the envy of his brother Professors and other literary characters in Scotland, as I could perceive from the sneers and depreciating remarks which they did not scruple to indulge themselves in even before us young men his Pupils. He had a son, who at this time was a sickly boy about twelve years old, but a wonder for precocious faculties and learning. The Father had taken great pains with him and was supposed to have pressed forward his education at the expence of his health. He lived to be an eminent man, and if I remember right to be one of the Professors of Marischal's College, Aberdeen, but died at an early period of life, and I fear the old Doctor had the pain to survive him.

The College Session of 1776-7 having terminated, the plan proposed for me at Aberdeen was accomplished, and I had to return to London to commence my professional studies. But I had to encounter, not for the first time, difficulties and mortifications from my poor Father's poverty, and inability to send me the remittance I wrote for, to pay my boarding house bill, &c., and the expence of my return. I had been frugal enough. The whole charge of my support and education at Aberdeen did not exceed perhaps £45 per Ann. or £50 at most; but this was more than he could easily and promptly supply. I was therefore detained some time by the want of money to clear my way. Meantime Mr. Nuccoll having business at Aberdeen, kindly brought my Sister Sibella with him to see Hannah and her brother William and other friends in that quarter, and with a kind invitation to me to accompany them on their return to Alloa, and take my passage to London from the Forth, after spending the remainder of the Summer with my Aunt and him. I cannot recollect whether his help was wanted to remove my pecuniary difficulties, or whether a remittance from my Father arrived in time; but I availed myself of his offer, and after a parting visit to my Sister Hannah and Aunt at

Peterhead, set off with him and Sibella for the South. I think at least the latter was of the party but am not sure whether she came with Mr. N. or whether my memory is not confounding with this journey one that I made with them at a later period. The seperation from my Sister Hannah and still more that from my Brother cost me many tears. The latter was become dearer to me than ever. His affectionate attentions and simpathy had formed my chief support during all my anxieties and all my bodily sufferings; and such was the sweetness of his temper that growing attachment to him was always the effect of closer intercourse. To bid him adieu for years was like seperation from a part of my own soul; and tho' Aberdeen had been but a cheerless residence to me, I left it in great depression of spirits, which my Uncle's kindness, and the various new objects we had to see in our journey, and the fine summer weather, could but slowly and imperfectly remove.

I sit down to spend half an hour in continuing this narrative on my 64th Birthday. How wonderful had been the conservatory care of a gracious Providence in preserving me to this advanced period of life, sickly tho' I was at the period to which my narrative has arrived (now above 45 years ago) and manifold though the diseases and perils from without to which I have been since exposed! I am brought to this age also with a portion of bodily strength hardly inferior to what I possessed in the prime of life, and blessed be God with an exemption hitherto perfect from all those painful maladies by which old men are so commonly annoyed, and with my faculties bodily and mental little impaired, my memory excepted. When I add to these, the many external comforts I enjoy, six dear children, two dear sons-in-law and four dear daughters-in-law, all dutiful and affectionate, and all I trust walking in the paths of piety and virtue as well as prudence, five little grandchildren to interest me in a new generation, kind and good fraternal connections, the warmest friendship and unbounded confidence of my dear Wilberforce, the review fills me with wonder as well as gratitude, and I trust I can truly add with deep humility. I feel my utter unworthiness of the least of all these mercies. Infinitely kind and gracious Benefactor, how much did I long abuse thy goodness! If thy forebearance and forgiveness had not been as great as thy bounty I should have been a monument of misery here, or should long ago have perished in my sins. Help me not only to adore and love these endearing attributes of thine, but to the best of my feeble power to imitate them in my heart and conduct towards my fellow creatures!!

Among all the blessings I enjoy the first is my knowledge, my *certain* knowledge from long experience, that "verily & indeed there is a God who governs the world" and intimately directs all the concerns of his rational and immortal creatures, that he wills my happiness, and that the course of his Providence towards me has all along been chiefly directed to the improvement of my moral state, with a view I doubt not to the preparing me for, and bestowing upon me, after this life, those joys which eye has not seen nor ear heard, neither has it entered into the heart of man to conceive. But then—awful thought! I may defeat these beneficent aims. Yes—my will is free. Heavenly Father, help me to fall in with thy gracious purposes. May thy love constrain me to give to thee my whole heart, and to present myself henceforth a willing living sacrifice to thee. May it be my daily meat and drink, my joy and comfort, to do thy holy will and "to have respect to all thy commandments." I have been looking anew today at one of the many good books which my dear Sally put into my hands, *Flavel*[1] *on Providence*, and was much impressed with the following passage in his Preface: "O what a history might we compile of our own experiences, whilst with a melting heart we trace the footsteps of Providence all along the way it has led us to this day; and make our remarks upon its more eminent performances for us in the several stages of our life. Here it prevented, and there it delivered, and there it corrected.

---

[1] John Flavel (1630?-1691), Presbyterian divine who preached at Dartmouth; author of numerous widely read works marked by strong evangelical sentiments. There are at least six editions of his collected works, the latest in six volumes in 1797. Stephen refers to one of the most popular of Flavel's works, *Divine Conduct: or the Mysterie of Providence: Wherein the Being and Efficacy of Providence is Asserted and Vindicated*, etc. (1678), of which the British Museum has two editions of the 17th century, five editions in the 18th century, and four editions in the 19th century, the latest of date 1837, and an abridgment of date 1814.

There was the poison, and there was the antidote. This Providence raised a dismal cloud and that dispelled it again. Here a want, and there a supply; this relation withered, and that springing up in its room. Words cannot express the high delights and gratifications a pious heart may find in such reviews as these."

My constitution has always been affected in a much more than ordinary degree by local influences and changes of air. The effects on my health and spirits of a removal from Aberdeen to a dry inland atmosphere were immediate and wonderful. I seemed to have left all my maladies behind me in the first day's journey southward. We slept at Cupar of Angus[1] and I remember to this hour the delight with which I felt our rising early the next morning to pursue our journey, the return of genial and comfortable feelings to which since I left England eighteen or twenty months before I had been a stranger. My animal sensations were so kindly and my spirits so light and gay that the seperation from my dear Brother had no longer a depressing power; and I went forward in that frame of mind which (blessed be God) has always been most natural to me, a state in which our day dreams are all of a cheerful kind. The pleasures of hope and imagination have been mine through life in a preeminent degree except when bodily disease or recent wounds of the heart have given them a short-lived interruption.

Nothing could exceed the kindness of the reception which I met with from my Aunt Nuccoll at Alloa. She insisted on detaining me there till the Autumn, in order to nurse me and restore me in better health to my Father, for tho' my diseases had in fact been left at Aberdeen, their effect on my appearance was still alarming. I was pale and emaciated, and tho' all pulmonary complaints had long subsided she still feared that I was in danger of a relapse into consumption. The then popular resource in such cases was drinking goat whey in highland situations; and Blair Logie about five miles from Alloa was a favorite resort for the purpose. She insisted therefore on my riding every morning to that place to drink goat whey, which I did for several weeks with

---

[1] A town on the border of Angus and Perth, so called to distinguish it from Cupar in Fife.

much apparent benefit, gradually increasing in flesh or rather becoming less of a skeleton than at my arrival. The true causes, however, were, as I believe, the more genial atmosphere which I breathed and the more generous regimen of my Uncle's table than that of the Aberdeen boarding house. A glass or two of wine or punch after dinner now aided my weak digestion, and those spasmodic affections in the stomach and bowels by which I had been so long annoyed were much abated in violence and returned at far more distant intervals.

In addition to my Aunt's and Uncle's kindness I had the society of my dear Sister Sibella to cheer me during my long stay at Alloa. She was then a sprightly girl about twelve years old, not having yet arrived at an age to excite the unhappy peculiarities of Mrs. N.'s feeling towards her own sex, was very happily circumstanced, full of spirits, and, as she has ever continued to be, tenderly attached to all her relations. No natural Parents could be fonder or more indulgent than Mr. and Mrs. N. then were to her. The family therefore had nothing in it but what was pleasant to my feelings if I except poor Mrs. N.'s incessant abuse of my kind Aunt in the North, and the very difficult task I had of at once avoiding offence by too decided a defence of the accused and not violating both sincerity and gratitude by express or tacit acquiescence. It would not be easy to give an adequate idea of the force of those angry and vindictive feelings which this otherwise kind and generous woman indulged against her Sister and Mr. Calder. She had much natural eloquence, and it was incessantly employed on the single subject of her quarrel with them. It was her theme of conversation every day, and all her trivial and imaginary subjects of complaint were drawn out in endless detail and aggravated till they appeared to her own disturbed fancy as the most atrocious wrongs and crimes. It was an instructive lesson, by which I ought to have profited, and believe I in some measure did so. It has made me perhaps more watchful against propensities of the same kind than I should have otherwise been. Mr. N., as I could well perceive, disliked these invectives not less than I did; but his easy temper and love of peace obliged him to be silent or not directly to oppose. Indeed, such was the ingenuity of my Aunt and the ascendancy of her masculine understanding over his, that she had brought him far enough into her views to make him think ill of her Sister and sincerely to fall in with her resentments tho' in his own meek and moderate way. It was her violence only that he disapproved. He was a worthy, kind hearted man, and a rational straight-headed man too, but had great deference for my Aunt's judgment; and she ruled him not less by affection, too, for a more obsequiously kind and courteous wife could not well be imagined. If she ever opposed his opinions or his will, it was only to make him take part in her quarrels with her female relations and friends, and that favorite point soon or late she was sure to gain, as my poor Sisters, tho' objects of his warm affection, afterwards painfully found.

During my stay at Alloa Mr. Nuccoll and I made excursion to Glasgow and other places, and he introduced me to relations and family friends in the South of Scotland, by all of whom I was kindly received. I was much pleased with my Aunt Stephen, the wife of my Uncle Alexander, my Father's eldest Brother. She was a very amiable woman, well bred, and of pleasing manners, but I fear not fortunate in her marriage with my Uncle. They were childless, and he lived much from home, being sought after as a man of companionable qualities and superior understanding, while she spent much of her time with her relations, the Bruces of Pitfools and Clarkmannon. One of these, her Aunt as I recollect, was a venerable, interesting old Lady, the Mistress of Clarkmannon Castle, an antient structure near Alloa which I visited more than once. She was lineally descended, as the family held, from King Robert Bruce, whose sword of State and other remains of his regalia were still preserved in the Castle, and the old Lady humourously affected still to possess some of his royal rights, among them that of conferring the honor of Knighthood, which I received from her in due form. My courage was afterwards put to the proof, tho' not by mortal foe; for the Castle was reputed to be haunted, a report which its antique and romantic appearance lent some countenance to; and I had not at that time conquered the fear of ghosts. I did not lodge there indeed, but in a late evening return through the avenues of old stately trees in the neighbouring Park was in some dread of rencontring the far-famed spectres. Among the stories of their appearance my Uncle Stephen, a man of very grave and sturdy character, was the Author of one that gained on his authority general credit, and which I dare say he himself believed. Lodging there one night in his way from Glasgow to Edinburgh, he was put in the room which was the reputed chamber of the Ghost and in which there was a blazing fire. He went to bed, having previously locked the door; but before he fell asleep a gleam of light or rustling noise, I forget which, induced him to draw the curtain back, when he perceived before him a figure like a woman in her chemise. He thought it was a servant and sprang from the bed; but she was gone. He searched the room but could find no trace of her nor any entrance or outlet by which she could have entered or retreated and found the door still locked. He lay down again willing to believe it an illusion. But soon after the vision was repeated. He again sprang from the bed with the same result. He hesitated about alarming the family, but was ashamed; for he had sat up after all the servants and must have disturbed all the Ladies in their sleep. He therefore lay down drawing the curtains close and hauled the sheet over his face, resolving to see no more. Of course it was imagination or a trick, for there was here no conceivable end in any such visit from a ghost. But I did not think so with any assurance at that time, and the character of the narrator, much more sceptical I fear than superstitious, gave more credence to his account than such tales usually claim.

After spending two Months not unpleasantly in the South of Scotland, I took leave of my kind friends at Alloa, parting with my dear Sister with many tears on both sides, but promising to see them again before I went to the West Indies, and embarked on the Firth of Forth for London, where I arrived after a week's passage, not without severe sufferings from sea sickness and other discomforts of the sea.

Chapter Six

[1777–1779]

MANY of course were the painful recollections that accompanied me in my walk to Stoke Newington; nor were my anticipations of the most pleasing kind, except that I was again to see the two dear little fellow orphans I had left there, for as to my poor Father, we had never been on those terms of ease and familiarity together that promised much pleasure on either side in our re-domestication together, which I supposed would now for some years take place. But the home, and the state of things I found in it, were below my expectations, and beyond my fears. Instead of the genteel and pleasant residence I had left in that Village two years before, I found that the family had removed to a cottage on the Common little better than a labourer's or rather a petty Farmer's house, except that it was surrounded by a garden, and with a brook in front dividing it from the road; and there I found my Sister Betsy and Brother John as far in their appearance and manners almost from the children of gentlemen, as the House from a gentleman's abode. They were allowed to run at large on the Common and to play with the children whom they found there, as well as to talk with the servants; and indeed during almost the whole of every day but Sunday, they could have no other Society, my Father going daily to Town and generally dining there. The servant, Catharine White, who had come into the family in Dorsetshire when a girl, and lived with my dear Mother till her death, still continued to be the chief, or rather I think the only, female domestic, and tho' very kind to the children, was of course ill qualified to perform the functions of a Mother or governess in forming their manners or their minds. They had in consequence become vulgar even to a ludicrous degree. I still remind my Sister Elizabeth, now Mrs. Milner, that she was an adept at riding pigs on the Common, and John, that in taking a walk with me he proposed to me to go into an alehouse to drink a pint of porter adding in the true carman's stile, that "he *would be a* penny, if I would *be the* other." Tho' the former was only between 8 and 9 years old, and the latter just turned of 6, my fraternal feelings were naturally alarmed, and I felt new gratitude to that gracious Providence which had rescued my elder Sisters from the same lot by placing them with their Aunts in Scotland. My poor Father's neglect did not proceed from want of affection. He was evidently fond of the poor children to excess, and had indulged John in particular so much that the boy took with him whatever saucy liberties he pleased; but his parental affection, as usual with him, was very improvident; and indeed such were his necessities and embarrassments that he would not have found it easy to take the best course for the children, that of placing them at proper schools. The fashion of Preparatory Schools for children of their ages had not then got up; and day schools were ill fitted to their cause; but at one of these, then called an "Old Woman's School" they had, I think, been for some time placed.

My poor Father himself had declined in manners and appearance not less than his children. I was shocked to find in him instead of his former strength, visible marks of bad health and a breaking constitution. His habits also were much deteriorated. He had taken to smoaking tobacco and carried it to great excess. His use of porter and spirituous liquors had increased, and his appetite was worse than ever, bad tho' it had at all times been. His intellectual powers were also plainly in their wane, and I soon found there was a proportionate falling off in the stile of society that he frequented and the kinds of business in which he was consulted and employed. There was one client, Captn. Davie, formerly of the East India Company's Service, who was become his inseperable companion, living in his house and accompanying him daily in his walks to and from Town. Captn. D. had been oppressed by Govr. Verelst[1] and the Council of Bengal. Having been led with very many other officers to quit the

---

[1] Harry Verelst (d. 1785) was governor of Bengal 1767–1769 carrying out Clive's policy. He returned to England in 1770 and was ruined by litigation raised by the people whom he had opposed in Bengal. He published a narrative in justification of his administration, *English Government in Bengal* (1772).

service in disgust on account of a general reduction of their pay or emoluments, he had settled at Oude, on the invitation of the Nabob of that Province, who gave to him and Captn. Nicholl, his Friend, great commercial privileges with a view to make their fortunes. Nicholl had at a former period commanded a detachment of the Company's Troops stationed at Oude, ostensibly a guard of honor to the Nabob, but in reality his Keepers; and instead of extorting money from him by an abuse of that delicate trust like some Predecessors in it, had treated him with disinterested liberality and perfect respect. The Nabob from a grateful sense of this had said to him when removed from that station, "If ever you quit the Company's Army and will come settle here I will provide for and enrich you." Accordingly he gave to Captn. Nicholl and his friend Davie a *Dustuck* or licence to trade free of duties throughout his dominions, in which the duties on merchandize were exceedingly high, I think on an average near 50 Pr. Ct. With true Asiatic principles he said to them at the same time, "Gentlemen I hope you will know how to turn this privilege to the best account," alluding to proposals which were immediately made to them by Armenian and other Merchants to give them large sums or participations of profit for liberty to trade in their names. Profiting by this hint they were in the way of soon fulfilling their Princely Patron's design by acquiring great fortunes, when Governor Verelst and the Council of Calcutta, jealous of their favour with the Nabob, or vindictive for their resignation, sent orders to the Commander of the Company's forces at Oude to seize them and send them Prisoners to Fort William. This was accordingly done, and with circumstances as I recollect of needless severity to them, as well as disrespect to the Nabob. Arrived at Calcutta, they were sent compulsorily on board one of the Company's Ships to England without trial or the imputation of a crime except that of their residing and trading within the limits of the Company's Charter without permission of the Company to do so. Captn. Nicholl brought his action for this against Verelst and others of the Council on their return to England, and Davie had taken the same course originally; but the actions were pertinaciously defended, and as was understood at the Company's expence, their right to send all British subjects from India without any investigation of the political grounds for it being in effect the question to be tried. Bills of Injunction were filed, Commissions to take evidence sent to India, and the whole game of litigation so obstinately played that poor Nicholl could not bring his suit to a final decision for many years. The question was at last decided against him; he was compleatly ruined but compassionately allowed to go again to India and resume his military rank there. Captn. Davie, when wearied with the tedious litigation, applied to my Father for advice and on his opinion indicted Verelst and the rest for false imprisonment, relying that in case of conviction they would be disposed to make him proper compensation, to avoid the judgment of the Court. I do not distinctly recollect what were the real or supposed advantages of this form of proceeding in exchange for the action (which he was of course obliged in consequence to discontinue) but believe it was expected to cut off the delay of the Commission to India under a presumption that the Court of Kings Bench must proceed to the trial of an Indictment without waiting for evidence from that Country and that the Court of Chancery would have no jurisdiction to stop the proceedings by Injunction or grant a Commission to take evidence as it had done in the civil suits. The Act impowering the Court of Kings Bench to issue such Commission in suits or prosecuttions for acts done in India had not then I think been made, or else being subsequent to the transactions in question was not supposed to extend to the case. Nevertheless the Indictment being found, the Defendants applied to that Court; but whether under the Act, or by way of putting off the trial in order to compel the Prosecutor to consent to a Commission I do not recollect. They made affidavits, however, stating certain facts in their defence and that they were advised and believed they could not safely proceed to trial without evidence to be obtained from India. Hereupon my Father (the Court having given effect to the application) recommended an Indictment for Perjury, and the Grand Jury found the Bill. The proceeding was certainly violent enough. But it produced the desired effect; for tho' the Defendants were acquitted on this Indictment, they were previously advised to consent by their Counsel to meet the Indictment for false imprisonment on the evidence to be obtained in this Country. I cannot recollect or did not learn in what view that advice was given. But if I remember right both Indictments came on for trial the same day, and an acquittal of the Perjury was consented to by Captn. Davie's Counsel. Probably, therefore, it was to take off from the minds of the Jury the impression that the unfortunate Prosecutor would be cut off from the hope of redress by the effect of the affidavit if a conviction did not follow, and to take credit for some liberality and compassion. There was another circumstance which probably led to it. One of the Defendants, Sir Robert Barker, had not joined in the application for delay, or in the affidavit; but had made his peace with the prosecutor and submitted to a conviction for the false imprisonment upon an engagement that he should not be brought up for judgment unless the other Defendants should be convicted. Upon these terms, into which I believe he was led by compassion, he advanced considerable sums to poor Davie, amounting altogether I think to £1200, to enable him to carry on the proceedings against the rest, and support himself during the tedious litigation, Davie agreeing to give credit for it out of any compensation, or the share of any fine, that he might recover from the Defendants collectively. On the trial of the Indictment for false imprisonment the Defendants were all convicted. This was no impeachment of the decision in Nicholl's case, which is somewhere reported. Indeed if I remember right the latter had not then been brought to trial. There was this material distinction between them: that Davie had originally gone to India as a free Merchant, he having been bred to the Sea service, and tho' he afterwards entered into the Army, his Licence which had never been revoked was held to have made his removal from India illegal. The Court however regarded the political considerations on which the Governor and Council acted as having much extenuated their conduct, and therefore tho' they recommended a compensation to the Prosecutor as the alternative to a serious fine, they afterwards on Davie's refusing £2000 (which was not equal to a fifth part of his expectations and actual losses) intimated an opinion that this was enough.

The poor Man in consequence tho' victorious in the contest was compleatly ruined. He had only a balance of about £800 to receive; and his debts contracted during many years of litigation largely exceeded that amount, so that he was obliged immediately after to abscond and go to the Continent for fear of an arrest.

I have been the more particular in stating these facts not only because the sequel as it affected the unfortunate man himself was interesting, and of a Providential character, as will be hereafter seen, but because they have an important connection with my family narrative.

Captn. Davie, as I have mentioned, was become an inmate of my Father's house. He was greatly attached to him, and I lament to say their constant association was not friendly to poor D's habits, for a daily resort to Taverns, Coffee Houses and Eating Houses where my Father's business was transacted in Town led him into frequent intemperance. What to my Father's strong constitution might not amount to excess, or at least not to intoxication, became inebriety in his companion, who had also contracted the habit of smoaking tobacco, and having no employment for his mind felt the effects of such a course of life the more injuriously. I regretted it the more because he was a kind hearted generous fellow and much attached to the children and to myself.

Under such family circumstances, I was not sorry to find that my Father's plans for me were such as would make me rather an occasional guest than a resident in his cottage. He proposed that I should have lodgings in Town, for the convenience not only of better assisting him in his business, and thereby learning something of the practice of the law, but also attending the Courts for my professional improvement. Accordingly some rooms were taken for me in a Court behind the Royal Exchange as the part of the town where his business principally lay, and not far from the house of Mr. Fletcher, the Attorney in whose name he conducted whatever suits he was employed in, and who engaged to open to me all the means of instruction that were to be found in his office. These means were neither very copious nor very respectable. Fletcher had little business beyond what he did for my

Father, and what they had between them was not of the best kind in general; for their clients were in general men in embarrassed circumstances, whom they had to extricate from their difficulties by negotiations and compromises with their creditors, and sometimes, I lament to say, by such dilatory expedients as the law affords when men are sued for their debts and have no present means of payment. Yet I obtained in acting as my Father's clerk in Fletcher's name and under his directions some knowledge of the business of an Attorney and Solicitor which was afterwards of essential use to me in the West Indies, where I had to practice in all the branches of the legal profession, and some specific practical notions for the want of which many a man, I believe, has been perplexed at his outset at the Bar and ultimately failed of success. In this instance, as in many others, I can look back with surprise and thankfulness on the means which a kind Providence employed to prepare for me the success in life that I have obtained notwithstanding my great disadvantages, supplying the defects of my education, and removing the exterior difficulties in my path, just to the degree which I can see to have been absolutely necessary, and no further. From my Father's rapidly increasing infirmities both of body and mind, the charge of all his business soon devolved on me. It was a little all. But it was miscellaneous, comprising conveyancing and Sessions business, as well as occasional practice in all the Courts of Westminster. I acquired, therefore, a smattering of everything, just what I afterwards wanted in the Colonial Field, and what I learnt was fixed in my memory by the peculiar and impressive means of its acquisition. Fletcher was a well-taught skilful practitioner, and for his own case was very willing to put me in the way of learning how to do whatever was wanted, referring me to the proper practical guides and supplying me with precedents, &c. Nor was I slow to learn. At the same time I read some of the elementary writers on both the civil and English law, but in a very cursory and idle way, and by no means in this respect made an industrious use of my time.

While I was thus employed my hours of relaxation, which were too numerous and generally comprised every evening after eight o'clock, were not unpleasantly spent. I had many acquaintances of my own age, chiefly young men whom I had known in the mercantile profession, or in physic, or in their way to the East and West Indies; and with some of these I often spent my evenings either at each other's rooms or at chop houses and other houses of public resort where we supped in an œconomical way. I was a particular favorite among them, for I had good spirits and cordiality and better powers of conversation perhaps than my Scotch Friends in general possessed. Among them were two sensible and pleasant men MacLeod, now Rector of Soho, and my late departed friend Dr. Lindsay. The present Dr. Livingstone of Aberdeen was also of the number, a very vivacious good-tempered young man at that time, but wild and imprudent in his conduct. He had suddenly disappeared from Edinburgh where he was studying Physic; and his Parents were greatly distressed, not knowing what had become of him, and fearing some fatal accident or a fit of insanity, to which some of his family had been subject. As it was suspected that he had gone towards London, Dr. Livingstone, the Father, wrote to me intreating me to get some account of him if possible, and by an accident I was happily enabled to do so by return of post. He had secreted himself from every Friend in the Metropolis, but an acquaintance of mine who knew his person had said to me a day or two before, "I could almost swear I saw William Livingstone to-day," which I had told him was impossible. I now went in quest of my informant and was enabled by circumstances to trace the fugitive to a lodging in Newgate Street. I burst in upon him, and the first effect was a long fit of laughter on both sides; but my remonstrances soon brought him to regret seriously the pain he had given his Parents, and to write a penitential letter to his Father putting himself at his disposal. He could give me no better reason for his elopement than that he was suddenly seized with a desire to see London which he could not possibly resist, had he been sure that death would be the consequence. I was nevertheless by spending that and part of many following days with him, perfectly convinced that he was quite in a sound mind. The old Doctor wisely made a virtue of necessity and saved his son's credit as much as possible by directing him to stay and walk the Hospitals in London, at the same time expressing so strong a wish that he should be much in society with me that a grateful sense of the kind attentions of the Family to my brother and myself at Aberdeen concurred with my real regard for this volatile young friend to induce me to spend with him many of my Evening hours. He has since become a steady, prudent character and has long been one of the most eminent physicians in the North of Scotland, but what is very singular

Octe. 13. 1822. Dell Cottage Missenden.

A striking coincidence—I was interrupted so suddenly that I had not time to finish the above paragraph. I have since been spending a week in London, and while there received a letter from Aberdeen with a formal intimation of Dr. Livingstone's death, which happened on the 4th. Instt.—perhaps the very day on which the above was written. When writing it I had not heard of his being ill and was about to notice that he was almost the only friend of that period of my life who had not already passed into the unseen world before me. What an awful admonition this!! In like manner perhaps will this narrative of my own life be cut short while my mind is intent on some unfinished and probably trivial incident. If so, there will be no pen to resume it. What the value of these Memoirs may be to those I write for is known only to Him "who sees the end from the beginning," but if there be a rational hope of their utility it behoves me to wander less and to make quicker progress.

I was proceeding to notice that my now departed friend had strangely at different periods of his life, since he became a practising Physician even, and up to the latest accounts I had of him, repeated the eccentric measure I had described, suddenly disappearing from his home, lately the seat of his very extensive practice in Aberdeen, without any known or assignable reason, and coming as has been supposed to England, but hiding himself, so that nobody, since the first instance in which I was his discoverer, has ever been able to find out where he went to. After long absence, generally of many months duration, he has returned without any apparent alteration in his person or manners, but never disclosing to anybody the cause of such mysterious conduct. These extraordinary circumstances, coupled with the known fact of one of his Sisters having been insane, naturally raised and long upheld the report that he was liable to temporary derangements of mind, and concealed himself or was concealed in distant parts of the country, till his recovery, in order to preserve his professional interest. But to this hypothesis (which I know to have been in the first instance at least groundless) insuperable difficulties were progressively opposed, till at length it was given up by all who knew him. These difficulties were, first, that his Wife, after he married, was thrown into the utmost distress by his next flight and took the measures proper to discover his course and his place of retreat with great anxiety, but in vain; and tho' he was a kind husband, and in other respects gave her no cause of complaint, he repeatedly treated her in the same way and on his returns observed towards her an impenetrable secrecy. In the next place he had a confidential manservant, who always went with and returned with him, but from whom all the solicitations and arts that could be tried could ever extort his Master's secret. His wife dying, he married again, and now a new phenomenon occurred. His second wife, finding she could not prevent these periodical freaks, wisely perhaps, gave in to them. She contrived to discover when he was about to set off, and so managed, by what means is unknown, as to accompany and stay with him till his return; and from the time she began this system was as mysterious and impenetrable as himself and his manservant. Her conduct, it must be admitted, is more reconcilable to the notion of his withdrawing to hide insanity than that of the manservant, who would naturally have shrunk from the responsibility of his situation when he found his Master no longer competent to act for himself. But there were other circumstances, the nature of which I forget, that demonstrated progressively to his Friends and Patients that he had during his absence and occultation acted as a free and rational agent; and in one instance, I think, or more, he was casually met with by persons in this country who were able to vouch for his perfect sanity as I was on the first occasion. So it was that the people of Aberdeen and its neighbourhood were at length quite satisfied on that point, and so great was their confidence in him as a Physician that notwithstanding the frequent inconvenience to his Patients from these strangely fugitive habits, he did not lose perceptibly any of his ordinary large share of practice, except during absence, but resumed it always on his return.

I have a surmise and a theory of my own to account for this extraordinary and seemingly anomalous case. I have known more than one person with hereditary predispositions to insanity, strongly addicted to similar changes of place, and am inclined to believe, from circumstances connected with those cases, that the indulgence of the propensity, while indulged, retarded in some of those cases, and has prevented in one of them, the actual attack of the malady. Livingstone, who was a sensible man and good Physician, may have been conscious periodically of an approaching danger of this kind, and may have always prevented it by travelling Southward, and remaining absent till the danger ceased. I know that his Father, a very able Physician, took the Sister from Aberdeen to England for a similar purpose; but she became insane on the journey. If such was my poor friend's motive of course he could not avow it, and his duties in life precluding any other assignable motive of his sudden flights a mysterious silence may have been his only resource.

Alas poor Livingstone! I have not the consolation of believing that his lengthened life had made him, on the Christian standard, more fit to die. He was, I fear, like most Scotch Physicians, a sceptic in religion. Some years ago I sent him a long and serious letter on that most important of all subjects, availing myself of our early friendship, and even of our mutual sins in our youth against each other's spiritual interest, to speak freely, but affectionately, and as I thought quite inoffensively, to him of eternal things. But I never heard from him in return; and he was in England afterwards, as I learned, and even in London, without calling upon me. May God be merciful to him, and to me a Sinner!

If it were not necessary to avoid digressions I could give interesting and amusing and perhaps even instructive accounts of the other characters with whom I at this time

associated. Among them was Alexander Stephens,[1] Son of
the Provost at Elgin and a distant cousin of my Father, tho'
he spelt his name with a final *s* (as indeed my Uncle William
Stephen used latterly to do). This quondam Friend was then
a very handsome fine young man, then recently from Scotland, which he had left contrary to his Father's choice to
become a student of law in London instead of a Merchant in
Elgin. He was a lively romantic fellow, ridiculously conceited
of his own capacity as a Poet, &c., and with an openness
and cordiality of manners that made him on the whole not
only an amusing companion to me, but inclined me pretty
strongly to form with him the ties of friendship. He courted
my company a good deal, and too often made me idle. But
he was licencious, extravagant, irreligious, and as I progressively discovered, not only undutiful to his Parents, but
regardless of probity and justice in his dealings with others,
whenever he could obtain credit to supply the wants in
which his expensive pleasures and vanities involved him. I
was twice the means of saving him from a prison. On one
occasion on my calling at his lodgings in the evening a Bailiff
crossed the Street as I knocked at the door, asked if my name
was not Stephen, and on my answering in the affirmative
arrested me. His employer, who was within sight, ran up and
told him he was wrong, on which he let me go with many
apologies, to which I made replies sufficiently indignant;
but on finding my friend was not at home, I immediately
went in quest of him, with difficulty found him, and prevented his going home to fall into the Bailiff's hands. On
another occasion I have with shame to acknowledge rescuing
him from Prison by a falsehood. He was arrested in my company in Cornhill, and while he was surrendering himself in
speechless consternation, I burst into an affected laugh
saying "*Montague*, this is a good joke" he took the hint and
we both acted the imposture so naturally as fully to deceive

---

[1] Alexander Stephens (1757–1821), biographical and miscellaneous writer,
best known as author of *History of the Wars Which Grew Out of the French Revolution* (2 vols. 4to, 1803) and of *Memoirs of John Horne Tooke* (2 vols. 1813) and as
editor of the first five volumes of *Annual Biography and Obituary*. Both the man
and his books are more respectable than James Stephen would allow. By the
time Stephen wrote these *Memoirs* he had been a Tory politician and the friend
of Wilberforce, and he had little tolerance for libertarian Whigs.

the Officer and make him believe he had committed a dangerous mistake. He beg'd *Captn. Montague's* pardon very humbly, and felt himself very fortunate in his consenting to overlook the unintentional trespass. In short he got away, when there were, as we knew, detainers enough likely to follow the arrest to keep him a prisoner for years or for life. The Plaintiff, who had seen the arrest, brought Action against the Sheriff for an escape, but not being able to prove the facts, was non-suited and had the costs to pay. It is useful tho' humiliating to look back on a low moral standard from which our own conscience has been raised. I lament to say that this dishonesty, injustice, and falsehood did not appear to me at the time as wrong or offensive in the sight of God. The end of rescuing a friend from distress and ruin seemed to me to justify, or at least excuse the act; and I was not slow to boast of the artifice to our common friends, instead of blushing for and hiding it. Nor did one of them regard it as blameable. At least no one expressed the just censure it deserved.

How many and great were the dangers from which a gracious Providence at this time and many subsequent periods preserved me in my intercourse with the vicious! Alexander Stephens was a companion my intimacy with whom threatened consequences ruinous to my morals, to my character, and my peace. He was not less imprudent and thoughtless than licencious, and without meaning to corrupt me led me more than once into company and situations from which it was not easy to escape with innocence or safety. I was, for instance, the confidant of a connection he had formed with a woman of great personal attractions and to whom he was romantically attached tho' he knew her to be vicious. He might possibly have married her, if her behaviour towards me had not convinced him as well as myself that it was my own choice that I was not a favoured rival. On another occasion he introduced me to a Billiard Room where a fashionably dressed Man soon joined us and by looking over and occasionally praising our play, and afterwards with the air of a novice proposing to play a hit or two with Stephens for the tables, and pretending awkwardness, &c., soon convinced him as well as me that he was a sharper intent upon cheating us. Stephens whispered to me to humour him, and divert ourselves by observing and balking his stratagems; and I had no objection to such amusement. Accordingly the fellow shewed himself plainly enough; but when he would have led us on to deep play we disappointed him by resolving to play no more. Unwilling to lose such promising young dupes he in a manner forced himself on us to take coffee with us in a neighbouring Coffee House to which he heard us propose to adjourn; and Stephens, contrary to my inclination, suffered him to go and sit with us there. We soon found what was his further purpose. With artifices of the usual kind and which men who had read novels and knew London could not fail to detect, he tried to decoy us to a nocturnal gaming house in Pall Mall, and Stephens carried his curiosity so far as to resolve not only to go, but to take me with him if possible. This I would not consent to, and after calling Stephens aside and strongly remonstrating with him against his purpose in vain, I left them together. Stephens assured me that he would not be prevailed on to play; but the next Morning I found that he had been strip'd of all he had. I fear it was only his initiation in a course that he afterwards, banefully to himself, if not dishonorably, pursued.

It fared with this volatile and imprudent young man as it usually does with those who for their pleasures frequent the company of profligate women and men. They do not stop with the indulgence of those sinful propensities for which they first formed such society, but gradually become corrupted in other points of character, imbibing the bad principles of those associates, and losing progressively the sense of probity and honor. Such I had soon too much reason to fear was the case with Alexander Stephens. He began to relieve his necessities by various mean and dishonest shifts, borrowing from friends, as well as contracting debts with tradesmen, by holding out delusive representations as to his future means of payment, and in one instance, tho' after my acquaintance with him had ceased, he went so far as to bring on himself a criminal prosecution and to be tried at the Westminster Sessions either for a fraud or felony, I forget which. He was acquitted; but the facts were disgraceful enough, he having been an accomplice at least in forcing a tradesman to leave at a Lady's lodgings goods which he had made for her under a promise of payment on delivery and turning him out of the house without his money. How the case was softened notwithstanding into an acquittal I forget. Long before this I had not only ceased to be intimate with him but wholly drop'd his acquaintance. I have not always observed that wise and most important maxim, *"Where you can read no morals, find no friend."* Yet it is but justice to myself, or rather it is but gratitude to the Almighty (to whose grace and providence I owe all that is right in my own sinful heart) to say that my regards or likings never long survive my esteem. With all the bad things I have done I have been preserved from the depravity of "taking pleasure in those who do them." The opposite quality, that of loving good men and courting their friendship, has under the blessing of God been the chief source of all my happiness in life and of all the little in my heart and conduct that can in any degree warrant the hope of my happiness in the life to come. At this period, low tho' my standard was, I gradually found Alexr. Stephens to be unworthy of my esteem or confidence. I must admit, however, on recollection that our intimacy was partly broken by his ceasing in great measure to court my company and that of his old companions in the City, our mutual friends, upon his attaining to much apparent prosperity at the West End of the Town, and living in a stile of fashion and expence far above our humble level. He became on a sudden not only conspicuous, in his dress and other outward tokens of affluence such as driving a Phaeton, &c., but as all who knew him reported, had plenty of money at command tho' without any visible means of acquiring it, circumstances which, combined with his frequent visits to a rich old Dowress who had a splendid seat near Town, excited surmises unfavorable to her character and highly degrading to his. From about this time he and I ceased to be on speaking terms almost, generally passing each other when we met with a distant salute; but to finish my account of him, he has since my last return from the West Indies made several advances towards a renewal of intimacy, and apparently with better pretentions to my countenance

as a kinsman, for he had married a Lady of respectable connections and some fortune, and had during many years been
living in a prudent and not uncreditable way. But I had no
inclination to renew my acquaintance with him beyond a
formal call or two on each side when we happened to be
neighbours. I found him to be a professed and violent
democrat, and I fear also an Infidel. He was a great intimate
by his own account of Horne Tooke,[1] Burdett,[2] and all the
heads of the Mob Party, and made no secret of his revolutionary and republican views. He was become also a political
writer, was patronized by Phillips[3] the democrat Bookseller,
and wrote a History of the late Wars, a work of no character,
and of which from the name I had once or twice the mortification to be thought the Author. He died, as I saw by the
Newspapers, a year or two ago. May he have been better
prepared for that awful change than I have any reason to
hope he was. Alas! the example he had from me during our
early intimacy was not qualified to do him much good; and
if I was or yet am in any manner better than he was, how
many advantages and what abundant means of grace have I
had of which he was probably destitute. May God be merciful
to him, and to me a Sinner!

About the time to which my narrative of my own life is
brought down I formed another intimacy the consequences
of which to me have been very painful and very instructive.

Mr. Fletcher had a young Irish Clerk, named Charles
Mc.Carthy, with whom in transacting business for my

[1] John Horne Tooke (1736–1812), politician and philologist; author of *A
Letter on Parliamentary Reform* (1782) and *The Diversions of Purley* (1786); an
independent radical who first supported and then quarrelled with Wilkes; later
supported Pitt against Fox; was jailed for a year (1777–1778) for soliciting
subscriptions for the relief of relatives of the Americans "murdered by the
King's troops at Lexington and Concord"; was in 1794 tried for high treason
because of republican opinions but was acquitted.

[2] Sir Francis Burdett (1770–1844), politician and radical agitator for reform
of Parliament; M.P. 1796–1804 and 1807–1844; friend and disciple of John
Horne Tooke; twice imprisoned for incendiary speeches against the government; moved for universal male suffrage, equal electoral districts, and annual
parliaments as early as 1817; author of laws removing disabilities of Catholics.

[3] Sir Richard Phillips (1767–1840), author, bookseller, publisher; before
coming to London a schoolmaster, hosier, stationer, bookseller, and patent-
medicine vendor; imprisoned 1793 for selling Paine's *Rights of Man*; proprietor
of the Leicester *Herald* (1792) and the *Monthly Magazine* (1796); friend of
Priestley, Orator Hunt, and other radicals.

8

Father I was naturally brought into acquaintance. Regarding me as his Superior in life he was very assiduous to please me, and very grateful for such little courtesies and civilities as I shewed him in return, so that a mutual good will and intimacy sprang up between us. I was not too proud to ask him now and then to a Sunday dinner at Stoke Newington, and my Father received him kindly there, which he regarded as a great honor, tho' certainly we were in point of fortune and outward appearances no very elevated persons.

Not long after this intimacy commenced there arrived from Ireland a brother of this young man, called Felix, whom he had sent for with a view of his getting into employment here in the same line with himself. He had been educated for a Priest, they being of a Catholic family, but declining that profession had no better prospect in life than his brother's invitation opened. Their Parents were poor Farmers in the County of Cork, but counted themselves gentry by birth, as being able to trace their descent from the Chiefs of the McCarthys, one of the most ancient of the Irish families. Probably every McCarthy in Ireland almost can do the same; and it is one effect of the confiscations in Cromwell's time and at former periods, that most of the poor Irish who are boastful of their blood, conceive also that their want of landed property is attributable only to their Ancestors having been dispossessed of it by English tyranny and usurpation, not caring to consider how many thousands descended from the same stock would have been in the line of inheritance before them. If Liberal and aspiring feelings are sometimes the growth of such prejudices, so are indolence and discontent. To the two McCarthy's, however, at this time of life they produced the former only without the latter. Charles was very industrious in his humble line, and content with it. Felix, tho' a good classic, or at least Latinist, was disposed to labour about the same way; and both had the liberal and honorary feelings of gentlemen, which poor Charles retained and acted up to, to the end of his life.

Felix was soon introduced to me, and I found him a character in more than an ordinary degree interesting and amusing. The usual characteristics of a young Irishman were so prominent in him as to approach to the burlesque. As yet a stranger to the manners of the world, he neither knew nor sought to hide his natural feelings, which had all the warmth and vivacity common to his countrymen, and he had a blundering naivete in his language and manner which were at once prepossessing and ridiculous. Tho' far from deficient in understanding he could hardly speak on any subject without exciting risible emotions. He would have been a rash man, however, who should have laughed at *Phelim* (such is the Irish conversion of Felix, and the name we then called him) without first gaining a hold on his affections (which at this time was no difficult task), for tho' he would do any thing or indure any thing for a man he was attached to, he was irascible and impetuous in his resentment when he thought himself insulted or despised, and both from his courage and his strength was a dangerous man to quarrel with. I have known men as brave, but never one, I think, with so much of what is called constitutional courage. It is common to say of a Man of that character "he would take a lion by the beard," but Phelim McCarthy was likely not only to do this, but vanquish him too. His stature, I think, was six feet three or four inches and his frame fitted to unite agility with strength beyond that of any other man I ever saw. He would vault like a deer, and his grasp was irresistable. Being at Vauxhall Gardens when the Prizefighting Champion of the day, Mendoza,[1] was insulting some gentlemen and keeping them aloof by the terror of his prowess, Felix McCarthy step'd in, though he had no concern in the quarrel, seized the champion with his long extended arm, and bore him off in spite of all his blows and struggles to the watch house. Nor did he let these talents of his rust for want of use. At the time I speak of, and for a year or two after at least, he had a romantic generosity that made him a perfect Quixote in getting into broils by interposing on behalf of the weaker and (as he supposed always from that circumstance) the injured party. If he saw a fight or riot in the Street, he was almost sure to interpose, sometimes at the cost

[1] Stephen must be in error here. Daniel Mendoza (1764–1836) fought his first important match in 1787 and was not thought of as "Champion" until after his second victory over Richard Humphries in 1789. He could have been a street-corner bully in 1781, when he was seventeen years old; but the likelihood is that Stephen's memory for names was at fault.

of being severely beaten by a concourse of assailants, once I remember at that of nearly losing his life by a stab from one of the pickpockets, a whole gang of whom were his opponents, and on another occasion he received contusions enough to kill a weaker man, in rescuing a turnpike-gateman at Kennington from a band of desperadoes who had broken his arm, and would probably have murdered him but for M.'s interference. I saw one of them afterwards, when under prosecution for the offence, a Distiller's Drayman or Porter of Herculean dimensions, but who it appeared was indebted to the help of his companions for his extrication from M.'s hands, who singly fought them all. I could mention still more extraordinary traits of the same kind which I shall probably find incidental to my story hereafter.

A man of this character was naturally exposed to great moral as well as physical dangers in London. But his vicious propensities were at this time under the salutary and only effectual curb of religion. He was a sincere and zealous Catholic, and tho' he had declined to take Priest's orders it was only, as I think he confessed, from the fear of not being able to observe the vows. It is an unjust prejudice to suppose that the Romish faith is never friendly to morals. In the education of youth, especially when they arrive at manhood under college discipline, it is more so than that of Protestants. The *confessional* is an instrument of mighty power at that critical time of life, the passage from the schoolboy to the man. My early familiarity with young Irishmen educated at the Jesuits' Colleges or other Catholic Schools let me into secrets as to the use of this sacrament of the Romish Church which I cannot with delicacy unfold. I will only say that faithful and judicious Tutors of that persuasion, if themselves Priests, or if they have the aid of sensible Confessers, do accomplish the difficult task of sending young men undebauched and pure into the world and armed too with principles and feelings capable of sustaining them some time at least against subsequent temptations. With all my dislike and contempt for Catholic superstitions, and few men feel more of them, I must do the religion this justice. Felix McCarthy had this benefit from his faith. He was at this time uncorrupted and had a salutary dread of falling into those sins to which his constitution most exposed him. But it could not be expected that the moral effects of his faith should be unaccompanied with zeal for its doctrines and its superstitious observances. He was a bigotted Catholic in all points, and I believe regarded eating meat on a Fast Day, without a dispensation from the Church, as not less sinful than those really criminal sensualities from which he had been taught to abstain.

I mention these latter traits of his character for the sake of confessing sins that I committed against him, of which I am deeply conscious, and for which I have been severely scourged. Never, my dear children, and my grandchildren, or other descendants, to whom these sheets may come, never, I conjure you, unsettle the faith of any weak or erring fellow Christian, unless in the serious, charitable attempt to give him a better. Never treat with mirth or levity, and for the mere sake of diversion or idle conversation, things that he holds sacred. Still less invite or lead him to violate his own conscience in matters which he regards as sinful, tho' *you* hold them indifferent. Remember the charitable precepts, and amiable sentiment of St. Paul, who "would rather not have eat meat while the world stood, than make his brother to offend." 1. Cor: 8—cap. You know not how much the whole fabrick of his Christianity may be unsettled and shaken by loosening the hold of one superstitious tenet in a light and heedless way. I did not, alas, thus reason and act in the case of Felix McCarthy, over whom my influence soon became very great; for I treated him, like his brother, with a kindness and courtesy that quite won his heart. Charles who had a good deal of drollery, and on whom his religion had begun to sit very light, loved to amuse himself and me at Felix's expence, by exposing and laughing at his strictness, and what I thought his ridiculous superstitions; as for instance when we met together on a Friday or other Fast day, and Felix would not partake of our fare, which the other did without scruple. Once or twice I remember his going further, and speaking with levity and ridicule, either of the practices of the Priests, or something else held sacred by Felix, who was greatly shocked at it and reproved him with much severity while I was inconsiderate and sinful enough to laugh at the contrast between the waggery of the one and the superstitions of the other. Charles did not escape his share of the scourge for this misconduct. He lived to smart severely from the vices of this brother and to repent (I hope) for having contributed to laugh him out of his once happy religious impressions.

Occupied with my Father's business, and with my own professional studies through the day, and generally, with some or one of these companions for an hour or two in the evening, my time passed not unpleasantly for some months after my return from Scotland. Indeed, the pleasure of health to which I had so long been a stranger in that Country, was alone no small enjoyment, tho' one of which I had not been conscious before its interruption. Such is our ordinary ingratitude for the blessings of Providence. The most indebted are the most insensible of what they owe; and afflictions are necessary, not only to make us humble, but to teach us the value of the good things we possess. Well had it been for me if my restored comforts had not been abused, and if gratitude for life preserved and health regained had engaged me to a steady obedience to the laws of my Heavenly Benefactor! My spiritual state at this time was such as it is neither pleasant nor easy to describe. I feared God and thought sometimes that I loved him. I was far from neglecting private prayer and generally if not always attended public worship regularly on the Sabbath. I abstained also from some sins to which I was strongly tempted; but it was more from a sense of prudence than of duty, and from the fear of God's vengeance than from a desire of his favor; and I was always ready to submit to more than ordinary temptation, and even secretly desirous of meeting it, as a fancied excuse for those indulgences from which I most unwillingly refrained. As to the duties of maintaining purity in the heart, of binding the tongue, and of abstaining from the appearance of evil, I transgressed against them every day, and almost without compunction. So far too was I from observing the precept of not laying a stumbling block in a Brother's way or causing him to offend by ill example that I can too well remember the wretched inverted hypocrisy of concealing from my young companions my reluctant obedience to some of God's laws, and affecting to be worse than I was. Still, however, I was by Divine mercy enabled to retain that part of my character which I desire particularly to mark in these memoirs because God has made it the chief source to me of all his temporal and spiritual blessings; a strong antipathy to vice, and love of virtue *in others*. I remember one instance of it about this time in the disgust I felt at a young clergyman, a schoolfellow of mine, because when I brought him to one of our evening Parties, he forgot what belonged to his sacred professions so far as to talk indecently and profanely. He was my companion no more. On the other hand I clung to Lindsay and MacLeod, because I regarded them as good and pious men. My standard, it is true, was by no means high, and therefore I had some companions by no means correct in their morals; but I gave them credit for being well principled in the main, and when I saw a man grossly licencious, he ceased to be an object of my regard, unless when I fancied, as I was once or twice foolish and unfortunate enough to do, that there were strong virtues in the character to counterpoise and redeem its faults. I had not yet learnt what a fraternity there is among the vices, and that a man who lives in the allowed systematic violation of one of God's laws is not to be relied on for his observance of the rest, except during the absence of temptation.

It is high time that I should notice an event which is of prominent importance in the history of my heart and of my life, the renewal of my acquaintance with my dear Nancy. Notwithstanding the offence my pride had received from her as before related, my early attachment to her had not been entirely obliterated in my heart, and I could not help feeling an interest more tender than curiosity that prompted me after my return to England to enquire about her.

Kensington Gore April 4, 1824
Another very long pause has occurred in this lengthy narrative. Eighteen months, I think, have elapsed since the last paragraph was written. The main cause of interruption has been one that may serve to excuse it. I have been more arduously employed than usual in the cause of the poor Colonial Slaves. Among other labours for them I have been

occupied at almost every hour I could find for voluntary desk work with my *Delineation of Slavery*,[1] the first volume of which I published in February last, and with numerous other urgent employments of my pen in the same righteous and deeply interesting cause, so that whenever I wished to unlock this Book and proceed with these Memoirs, conscience has suggested to me some work of charity in that line which seemed intitled to a preference. The same impediment, I fear, is likely much and often to recur. The hope of ultimate success in the efforts that are now making by the Friends of that great cause and the partial advantages we have gained are new motives for energetic perseverance; and while the contest continues my time and my pen are not likely to be much at my command for any private purpose. Yet with God's permission I will occasionally endeavour to make further progress in this work that the object of it may not finally be lost.

That part of my Narrative to which I had arrived was a very interesting one, and the recollections it excited, tho' mixed with melancholly associations, not unpleasant to a mind that is much accustomed to court with a nameless pensive pleasure the memory of its bereaved affections, and to love the haunts where from visible images it is most sure—

To meet the ghosts of its departed joys.[2]

Vanity had always whispered doubts to me whether my dear Nancy's offensive conduct on my attempt to renew our intercourse had not been the result of painful compulsion, and whether her heart had not remained faithful to me notwithstanding our long seperation; and I at length resolved that I would attempt to see her again to solve that doubt, but in such a way as to save my pride from further mortification if I found her really indifferent towards me. The resolution was soon after confirmed by information which if I had been more worldly or more prudent might have served to

[1] The first volume of Stephen's *Slavery of the British West India Colonies Delineated* appeared in February, 1824; the second volume in 1830.

[2] Young, *Night Thoughts*, Night I, ll. 229–230. Stephen is adapting to his purpose two lines which read

"... and meet the ghosts
Of my departed joys: a numerous train."

change it. I accidentally met with a Gentleman, Captn. McWilliams, whom I recollected as a visitor and Friend of Mr. Stent, and seized the opportunity of asking with an affected air of careless curiosity what had become of the Stent family in whose house I had met him formally at Walnut-tree Walk. In reply I learned from him that Mr. Stent in consequence of some heavy losses had been much reduced in his circumstances and nearly ruined, tho' he was still carrying on his business as a Stock Broker; that my old friend Thom had also been unfortunate, for that after some desperate services in the Man of War he served in on the Coast of America, in which he had behaved very gallantly, he was taken Prisoner by the Enemy on board a Prize vessel which he had been put in charge of; and there being no cartel, had remained as a Prisoner on parole among the rebels for two years, tho' then at liberty and again in service on a foreign station; and as to my dear Nancy that she was still single, and living with her friend Mrs. Thomas as a Boarder in her family near Vauxhall, but had suffered great afflictions as well from ill health as from the family misfortunes.

Simpathy with my dear Nancy now strengthened the other feelings that prompted me to see her if possible, but at the same time made me the more cautious of taking any course that might embarrass or distress her. The plan, therefore, which I adopted was to watch for an opportunity of meeting her as if by accident near Mrs. Thomas's house, if she ever walked out in its then retired neighbourhood alone. Having reconnoitered the house and its environs I found post for observation. It was nearly surrounded with nursery grounds; and on the opposite side of one of these which directly fronted Mrs. Thomas's door stood a public house, much frequented on Sundays, as having booths and a garden for tea drinkers, but on other days commonly pretty empty of guests. In the first floor of this House I found a room the windows of which commanded a full view across the nursery ground of my dear Nancy's place of abode and of a retired path through which she was likely to pass if she ever came out to walk. Here, therefore, I took my stand the first fine afternoon that I could disengage myself for the purpose, and calling for tea, the sipping of which was easily protracted for two hours or more, watched closely at least so long at the window, riveting my eyes on the door from which I hoped she might sally. I had also provided myself with a pocket spyglass with which I carefully examined every female that appeared in the adjoining path. But after staying till the day began to fade into twilight (it was Springtime) and until it was too late to leave a hope of her quitting home alone, I was obliged to retire disappointed. The experiment, however, was renewed at an early day, and reiterated almost as often as business permitted me to go over in good weather at a proper hour to Vauxhall. Wearied at length with many tedious and fruitless efforts, fearful of observation, and despairing nearly of success, I should probably have relinquished my purpose altogether, or adopted some more open course to obtain an interview or a letter; but when I was about quitting my window, probably for the last time, the door on which my eyes had long been anxiously fixed at length opened, and a lady descended the steps whose stature and gait, as my fluttering heart told me, indicated her to be the interesting object of my search. I was transported and agitated still more when I perceived that she was not accompanied or followed, and took her way in the direction of Lambeth down the retired path that I have noticed, which was crossed by another at a short distance leading towards the House I sat in. I hastened out to throw myself in her way; but she had turned at the crossing in the opposite way. I had therefore to follow and overtake her, in doing which I had leisure to recognize more fully the well known figure of my once much loved Nancy. So much the better for my purpose, for such was the alteration in her face that had I met her front to front I might have passed her as a stranger. Nothing at least but the having seen her come from Ms. T.'s house would have assured me that she was identically the same young lady whose image had seven years before been so deeply printed in my heart till her well known voice confirmed it. The change certainly was not for the better. My amorous imagination had no doubt coloured highly the impressions of memory, and given her beauties that she never possessed; but the real deterioration was great.

The bloom of fifteen had faded, her naturally fair and clear complexion had become a sickly white or wan, and her skin had lost its clearness through the effects of a scorbutic or cutaneous complaint by which she had been much annoyed two or three years before, and which had not yet entirely disappeared. Her features in general were never good, and perhaps had suffered little change, but their defects at least had escaped my observation in the girl, tho' I saw them now in the woman. Her eyes, however, which to my taste, or rather let me say to my *feelings*, are the feature of most attraction when good, had lost none of their charms. They were as full of intelligence, animation, and tender expression as ever. Her person was pleasing; and her hair had improved, having changed from red into auburn. Such did I find my dear Nancy at this interview pregnant with consequences the most momentous to both our fates.

When I passed her, and fixing my eyes on hers, called her by her name, she started and trembled with surprise, and could hardly find utterance for her next emotions, which were great alarm at my presence and an earnest desire that I would leave her without delay. On my part I said all that was most proper to compose and soothe her, but declared my determination not to part with her without some further conversation, in a way so resolute tho' respectful that she soon saw denial was in vain and instead of going on to the House of a neighbouring friend with whom she was going to make tea, agreed to prolong her walk and allowed me to attend her. The sun was still above the horizon, and so interesting a conversation ensued that I believe he had long set before her repeated intreaties induced me to allow her to go home, whither of course I escorted her as near as I could do without being seen by the family.

If my object in these memoirs were to entertain and interest, rather than instruct and improve, I would endeavour to recollect and detail the particulars of that interesting conversation and to trace the steps by which in some subsequent interviews my dear Nancy and I were not only reconciled to each other but replaced on the footing of lovers avowing a mutual attachment. But I must endeavour to confine myself to such of those particulars as the connection and right apprehension of my narrative may make it necessary to state.

There was at first much of reciprocal upbraidings and explanations in respect of past conduct; and tho' I was easily satisfied with her excuse as to the unkind and mortifying manner in which my last letter had been answered and returned through my Father's hands, for I found it was as I suspected, conduct imperatively prescribed to her by her Father and Mrs. Thomas, she was not so readily disposed to pardon my insulting reply, and still less my disrespectful treatment of her Father. It is but just to her memory, dear woman, to say that notwithstanding those breaches of filial duty into which her love for me and my too powerful influence led her, she ever entertained for that Parent the liveliest affection; and on this as on other occasions, resented far more strongly any disrespect to him than any wrong or insult to herself. At length what could not be justified was confessed and forgiven; and I could plainly perceive before even the end of our first interview that the flame of our early attachment would not be more difficult to rekindle in my dear Nancy's bosom than in my own. Still there was something in her manner that I did not altogether understand. At least so I fancied upon recollection, after a discovery that I shall hereafter relate. That she should shrink from the renewal of disobedience to her beloved Father was natural enough, but there was an *ultra feeling* not only in regard to him, but to her Friend Mrs. Thomas, and an excess of uneasiness as to the consequences of her meeting me being discovered by the latter, that I found it harder to combat than from the evident state of her feelings towards me might have been expected. Her attachment to that friend, however, was so strong and well founded as to make it natural she should be alarmed at the danger of incurring her displeasure. They had long lived together as Mother and daughter with mutual satisfaction, and Mrs. Thomas was a woman of distinguished piety as well as general merit and amiable manners.

Notwithstanding all these opposing feelings my dear Nancy's faithful and susceptible heart pleaded so strongly on my side that I prevailed upon her to give me a second, third, and several other interviews, till all reserve was at an end on her part as well as mine and our early engagement tacitly renewed by an avowal of mutual attachment. She had a married female friend who being let into her confidence assisted us in our meetings by evening visits at her house, and when this could not be easily done, I prevailed upon her sometimes to indulge me with a short interview in a nursery garden near her house, in which she had the privilege of walking.

But my Friend, her brother, Thom's arrival from America at this critical period opened to us new facilities; and indeed but for this event I should probably not have been able so far to overcome the fears and anxieties of his Sister as to prevail on her to continue our private intercourse. Thom and I met with all the warmth of early friendship. He had become a fine handsome fellow but retained the same kindness and openness of character which distinguished him when a boy and the same predilection for myself as when we were school companions. He was, as I could perceive, uneasy at the renewal of the attachment between his Sister and me; but he had always such an easiness of temper and such a sailorlike propensity to enjoy the present moment heedless of future consequences, that he did not stand out against my wishes or deny himself the pleasure of my society for that cause, but on the contrary consented to bring his Sister to Parties proposed by me for them at the Theatres and other public places, when he knew it was my purpose to join them. On her part her fondness for her Brother was so great that if he had proposed to her a thing very unpleasant she would hardly have refused him, how much less what I believe, dear woman, was the greatest enjoyment earth could afford her, the enjoying at once his society and mine and witnessing our mutual Friendship.

His company was not at all times equally convenient. Of course it was only on a few of the many evenings we spent together that my dear Nancy could be of the Party. On other occasions, he was glad to join MacLeod, Lindsay, and me, and other friends to whom I introduced him at places we sometimes supped at together; but Thom was so volatile and had so much of the ordinary character of a Seaman on shore, that he did not always keep within the bounds of

temperance, and thought it rather an improvement of an
Evening Party to end it by some riotous means such as "*un-
shipping*" the lamps in the hands of the watchman. His stay
in London, however, was not very long. It was war time;
and his leave of absence being expired, he returned to his
Ship, which was ordered, I think, to the African Station.
During his stay on shore at this time he fell in love with a
young Lady with whom he got acquainted at the maternal
home of a brother officer, and whom he described to me as a
perfect Venus. His Sister also, who had been introduced to
her through his means, spoke in strong terms of her personal
attractions. I shall have to mention this lady again hereafter. At present I will only add that my Friend's addresses
to her were rejected, and that he went away in consequence
very disconsolate, tho' encouraged by my advice not to
despair of future success if he met with preferment in the
service.

It was not long after his departure that an ecclaircissement
took place which too well explained his visible uneasiness in
regard to the renewed intercourse between my dear Nancy
and me. I was preparing one afternoon to meet her, pursuant
to an appointment I had prevailed on her to make, when I
received a letter that overwhelmed me with surprise and
consternation. It told me in effect that we must meet no
more for ever. No intelligible reason was given; but some
invincible one was hinted at, in terms not less mysterious than
decisive. That it was no change in her own feelings was
manifest, nor any supposed fault on my part; for her
language was of the tenderest kind, and imported that she
was acting under a cruel necessity and renouncing all her
hopes of happiness in life, from a sense of inexorable duty.
Deep self-condemnation for having permitted the renewal
of our intercourse, as deep a sense of having cruelly wronged
me in doing so, supplications for my forgiveness, and earnest
prayers for my happiness, were all expressed in the most
impassioned terms; but the sad practical conclusion that I
must see her no more was the only part of her meaning
clearly expressed, tho' that was announced in so peremptory
a manner as seemed to preclude every hope and every
attempt to change it. Wounded pride and anger at first

prevailed over all softer emotions, and I was disposed for a while to take her at her word, to regard her as an unprincipled jilt and cast her out of my heart for ever; but every successive perusal of the letter more and more convinced me that these feelings were injurious; and when I recollected the numerous and strong indications of a tender attachment for me which I had lately seen in her, and reflected on her general character in which there was much of native warmth and openness, but not a shade of fickleness, levity or artifice, I found it impossible to doubt that her present conduct was imposed upon her by some strong necessity, and that she merited compassion rather than blame for it. Of what kind that necessity was I could form no conjecture. That she had not renewed her intercourse with me without being prepared for disobedience to her Father if he should hear of and forbid it was, alas, too certain. She always indeed loved her Father fondly. It was, I may say, a prominent feature in her character and the idea of his resentment was extremely painful to her; but having found her attachment to me too powerful for these right feelings she was not likely thus suddenly and decidedly to have reversed her conduct from a sense of filial duty. Besides I found from the date of the letter or otherwise that she was with Mrs. Moss, her Mother's Sister, in Lambeth where I knew Mr. Stent's influence was not likely to be present, because this Lady, like the rest of Mrs. S.'s family, had taken part with her against him, believing or injuriously professing to believe that her conduct had not been guilty and throwing the blame of the seperation on him. They were consequently at open and irreconcilable variance, tho' Mr. S. had good naturedly not prohibited his children from visiting this maternal Aunt, and I believe connived at their sometimes seeing their Mother at her house. He was always kind and indulgent even to a fault, and I believe I have before noticed the extraordinary character of this woman, who notwithstanding her great and indubitable crime acted in all other respects with such strict propriety and delicacy as to stand high with all who were not certain of her guilt. Her manners were so unexceptionable, and she was so eminently gifted with good sense, that far from exciting disrespect or suspicion, she had maintained a powerful influence over the minds of her relatives in general, and probably her injured husband knew and relied upon this character sufficiently to be assured that his children would receive no prejudice at her hands. I nevertheless regard it as wrong in him to have allowed any such intercourse if he knowingly did so, of which I have some doubt. I never asked any explanations, I think, from my dear Nancy on this delicate and to her very painful subject. Perhaps from like feelings they never spoke to their Father, nor he to them about it; and when the Mother was brought into their company at their Aunt's they may have thought it better to assume, than to ascertain, that he did not mean to prevent it. I doubt not, however, this may have been, that my dear Nancy's conduct in the matter was sanctioned by the advice of her worthy friend Mrs. Thomas, who for her own part had renounced all intercourse with the Mother and therefore could have no bias in her favor. After some painful struggles between pride on the one hand and tender feelings combined with an anxious curiosity on the other, I resolved that before in compliance with my dear Nancy's request I gave her up for ever I would insist on an interview with her and learn from her own lips the cause of her present conduct. Accordingly I went over to the neighbourhood of her Aunt Moss and sent a letter to her there intimating that resolution, and in terms sufficiently decisive to preclude the hope that I would admit of either refusal or delay. I waited near an hour at a neighbouring tavern in the most painful suspense, until my Messenger returned bringing me a letter from Mrs. S. in which I was told that her daughter was too ill to answer my letter for herself but would see me for a short time in her presence. I hastened to the house and was soon shewn into a room where I found them both together, but my dear Nancy in a state of pitiable distress, unable to raise her eyes to mine or to speak a word from the sobs that choaked her utterance. She had evidently been shedding floods of tears, and her agitated frame shewed the sufferings under which she still laboured. Mrs. S., whose person still retained much of its attractions, received me very kindly as an old friend and favourite of hers, and displayed much sensibility for her daughter's feelings and mine, but at the same time told me in the most decisive terms that it was absolutely necessary this unfortunate attachment should be conquered by us both. On my demanding the reason she saved my dear Nancy the pain of giving the explanation by telling me that before the renewal of our acquaintance and while her daughter thought herself no more remembered by me, she had consented to become the wife of another Man, no other than the son of her Friend and Guardian, Mrs. Thomas, who as they had now just heard was on his passage from the West Indies expecting the performance of that engagement. This information, of course, was quite enough for me. Tho' my heart beat high with pride and indignation, I disdained reproaches or complaint, but rose to take my leave. But my eye no doubt spoke what my tongue abstained from. My dear Nancy could not sustain it. She burst into the most piercing explanations of anguish and self-reproach conjuring me to believe that her heart was wholly mine and that in resigning me she took leave of every hope of happiness in life and gave herself up to misery and despair. It was impossible not to be moved by her distress, but my delicacy and pride were so much hurt at her supposed infidelity that I restrained every tender emotion and would have left her in that agitated state if her Mother had not detained me by explanations which she rightly thought would mitigate my resentment, but erroneously that they would lead to a mutual and peaceful acquiescence in her purpose. The facts, as she truly explained them to me, were these. Mr. James Thomas, as the son of her Father's old and intimate friends, had been her daughter's familiar companion in childhood, and till he went, I think in the mercantile line, to Grenada, from which he had not since returned. There never had before his departure been any attachment of an amorous kind between my dear Nancy and him, but a friendship resembling that which subsists between a brother and sister; and this had naturally led to a frequent correspondence in his absence, especially after she became one of his Father and Mother's family. Latterly the correspondence on his part had assumed a warmer character. His regard for her had, I doubt not, been augmented by his Mother's account of her conduct since the disastrous event that had placed her under her own protec-

tion, and by Mrs. Thomas's esteem and affection for her,
which I know were very great. At length he professed his
wish for a union with her, and my dear Nancy's consent was
naturally not very hard to obtain, assisted as he was not
only by long established confidence and friendship, but by
the powerful influence of his Mother. At that time all her
early feelings towards me had subsided, or rather given
place to a sense of resentment for my disrespectful treatment
of her Father and herself; nor had she any reason to suppose
that my boyish feelings had been in any degree retained or
that she should ever hear of me again. I knew enough of the
case (well remembering that in my visits at Walnut-tree Walk
I often met James Thomas, a lad about my own age who was
like a son in the family) to perceive how natural this explanation was, nor could I entertain a doubt of its truth; but
admitting that I had no cause of complaint in the formation
of such engagement, its concealment from me of course
appeared not only unjust but cruel, and a wanton trespass
on my peace. Why was I not told when I first attempted to
renew my intercourse with her that this decisive objection to
it had arisen? Here, however, Mrs. S. had more to say in
extenuation of her daughter's conduct than it was wise to
bring forward to me. Her heart at our first interview had
too strongly recognized my earlier claims upon it. She could
not do herself the violence to divulge what she knew would
banish me for ever. She had ever since maintained a painful
struggle with herself, resolving often to disclose the unhappy
secret and bid me a final adieu, and failing as often in her
resolution, from feeling that it was more than she could
sustain, and from doubting also whether justice to Mr.
Thomas did not require that she should break off with him
instead of me, and not give him her hand while her heart was
irrecoverably mine. No doubt she had also deceived herself
with a doubt whether her prior engagements to me did not
invalidate her promise to him, tho' the former were made
when we were almost too young to have morally a contracting power and in opposition to parental authority, while the
latter was made between adult parties and with the approbation of Parents on both sides. The heart is a licencious
casuist in such circumstances, and it might seem to my

poor Nancy that our release of those early engagements,
being the effect of compulsion on her side and misconception
on mine, was no dissolution in conscience of the tie. There
were circumstances, however, in the case that made her
conduct harder to defend as to the past, but which Mrs. S.
was obliged to state in justification of her present purpose.
The proposed union was part of a plan which had been concerted for the return of young Mr. Thomas and his settlement
in his native land. Both the Fathers, and some relations of the
Thomases, I believe, the Broughtons, one of whom, Bryan
Broughton, was then Secretary to the Prime Minister Lord
North, were to contribute their assistance to establish the
young man as a Merchant in London. Whether he had been
unsuccessful in the West Indies, or found the climate injurious
to his health, or what else was the cause of his wishing to
quit it finally. I do not recollect; but his settling here had
been resolved on; and he was then, I think, actually on his
passage, and both he and his Parents were looking forward
with joy to his establishment in business and settlement in
marriage soon after his arrival. I do not think it right to
suppress these circumstances or any thing else that tends to
my dear Nancy's inculpation in the case; for the main
object of these memoirs is to illustrate the ways of Providence;
and if her fault was great, so, it will be soon seen, were
chastisements. To spare her memory would be much more to
diminish my own reproach as will also soon be seen. But let
me avoid anticipations. Mrs. S., after thus developing the
mystery of the letter which under her urgent advice, and
that of Mrs. Moss, my poor Nancy had been induced to
write, set herself to defend that measure and to reason me
into acquiescence and certainly used the best topics of
persuasion by appealing less to my prudence than my
generosity and compassion, and to my regard for the credit
and welfare of her daughter. If I persisted in drawing her
from the path of duty, or if all intercourse between us were
not finally renounced, it would be absolutely necessary
without further delay to apprize both her Father and Mrs.
Thomas of our conduct. Hitherto both were ignorant that
our acquaintance was renewed. My poor Nancy had wholly
concealed it, not only from her Father, but from that kind

and excellent friend with whom in no other case had she any reserve; and only from the intolerable pain of the dilemma in which she consequently found herself had cast herself at length on her Aunt and her Mother for advice. But they, as Mrs. S. justly thought, were bound to insist on an immediate discovery both to Mrs. Thomas and Mr. Stent unless we mutually promised to see each other no more; and yet cruel to my dear Nancy would be the effects of the disclosure. Independently of her Father's resentment, it must put an immediate end to her connection with Mrs. Thomas, deprive her of a protectress whose loss could not be supplied, and make her an outcast from that circle of Friends in which she then moved, *viz.*, the Miss Broughtons and the other connections of the Thomas family who formed her only eligible companions and intimates, but who would not fail to resent her conduct and turn their backs upon her. Mrs. S. mixed with pathetic appeals to my feelings on such a prospect, complimentary, and I dare say sincere, professions of her regard and esteem for myself, declaring that if I were in a situation to rescue her daughter from those painful consequences, or had any rational prospect of soon being able to do so, her preference for me would give her the greatest pleasure, but knowing the contrary she hoped I would be too generous to persist in a course which would subject the woman I loved to misery and ruin.

These arguments were not lost upon me. There was an end of pride and resentment. Indeed the state of my poor Nancy, who during this conversation had contrived silently to indulge the anguish of her mind in tears and sobs till she was quite exhausted, might have moved a sterner heart. I expressed my entire forgiveness and acquiescence in whatever she resolved. In my turn I gave way to tears, and elevated by the consciousness of intending a generous sacrifice unbosomed myself in a strain that I believe was eloquent and am sure was deeply impressive on both my hearers. Far from concealing my bad prospects in life, I stated not only my own, but those of my fellow orphans, and frankly declared, as I had previously done to my dear Nancy, that I regarded them as my own children and would never marry till I was able to rescue them, my sisters at least, from dependency or want. At the same time I professed, what I always felt, a confidence of success in life through my own professional exertions, but admitted that there could be no question as to the imprudence of her daughter's preferring such distant and doubtful prospects, to an immediate establishment in marriage; especially considering the painful consequences of a breach with Mrs. Thomas and of her Father's displeasure. With these sentiments I was about to take my leave; but the Mother as well as the daughter was greatly moved, and tho' the former would have allowed me to depart, the latter fell into a state that frightened us both from our purpose. I find it difficult to describe the scene that followed. She was relieved, I think, by a fainting fit, as well as total exhaustion. Her Aunt, if I remember right, was added to the party. At length when composure was restored in some degree, Mrs. S., alarmed from what she had seen on this occasion, and no doubt on former ones also, of the strength of her daughter's feelings on the subject, was afraid to press her purpose any further, and frankly declared that she felt it impossible to do so, and found it necessary to acquiesce in the continuance of our mutual attachment and intercourse, contrary tho' she considered them to the plainest principles of prudence. But she added that an immediate ecclaircissement with the Thomases and Mr. Stent was unavoidable and that my dear Nancy must not return to her home till this had taken place. Truly painful to her though this discovery in prospect was, it was readily agreed to; and we both felt like persons reprieved from immediate death. Our attachment even seemed to us to have received a sanction that made it more interesting and delightful from the consent of this Parent, constrained tho' that had been, and notwithstanding the misconduct by which she had renounced the rights of the parental relation. Won by her kindness and the praises she bestowed on my conduct for its generosity, &c., and the recollection of her old partiality towards me, I was disposed to fall under the same fascination which she spread over the minds of her relations, and to regard her with esteem and respect, as well as affection, imputing her known sin unjustly to extreme provocation from her much injured husband, to whose character I was then a stranger. We parted in the kindest manner, and I really believe she felt towards me as an affectionate Mother.

My poor dear Nancy had immediately after to sustain the deep affliction of a final breach with the Thomas family, and of forfeiting the esteem and regard of her pious and affectionate Guardian. The discovery was made. The mode of it I think was by letter, and she returned to her home no more. Her Father's resentment also, alas! was another bitter draught, and from his presence too she was long excluded. Distant tho' the time now is, and immaterial to *her* tho' all her human sufferings have become, I cannot without grief remember what she endured for my sake; but I ought with far greater pain to contemplate the sinful cause: the breaches of duty which I had induced her to commit. Without my instigation and the too powerful hold that I had upon her heart, she would never, I verily believe, have been undutiful to her Father or inconsistent in her conduct with the attachment and gratitude which she warmly felt towards her adopted Mother, Mrs. Thomas. I trust that she has been pardoned by the Most High for these and all other the sins whereof I was the Author or the Accomplice. Scarcely a day has passed since her death, now twenty-eight years ago, in which my prayers have not been addressed to him for her forgiveness and the felicity of her departed spirit. This may be, and probably is, unwarranted by the Scriptures; but it is a point on which, like that great man Dr. Johnson,[1] I am more than half a Catholic. I know from blessed experience what the efficacy of prayer is on *this* side the grave. The proofs I have had of it during a long life, and still daily experience, are astonishing and numberless. Without exaggeration I could almost as easily doubt of my own existence as of this delightful truth. Shall we then forbear to pray for the departed spirits of those we fondly loved? and shall we thus abstain even from including them in our prayers for forgiveness of those sins whereof we were jointly guilty, and into which we ourselves seduced them? Nothing short of a

[1] See Boswell's *Life of Johnson* (Birkbeck Hill edition), I, 278, where Johnson's prayer is quoted: "And O Lord, so far as it may be lawful in me, I commend to thy fatherly goodness the soul of my departed wife; beseeching thee to grant her whatever is best in her present state, and finally to receive her to eternal happiness." Also, *ibid.*, II, 120, 186–187.

positive prohibition from Heaven, I think, could warrant
the omission. But, I bless God, there is no such prohibition.
A protestant theologian may reason against it, from the
extreme, final, and irreversible nature of that state into which
we pass at death; but a Catholic would deny his premises, as
well as his conclusion; and I confess that of all the Catholic
doctrines which we have disclaimed, that of purgatory seems
to me the least unworthy to have been retained. It may be
beside the Scripture revelation; but not I think *against* it.
The foul abuse made of it by Priestcraft is no impeachment
of its truth; for what truth, however certain and fundamental
to Christian faith, is not liable to the same objection? I am
not easily reasoned out of, or reasoned into, any tenet as to
the things unseen, by *inference from* the sacred text. To what is
"plainly declared in" and not what is *"proveable from"* it, I
yield a full assent; for we always reason rashly, if not pre-
sumptuously, when the subject is beyond our comprehen-
sion, as things spiritual commonly are. But if we are to be
"wise beyond what is written" it ought not to be for the
purpose of condemning any opinion consonant to natural
religion and necessary for the consolation and support of
feeling and pious minds. I will not point out the application
of these remarks, nor enlarge further here on this very
important and interesting subject. I think my dear Sally's
views on it were like my own. She knew that I often prayed
for the former Partner of my heart and did not find fault
with it as she always faithfully did with what she regarded
as religious errors; but on the contrary once said to me, "My
dear Stephen, will you pray also for *me*, when I am gone?"
Yes! exalted Spirit! I *do* pray for thee also daily; tho' I can
recollect but very few, and very venial faults, to ask forgiveness for on thy behalf. More congruous perhaps with my
sincere impressions is the prayer that thy felicity may be
increased, and thy crown of glory brightened, by the success
of thy pious labours of love for my own immortal interests,
and those of my children! On reviewing the terms of this
digression, I perceive that they may probably be construed
as a profession of my belief in the Catholic doctrine of
purgatory. *That* is not my meaning. My views on this
subject cannot be compendiously, nor perhaps usefully

explained. Unless an explanation of them shall be given by my pen before I die, let me be here understood simply to mean that prayers for departed friends are not inconsistent in my opinion with anything that we are bound as Christians to believe.

I do not recollect having been informed by my dear Nancy of what passed between her Father and her on the discovery. She thought it best perhaps to spare me and herself the pain of such a communication, which might have tended to widen the breach she was most desirous to close. The result, however, was that he placed her as a boarder with a Widow Lady of the name of Heath, and left her tacitly, if not expresssly at liberty in regard to such future intercourse with me as without any breach of prudence or propriety might be allowed. So I infer at least from her conduct; for she no longer regarded the meeting me, or receiving my visits, as any violation of her filial duties. The only question was how we could often see each other with decorum. All difficulty in this respect was soon removed. Mrs. Heath, who had received my dear Nancy as a boarder not altogether from mercenary motives, but more from the want of society, became much attached to her, and being let into the secret of our engagement to each other, willingly favoured our interviews at her house. I naturally in return paid my court to the old lady, and soon became a great favorite with her, so much so that she at length forced on me the hospitalities of her table beyond any degree that I could well reconcile to delicacy my acceptance of them. Having no child or near relation, and being in very easy circumstances, she thought nothing of the expence that such kindness must have sometimes occasioned, and found her domestic comforts materially enhanced by my visits. I brought her the news of the town (for she lived in Walcott Place, then regarded as a retired rural situation) read to her and my dear Nancy while they worked, was an oracle of taste and information in the old Lady's esteem, and not rarely made a fourth at whist when an intimate friend of hers who managed her affairs came to dine or spend the Evening.

In short if I had gone there every day in the week she would have given me a hearty welcome.

With such facilities of course I spent much time at Walcott Place that ought to have been more profitably employed. My law books were too often laid aside, and if my poor Father's business was sufficiently attended to, it was because its demands on my time were small and were rapidly declining. It was in fact but a short time after the events last narrated that he continued in business at all. His health became so bad that he was at length unable to come to town except on pressing occasions, and both mind and body progressively fell into such debility and lassitude that he was incapable of any exertion and for the most part shrunk from all intercourse with clients or friends, shutting himself up in his cottage on Stoke Newington Common. Tho' I had long seen that his health was declining, the slowness of the progress, and his own silence on the subject prevented my apprehending any immediate danger; but my friend Livingstone, going with me one day to see him, was greatly struck with the deterioration that had taken place since their last interview, and opened my eyes to the true nature of the case. It was plain to his professional judgment that the liver was diseased, and a fatal termination probably at no great distance. I forget whether it was before or after this discovery that my Brother William, having learnt in Edinbro' that our Father was declining in health, and I think also of his wish to see him, came to London to visit and attend him. He also thought very badly of the case; but if I rightly remember was obliged to return to his medical studies without waiting for the result. I think that the event at that time was not expected very soon, and was in fact delayed afterwards for several weeks at least. As soon as my eyes were opened to the danger, I obtained for him by Livingstone's suggestion the advice of Dr. Saunders,[1] then the Physician in first repute for bilious diseases, who saw him several times and prescribed for him, but with no permanent good effect. The Doctor's prognostic, as I learned from Livingstone, was that he might linger a long time but could not possibly recover. To the Patient himself as usual nothing of that kind was

[1] William Saunders (1743–1817), physician to Guy's Hospital, London, 1770–1802; FRCP, 1790; physician to George, Prince of Wales, 1807; first president of the Royal Medical and Chirurgical Society, 1805.

said; and I doubt whether my poor Father was himself aware that he was in any great or early danger. Self deception seems to be a law of our Nature in such cases. If he had any apprehensions he never mentioned them to me; indeed he was systematically reserved on subjects that were afflicting to him, at least towards his children, and valued himself on fortitude or indifference under sufferings. "I have had many troubles in my offer (he used to say) but never accepted any of them." It was, I remember, an anxious question with me whether I ought not to disclose to him the danger of his situation, and I sometimes had nearly made up my mind to do so, but always postponed, when with him, the painful task. My filial anxieties were not engaged by his bodily sufferings alone, or the prospect of their fatal termination. I knew that if he should recover, or even hold out for any considerable time, absolute want was his inevitable lot. He also knew it; tho' I kept back from him in some measure the extremity of the case, as I was in a small degree able to do, from his having of late made me his sole cashier, and devolved on me the entire charge of his affairs. Often do I look back on the wonderful care of Providence in supplying his necessities for many years, as well before as after my dear Mother's death, contrary to all probability, by sending from time to time unexpected resources; which generally arrived when to all appearance we were on the eve of extreme distress. In many instances did I look around me in vain to discover if I could a single ray of hope, one cheering tho' slight probability, of our finding means to sustain the family, even for a month to come. Not only money but credit was wanting for the purpose. The tradesmen that supplied us with the necessaries of life, uneasy from the amount of unpaid bills, refused to trust him any longer: and legal coercion was sometimes threatened which if resorted to would have sent him to a prison. But uniformly when the hour of compleat and hopeless ruin seemed to have arrived, some unlooked for supply drop'd on us like manna from the clouds, and was sometimes large enough for a temporary extrication from our difficulties by the payment of debts, &c., tho' very rarely beyond the immediate necessities of the case. To explain the means would be tedious and painful; they were various;

James Stephen, father of James Stephen
the author of the Memoirs

but all or for the most part, not only unconcerted by us, but such as are usually called not only accidental but extraordinary. I mean the occurrence of which at such times of need was beyond all reasonable calculation. My dear Mother had often called my attention to such events as proofs of a presiding Providence; and I had seen so many of them, that I had become accustomed to expect resources, tho' unable to conjecture from what quarter they would come, merely from our urgent need of them. But at the period of which I am speaking our prospects had become gloomy and hopeless beyond all former experience. In my Father's helpless state he could not place himself, so to speak, in Fortune's way; he had no longer any business my care of which could recruit the small remaining fund in my hands, and among the debts he owed there was one which I found it would take the whole of that fund, about £40 as I best remember, to discharge, while its immediate payment had become necessary to save him from an execution. This debt was an arrear of rent due to his Landlord, a wealthy but unfeeling man, who upon the non-payment of a bill or note given for it, had obtained a judgment, and was about to send an execution into the House. I too well remember my poor dear Father, who was then at length confined for the most part to his bed, sending for me on receiving notice of this intention, and that I had the pain to find him, for the first time I think, alarmed at the near prospect of distress and want. His mind, broken down by sickness, was less than usually firm, and he told me in a plaintive way that he feared he should have his bed sold from under him, or something to that effect. Tho' my apprehensions were like his own, I disguised my real feelings, assumed an air of cheerful confidence, earnestly requested him to make his mind easy, and assured him that he should never know either distresss or want. Animated at the moment by a strong sense of filial duty and a resolution to make my words good, I forgot the impotence of my situation and induced him to forget it too. He seemed quite tranquillized by my assurances and mentioned the subject no more.

On reflecting what was to be done I saw no more promising course than to try to soften the creditor by disclosing to him the compassionable nature of the case; but knowing that I had to deal with a coarse and unfeeling man, and that unless he were satisfied in the first instance of the safety of his debt no mercy could be hoped for from him, I thought it best in the first place to call on his Attornies and engage their feelings if possible in my favor. They were entire strangers to me, but respectable men, the Messrs. Wadeson brothers, the last survivor of whom not long since attended me in my office as Solicitor in a cause referred to me but is now, I believe, no more. When informed by me that the defendant into whose house they were going to send an execution was on his death bed (for he was at length unable to rise and manifestly could not hold out long) and that they might hasten his end but could hardly perhaps finish the harsh proceeding before his dissolution, they very kindly listened to my solicitation and promised to mediate with their client. They accordingly sent for him, and on his arrival did all they could to second my purpose, but in vain. I observed to him that his debt was quite safe, because the furniture in the house would more than cover it, and that he being the Landlord, as well as the only judgment creditor, was in no danger of any preference being obtained to his prejudice. His attornies good-naturedly forbore to point out the only possible flaw in this security, that of my making away with the furniture, which under the circumstances and from what they saw of my feelings, they probably regarded as no reasonable cause of distrust; nor did the Man himself profess any apprehension on that score. But it was in vain that I attempted to move him by the distressing circumstances of the case, and besought him not to embitter the last moments of a dying man and to aggravate the feelings of his children who were soon to be destitute orphans. My language, I doubt not, was eloquent, for it came from the heart, and I remember it had a visibly powerful effect on the minds of the Wadesons. But their client was a perfect Shylock. He did not scruple to avow the revenge which combined with his avarice, because my Father had disputed, on some ground which I forget, his title to the house, and inexorably insisted on the execution being immediately sent in unless the debt was paid. When I found it impossible to move him from this relentless purpose, even by those tears which the prospect of my poor Father's impending fate forced me to shed profusely, I was agitated by less kindly emotions. Indignation succeeded to grief, and I reproached the obdurate man in terms that led him hastily to retreat. The Attornies behaved with great feeling throughout, and tho' forced to follow their Client's instructions they either gave a short delay or pointed out that an interval would necessarily elapse before the execution could be sent in during which I might try to raise the money. Before the expiration of the time, this was effected and the debt paid. I forget whether it was by the application of the small fund which was all that was left to sustain our daily expences, or by the aid of my dear Brother, who either then or immediately after consulted his filial and fraternal feelings by giving or sending to us about £50, I think, recently remitted to him by his Uncle for his own support. In doing so he risked, but I believe in no degree incurred, his Uncle's displeasure. About this time he came again, I think, from Edinburgh, on account of our distressing situation; but whether he arrived before or immediately after our poor Father's death I cannot clearly remember.

Chapter Seven

[1779–1781]

THAT event was still nearer than I apprehended. The case is usually so both with the Patient and his family in lingering diseases. I had recently been in his room and thought from appearances he was rather worse than common, and was again painfully deliberating with myself whether I ought not to apprize him of the imminent danger he was in and suggest to him such thoughts as might possibly induce him to send for a clergyman or in some other way prepare himself for his approaching change. In order to make up my mind on this point I went out on the Common in front of his house, and took two or three long turns, during which I came to the resolution to perform that painful duty, and I think was returning for the purpose, when I saw the window of his bedroom hastily opened and an arm waving a handkerchief to me from it. Alarmed at the signal, I ran towards the house and hastened to his chamber; but my poor dear Father had breathed his last. The final struggle of Nature must have been very short, and his departure easy, for Kitty, the servant who was in the room with him, had made the signal to me as soon as she perceived any convulsive symptom.[1]

Tho' I have never laid much stress on death-bed preparations, my feelings on this sad event were aggravated by the doubt whether I had not neglected a sacred filial duty. It is not the only fault of the kind that I shall have to record against myself in these Memoirs. In truth there is no duty from which I shrink so much, or which I have so uniformly neglected. May God of his great mercy pardon these and all my sins.

I had not on this occasion much leisure for the indulgence either of sorrow or remorse. Active duties of a difficult kind thronged immediately upon me and admitted of no delay.

[1] Leslie Stephen gives the date of the elder Stephen's burial as September 9, 1779.

The decent interment of my poor dear Father's remains was hardly a more pressing concern than the breaking up his domestic establishment, the discharge of his servants, and giving up the House to the landlord, and, as necessary means of all, the selling his Household furniture, the only property he had left. I had not the means even of providing for the funeral, which was in the most frugal stile that decency allowed, otherwise than by employing the village undertaker to appraise and sell the furniture, and assuring him of payment out of the first proceeds. My dear Brother William, who at this time, if not before, arrived from Scotland, assisted me in the last duties to our deceased Parent. We laid his body in the same spot in the Church Yard of Stoke Newington where that of my dear Mother had been interred, and where I have since sunk a vault, and erected a plain granite monument or tomb, and deposited the remains of four other beloved relatives, and where I expect that e'er long my own dust and that of my dear Wilberforce will mix with theirs. See my reflections on the interment of my dear Mother in that spot. My Brother and I and our two little fellow orphans with the Servants were the only attendants but the humble solemnity was not unaccompanied with the feelings that properly belong to it. Among them on my part, and my dear Bill's too, I doubt not, were those towards the children of renewed adoption and parentage. We felt that we were now their only Guardians; we knew not that any other human ones would be found; but forgetting the impotency of my own situation which (adult age excepted) was hardly less destitute and helpless than theirs, I resolved that they should find in me a second Father; I seconded the resolve with prayer, and felt a firm confidence that it would not be fruitless.

My dear Brother and I had deliberated before with much anxiety on the course we had to take in regard to them. The best or only hope we had was that the affection and compassion of our Aunt and Uncle Nuccoll or of our Uncle Milner would prove a resource for them, to the extent of sustenance and education during their tender years, or till we were able to sustain them. But of this we had reasonable doubts; for tho' our Aunt's kindred feelings and generosity were great, and well seconded by Mr. Nuccoll, who was a kind, liberal man and most indulgent husband, his circumstances were not affluent, his family establishment was small and frugal, and having already adopted our Sister Sibella, it seemed too much to expect that he would also take the charge of two other children, a boy about seven and a girl about nine years old who were not his own blood relations. The latter was not the case with Mr. Milner, and their Mother had stood high in his regard and esteem; but after her death all family intercourse with him had ceased, except that I had once seen him in his way through London. His circumstances indeed were easy, and as we then supposed affluent; and he had but one Son, whose kindness and liberality of character we knew. But Mrs. Milner was so much annoyed with chronical complaints of a nervous kind, and so little, from her consequent habits, fit to sustain the noise and trouble of children in her family that we could not but regard an offer to receive those little orphans into it as no very probable fruit of simpathy from them. Except these relations, and our Uncle William who was in the West Indies, and who was likely to think he had done enough for my Father's family in adopting his eldest son, there was no relative near or remote from whom we could hope assistance. We felt that under these circumstances it would be wrong for us to *ask* any thing in either quarter; but that we ought only to state without reserve the destitute situation in which the family was left and wait to see whether any and what help would be offered. This we accordingly did without delay, my Brother writing fully on the subject to Mrs. Nuccoll and I to Mr. Milner. While waiting for their answers we sold the furniture as agreed, discharged the Servants, and gave up the House, removing with the children to a small set of Chambers in an Attic story at Lyons Inn. I had taken them, if I remember right, a short time before the time when my Father's recovery was quite despaired of and his end visibly approaching, but if so they had not been furnished; for the means we took to prepare them for our immediate reception was to redeem at the appraised value some beds and other necessary articles from the undertaker who bought the rest, for which purpose, and our immediate subsistence, my

Brother applied some money that he had brought with him,
or was able to take up from his Uncle's correspondent in
advance of his stated allowance. Having applied to the last
farthing all that my Father's effects produced in paying for
the funeral and servants' wages, I was painfully obliged to
leave some debts which I understood or supposed that he
owed to the tradesmen and shopkeepers in the village undis-
charged, but so notorious was our destitute situation that
we were neither complained of, nor applied to on the subject. It was a blameable oversight in me not to ascertain and
make a memorandum of what they were. After my return
from the West Indies I made enquiries with a view to their
payment but could not discover a single creditor. The two
or three persons whom I knew him to have dealt with were
either dead or removed, to what places I could not learn. On
reflection I thought it doubtful whether he in fact left any
such debts, and believe if he did they were very trifling, or I
should otherwise have heard of them. His known poverty and
embarrassments during his last illness probably induced the
tradesmen to keep short scores with him. In saying that we
discharged the Servants I should have excepted Kitty White,
an old one who had lived with my Mother many years and
continued with my Father till his death. She had a maternal
affection for the children, and we brought her with them to
Lyons Inn. I recollect also another inaccuracy which I must
from its connection with subsequent events correct. Her
wages, and those of another servant, were by their consent
left unpaid, that we might be able to redeem more of the
furniture that was wanted at Lyons Inn. We concluded that
our stay there would be very short, and it was to be sold
when no longer wanted there to satisfy those demands. As the
rent of the chambers was only £10 a year, this was a cheaper
course than taking furnished lodgings.

The answer from Mr. and Mrs. Nuccoll was very kind and
affectionate and expressed much anxiety to learn what were
my plans for myself and the children, with a wish to do any
thing in their power for our assistance, in which they concluded Mr. Milner would concur; and when we should have
consulted with him and our relations in England they
desired to hear what was thought best for the children. I

9

think there was also an intimation that they supposed Mr. and Mrs. M. would offer to take one at least of the children under their charge.

My dear Bill and I were now much embarrassed and disheartened; for tho' we had no reason to be dissatisfied with this letter, or to despair from it of their coming forward effectually in the sequel, it was plain that they meant in the first instance to put the feelings of our maternal relatives to the proof; and we had waited a week or more beyond the return of post without receiving any answer from Mr. Milner. At length a letter came from him by which we found the delay had partly arisen from his being at Comberton in Cambridgeshire whereas my letter had been sent to Poole in Dorsetshire, where I supposed him then to be. His stile was chillingly cold, and there was an expression in it which cut me to the heart; for he expressed surprise at what I had stated of my Father's circumstances, as he was well informed that not long before he had a considerable sum at his Bankers. Taken with the context it seemed to me to imply a distrust of my veracity and integrity. My Uncle, tho' a generous and affectionate man, by whom I had always been treated with kindness, had a weakness by general repute in the family very incongruous with the general liberality of his character. He was very apt to conceive unjust and even extravagant suspicions. Both my Brother and I therefore were inclined to take this very unseasonable intimation in an offensive sense, and I felt so indignantly upon it that had my own interest only been in question he would have heard from me no more. But the rest of his letter, tho' it contained no offer of assistance as to the children, was not calculated to convince me, still less to convince our friends in Scotland, that such assistance was hopeless. It expressed a desire to be informed what plans we had for them, and also what I proposed to do in my own case. I felt myself therefore compelled for their sakes to suppress my feelings; to take what he had said in an inoffensive sense, and content myself with such explanations respecting my Father's affairs as were calculated to remove his suspicions, if he really entertained them. As to our plans for the children, the answer of course was that we could form none, that we had expected some advice on that subject from the only friends to whom we could look for present means for their support, and that our Friends in Scotland waited to hear whether our Mother's relations had any thing to suggest on that subject. Such, I believe, was in substance the tenour of my reply on the enquiry as to the children. For my own part I told him I was determined that I would shift for myself, and not add in any way to the burthen which my helpless fellow orphans must inavoidably impose upon others, and that my plan was immediately to go to America and offer my services to General Washington as a Volunteer in the Army under his command.[1] Such was in fact my resolution. My dear Brother had in vain endeavoured, even with tears, to dissuade me from it; for I saw no other way in which, without renouncing my rank in life as a gentleman (to which I proudly deemed myself not less intitled than if I had been born to affluence) I could hope to earn my own bread, and avoid the mortification of dependency. I was enthusiastically attached to the cause of the revolted colonies, which I deemed to be that of liberty throughout the world, and thought that even the British Constitution itself depended on their success. I felt no scruple whatever as to the violating my allegiance. On the contrary I thought it would be meritorious so to promote the best interests of my Country in opposition to her misdirected arms; and I vainly gave myself credit for talents that would raise me to eminence and military renown. I reckoned also on being more likely to find means in that new country than in England of providing thereafter for my Sisters and younger brother. At worst, if I could get a passage to America (on which I not without some reason relied) I should be able, as I thought, to avoid want and to find a path either to independency or an honorable death. In this as in a hundred other instances I have lived to learn into what misery and sure destruction I should have plunged if a gracious Providence had not superseded my own designs. The climate and the hardships of the service would have ruined my health and brought me to my grave in a single campaign; and when brought into con-

[1] Here, sometime after September 9, 1779, Stephen was still planning to go to America. See above, p. 157.

tact with those slave-driving champions of liberty and
justice, there would have been an end of the delusions which
had given to them my simpathy and made me a willing
victim to their cause. When Mr. and Mrs. Nuccoll found
that nothing was proposed for the children by their Mother's
relations, they did not leave us longer in doubt as to their
own kind and generous intentions but wrote to us that they
would willingly take charge of them both and requested that
my Brother would bring them to Edinburgh with him on his
return, for which he had soon to prepare.

The offer, of course, was on our part gratefully accepted,
and Mr. Milner was informed that this subject of our
fraternal anxiety was happily removed. In reply he expressed
his satisfaction on that score, but added professions of concern on my account and an invitation to me to come to
Comberton that he might talk with me about my plans in
life. I was by no means willing to go. Tho' the stile of this
letter was kind enough, I had not forgot that of the former
one and felt a strong disinclination to accept or to appear
willing to accept any assistance in that quarter. But my dear
Brother in his affectionate anxiety so earnestly intreated me
at least to go to Comberton and hear whether Mr. Milner
had any thing to propose for my benefit, that in compliance
with his solicitations I vanquished my repugnance to the
visit. He walked with me to Ware, where we slept, and the
next morning I proceeded alone to Comberton in the same
way. Well do I remember to this hour that solitary journey
and some of my reveries by the way. The conference to which
I was going was likely to have a most important influence on
my human destiny; but my spirits were then buoyant and
my imagination warm, and I had little or no anxiety.

My reception from my Uncle Milner was kind and obliging. I saw for the first time that House in which I have since
spent so many pleasant days, and even the kind hospitalities
of my dear Brother-in-law and Sister, its present owners,
could not exceed those I then met with from my Uncle, who
was living there without his family. It is due to his memory
to say that he had a delicate sense of what liberality required
in his personal deportment towards those on whom he had
conferred or meant to confer obligations. His mind was far

from a vulgar one, tho' he had his faults and among them that which I have already noticed, as I found afterwards to my cost. The cordiality of his manner and conversation soon dispelled the unpleasant feelings which his first letter had excited, and when he entered on the subject on which he had desired to talk with me it was in a way entirely to satisfy my self love and inspire me with confidence in his friendly feelings and intentions. He explained frankly to me the reasons which had prevented his offering to take one or both the children into his family, which turned chiefly on considerations regarding my Aunt's state of health and habits; and I was able without insincerity to admit their justice and force. But as to my own case he professed an earnest desire to give me all the assistance that might be necessary to enable me to follow up the plan of life which I had been hitherto pursuing. He spoke of my talents in a very flattering way, and thought that regard not only to my own interest but that of my fellow orphans should forbid my quitting the path of a profession in which I might reasonably promise myself such success as would enable me amply to provide both for myself and them. He entered into very full and free explanations as to his circumstances, which I found to be by no means so affluent or easy as I had before supposed; and the general effect was that he certainly had not much if any thing to spare out of his income, especially as he had to provide for the expences of his Son, then a fellow-commoner at St. Johns. But he concluded by saying that he could, and very willingly would, supply me with such a moderate allowance as with œconomy and prudence on my part might enable me to make my way to the bar.

I thanked him heartily for the offer, but declined to accept it, observing on the doubtfulness as well as distance in that direction of the independency which I was impatient to obtain and the certainty that if I could get to America I should, by entering as a volunteer under Washington, cease to be a burthen to my friends at least, and perhaps advance myself honorably in the world. If he would kindly furnish me with the means of fitting myself out decently and paying my passage money, it was assistance that I would willingly and gratefully accept; but as to the being for years a

burthen on his purse the explanations he had given were
new and powerful reasons with me for declining it. In reply
he pointed out very strong objections to my American plan,
such as could not but painfully chill my sanguine hopes and
truly enough represented it as what would be throwing
away my best chance of usefulness in life and most probably
life itself. He was a sensible man who knew well how to put
his ideas in a strong and impressive shape; and his kindness
was still more persuasive with me than his arguments. Yet I
slowly and with difficulty gave way. When I began to do so
he pressed me to consider and state what annual sum at the
lowest might suffice for my support, independently of the
charges that would attend my admission to the bar, proposing as a means of reducing the expence that I should spend
my vacation time in his family. I cannot recollect certainly
on which side it was, but think on his, that fifty pounds or
guineas per ann. was at last mentioned as a sum that might
possibly suffice. On my part, when my great opposition to
the plan in the abstract was subdued I naturally wished to
place the allowance on the lowest possible scale, and tho' I
felt that it would be extremely difficult to live on fifty pounds
a year as a law student, I certainly did not object to it as too
low. At that time it would have gone further than £100
a year at the present day. After much unfeigned reluctance
on my side and much kind solicitation on his, it was at
length settled between us that I should renounce my American scheme and sit down in London to prepare myself for the
bar by attending the Courts, &c., and keeping my terms to
the end of my course at Lincoln's Inn and that to enable
me to do this he should remit to me £50 or guineas per Ann.,
by quarterly portions. As the chambers we had taken in
Lyons Inn were so very cheap, it was his opinion and mine
that I had better keep them and live at Eating Houses (as
I well knew how very frugally to do) as a cheaper plan than
boarding and more consistent with the view of œconomising
by spending the vacations with him. This, however, obliged
me fully to explain to him that the furniture there was liable
for the servants' wages and must be sold to satisfy them unless
I had other means of doing so; and as he still approved of my
keeping the chambers I fully expected that at parting he

would put into my hand with a Quarter's allowance in advance the amount also of what was due to the servants. In this I was disappointed. He parted from me very cordially but gave me no money nor said any thing on the subject. I concluded, however, that it was because he had no money in the House, and that I should hear from him with a remittance soon after my return to London.

My dear Brother was overjoyed with the report that I brought back. He thought indeed the allowance too small, but hoped that it would be in his power after his settlement in the West Indies at least to supply what might be deficient. Meantime the great objects of his fraternal anxiety were attained. I was not to throw away my life by going to America, and I was to prosecute that professional plan in which he relied on my success. There was another person whose heart was much relieved and elated by the same result. I have long forborne to speak of my dear Nancy, but it is needless to say how deeply she simpathised with my sorrows and how lively an interest she had taken in my journey to Cambridge. She could judge little what on the death of my Father was best to be done, but was naturally very averse to my projected migration; and it was enough to insure her satisfaction with the plan I had embraced that for some years at least I should be near her. Of course the same consideration was powerful with me, and her feelings had a strong influence on my decision; without it perhaps the proud dislike of dependency, and the romantic views that inclined me to migrate, would not have yielded to my Uncle's arguments. The recent renewal of my tender attachments to and intercourse with her was one of the means which a gracious Providence had prepared to rescue me from the wretchedness and destruction that I should probably have met with in America, and to retain me in a professional plan pregnant with future blessings to me and the rest of my dear Mother's children.[1]

My dear Nancy was also to me at this period a great and necessary consolation, for immediately after my return from Cambridge I had the pain to part with my beloved Brother and the two little ones who now, from our mutual misfortune

[1] This is Stephen's last mention of the possibility of going to America.

and necessities, as well as much intercourse with them at their interesting ages, had a very fast hold on my affections. My kind and pleasant companion, Livingstone, also was to return to Scotland with them, having finished his medical course in London. Under bereavings my heart clung fondly to the resource that my dear Nancy's affection and Society held forth to me, and my dear kind Brother was as much relieved as myself by the knowledge that he did not leave me without such a tender and faithful friend to supply his place. I had no secret with him on that or any other subject. I had introduced him to her, and they were mutually pleased with each other; and such was his uniform indulgence for all my feelings (of which he well knew the force) that he never once hinted to me, tho' he must have seen, that such an attachment was premature and imprudent. Sad was that morning when I accompanied this amiable Brother, our friend Livingstone, and the poor children to the wharf, saw them on board a vessel bound for Leith, and gave them a long adieu. The children seemed to feel the seperation not less keenly than the rest of us. They clung to me and wetted my face with their tears. For my part the scene painfully reminded me of that which I have herein before described, my parting with the two elder girls soon after the loss of our dear Mother; and it seemed to me as if in thus resigning the remaining objects of her dying charge, no more personally to protect their helpless innocence or watch over their opening minds, I was deserting, tho' from a cruel necessity, the duties I had vowed to her. Reason, indeed, soon checked that error of the fancy. I was no free agent in the seperation, and it was manifestly for their good. My hope also of future usefulness to them demanded that I should be where they could not remain. The parting with my dear Bill was a sorrow that I had known repeatedly before, but iteration had not lessened its severity. He was always my best-loved companion as well as my kindest friend.

My first resource in all such afflictions, next to the relief of tear shedding, is prayer. Both were used on this occasion very copiously; but my prayers were not wholly of a kind perhaps to be approved. There was more in them, I fear, of an earnest desire to reunite with these beloved relatives in the present life, and for their temporal welfare and happiness, than for those spiritual blessings to which our prayers, whether for ourselves or others, should chiefly be directed. Yet it has pleased God often and wonderfully, yes *very* often and *very* VERY wonderfully, to answer my prayers for temporal objects. Is it because my feeble faith has always stood pre-eminently in need of such confirmation? Is it that I may love him more and thereby be led to aspire more after Heavenly things? Both no doubt; and the latter object, as well as the former, is I hope in some small degree accomplished.

I dare say that I did not sleep before I had seen my dear Nancy, and found in her tender simpathy the best human balm for my wounded mind. Her Society, which I no longer found any difficulty in obtaining, soon soothed my sorrows, and gave pleasing occupation to at least as much time as I could justifiably take from my business as a law student.

I found, however, immediately after my Brother's departure, matter of much embarrassment and disquietude in my Uncle Milner's conduct. No remittance, no letter, arrived from him, while the Servants were waiting for their wages, and one of them, Kitty White, was unable to go to her Friends in Dorsetshire, as she proposed, for want of means to provide her with some necessaries, and pay the expences of her journey. I had no money left for this purpose and very little to answer my daily expences; tho' my Brother had left with me all the little he could spare; nor had I any resource but to sell the furniture, which would have obliged me to give up the Chambers, and thereby to reverse the plan so recently settled with my Uncle. Having so fully apprised him of the circumstances, he must, I concluded, be as well aware as I was myself, that I could not go on without an immediate supply of money. It might seem, therefore, I felt, like a complaint or rebuke if I were to write him of the difficulties I was placed in. I resolved therefore to avoid doing so as long as I could possibly hold out, and waited in daily expectation of a letter from him, till I found that actual distress, both to the servants and myself, must be the effect of a longer delay. When I wrote at last, I could not bring myself to make a direct and absolute request for money. I therefore, after clearly stating the necessities of my situation, especially in what regarded the servants, observed that if he thought fit I could sell the furniture for as much as would pay them off and leave me a small fund in hand for my current expences, but in that case must part with the chambers (which I had taken only for three months certain) and adopt the plan of lodging and boarding in a private family. To my great surprise and consternation, I received no answer to this letter, either in course of post, as I had requested, or for several days after.

I forget whether I wrote a second time, but believe I did, apprising him also that I had enquired as to the terms on which I could be boarded and lodged in a decent private family, and found it would be £40 a year. At length, when I was reduced to extremities, a letter arrived explaining in some measure the delay in answering my first, by his absence from home, but containing no remittance or any other solution of my difficulties except the permission to take what course I thought best. In effect he left me no choice, while desiring me to choose for myself and, what stung me still more, he remarked on the terms of boarding which I had mentioned, that when he himself was a boarder in London the terms were much lower, I think he said £20 a year—manifestly implying that my views were extravagant. I now began to feel very painfully the sense of dependency and to anticipate consequences of my situation such as very soon ensued, but felt that it was due to myself and my fellow orphans to practise all possible forbearance and if I could not retain the patronage which sat uneasily upon me, at least to take care that I was not put in the wrong in the estimate of impartial friends. I therefore restrained my feelings and said nothing in reply that could possibly give offence, but merely expressed the necessity that I found of giving up the chambers and my willingness to become a boarder in any House that by his assistance could be found in which I might be received on cheaper terms.

There being now no time to lose, I immediately sold the furniture of my chambers to the same Tradesman who had provided my Father's funeral, and though I believe that compassion prevented his taking any unfair advantage, I found it would barely suffice to pay the Servants what remained due for wages to discharge the rent, and leave me a very few pounds, I believe not more than three or four in hand.

A concurrent object of no less urgency was to find a family into which I might immediately be received as a lodger and boarder; and upon this point, as indeed on every other of any interest, I naturally consulted with my dear Nancy, now my only bosom friend on the spot, whose lively simpathy in my recent sorrows and discomforts had been my chief consolation and had endeared her to me, if possible, more than ever; and by one of those important incidents, called chances, on which the good and evil of our lives often mainly depend, I found her on this occasion, fortunately as I thought, able to give me the very information and assistance of which I stood urgently in need.

I have mentioned that my old friend, her Brother, had, prior to his departure on his last voyage, fallen violently in love with a young Lady who had rejected his addresses, and of this young Lady it now becomes necessary for me to give some account. As she will often be mentioned hereafter I must give her a name, but it must be a fictitious one, and I will call her *Maria Rivers*.[1] Miss Rivers was the reputed niece of a Doctor Lennox (this name also is fictitious) who was an old physician of a very respectable family, but a younger Brother, and who not having, I presume, been very successful in practice, had lived a batchellor and retired at the approach of old age with but a very small fortune, his original patrimony, to spend the rest of his days in a Village near London. In fact Maria was his illegitimate daughter and by a married lady, but under circumstances of some extenuation. I have heard enough of her to hope she was a sincere penitent, and she did not survive her transgression very many years. The Doctor acted towards the unfortunate offspring of their crime the part of a tender and liberal parent, tho' perhaps not a discreet one. He resolved to give her what in his own estimate was the best of educations, and to that end, as well as the better to conceal her true extraction, placed her till the age of 12 or 13 in a convent in France and from that period till about 17 at an eminent Lady's boarding school

---

[1] I have been unable to find any clue to the identity behind this fictitious name.

near London, when having, in addition to a fluent command of the French language, enough of what are usually called accomplishments, she was taken home to live with her reputed Uncle a year or two before the time when my friend Tom first became acquainted with her. The old Gentlemen having become a prey to the gout and other infirmities, a woman, whom I will call Mrs. Hamilton, of fawning manners, but of a mercenary and designing character, had contrived for many years to obtain a strong hold on his confidence and attachment, not I believe by any criminal means, but by the ordinary parasitical arts of humble friends and dependants. Her husband, who had failed in business, was struggling to reestablish himself in it on a small scale, probably with the Doctor's assistance; and while he was thus employed in London, she devoted herself to Doctor Lennox's service, in fact as a housekeeper and nurse, but ostensibly as the Mistress of the House in which, tho' kept wholly at his expence, he chose to be regarded only as a lodger and boarder for his greater ease and convenience, Mr. Hamilton sleeping there and managing as his own the external concerns of the establishment. A grown-up daughter of theirs tolerably well educated also made a part of the family; and their son, a Midshipman in the Navy, also lived in it during his short visits when in port to his Parents. Such was the home to which Miss Rivers was brought when her boarding school education was finished; and as the old Man's love for her was extreme, these his dependants naturally paid their humble and assiduous court to her. She was also apparently a great favorite with Mr. Lennox, the Doctor's elder brother, who like him had lived a batchellor and was a very wealthy man, not only from inheriting the family estate, but from successful practice at the bar from which he had long retired. He was affectionately attached to the Doctor, to whom it was understood he meant to leave his fortune, and had led him and Maria to expect that in the event of the Doctor (whose income was chiefly for life only) dying first, he would amply provide for her. She was therefore considered as an Heiress and taught to look forward to affluence.

A few months prior to the period to which I have brought my narrative Dr. Lennox died, and a will was found whereby he had left to Mrs. Hamilton no inconsiderable part (a half I think) of the property he had power to dispose of, including the House and furniture, altho' the rest was but a very slender provision for a young Lady brought up as Miss Rivers had been; but he doubtless relied that his Brother's affection would be an ample resource for her, and it was probably for her sake that he wished to enable the Hamiltons to keep up the establishment, for it was his desire that she should continue to live with them. She accordingly resolved to do so. Indeed, she had no other friends under whose protection she could be placed; for her Uncle, Mr. Lennox, who was for the most part confined to his room by the infirmities of age, had no female in his family and had a male inmate to whose management he had committed himself almost as implicitly as his Brother had to the Hamiltons. It was not long, however, before these found themselves unable to keep up the establishment without further aid than such an allowance for Miss Rivers's board as her small fortune would afford, and they resolved to take two other boarders, and accordingly let some of their best accomodations to a gentleman whom I will call Major Berkeley, an old officer who had spent a great part of his life in the East Indies.

My dear Nancy, who then lived in the same neighbourhood and had for her Brother's sake as well as Miss Rivers's, whom she much liked, cultivated an intimacy with that young lady, knew all these particulars; and on my consulting her she kindly suggested that if Mrs. H. could be prevailed on to accept me as a boarder the situation would be a more pleasant one than any other I was likely to find. That it would not only place me very near to her but thro' her intimacy with Miss R. bring us frequently together was naturally with us both a powerful recommendation; but we had reason to doubt not only whether the terms would be low enough for my purse, but also whether my age might not be thought objectionable, tho' Major Berkeley's had been thought to remove any objection in his case to a male boarder. We resolved, however, to try, and my dear Nancy was so good and zealous a mediator that all difficulties, if any were raised, were soon surmounted. I doubt not that the disclosure of our engagement, together with her very partial

account of my character and manners, contributed to reconcile the Hamiltons to what they must otherwise have regarded as an impropriety, tho' Maria's warm approbation
of such an addition to the family Party might seem an additional excuse. As to the terms, my requiring only a bedroom
and other arrangements, reduced them I think to forty
guineas or a little more, and tho' I feared that they were
more than I should long be able to afford I resolved to make
the experiment for a quarter at least, since it would not be
easy to find any other situation so speedily as my necessity
required. I was introduced therefore to Mrs. Hamilton, and
she agreed to receive me in a few days.

Before I could take a final leave of my chambers at Lyons
Inn I had a troublesome duty to perform. I had deposited
there without examination or arrangement a great mass of
papers found in my Father's possession at his death; and as
many of them belonged to persons who had been his Clients,
it was necessary to examine them in order to return any of
them that might be of value to their respective owners. In
this work I was assisted by Felix MacCarthy, the young
Irishman before mentioned, who had during my recent
misfortunes and anxieties manifested towards me a warm
and faithful attachment, and who having latterly acted as
our clerk was well qualified for the purpose. We selected all
the papers that were to be sent to others, and then finding
a great accumulation of old family accounts and papers of
no use, threw them after a very cursory inspection on a large
pile on the floor to be burnt, when just as we were finishing
our work a small piece of paper rolled down from the heap
that attracted Mc.Carthy's eye from the subscription that it
bore of Catherine White, the faithful servant before mentioned. He handed it to me; and we both, I believe, read it
several times before we could trust our own eyesight as to
the strange contents. To my great surprise and consternation it was a full and explicit receipt to my Father for her
wages paid by him to a period only two months before his
death, whereas she had claimed and I had paid them as
being two years in arrear. Such a fraud, committed under
such circumstances, by one whom I regarded rather as an
old faithful friend than a servant, was enough to excite in me

not only astonishment but horror. Had a viper fallen from the pile and bit me I could scarcely have shrunk from it with greater wonder and dismay. My surprise was increased by the strange coincidence of my Father having, contrary to his ordinary habits, taken and preserved such a voucher; and when a subsequent effect of the discovery comes to be stated, the occurrence will be seen to have a strikingly providential character. Mc.Carthy, not less astonished and indignant than myself, was for exposing the woman who had so basely defrauded me at so interesting and distressing a conjuncture, by sending the receipt to my Uncle in Dorsetshire, whither she had just returned to her relations; for she was likely to be well received and recommended there on account of her long supposed fidelity to our unfortunate family. My own feelings at first inclined to me to that course; but better ones soon succeeded and prevailed. I recollected her long services to my deceased Parents, which notwithstanding this dis-covery, I believed to have been in general faithful and pro-longed from affectionate attachment to the family. At all events, I felt that to abstain from ruining her character was due if not to gratitude, at least to generosity and charity. I therefore injoined secrecy to Mc.Carthy, and carefully putting up the paper, resolved to say nothing of her fault, even to herself. This little incident was of no small importance to my future welfare, as will be hereafter seen, and it pleased Heaven in this, as in other instances, to reward me for right conduct, tho' in an indirect manner and one far beyond the reach of human foresight, as I shall shew in the proper place.

Having finished my preparations for leaving Lyons Inn I gave up my chambers, and I removed to Mrs. Hamilton's just before the commencement of the winter season, carrying with me all the little property I possessed in the world, a few professional books, a scanty stock of cloaths, and I think three or four guineas, but relying of course on an early supply from my Uncle Milner, to whom I wrote with a particular account of these proceedings, and of the plan which I had been obliged to adopt, submitting the prosecu-tion or change of it entirely to his judgment and choice.

I soon found my new situation a more pleasant one than I had ever before known, and could perceive that to all but one in the family, my society was a gratifying acquisition. The ladies found in me a companion desirous to entertain and oblige; and scanty tho' my education had been, I was so well versed in all that light reading that women usually take an interest in, and had seen so much of the world, and with all knew so well how to address myself to their taste and make the most of my qualification, that they all became very fond of my company, and it was not easy to escape from the dining parlour so soon after our meals as my studies or other avocations required. The exception was Major Berkeley, to whom I could easily see that I was by no means acceptable. He was a sensible old man, one who at least had passed the meridian of life some years, and from long residence in the East Indies was still older in constitution, and of a vale-tudinary habit. His manners in general had the polish or correctness that belongs to a veteran officer; but at the same time he had a reserve that savoured of pride or self conse-quence, and no small share of dogmatism and obstinacy in advancing and maintaining his opinions. To these latter propensities I was not always disposed to give way, but while I treated him with the respect due to his years, frequently dissented from his opinions (which on political subjects were generally opposed to my own.) This he naturally disliked, especially as he commonly found me, in point of volubility at least, an overmatch for him in argument. He had pre-viously, I suppose, been looked up to as an oracle by the Ladies, and so ill relished any diminution of his intellectual importance in their eyes that he began soon to disrelish our after dinner conversations and to retire pretty generally to his own room soon after the cloth was drawn.

Of the most interesting member of the family circle, Miss Rivers, I had no such cause of complaint. As it was through her friendship with my dear Nancy that I had been intro-duced to it, and with prepossessions that she had been inspired with as to my character by that very partial friend, I found myself from the first treated by her with the most favorable attention and could soon perceive that of all the family she was the most pleased with my Society.

This young Lady was then, I think, an object of as great and general attraction as any female I have ever known. I forget whether she was in her nineteenth or twentieth year, but she was in the full bloom of her beauty. Her stature exceeded the middle size, and her person was finely formed and graceful. Her features, without perfect regularity, were extremely pleasing, and had an animated playful expression well according with her character. Her hair was dark brown, and her skin the clearest and softest that I ever saw, with a complexion in which delicacy was united with the finest glow of health. In respect of that advantage she was indeed a perfect Hebe. Few women or men, I believe, were ever blessed with so fine a constitution, and she owed to it a peculiar charm, one at least which I do not recollect in any other woman : a visible self enjoyment, shewing itself not only in the absence of all restlessness or irritability of nerves, but in the zest of every pleasure or amusement, in the elasticity and ease of every motion, and in constant cheerfulness and complacency. I have thought of her when recollecting Dr. Paley's pleasing remark on the benignity of the Creator as displayed in the animal enjoyment of a healthful Infant to whom even the involuntary action of the bodily frame itself in the different secretions, &c., is a source of agreeable and joyous sensations. Maria Rivers seemed to be constantly in that festive state of feelings.

As to her mind, it is not easy to class or describe it either in respect of intellectual character or morals. She conversed and wrote, generally speaking, like a well-educated woman, and was sometimes arch and even witty. Her taste and judgment, I think, were not at all below par. Yet her natural hilarity made her often say and do inconsiderate and foolish things. There was a naiveté in her manners that made such things in her rather amusing and pleasing than offensive; and I think she would have been less interesting, and less generally admired if she had been more uniformly judicious and correct.

I could soon perceive that Miss Rivers had little respect for Mrs. Hamilton or deference for her opinions. Nor was this blameable; for she was much her inferior in education and manners, and perhaps also in good sense. I saw also that there was not friendship, tho' no positive disagreement between her and Miss Hamilton, who was insipid and

apparently reserved, and that tho' she occasionally visited
Mr. Lennox, her Father's Brother, an old gentleman broken
with infirmities, she had in truth no friend or confidant
nearer to her in regard than my dear Nancy, whom she often
saw. I was soon satisfied also that she had no attachment of
an amorous kind. There was mention indeed of more than
one gentleman who were her professed admirers, but from
her jocose treatment of the subject, and her manner when I
saw one of them in her company, I was reasonably sure of
her heart being quite disengaged. I thought therefore my
friend Tom's case not quite hopeless, and was confirmed in
my resolution to help him by my influence if possible, and
with that view to cultivate her confidence and favour.

The latter, tho' a dangerous, was not a difficult work.
Maria's predilection for my company and conversation
soon became perceptible not only to myself but to Mrs.
Hamilton and her daughter, and still sooner perhaps to
Major Berkeley, who I believe gave them a caution on the
subject. Tho' his years precluded his having any views of
engaging Miss Rivers's affections himself, he admired her
much and always treated her with obsequious respect and
attention. He was naturally, therefore, mortified and envious
at perceiving how much more acceptable my society was to
her than his own; and perhaps he had better motives. The
dissatisfaction of the Hamiltons on the same score was not
wholly disinterested. Mr. Hamilton, Junior, who was a
Midshipman on board the same ship with my friend Tom
on his last voyage and had introduced him to the family, as I
understood, was one of the many who admired Miss Rivers;
and his Mother, as I had reason to suspect, flattered herself
that when he obtained promotion he might be a successful
suitor to her ward. Whether so or not, she and the rest of the
family discovered by their change of manners towards me,
and expressly avowed, as I afterwards learned, to Miss
Rivers, their dislike of the growing intimacy between us, and
their suspicion that notwithstanding my engagement to Miss
Stent, I was trying to win, and had actually won, her
affections. The old woman gave the broadest hints she could
venture upon of that surmise. Neither Maria nor I, however,
cared much for their opinion or good will; and being con-

scious of intending nothing inconsistent with honour and justice towards my dear Nancy, I regarded the suspicion as a wrong. That dear woman, relying implicitly on my fidelity, was so far from apprehending danger that she continued occasionally to bring Miss Rivers and me together at her own home or on Parties of walking or other recreations abroad. One of them in particular I have many reasons for remembering. It was to hear a debate at Coachmakers Hall,[1] which with other places of a like kind was at that time a very fashionable resort for ladies as well as Gentlemen. Coachmakers Hall was the most celebrated of all those schools of eloquence, as they were called, it containing the largest audience—I think from 1500 to 2000 persons—and being frequented by many speakers at that time of great talents, and who have since become eminent in professional and Parliamentary life. Among them were Erskine,[2] Dallas,[3] Garrow,[4] Lord Lauderdale,[5] Emmett,[6] the Irish Conspirator, &c. The Ladies knowing that I went there occasionally, desired me to convey them to the gallery at an approaching meeting, and I promised readily to do so. Miss Hamilton also was to be of the Party. Conceiving a wish to

[1] Coachmakers' Hall in Noble Street belonged to the Coach and Coach Harness Makers, one of the minor livery companies. The hall as Stephen knew it had been the property of the Coachmakers since 1703. The company, not being wealthy and having a hall which would seat more than a thousand people —it was probably not quite so large as Stephen remembered it—rented it during the week to auction sales and to meetings of such debating societies as Stephen attended, and on Sundays to dissenters as a place of worship. It was a meeting in Coachmakers' Hall in 1780, addressed by Lord George Gordon, that led to the Gordon No Popery riots. The hall was rebuilt in 1867.

[2] Thomas Erskine, first Baron Erskine (1750–1823), lord chancellor (1806–1807); obtained a verdict of "not guilty" for Lord George Gordon 1781; M.P. 1783–1806.

[3] Sir Robert Dallas (1756–1824), judge; made reputation as counsel for Warren Hastings 1787; counsel for Lord George Gordon when the latter was convicted for libel 1788; M.P. 1802–1824.

[4] Sir William Garrow (1760–1840), baron of the exchequer 1817–1832; made reputation by prosecution of Aiken for stealing a bill of exchange 1784; M.P. and distinguished lawyer.

[5] James Maitland, 8th Earl of Lauderdale (1759–1830), lawyer and statesman; one of the founders of the Society of the Friends of the People 1792; author of *Inquiry into the Nature and Origin of Public Wealth* (1804).

[6] Stephen is clearly wrong about Robert Emmet (1778–1803), United Irishman who was executed in 1803. Emmet would have been only three years old in 1781.

shew them how well I could speak in public, I enquired what the subject was to be, and found that it was *negro slavery*, the question being whether it could be defended on principles of humanity and justice or something to that effect. The subject was new to my mind, except the little I had heard of it from my Brother; but I resolved to consider it thoroughly to prepare a set speech, and to surprise the Ladies by their finding me among the Orators. This required some courage; for I had before made an attempt there which had been but ill received, tho' I had taken much pains to prepare an elaborate speech. But then the subject was dry, and I had been oppressed by diffidence on rising to speak, and broke my own line of argument. On negro slavery I found it not hard to devise topics and frame arguments and language likely to be well received by a popular auditory, but was so much afraid of my own fears that when the expected evening came, and I had placed the ladies in the gallery, I had much difficulty to resolve on executing my purpose. The room was crowded to excess in every part, and there were speakers with whom I had not the vanity to think I could cope without failing and sinking in the eyes of those whom it was my too anxious desire to be admired by. On this occasion, however, I was befriended in my need, and I have often since been, by the warmth of feeling excited by opposition in a cause that I had sincerely embraced. Some eminent speaker, I think it was Dallas, had made an able defence of negro slavery, to which I felt that much of my prepared matter would be a pertinent reply, but new matter at the same time suggested itself to my mind and being warmed beyond the fear of my auditory, I felt that I could trust myself even with extemporary language and arrangement, which was necessary to the best effect. I rose, and made a Speech, the best, and by far the best received, of any I ever made in my life. Ardour and indignation gave me language and arguments superior to those I had preconceived, and yet I was able to weave in the best part of these with happy effect. From the first paragraph to the last, I was received at intervals with thundering bursts of applause; when I sat down they were long reiterated in louder peals than Coachmakers Hall perhaps had ever been shook with; and the compliments of the Speakers on both sides who followed were almost too strong for my own vanity to digest. Negro slavery was condemned by a majority, I believe, of fifty to one; and when the meeting broke up the general curiosity was to see me and learn my name. Need I say how great my triumph was to find my dear Nancy and Miss Rivers quite overwhelmed with surprise and joy? In our way home I heard and saw enough of their feelings almost to turn my brain with delight; and I think it was on this occasion that I first saw clearly that Maria regarded me with more than the feelings of a *friend*. It was also, I believe, about the same time that I began to perceive in my poor dear Nancy some symptoms of uneasiness on the score of the visible partiality of Miss R. towards me, which the latter probably made no secret of in their private conversations, while conscious of no purpose or feelings with which her friend had cause to be discontent. But to my anxious eyes, it was e'er long manifest that their friendship was on the wane, or at least that they were not so much at ease together, or so fond of each other's company, as before. What my conduct ought to have been on these discoveries is plain enough. Prudence, honour, and tenderness for the dear woman who had given me her fond affections should have concurred to make me shun the company of Miss R. as much as possible and cease to pay her any further attentions than mere civility required. Nor did reason and conscience fail to suggest this to me. "But the heart is treacherous above all things."[1] Mine had taken a part in the question deeper than I was then aware, and it betrayed my judgment and my better feelings on this occasion strangely. Perfidy to my dear Nancy and my friend her Brother was a crime of which I thought myself so utterly incapable that I thought it no duty to shun temptation. I even felt it such a wrong to my character when some symptoms of distrust appeared in her that it seemed to absolve me from the unkindness of not doing all I could to remove it. As to Miss R's feelings, I was absurd enough to think that they would lead only to a friendship and confidence that would be very happy for her in her unprotected situation,

[1] *Jeremiah*, 17:9, which in the Authorized Version reads: "The heart is deceitful above all things, and desperately wicked."

and which I might so use in favor of my friend Tom as on his expected return and preferment to accomplish his dearest wishes. Had I gone earnestly and sincerely to the Fountain of Wisdom for advice, I should have been rescued from this delusion, but if I made it at this time a subject of prayer at all, as I most probably did, it must have been in the spirit of hypocrisy, that species of it by which we deceive ourselves, rather than others. I must have asked God's direction with a secret purpose of following my own self will, rather than submitting myself implicitly to his guidance. My prayers therefore must have been an offence to him and were justly rejected. Pride and resentment towards the Hamiltons assisted to confirm me in the wrong; for they soon after began systematically to thwart me in every attempt to engage Miss Rivers in conversation and to treat me so coolly that I saw it would be necessary to quit their house at the Quarter's end, then nearly approaching. I could discover also that variance had sprung up between Maria and them, and that her usual chearfulness sometimes gave way to mellancholly or uneasiness, of both which I could too well divine the cause. Major Berkeley also, who plainly was of our Hostess's party, continued indeed his usual courtesies to Miss Rivers, but was more stiff and reserved than ever towards me, and was evidently restrained from treating me disrespectfully only by his prudence; for I was not slow to repel every approach towards offence from him, in a way that must have shewn him it would be dangerous so to indulge his ill will.

I forget whether Mrs. Hamilton or I first broke the ice as to my removal, but it was resolved that I should leave her family at the Quarter's end, and to all but Maria and me its approach was no subject of regret. Even to me, indeed, it would have been a relief, and my removal would perhaps have preceded that period, but for some very unpleasant and embarrassing occurrences which I must next proceed to narrate.

To my great surprise and alarm, my Uncle Milner had never made any reply to my letter written to him on my leaving Lyons Inn tho' he must have known from the fact contained in it that I must be by that time much at a loss

for money. Four or five months had elapsed since he had
taken my support on himself by his own pressing solicitations,
and as yet he had not given me a shilling. It was with extreme
reluctance and humiliation that I had to remind him of the
omission, but there was no alternative or means of further
delay, for without a remittance from him I could not
possibly clear scores with Mrs. Hamilton. I therefore wrote
to him and, without any complaint of his neglect, or any
expression that could be construed into dissatisfaction, merely
reminded him that the allowance he had kindly promised to
allow me quarterly was in arrear, and that I was under the
necessity of troubling him for it in order to pay for my board
and lodgings. To my consternation some posts elapsed without any reply to this letter, and I should have been disgraced at Mrs. Hamilton's from inability to pay her bill and
remove, but for an unexpected resource in the kindness of
the two Mc.Carthys, my Father's quondam clerks, and then
still my humble much attached friends, to whom, without
expecting help from them, I revealed my painful situation.
They were both clerks at that time to Attornies, and tho'
Felix, my chief confidant, was not prudent enough, ever
almost, to have a guinea in store, he knew that his Brother
Charles, a more provident character, had saved a good many
pounds. My necessities were no sooner made known by the
former to the latter than he sent me the sum I wanted, and
I consented to borrow it till a remittance from my Uncle
should arrive. But Felix did not stop here. He had formed
an acquaintance with a Mr. Leoni, an Italian Teacher who
had then a large house, now Spode's warehouse, in Portugal
Street, Lincolns Inn, and was desirous of taking some
gentlemen as lodgers and boarders; and by his recommendation Leoni agreed immediately to receive me, on terms as
low or lower than Mrs. Hamilton's.

I was enabled, therefore, not only to settle with Mrs. H.
but to remove at once, and with credit for another quarter,
without my hearing from Mr. Milner; and I was obliged, if
I rightly remember, to send him another letter to ascertain
that the last had not miscarried. At last his answer arrived,
and was one that overwhelmed me with astonishment and
indignation. More than once did I read it before I could be

well satisfied that my senses did not deceive me. It enclosed an order on a gentleman in London for £15 but accompanied with language of studied insult and opprobrious accusation. He tauntingly recommended to me "not in future to carry the arts of my profession into my private life," meaning not to practice falsehood and deceit, and then proceeded to charge me in positive terms with a foul and detestable fraud in the account I had sent him on quitting Lyons Inn, asserting that instead of having paid the servants by selling the furniture and applying the proceeds that way as I had pretended, I had left Kitty White wholly unpaid "so that she had been obliged to borrow money from one Sister to carry her into Dorsetshire and from another to carry her back again to London"!!!

It is easier to conceive than to describe the emotions that agitated my mind for hours after reading this letter. The most painful and predominant by far was indignation at its author; for tho' the crime in which I had detected Kitty White made it probable enough that she had really devised such a calumnious falsehood for the purpose of obtaining money from her Sisters, and that the latter had reported it to Mr. Milner, this did not seem to me an excuse, or even palliation of his conduct. To credit such an accusation, implying, as it did, complicated fraud and villainy and baseness, to treat me in consequence of it with the most galling and cruel neglect for months past, and now to insult me, under a dependency which he himself had induced me contrary to my own ingenuous feelings to contract, by arraigning me on that horrible charge, putting it as one that he certainly knew to be true, and to suppose that I would receive his money after all and continue to subsist at his expence, were all together not less offensive to my feelings than if to get rid of me he had himself invented the lie. That his cruel treatment of me was directed to that end, whether he believed the slanderous tale or not, seemed to me beyond a doubt, since his indelicate and unfeeling neglect had long preceded the settlement with the servants at Lyons Inn to which the charge related. I thought it now manifest that he had repented his friendly offer almost from the moment when he had prevailed over my reluctance to accept it, and that to

save his own credit and his money together he was resolved
to make the breach he desired between us my own act by
such treatment of me as no liberal spirit could brook. Most
probably this construction was unjust to him, or at least unfounded in truth; for Mr. Milner, tho' much addicted to suspicion and caprice, was not an ungenerous man. But looking
back on the facts now, so very many years after every resentful feeling has been buried, first in a cordial reconciliation
and since in his grave, I am quite at a loss to account for his
entire conduct towards me upon any justifiable or excusable
ground. The subject was too tender and delicate to be any
topic of enquiry with my dear friend and brother his son,
even since we became so nearly connected, but if any
explanation had been known to him at all justificatory of his
Father, I am persuaded he would have found means,
through my Sister or otherwise, to put me in possession of it.

Of whatever extenuation my Uncle's conduct might be
capable one thing was too clear to my judgment as well as
my feelings to admit of a moments hesitation. It was impossible for me ever to accept any favor at his hands, or not at
once to renounce my dependency upon him. The very
speedy and apparently certain consequences of not abandon-
ing all my professional prospects, but falling into want and
distress, did not pause me for an instant in the resolution to
break with him for ever; and I resolved even to take such
a tone as would make it impossible that the breach should
ever be closed, foreseeing that I might otherwise have to
fear the interposition of mutual relatives or friends, and
feeling that neither want nor any other evil would be half
so intolerable as the incurring any future obligation in that
quarter. The proper mode of self defence against his opprobrious charge was not so obvious. I remembered with
gratitude to Providence the singular discovery of Kitty
White's receipt to my Father, which I had carefully preserved and which I felt would be a sure instrument of either
compelling her to do me justice or destroying her credit.
Without it, I might have stood at her mercy; for I had taken
no receipt for the wages paid to her, without a witness, by
myself. I should as soon have thought of taking such security
against a sister or parent. I at first thought therefore of send-

ing immediately to Mr. Milner that evidence of her dishonesty and falsehood. But a little reflection changed this
purpose. She might not in truth have said what Mr. M.
asserted; it might be only his own injurious construction of
the fact of her having borrowed money of the Sister in his
neighbourhood if she had really done so, or might not even
have that slight foundation. At all events I felt it would be
wrong to reverse my former mercy and forbearance and to
ruin her character, untill I had given her an opportunity to
clear herself of the new imputed offence if she could. Besides,
without her confession, my defence might be incompleat,
in Mr. M.'s jaundiced eyes. To prove that my Father had
paid her the wages in question, and that therefore she had
no cause of complaint, would not have proved that I paid
them over again to her after his death. I resolved therefore in
the first instance to demand a receipt from her for what I had
paid at Lyons Inn, telling her the charge made against me
on her authority as my reason for it, and that if she gave the
one, and denied the other, I would still keep the secret of her
crime both from Mr. Milner and her relations. I considered
further, however, that if she had really been guilty of the
imputed calumny it was most probable she would refuse to
give a receipt for her own confession and disgrace; and as this
might place me in an an awkward predicament, it was necessary to apprize her that her character was in my power.
Finding on enquiry that she had gone into service in Essex,
I wrote requiring her immediately to come to me in London,
and in a stile to assure her compliance, and employed the
interval in preparing a reply to Mr. Milner, with the
deliberation that the importance of its probable consequences
deserved. When she arrived I was relieved from all anxiety
as to the means of self justification. She gave me a receipt in
terms of my own dictation acknowledging the having
received the sum paid for wages on my discharging her at
Lyons Inn. I think she did this before I produced to her the
evidence I possessed of her dishonesty; but my application
to her had been in a stile from which she most probably
inferred my possession of that paper. Either before or after
complying with my demand, I forget which, she affected to
feel herself much hurt at my having used language implying

a doubt of her integrity, and a power of exposing her character, so that I was obliged to produce the receipt in my own justification, and tho' silenced and abashed she did not seem much surprised at seeing it. She solemnly denied having ever said a word to Mr. Milner or any one else, of the kind alleged by him, and appealed to her Sisters, whose good and pious characters I knew, that she had not denied but freely mentioned to them the payment I had made to her; but as to the previous fraud, it was too plain for dispute and she thankfully embraced my offer to keep the matter secret from her Sisters and all who knew her, Mr. Milner not excepted. I was not indisposed to believe her protestations, for the worst view of my Uncle's conduct was the best for my feelings and my purpose, and my letter to him therefore did not merely inclose her receipt in testimony of my innocence but announced her total denial of the charge and put him on the proof that he had any authority for the opprobrious accusation he had made. It was in other respects as pungent a retort, tho' without disrespectful *terms*, as my powers of composition could make it, containing a full statement of all his unkind and indelicate conduct towards me, and avowing my conviction that tho' momentary feelings of compassion had led him to press on me an offer of support, he had immediately after its reluctant acceptance, repented of it, and resolved to get rid of me by such treatment as would make dependency on him intolerable to any liberal or ingenuous feelings. I returned him his Order for money and declared that no extremity of fortune should ever induce me again to receive an obligation at his hands. Having finished my letter and copied it for the information of my dear Brother and other friends, I dispatched it with the feelings of a man who had just laid down a galling yoke or filed off his fetters, regardless for the moment of the destitute and hopeless situation in which it left me. My prospects, to be sure, were gloomy enough. I had not a guinea in the world, nor any means of self support in possession or expectancy, nor a friend from whom I had any rational hope of assistance except perhaps from those friends whom I was resolved not to accept it from if offered, for the sake of those four little fellow orphans with whom they were already burthened. My dear Brother was then, I think, on his voyage to the West Indies. Our Uncle there, his Patron, finding his health a little on the decline and wishing to return as early as possible to Europe, had suddenly sent for him before he had finished his course at Edinbro' in order to introduce him into practice under himself before his retirement. I had one very estimable and respectable friend, however, in London who, tho' unable to assist me in a worldly way, being herself a Widow in difficult or very narrow circumstances, gave me what I valued more, her kind simpathy and the sanction of her judicious opinion in the decisive step I had taken. This was Mrs. Forbes, my Mother's Friend, of whom I have formerly spoken. When I shewed her the correspondance she shed tears and said that she rather approved than blamed the course I had taken. "If," added she, "after Mr. Milner's conduct, there could have been a hope of any lasting benefit from him, I should have wished you to sacrifice your feelings to your interest; but I am satisfied that no forbearance or concession on your part could long have prevented a rupture with a man capable of treating you in that cruel and ungenerous way. I am not sorry therefore that the connection is broken." At parting she slipped two guineas into my hand saying, "My dear James, there is a Widow's mite, and I heartily wish I had it in my power to give you any effectual assistance of that kind." I would fain have declined the gift, and long refused to accept it, till I found the refusal gave her so much pain that I was obliged to comply, tho' I too well knew she had nothing she could easily spare.

It was, of course, necessary that I should apprise my relations in Scotland of this unfortunate change in my situation and prospects, which I did by sending them copies of Mr. Milner's letter and mine; but my conduct did not meet with them the same approbation that it received from Mrs. Forbes; nor indeed did I hope that it would. Prudence is more honored than any other of the virtues in that Country; and tho' my Aunt and Uncle Nuccoll were not only kind but generous people, I knew that they had a strong tincture of this national characteristic and would be too much alarmed at my renouncing my only means of subsistence and professional education to enter fairly into the feelings that had constrained me to act as I did. It was with much more pain than surprise therefore that I received a letter from them lamenting and blaming my conduct in "casting off," as they called it, my Uncle Milner, and earnestly advising me to attempt a reconciliation with him, in which Mr. Nuccoll offered himself as a mediator. This, of course, I most resolutely declined, tho' in terms of grateful and heartfelt respect, endeavouring to convince them that the attempt if made would certainly be fruitless, and that in fact it was Mr M. who had cast off *me*, tho' by ungenerous and insidious means he had contrived to avoid the express retractation of his promises, and make the breach in point of form my own. Mrs. Nuccoll, who had good sense, as well as affection for me, was probably convinced by my reasoning and brought her husband, as she generally did, to her opinion, for I had a kind reply, acquiescing in my determination, enquiring anxiously what new plan of life could be formed for me, and offering pecuniary assistance for my present support. I was much affected by their kindness, but was resolved and told them decidedly that I would never consent, whatever might be my fate, to add to the burthen on their affection and generosity which three of my helpless fellow orphans already formed.

Relieved by these ecclaircissements from the most painful of my feelings, and by Mr. Milner's silence from the fear of any relenting on his part, I cast my eyes on every side for some expedient by which it might be possible to sustain myself till I could hear from my dear Brother William, to whom of course I wrote fully by the first Packet. I had a certainty that if he succeeded in his profession his first object would be to help me into mine; and if I had possessed the means of executing the plan Mr. Milner had induced me to abandon, that of going to America and volunteering under Washington, I should have thought it wronging his affectionate heart to do so, without giving him an opportunity to prevent it if he could. It was, if I remember right, to his affectionate efforts that I owed the means of repaying the loan I had contracted on quitting Mrs. Hamilton's, he having saved so much for me before his departure out of the money allowed him by his Uncle. But five or six months

must elapse before I could hear from him, and how to subsist in the meantime was a problem I could not immediately
solve. My situation soon became more difficult by the
necessity of quitting Leoni's. I found him not only to be a
bad and despicable character, but so indigent and embarrassed in his circumstances that his table, wretchedly supplied from the first, was occasionally from his want of money
and credit left wholly unfurnished, and his house not only a
very uncomfortable but hardly a creditable abode. In
addition to his employment in teaching Italian and French,
chiefly at Boarding Schools for young ladies, he had established, as I found, a kind of private Register Office for
supplying such schools with female assistants and providing
these with situations; but he had vices which I believe con-
sumed his gains, and I heard so much of his conduct with
some of the young women whom he recommended to his
employers, as to be shocked at the knowledge that young
ladies were placed under their care. In short I found cause to
regard him with aversion and disgust and would have quitted
his house without delay if I had possessed the means of doing
so by paying his bill. I did, in fact, leave him some time
before the Quarter's end, but the course I was obliged to take
was the leaving behind me most of my cloaths, &c., and
under pretext of a journey leaving accounts unsettled till my
return. I took a very humble lodging in a retired situation
about three Miles from town and resolved to keep myself
out of his sight till I could return with the means of putting
myself out of his debt. The few shillings weekly that I had to
pay for my room and the charge of my very frugal meals
were supplied chiefly through the faithful attachment of
Felix Mc.Carthy, with whom I had no reserve and who not
only offered but forced me to accept all the little money he
could command. He was still clerk to an Attorney and had
saved, as he represented from time to time what he gave me,
out of his weekly or monthly salary, tho' I think it afterwards appeared he got it from his Brother Charles for the
purpose, they both knowing that I should not so easily have
been brought to accept it from the latter. I had the less
scruple to accept such help from Felix knowing that he was
so careless of his interest and so warmly attached to me that

I could not do him a greater pleasure. Such at least was my then opinion of his character, and I still think I was not mistaken, tho' it was afterwards strangely reversed in every estimable point. This slender resource, which did not, I think, altogether exceed four or five pounds, was soon exhausted, and I was afterwards reduced to such straights that after pawning my watch, &c., I was more than once nearly reduced to actual hunger. I remember once expending my last sixpence at a public house on a slice of bread and cheese and pint of porter, as the best substitutes I could find for a meat dinner. Yet I never was despondent or very anxious for the future, but always retained a strong trust in Providence that my wants would be supplied.

Chapter Eight

[1781]

THIS confidence was at length justified by events, at a time when my situation was come to the worst, and my human prospects to the darkest pitch, and that in a way quite beside my own contrivance and calculations.

The *Morning Post* was at that time the reigning newspaper of the day. It was edited by an able and witty, but profligate man, then called Parson Bate,[1] since the Reverend Sir Henry Bate-Dudley, Bart., Prebendary of Ely, &c., who by his prowess as a noted bruiser and duellist, not less than by the power of his pen, was become a very conspicuous and formidable character. His domineering spirit had so much subdued the Proprietors of the Paper, among whom were Alderman Skinner[2] and some other individuals of pecuniary consequence, that he was allowed to conduct it without controul as to its political tone or otherwise; and I doubt not made it subservient to his own interests in many improper ways. Mr. Joseph Richardson,[3] who was afterwards well known in the political world, having been brought into Parliament by the Whig Party, and being, to his misfortune, the favorite friend and companion of Sheridan, was at this time one of the two Parliamentary Reporters for the same Paper. He was a young man of great talents and acquirements who had distinguished himself at Cambridge; and the large share he was known to have in the *Rolliad*, the *Probationary Odes*, and other political *jeux d'esprit*, at a later period,

[1] Sir Henry Bate-Dudley (1745–1824), journalist; curate of Hendon from 1773; editor of *Morning Post* 1772–1780; proprietor of *Morning Herald* 1780–1781; imprisoned for libel 1781; called the "Fighting Parson" because of his numerous duels.

[2] Thomas Skinner was at the time of which Stephen was writing an Alderman of the City of London, and in 1784 was a Sheriff and author of *An Account of Some Alterations Attempted in the Duty and Office of the Sheriff of Middlesex and Sheriffs of the City of London, During the Sheriffalty of Sir Bernard Turner and Thomas Skinner, Esq.* (London, 1784).

[3] Joseph Richardson (1755–1803), author and M.P.; contributed to the *Rolliad* and *Probationary Odes*; assisted Sheridan in management of the Drury Lane Theatre.

is enough to prove that he was a very lively and witty writer. His conversational powers also were much admired; and the whole was set off by a handsome person and very gentlemanlike manners. He became a proprietor of the *Morning Post*, at the request, I believe, of Alderman Skinner, with whom he was intimate and who probably advanced him the money to purchase some shares in order to obtain support by his talents in the Committee of Proprietors, against the despotism and insolence of Bate. Richardson did at least give him and his party in the Committee such support; and Bate, finding himself controuled by a vote of that Body at one of their meetings, gave way to his resentment so far as to apply some opprobrious name to them all. Richardson in consequence demanded the retraction of the term, in respect of himself, and on Bate's refusing it sent him a challenge. They met, and Richardson was wounded in the arm, while his antagonist escaped unhurt through a foul contrivance, I believe, on the part of the latter. He brought as his second Mr. Dennis O'Brien, a well known *man of the Town*, who was his own obsequious creature, and Richardson was attended by a friend wholly unacquainted with such matters. I think it was Richard Wilson, commonly called Dick Wilson, now an eminent Solicitor, and who was Secretary successively to Lord Eldon[1] and Lord Erskine, till the latter lost the Seats.— The Parties met in Hyde Park, just at the dawn of day, when Bate, an experienced duellist and coldblooded ruffian, said, "Let us toss up for the first fire," and without waiting for an answer threw up a shilling, desiring Richardson to call head or tails. Richardson complying, said "heads," and Bate, without giving him or his second time to see which side fell uppermost, caught up the shilling and said, "You have lost, Sir." Richardson believed, as he himself told me, that it was a fraud, but he out of delicacy, and his Second from want of presence of mind, I presume, did not object to the proceeding. Bate next tried to intimidate his opponent in the most shameful and detestable manner. After pointing the pistol at him and taking a deliberate aim for some time, he com-

---

[1] John Scott, first Earl of Eldon (1751–1838) lord chancellor 1801–1806; 1807–1827; active opponent of parliamentary reform. For the short period between his two terms of office, Lord Erskine was the lord chancellor.

plained that he had not light enough to take his aim distinctly and proposed to walk aside for some time till the dawn was more advanced, with which, R's Second still not interposing, his own sense of honor and delicacy led him to comply. On approaching again, Bate levelled his pistol at him again for some time, then drew it back, affecting to feel a tightness about the shoulders of his coat that impeded his aim, and after distending his arms to stretch the coat, a third time pointed his pistol. At length the Ruffian, finding he could not vanquish the resolution of his antagonist, fired with so good an aim that had not Richardson's right arm covered his breast, the shot would most probably have been fatal. As it was, the wound gave safety to the reverend miscreant himself, for tho' R. fired, his arm of course could not well support and point the weapon. The Proprietors of the *Morning Post* were naturally so indignant at this brutal conduct, added to the former insolence, that they immediately dismissed Bate from the Editorship; and as Richardson did not choose to accept it, appointed a Mr. Jackman[1] in his stead. Bate, on the other hand, set up a rival paper, which he called the *Morning Herald*, and the two prints, tho' both on the Government side, daily loaded each other and their respective conductors with the most virulent abuse. Bate was able to draw over to his Party a very able and respectable man, Mr. Jas. Sherridan,[2] who reported the Debates of the House of Commons for the *Morning Post* but now undertook the same department in the *Herald*. Another reporter, therefore, was wanted in his stead for the *Morning Post*, and the appointment most providentially fell to my lot. Having so much acquaintance with Richardson as to have once dined in his company, and having formed some slight acquaintance also with the Printer of the *Morning Post*, at debating Societies which we both attended, and where he had formed a good opinion of my talents, I lost no time in applying for the situation and by Richardson's influence with the Proprietors obtained it. I did not conceal from him the unfortunate and necessitous circumstances in which I stood, and he in con-

---

[1] Isaac Jackman (fl. 1795), joint editor of *Morning Post* 1786–1795; author of several farces and comic operas.
[2] I have not been able to identify James Sherridan.

sequence interested himself so much in my favor as to overcome the objection that must have been felt to the intrusting
a department at once so important and difficult to a man who
had never before employed his pen in reporting or writing
for the press. The reporting Parliamentary debates was then
a business very different from what it has since become, and
far more arduous in its nature. No man was allowed to take
a note for the purpose. To use a pen or pencil in the Gallery
was deemed a high contempt, so much so that I once saw a
Gentleman taken into custody and turned indignantly out,
merely for taking down a figure or two with his pencil when
Lord North was opening his budget. We were obliged therefore to depend on memory alone and had no assistance in the
work, one Reporter for each House being all that any Paper
employed. For many years past, I believe between 30 and 40,
both Houses have relaxed that rule, and the consequence is
that every man who can write shorthand or take quick notes
is qualified for a Reporter. A further consequence is that
many different Reporters are employed by the Proprietors
of the Morning Papers, who when there is a long debate take
different portions of it, successively quitting the gallery at
different hours, so that the earlier speeches are composed
and set up, while the debate is still proceeding. Those who
write them may generally finish their work and retire to
rest at no very late hour, and even the Reporters of the latest
speeches need not often work above two hours, perhaps,
after the House breaks up. We, on the contrary, were
obliged to sit in the Gallery from the sitting of the House till
its adjournment, and afterwards, however late, to begin and
finish our work before we retired to rest. The Papers consequently went late to press after an important debate; but
this being a great disadvantage to them, both in their
advertising interests and their sale, the poor weary reporter
was always importuned for the utmost possible dispatch, and
quickness of composition was not less in request than strength
of memory and correctness of stile. This, tho' hard on the
Reporter, was good for the Public, when compared with the
present licencious system.[1] The Reporters now are able to

---

[1] The press gallery, with reporters allowed to take notes in shorthand, dates
from 1802.

gratify their political and personal predilections and anti-
pathies without inconvenience, and do in fact gratify them
with a shameful partiality and injustice; for by the help of
shorthand, or quick notation, they can carry away materials
enough to fill up twice or thrice as many columns as the
paper can afford for the debate; and they have time enough
for selecting from them at leisure. They consequently are able
to give the speeches of their favorites in the fullest, and the
speeches of those they disfavor in the most contracted form;
and the general impression of the debate is rather what they
choose to make it than what it actually made in the House;
wheras in my time the Reporter had an interest quite paramount to his party-spirited feelings, and to his personal considerations also, however strong they might be; and it was
an interest that inclined him decisively to fair and impartial
conduct. I mean the interest of his own ease and convenience, associated strongly with that of his own reputation
in his business. This will be obvious, if it is considered that to
give a fair account from memory is a simpler, easier, and
shorter process, than to blend truth with falsehood, by
altering the proportions and the effect of what we remember
to have heard. But it is further to be considered that the
memory will best retain that which, when heard, was the
most impressive; and consequently that in the effort to
report from recollection, the Reporter will be naturally led,
if not even irresistably drawn, to give preference and promi-
nency to those speeches or passages which produced the best
effect. He will inconsciously perhaps, and almost unavoidably, select the matter which best deserves selection. I speak
not here from theory but experience. I had my political
partialities, and strong ones. I disliked the Tory Speakers,
and was credulous enough to think that patriotism and high
moral principle were as much in the hearts of the Whig
Members as in their mouths; but I was impartial, because
without being so I must have increased the too heavy tax on
my memory and my time. No adequate view of the importance of these considerations will be taken by those who
imagine that a Newspaper Report is a full length picture of
any debate. More columns by far are allotted to this species
of intelligence in the Morning Papers than was usual in my

time except on the most important occasions; but still the
fullest report they can receive is but a brief abridgment of
what was actually said. As the greatest part must unavoidably be left out, there is a most dangerous latitude for
partiality, and the particular accuracy of the Note-taker
is far less valuable than the general fairness of the report as a
whole to which by dependency on memory we were so
strongly disposed or driven. Having digressed thus far, it may
be right to do justice to the real, and distinguish it from
the imaginary, merit of William Woodfall,[1] the then Printer
and Proprietor of the *Morning Chronicle*, who was regarded as
a perfect prodigy, and certainly possessed as a Reporter very
extraordinary talents. He published debates with greater
fulness and greater accuracy, too, than the use of shorthand
notes has since produced, and the memory which was supposed to be his sole resource was naturally a subject of
admiration and wonder. But we his contemporary fellow
labourers well knew the advantages he possessed, and which
reduced the apparently preternatural talent to intelligible
tho' certainly more than ordinary dimensions. Being absolute
Master of his own paper, and being inclined from vanity or
mistaken self interest to sacrifice all other considerations to
its reputation for Parliamentary reports, he used to publish
the day after an important or long debate in either House
several hours later than any other Morning Paper, and never
sent his Paper to press, or went himself to bed on such
occasions till he had read all the other reports and supplied
from them as far as he thought fit the omissions of his own.
We were all therefore in effect made tributary to the high
reputation of Woodfall. All were then, I think, pretty impartial and for the reasons here given could not be generally
otherwise; but Woodfall was so from system and was
deservedly admired for that good quality, as well as for his
superior fulness and correctness. Yet I am sorry to say he was
ill compensated for the sacrifices he made. The sale of his
Paper, and its advertizing interests, were greatly prejudiced

---

[1] William Woodfall (1746–1803), parliamentary reporter and dramatic critic
on the staff of the *Morning Chronicle* 1774–1789; established (1789) the *Diary*,
the first journal to give full reports of parliamentary proceedings on the morning
after they had taken place.

by his late publication of it; and all he got in return was the empty gratification of being praised and courted and caressed by Parliamentary Speakers of both Parties, of which I was often a witness. When he died, it was found that he had saved little or nothing by his long and arduous labours. His Widow and children were left in a state of indigence and pleaded his merits in vain, I believe, both with Government and the Public, in the hope of obtaining some provision or relief. Were public services always regarded in proportion to their real usefulness, the faithful and able reporter of Parliamentary Debates would not be thought less worthy of a pension than the civil or military servants of the State. But I am wandering too far from my narrative and anticipating topics more proper for its future stages.

Had I known beforehand all the difficulties of a Reporter's employment I should hardly have been bold enough to undertake it. As it was, I truly professed to Richardson my diffidence of my own qualifications for it. But he kindly encouraged me to try the experiment and gave me the satisfaction to hear that I should be under no subordination to the Editor but responsible for the conduct of my department to the Proprietors alone, with whom I knew I should have in him a powerful friend and supporter. As to my salary, it was to be 104 Guineas a year, or rather two Guineas per week, for to my great satisfaction I found it might be received weekly if I chose. I suppose the terms are lower now, in proportion at least to the reduced value of money, as the province is divided among many and much inferior men to the reporters of that day, very inferior, I fear, in moral character as well as general talents. To me, £109 per Ann. appeared an abundant income; and I did not scruple on the strength of it to take Chambers in the Temple, where I got a very comfortable set ready furnished, and free of all taxes for £30 a year. The nature of an employment, which obliged me to be extremely irregular in meals and often to be out beyond midnight, or till sunrise, at the printing house, was incompatible with private boarding or lodging in a family house. But my habits of expence had been pitched so low by early necessities, and I knew so well where and how to get my meals comfortably and œconomically in London when possessed of ready money for the purpose, that I found my weekly salary fully equal to my support.

Here let me pause for a while in my narrative, and look back with humble gratitude on the ways by which a gracious Providence has led me to all the advantages and blessings I have since enjoyed. If I had not found some means of self support at that period, my subsequent lot in life could not have been such as it has happily proved and might probably have been bad in the extreme. With all the guards that I had in principles and feelings, both right and wrong, against actions disgraceful in the sight of man, I dare not say that necessity might not have driven me to sinful and shameful expedients under the pressure of actual want; but if not, some desperate course, for instance that of inlisting in the army or navy, was the only probable resort. That I should, when such extremities were not only approaching, but so near that I could barely fend off their actual grasp from day to day, find *any* escape from them, would have been a signal mercy. How much more so that I found, at that critical moment, not only present and ample means of support, but such means as were peculiarly well calculated to promote my future success in life. Such was the nature of my new employment. I held it for little more than a year; but in no period of what may be called my education did I acquire so much of the habits, the information, and the talents that were instrumental to my subsequent welfare. I much wanted patience of labour, and it was forced upon me. I knew little or nothing of public or political business and of those various subjects closely connected with the science of law that come under discussion in Parliament; but this defect of information was supplied, and in the most impressive manner, by my having daily to record what I learned. I found also in several of my fellow labourers, well informed and sensible men from whose conversation I got much acquaintance with the living world and added materially to my small stock of knowledge in matters of fashionable literature and taste. Reviews of Books, of the Stage, of public exhibitions, &c., were parts of our business, when Parliament was not sitting, especially of such of the Reporters as edited in whole or part their respective Papers. Greatly did these things tend to counterpoise the

defects of my early education and to promote my credit and
success afterwards in West India practice. But above all by
far, I was benefited by the vigorous exercise of my memory
and powers of composition, for which a better school never
existed than the reporting *under the then regulations* for a
Morning Paper. Before the end of the Session I was
astonished at the facilities I had acquired in these respects;
for my memory was always the weakest of my intellectual
powers; and my pen, till put to its speed, in order to keep
the compositors at constant work in their midnight tasks and
expedite the publication of the paper, was, tho' a tolerably
correct, by no means a quick one. It should be added that
from the good Parliamentary speakers I naturally acquired
more of the art and the tact of argumentative warfare in
public speaking than I should otherwise have possessed; and
certainly it was to my powers of argument and elocution at
the bar, such as they were, that I owed all my professional
success.

When I compare these advantages and their fruits, not
only with the destitute and hopeless situation from which
my engagement with the Press relieved me, but with the
former dependency on Mr. Milner and the probable effects
of its continuance, I justly regard the rupture between him
and me not as a misfortune but a blessing. Uneasy and painful at the best must that connection have proved, and had it
continued till my call to the Bar I should have missed all
those advantages, necessary as I believe they were, to my
future success. Nor should I have entered with the same spirit
and energy into the professional efforts to which I was
afterwards called. There is a capacity and fitness for the
business of the World which is best attained by early
struggling for a subsistence, in dependency on a man's own
industry and address; but instead of this important talent,
I should have embarked in my profession with the depressed
and diffident spirit of a man who had long leaned on another
for support and had to try for the first time the awful experiment whether he could emerge from dependency, and
rescue himself from want by his own unassisted efforts. For
these and other reasons, I am convinced that had I passed
immediately from under the wing of Mr. Milner into my

profession, I should certainly have shared in it the failure of many, not the success of the few, still less that early and large success with which it pleased God to crown my scanty acquirements and talents, happily for myself and also for my fellow orphans. It is in these views that I recognize the hand of a rewarding Providence in my mercy and forbearance to poor Kitty White, as well as in the singular discovery of her crime. If I had exposed her, as indignation and selfish caution also, much tempted me to do, the breach with Mr. Milner probably never would have arisen. There would have been no place for the degrading suspicion on his part, coupled with the decisive self-vindication on mine, which led to my renouncing the connection and casting myself on my own resources.

Having recurred to the notice of this poor Woman's misconduct, let me thankfully mention that she afterwards became a sincere penitent and a pious Christian and is, I trust, now in Heaven. Had I disgraced her, the case might have been different, and her subsequent history is instructive, as well as pleasing. She had, as I believe was before remarked, a Sister named Pamela, now Mrs. Pamela Davis, widow, of Blue Anchor Square, Peckham, who was, even at that time, I believe, eminently religious and of the Methodistical school. She was, like Kitty, a domestic servant, but afterwards married a Man who had property enough to leave her a humble independency at his death; and she has since distinguished herself so greatly through Peckham and its neighbourhood by her usefulness to the Poor, both in their temporal and spiritual concerns, as to stand very high in the regard and respect not only of them, but of all her wealthy neighbours who walk in the same charitable path, so that many of them employ her as their Almoner, and there are few names there, if any, better known or esteemed than that of poor Widow Davis. It must, I believe, have been to this Sister that Kitty owed what may not improperly be called her conversion; and she in her turn (wonderful are the ways of Divine Providence) became a converter of others. She lived many years in the service of a clergyman, the Revd. Mr. Beuthin, as a nursery maid, and during that time or before must have acquired her religious feelings and opinions,

10*

but certainly not from her Master; for he was adverse to them, being like too many of the Established Clergy, extremely afraid of enthusiasm or Methodism, whichever name he gave it. He was a moral and amiable man who had a large family to bring up on a small income, either as Curate or Incumbent of some poor Benefice in the City, and he was very sensible of Kitty's value as a faithful servant, but much dissatisfied on finding that she had impressed on the minds of his children, as they advanced to manhood, her own religious principles and feelings. His eldest Son not only joined the Methodists but actually became a Preacher, and an eminent one among them, not, I believe, the Wesleyans, but some other Sect of that general denomination; and his Second Son, now my coal merchant, is zealous in the same persuasion, and I have heard them both gratefully ascribe to Kitty all their religious knowledge and serious impressions. She continued to live in their family, I think, till it was dispersed by the death of their Parents, or till her advanced age and infirmities made her unfit for service. I had the gratification of assisting their endeavours and her Sister's to make her last years comfortable; and after a long decline, which she bore with the patience of a humble Christian, she died in faith and peace.

This may also be a proper place to mention the other member of my poor Father's family at Stoke Newington, of whose history and character I have taken some notice before, and who was made in a striking manner the subject of a like happy change. Captn. Davie, as from his former rank in the E.I. Company's Service we called him, went to the Continent, on the termination of his long and unfortunate land suit, fearing lest creditors might arrest him, and also with a view to explore the best means of subsistence of which he had any hope by engaging if possible in the Service of the Imperial East India Company, then recently formed at Ostend. The Emperor of Germany had employed in its formation Mr. Boltz,[1] who was a friend and fellow sufferer of

[1] Willem or William Bolts (1740–1808), Dutch adventurer; entered Bengal civil service 1759; resigned the service, being reprimanded for using the East Indian Company's authority for private trading schemes 1764; departed to England 1768; wrote *Considerations on Indian Affairs, particularly Reflecting the Present State of Bengal and Its Dependencies* (2 vols. 4to., 1772–1775).

Davie's, having, like him, been sent from Bengal as a Prisoner by Govr. Verelst and his Council for having established a House of Trade in the Nabobship of Oude without licence from the English Company. Boltz also had prosecuted his oppressors at law in this Country (but, as I best recollect, without success) and had ultimately found a resource by transferring his knowledge and enterprize, which were great, to the Imperial Service, he being, I believe, a German by birth and the then Emperor Joseph being very desirous of supplanting our E.I. Company, at least in the supplying his own dominions with Indian goods. Unfortunately, as it seemed, for poor Davie, he found on his arrival at Ostend that his friend Boltz had sailed for India. He still, however, remained on the Continent, endeavouring tho' in vain to prosecute his object, and probably might have persevered till Boltz could be heard from, had not my Father's death and other circumstances cut off his pecuniary supplies or hopes of receiving them from this Country. He then came to England and, finding himself destitute of every means of present support here, took the resolution of engaging himself as an Officer on board of a large Privateer then fitting out in the River Thames to cruize against the French and Spaniards in the Channel. His nautical and military education together well qualified him to take the command of the Marines, which, I think, was the station he obtained. It was with my privity and cooperation just before I left Lyons Inn that this was done. I deeply regretted the necessity of such a measure; but there was no less desperate resort, and it was probable, as we thought, that he might soon gain Prize money enough to support himself in privacy on shore till Mr. Boltz's return to Europe. Providence here guided my unfortunate Friend to salutary and necessary discipline. He had the feelings of a gentleman and had originally, I believe, imbibed from his Scotch education the principles of a Christian, or at least a general knowledge of what the doctrines of the Gospel are. But whatever good impressions he had received in early life had, I fear, been obliterated, and he had acquired habits of indolence and intemperance to the great detriment of his health, a case apparently the more hopeless because he was a man not possessed of any great strength of mind, but had rather a slender capacity, and little resolution both in his mind and body. The first process of the cure was to disgust him with intemperance, profaneness, and depravity, by bringing him into contact with them in their most revolting forms, and in extremes to which he was yet a stranger. The Society he met with on board the Privateer was of the very worst sort. He found himself among a set of Demons, rather than men, and was so shocked with their conversation and manners, those of the Captain and Lieutenants included, that he could not long after, when we met, speak of them without consternation and horror. So intolerable was his situation that as soon as the Privateer returned from a short cruize he took the opportunity of being boarded by a Man of War's boat to enter himself on board her as an ordinary Seaman, and with all the hardships of that situation blessed God for his deliverance. He had changed his name when he entered on board the Privateer inverting it to David Thomas, and retaining that concealment he disclosed nothing of his past history to the officers of the Man of War, but submitted to his new duties with so much humility that he gained their favor and was promoted to the station of a petty officer, I think that of Armourer or Armourer's Mate. At first it was hard on him, as a man who had been long accustomed to the self-indulgent habits of a gentleman and even to the luxuries of the East and who had passed his fortieth year, not only to labour with his hands but to mess with the common Seamen and keep their nightly watches; but he soon found a compensation in the recovery of his bodily health and strength and still more in the resumption or first acquisition (I am not certain which) of Christian faith and peace. He found among his Messmates, if I remember right, some one or more of the followers of Wesley or Whitefield who inspired him with, or brought back to his mind, just views of the evil of sin, the necessity of redemption, and the efficacy of faith and prayer. He looked back with sincere penitence on his past life, regarded his misfortunes as merciful corrections from his Heavenly Father, and submitted to his hard lot with resignation and content. He wrote to me, however, at the first opportunity with information of his adventures and with a request that I would learn whether Mr. Boltz had yet returned to Europe and if so to apprize him of his unfortunate situation. This of course I did and finding that gentleman at Ostend addressed a letter to him with such an account of my poor Friend, his character and conduct, as was best calculated to call forth pity and esteem. Mr. Boltz very kindly met the call and wrote to me that if Captn. Davie would get his discharge from the Man of War and come to Ostend he would provide him with the means of going to India. I was not slow in communicating this good news, on the receipt of which poor David Thomas, as he was called, revealed his true name and rank in life and his past misfortune to his Captain. The Ship was then on some foreign Station, but his discharge was easily obtained, and I had the satisfaction to see my old Friend again in his way through London to Ostend so improved in all respects that I could hardly recognize him as the same person. His bilious and emaciated countenance was exchanged for a plump and florid face, and his figure and movements bespoke rejuvenescent health and strength; but the change in the inner man was manifestly still greater. His conversation was pious, correct, and edifying, and it seemed as if his intellectual faculties as well as his bodily condition had been renewed or greatly improved by his misfortunes. Mr. Boltz was as good as his word. He gave him a situation as officer of one of the Imperial East India men. On her arrival at Bengal poor Davie was kindly received by some of his old remaining Friends, and their simpathy with his misfortunes being adopted by the local Government, he was restored to the rank that he held in the Army before he quitted the service. I received at least one pious and affectionate letter from him breathing content, satisfaction, and gratitude to Divine Providence, but my own migration to the West Indies interrupted our correspondence, and he was soon after removed, I trust to a far happier world.

It is high time that I should resume that painfully interesting part of my narrative from which I broke off to relate my quarrel with Mr. Milner. That event, and its serious probable consequences, ought to have sobered my mind, and stop'd me in the imprudent course I was pursuing. There was at the same time a fair opportunity of putting an end to my dangerous intercourse with Miss Rivers; for having quitted Mrs. Hamilton's house on terms that precluded my visiting there, I could no longer see her at home; and my dear Nancy had ceased, as I observed, to favour our intimacy and begun to regard it with anxiety, not to say distrust. Reason and conscience did not fail to suggest to me the duty of yielding to these impediments; but the idea of seeing the lovely, interesting Maria no more, of repaying her too visible partiality with apparent coldness and contempt, and leaving her, unprotected and friendless as she was, to the influence of a low and mercenary woman, was too painful to be resolutely admitted and carried into practice. Instead, therefore, of shunning the places where I was likely to meet her eye, I was almost insensibly drawn in my walks to the neighbourhood, and even through the Street, in which she lived. Without directly plotting to see her, or avowing perhaps such a purpose to my own heart, I acted as if I had formed it. Justly are we punished in such cases for deceiving our own consciences and courting, rather than flying from, temptation. On one fatal morning, in passing by the house, I found Maria just issuing from the door, for the purpose of some call, I suppose, on a neighbour, or at a shop. The rencontre, unseen by any of the family, was plainly to her productive of emotions far from unpleasing or unkind, and on my part it was a temptation I was far from trying to withstand. On the contrary I improperly engaged her to prolong her walk to some neighbouring nursery grounds and a retired road beyond them, that I might hear all her news since our seperation; and she was not loth to communicate to me much of an unpleasant kind that had passed between her and the Hamiltons, of which it was plain that their dislike or jealousy of me on the one side, and her resentment of it on the other, had been the source. She did not scruple to avow to me that contempt for their mean and narrow-minded characters which I before perceived her to entertain; nor could I sincerely have combated that sentiment in her mind if I had been prudently disposed so to do; but my advice, as I hope and believe, was to avoid a breach with them at the expence of all practicable forbearance, on account of Mrs. Hamilton being

the Person to whose immediate charge her deceased Father
had commended her. Objectionable tho' her present situation was, no better or equally decorous one was in her choice.
Her Uncle, Mr. Lennox, was kind and affectionate in his
manner towards her when she called, as he wished her frequently to do; but he was in his dotage, had grown old in
the habits of a sensual and licencious Batchellor, had no
female in his family, or I believe in his intimacy, and had as
his inmate and toadeater a much younger man, who
governed his household, managed his affairs, and looked
forward, as was understood, to be the Legatee of most of the
property he possessed. No asylum therefore could be found
under the roof of this relative; and to her Father's more
remote relations Maria was a stranger, and her extraction
probably unknown. The too lively interest I felt in her
situation and prospects prompted me to enquire very particularly into these circumstances, and Maria informed me
of them with as little reserve as if I had been her Brother.
Behold me, then, placed in the perilous situation of being the
chosen, I might say, the sole friend and confidant of a
fascinating young woman, in the full bloom of beauty, and
by whom it was too clear that I was not only trusted but
beloved. Alas, it was too certain, also, tho' as yet I concealed
it from my own heart, that I loved her passionately in
return. One addition to the danger only was wanting, and
that also was by this fatal interview supplied. I mean the
expression of our mutual feelings to each other.

It was in the sincere (I *think* at least it was sincere) prosecution of my plan in favor of my friend Tom that this ecclaircissement arose. The opportunity seemed to be fair, and I
embraced it, of promoting my Friend's wishes by suggesting
that if she could be prevailed on to reward his faithful attachment she might probably soon find a happy deliverance from
the discomforts of her present situation, as we expected his
early return to England and that promotion as well as Prize
Money would so far reward his gallant services as to enable
him to offer her an acceptable settlement in life. I had on
one or more former occasions spoken of my Friend with the
praise he merited, and otherwise indirectly approached my
purpose; but this direct avowal of it was more than Maria

could bear. She stop'd me with a look of anger and reproach, declared her firm resolution never to accept Mr. Stent's addresses; and with much agitation attempted to turn away from and leave me. I was not wise or just enough to permit her to do so. I seized her hand, pressed it to my lips, and told her melting, expostulating eye with the language of my own, that she was not misunderstood. Indeed it would have seemed to me a cruel and affronting affectation to appear longer inconscious of her feelings, or not to save her female delicacy and pride by an avowal of my own. But I was far at the same time from admitting a thought of perfidy towards my dear Nancy. I foolishly thought there was no such sin in declaring to the lovely Maria, who well knew of my engagement, that this alone prevented my being an ardent supplicant for that happiness which she refused to bestow upon my Friend, and that if I wished her to become my Sister-in-law it was only because honor and justice forbade my following the emotions of my heart by aspiring to a still nearer and more tender connection. Maria both looked and said enough to shew that this obstacle was very painful to her, tho' she felt that it was decisive. "Yes," said she, "I know your engagement. You are in effect a married man, and we must meet no more." I did not dispute this consequence. It was obviously not less the dictate of prudence than of duty on both sides; and happy had it been for us both if we had adhered to it. Such was sincerely, perhaps, our mutual purpose at the moment. If I remember right, we kept it to the end of our long walk, which, however, was protracted to suspend the dreaded last adieu, with so much more of tender and interesting explanation, of love, regret, and grief, as tended to make the sacrifice still more painful, and more doubtful too. The self-devoted purpose seemed to give a license to mutual tenderness during the few minutes that were left to us, and my farewell was more than once sealed on her glowing cheek and fragrant lips without rebuke.

When the tumult of feeling had subsided and I had to converse in solitude with my own heart, my reflections were sufficiently painful. It was impossible to conceal from myself that fidelity to my dear Nancy had been violated, tho' not in the last degree, or in any irreparable way. To keep my hand for her, giving my heart to another, was neither acting up to my engagements nor what her fond and delicate feelings could possibly brook if known. When I reflected on the strength of her faithful attachment to me and the painful sacrifices she had made to it, I was shock'd at my own ingratitude and injustice. It was painful also to reflect that I must now practice reserve towards her between whose heart and mine simpathy and perfect confidence had so long and pleasingly prevailed. On the other hand, I reproached myself for having inspired, and confirmed by my declaration in the breast of poor Maria, a passion that could never be gratified and might poison her happiness for life. These painful bosom censures led me to prayer, and penitence, and earnest resolutions of amendment. I determined to avoid Miss Rivers's company in future and do justice if possible to my dear Nancy in my feelings as well as in my conduct. In truth my feelings towards the latter, strange tho' it may seem, were very little altered. It has been said that no Man can love two women at once; but I am confident this is an error. My love for Maria, however, was in kind different from that of which my dear Nancy had long been the object. It had more of passion, but less of every other ingredient that enters into a virtuous attachment between the sexes. There was, however, in both cases that which has always with me formed the first charm in a woman; they both loved me, and as I thought with equal warmth; and beyond doubt I loved them both, fondly loved them, in return.

By what means I was led in the first instance to depart from my right resolution I cannot distinctly recollect. Perhaps it was by meeting Maria again in my dear Nancy's company, for tho' their mutual friendship or intimacy had declined, they still occasionally visited each other. But I was not long just and wise enough to decline, or not to seek walks which she loved to take. I found a new source of self deception in the return of young Hamilton from sea and in the purpose which his family plainly shewed of getting Maria to receive his addresses. She reported to me at least enough to excite that suspicion, and it served me with an excuse to myself for keeping up my intercourse with her that my influence might be necessary to frustrate their purpose; for it seemed to me that it would be a shocking sacrifice if Maria should be betrayed into such a connection. There was no doubt a mixture of jealousy in that feeling, but I was self deceiver enough to suppose it a pure regard to Maria's credit and happiness that made me alarmed at the idea of the possibility that she should so throw herself away and attach herself for life to such illiberal and sordid persons as composed the Hamilton family. Besides I still felt or fancied myself to feel a wish to preserve her for my absent friend Tom; and if she could be induced to renounce her unfortunate attachment to me in favor of another, he, I thought, was at least as likely as young Hamilton to be and more deserved to be that happy man. By these and other self deceptions, conscience was silenced on my part, and as to poor Maria, neither that Monitor nor prudence were powerful enough with her to prevent this perilous relapse. To shun the company of the man she loved, now that she knew herself to be loved by him in return, and who was become her sole bosom confidant in all her cares and concerns, was a self denial far beyond her strength of mind. She freely indulged me therefore in those dangerous private interviews as often as I asked or sought them.

In one of these I had a sample of her character in point of thoughtlessness and imprudence that might have had fatal effects. The Hamiltons indulged their spleen against me often, in family conversations, either to vex her, or perhaps because they thought it a duty to her (as they well might) to lower me in her esteem; and the young officer since his return, foolishly and indelicately enough, began to join in such attacks, tho' I was a stranger to him, except perhaps having seen him once or twice before his last voyage in my friend Tom's company. Maria, of course, did not bear this very patiently; and some retort from her to young Hamilton putting him out of temper, he was rash enough to bid her "tell Mr. Stephen that he was an officer, or a gentleman (I forget which) and wore a sword." This Miss Rivers, in reporting to me as usual the family disputes the next time she met me, had the egregious folly to repeat. The consequence, I lament to say, was conduct on my part which but for the great mercy and long suffering of my much offended

Heavenly Father, might have finished my sinful career in a
dreadful way or covered me with blood-guiltiness for life.
I madly resolved to call the young man to account for it, tho'
from his profession it seemed highly probable that there
could be no other result than a duel. The execution of my
purpose was happily delayed from the want not only of
pistols but of some friend at hand whom it would be proper
to select as a Second. I knew a Lieutt. Edie, then quartered
with his Regiment at Dulwich, and went there in search of
him, but providentially he was gone from his Quarters, or
the corps had been removed to some other and distant
station so that I could not find him. I then recollected Captn.
Cox, an old friend of my Father's, and was able to borrow a
pair of pistols from him, but still was at a loss for a Second.
I cannot recollect whether Cox refused, or that to get the
pistols I was obliged to conceal that they were for my own
use, but I believe the latter. It was by Felix Mc.Carthy's
agency (who, Irishman like, was most prompt to assist my
purpose) that I got the pistols from Captn. Cox; but, he
being then an Attorney's clerk, we both felt that my *dignity*
would not allow of his being Second. I went therefore in
search of another friend, with the pistols in my pocket, and
in my way met my intended antagonist. Conceiving immediately, or having as I believe previously conceived, that the
best way to obtain a concession from a man of the sword was
rather to avoid mediation if possible, especially that of a
military second, so as to give him the hope of secresy, I
coldly saluted Mr. Hamilton, and on his returning it, stop'd
and turned with him, and no one else being near, addressed
him in a resolute tone as follows: "Mr. H., you and I have a
serious account to settle before we part. You sent me word
that you are a gentleman and wear a sword. Now Sir, I
wear no sword, nor know how to use one; but I have a pair
of pistols in my pocket, and one of them shall be immediately
at your service, if you will walk with me to a convenient
spot." He was plainly intimidated, and took the course of
denying that he had used the words or said anything to that
effect, to which I replied that I would accept the denial as
satisfaction provided he gave it me immediately under his
hand; otherwise not. With this condition he thought fit to

comply, and we went into the first public house, where I drew up and he signed a most distinct and positive denial that he had ever sent me such a message. Thus we parted, and I put the paper the same or the next day into Miss Rivers's hands, who, I fear, with my permission, produced and insulted him with it at the family table. It was impossible for me on this occasion not to disapprove Maria's conduct in my heart and compare it to her disadvantage with my dear Nancy's, for the latter hearing from some person that they had seen Mr. Hamilton and me walking down the road together (we had met at no great distance from her home) immediately took alarm, for tho' she had heard nothing of the message, she well knew there was bitter enmity between us. She therefore hastened out, regardless of every thing but my safety, and pursued the course we had taken with such speed that she arrived breathless at the door of the public house, but happily not till everything was over, and we were quitting the house.

Deep, and I trust, accepted has been the penitence and lively the gratitude with which I have a thousand times looked back on this incident of my life. I offered in it a grievous provocation to Almighty God, resisting the admonitions of my conscience at the time, for I was as well convinced then as now that duelling is a great and highly presumptuous sin; and on this occasion I was hurried on to it by pride and revenge and by the suggestions also of another guilty passion which would not suffer me to act otherwise than as a man of spirit in Maria's eyes, especially as the insult was meant for her, as well as myself. Most justly might I have been hurried into the immediate presence of the God I had offended, or incurred the guilt of murder, tho' I hope and believe it was my intention on this, as it certainly was on subsequent occasions of a like kind, not to take the life of my opponent. Most mercifully was I spared by the forbearance and long suffering of my ever gracious and compassionate Creator. Yet my crime, as will be seen, was not left unchastised; and severely too was it visited upon me, if this incident was necessary, as I think it was, to plunge me into the abyss of remorse and wretchedness into which I soon after fell.

One of its immediate consequences was an open and final rupture between Miss Rivers and the Hamilton family. The Mother with too much reason accused her of having exposed her to the loss of her only Son; and tho' both she and the young man affected to regard me as a desperado, against whom he did right not to stake himself, they were of course much chagrined at his having been so humbled and compelled to attest a known falsehood under his hand. Maria was not inclined, however, to make any concessions. An appeal therefore was made to her Uncle, Mr. Lennox, and it was determined that she should immediately quit Mrs. Hamilton's family, and go to reside as a Parlour boarder in the respectable lady's boarding school at Kensington at which she had finished her education. Another consequence which contributed much to the unhappy events that followed was her final loss of my dear Nancy's confidence and regard. It was impossible to conceal from the latter what had happened. There was no way of appeasing her alarm but by shewing her the paper in proof that the business was over; and this explained the immediate cause of quarrel. Justly did she condemn with severity the conduct that had brought me into danger on Maria's part as well as mine; and it was no longer possible to satisfy her that a mutual attachment between us, inconsistent with fidelity towards herself, did not subsist. The Friend with whom she lived heard of the matter and was discerning enough strongly to confirm her suspicion, and persuade her no longer to countenance or see a Person who was supplanting her in my affections, and as she supposed by deliberate perfidy. In the latter she exceeded the truth of the case. I believed, at least, that Maria was as innocent as my treacherous heart told me I myself was of any purpose inconsistent with my engagements to her former friend; and I was unjust enough to be dissatisfied with my poor Nancy for renouncing her society, as injurious to her honour and my own. It was to make her more the victim of an involuntary and hopeless passion for which my self love of course made ample allowances.

This rupture worked very unfortunately. It left me no means of ever seeing Maria again except by contrivance and alone, and yet to take a final leave of her after having been the means of severing her from all her friends, my dear Nancy included, and having subjected her also to her Uncle's displeasure, was more than my heart could bear to think of even in my most consciencious and rational hours. We were both at the same time relieved in some degree from the restraining sense of what was due to my poor Nancy while she acted with kindness and confidence. There was no longer any friendship between them to violate, or any confidence to betray.

MEMOIRS OF JAMES STEPHEN

written by himself

Volume 2d.

Begun at Missenden October 30: 1825

"Behold O Lord how that I am thy Servant. I am thy Servant; & the Son of thine handmaid; thou hast broken my bonds in sunder."[1]

"Praise the Lord O my Soul, & forget not all his benefits! Who forgiveth all thy sin; and healeth all thine infirmities. Who saveth thy life from destruction; and crowneth thee with mercy and loving kindness."[2]

---

[1] *Psalms,* 116: 14, Book of Common Prayer.
[2] *Psalms,* 103: 2–4, Book of Common Prayer.

Chapter Nine

[1781]

I WILL not continue my narrative in this Volume from the point of its interruption in the first. I had arrived at the border of some incidents in my life through which this retrospect cannot be led with perfect security to the feelings of others still living. Before I die this objection may possibly be removed; and I may then perhaps record, in some intermediate Book of small dimensions, events deeply humiliating to myself and highly instructive to others, which I now deem it right to suppress. But the most important part of my plan, the history of my own heart, would be imperfect and not sufficiently intelligible, if I were not to confess that I became a great sinner before God; that the young lady to whom I have given the name of Maria Rivers was an accomplice in the offense; that I was in consequence plunged into a labyrinth of guilt and misery from which my extrication was to human eyes almost impossible: and, but for the infinite mercy of God, I should at this moment have been the Author of the destruction, the temporal destruction at least, if not the eternal, of more than one fellow being who fondly loved me, and whom I fondly loved, and should have been justly regarded as one of the worst and most perfidious of mankind. From all these dreadful consequences the gracious Providence of God has wonderfully rescued me. He chastised me indeed, long and severely chastised me, but it was chiefly by the anguish, remorse, and terror of which I was the victim, and the privation of happiness that I might otherwise have enjoyed; and in the midst even of this correction he remembered mercy. At length these bitter fruits of sin, and a sense of dependency on his Providence for the averting those dreadful consequences with which others were imminently threatened, brought me to true repentance and gave me a victory over those guilty passions by which I had been so long enslaved. He then heard my earnest, indefatigable prayers and by a train of events the most improbable and

313

unexpected released me from the cruel bondage in which the enemy of my Soul had bound me, reversed all my gloomy prospects, and restored to me that peace and happiness that seemed to be forfeited forever. Not one of those evils that I so reasonably dreaded has fallen on me, or those who were likely to be the victims of my crimes. He has even brought good out of the evil, making some of the painful consequences of my sins the sources of my temporal prosperity. "He brought me out of the horrible pit, out of the mire and clay, and set my feet upon the rock, and ordered my goings; and put a new song in my mouth, even a thanksgiving unto our God." "I will thank thee O Lord my God with all my heart, and will praise thy name for evermore; for great is thy mercy towards me, and thou hast delivered my soul from the nethermost Hell."[1]

On considering how to resume my narrative without relating the events which it is my purpose to omit, I perceive that my plan of an entire chronological gap in it will throw me into confusion and that, to shew the dependency of subsequent events, I must find another course. I think, also, on further reflection that my fall will appear too sudden to be consistent with my real character, and not to be so instructive as it ought, if I do not trace a little further the steps that led to it. On the whole, it will perhaps be best to continue unbroken the main thread of my narrative, omitting only such incidents as, for the reason I have given, it may be proper to withhold; and perhaps I may find a way, by sinking only a few facts in my progress, to attain sufficiently the end I have in view. The smaller the suppression the less will be the contraction of that striking view of the Divine mercy towards me that I wish and ought to exhibit.

The close of my first volume left Maria on the point of removing to reside as a Parlour Boarder in the fashionable school at Kensington, where she had two or three years before finished her education. The ladies who kept it were pleasant women and much attached to her, and she therefore found her situation comfortable enough, except that it naturally opposed some difficulties to her intercourse with one whose society, alas, was too necessary to her happiness;

[1] *Psalms*, 40: 2–3, 86: 12–13, Book of Common Prayer.

and she was less disposed than ever to relinquish it. Means, however, were found to diminish this difficulty. She had some old friends in the neighbourhood whose daughter, some years older than herself, was very fond of her company; and they often walked out together. With this young lady and her Parents she contrived to make me acquainted, and I paid my court so well to them as soon to become a favorite. But unfortunately it did not satisfy Maria's feelings or mine to meet only at their tea table or elsewhere with third persons. We soon, therefore, relapsed into the dangerous practice of meeting to walk together in Kensington Gardens or some less frequented place in the neighbourhood, her frequent visits to the family I have mentioned serving as a blind for her walking out on such occasions alone. It may be thought that I could not often lead her into such appointments without a bad design. But the fact was otherwise. I cheated my own heart at least into the belief that, tho' certainly much gratified by such intercourse with a beautiful and interesting young woman who loved me, my motives were generous and pure. She had now no Guardian to watch over her, and no confidential friend on earth, but myself. Her person, character, and manners exposed her, as I reasonably thought, to great dangers; and against them her love for and confidence in me seemed to be a security of which it would be ungenerous and cruel to deprive her. In these views the sense of what was due to my poor, dear Nancy had unhappily lost much of its influence; for she, I thought, had, by renouncing Maria's friendship and society, created or aggravated the dilemma. There was a time when better views had so far prevailed with me that I should probably have changed my conduct, but for an unfortunate incident that determined me to persevere in it. One of Miss Rivers's former school fellows had married a Gentleman of family and fortune who resided on his Estate in the Country; and on her invitation Maria, about this time, made her a pretty long visit. The husband, who I believe was a man of fashionable vices, paid her particular attentions and at length acted in a way that shewed he had bad designs on her person. On our first interview after her return, she reported the circumstances to me and on my advice readily consented to act in a way that

put a final end to her acquaintance with him and his wife.
This naturally strengthened my feeling that her unprotected
situation demanded from me the continuance of our private
and confidential intercourse. Other feelings of a more selfish
kind were no doubt mixed up with this anxiety for her welfare; and reason, if fairly consulted, would have told me that
her character at least, if not her person, would be more
endangered by frequent private meetings with a man of 23,
engaged to another woman, than by any probable risks they
could save her from. I had not, however, wholly abandoned
the hope that on my friend Tom's return from sea the same
powerful influence might yet induce her to give her hand to
him, who was a handsome and engaging young man, and
that way put an end to all anxiety on her account. The
consciousness that I was really desirous to convert in his
favor, notwithstanding my enamoured feelings, the lover into
the friend and brother-in-law, fortified my dangerous self-
delusion.

Dec. 8. 1825

Since the last lines were written, and within a few days
past, an event has occurred[1] that gives a freshened interest in
my mind to all that relates to poor dear Maria and may
perhaps in its consequences materially alter the plan and
style of my narrative in all that relates to her; but I will not
anticipate any such change, and hope that the event will
only be productive of new causes for admiring and gratefully recording the conduct of a gracious Providence, and
the wonderful answers to prayer of which my life has been
one long-continued exhibition.

My private meetings with that young Lady became, after
her removal to Kensington, more frequent than before. They
were usually, as I have mentioned, in the less frequented
environs of her residence, where we met by previous arrangement and afterwards walked together. No small risk, certainly, to her character was incurred by them; and sometimes unpleasant rencontres might have served to shew us
their imprudence. On one occasion when I had appointed to
meet her at Bayswater, then a solitary road, tho' at midday,

[1] One can only guess at this event. Could it possibly be the death of Maria?

I saw a gentleman dressed like a military officer overtake
her just as we were meeting and say or do something in passing her that threw her into great agitation, so that when I
came up she was barely able in a faultering voice to tell me
he had grossly insulted her. He had passed on a few steps;
but I immediately assailed him with my cane and beat him
till it was bent almost to a right angle over his back, he
running and crying out, and I following him with the same
discipline till I was nearly breathless. Happily, perhaps, for
us both, nobody else was in sight, and he was glad to escape.
Otherwise, if he was really an officer, he might, poltroon tho'
he was, have been obliged to resent the indignity in a way
productive of fatal consequences. How much, how infinitely
much, do I owe to a merciful Providence in saving me from
such effects of my own irascibility and rashness!

I cannot recollect, nor is it material, whether this incident
preceded or followed the unhappy criminal result of these
dangerous meetings. To trace their progressive inflammation
of our mutual passion, and the steps by which they led to its
ultimate gratification, would be to trespass against delicacy
and decent reserve, as well as to cover myself with well
merited humiliation and shame. Maddened with admiration
of her person, I always forgot in her presence the resolutions
with which I met her and, instead of the friend and the
monitor, acted the part not only of a passionate lover but of
a seducer, bent on the destruction of her virtue. When we
parted, reason and conscience often for a while came to my
aid and sometimes suggested resolutions of seeing her no
more. But afterwards the very recollection of the improper
liberties I had taken aggravated my fears of her being
exposed to ruin by others if I should desert her and deprive
her of what I insanely thought her best security, her unbounded confidence in, and fond attachment to, myself.
Nor was it in her absence only that feelings of compunction
and disinterested regard for her welfare had a right tho'
transitory influence. Often for a while did I talk with her in
a strain of self-reproach and tender admonition, professing
sincerely my concern for having given way at the last interview to feelings inconsistent with that engagement to my
dear Nancy which made them criminal on my part and

dangerous to us both; and yet, in a few minutes perhaps, I relapsed into the same fault and prepared for myself new remorse when released from the fascination of her beauty. Had I been a steady and determined villain her danger would have probably been less. She might have seen my drift and been put on her guard against me; for it would hardly have been possible to act the part I did if my right intentions, tho' transitory and inconsistent, had not been sincere. But in the sight of God, my conduct was scarcely the less guilty for these vibrations between right and wrong than if my purpose had been deliberately and uniformly bad. It was an impious alternation of penitence and relapse. I wilfully equivocated with my own conscience and returned to the influence of temptation long after experience had taught me my inability to resist it. In short, my guilt, as well as my infatuation, was gross; and the details which delicacy would suffice to make me suppress would, if given, make me more odious and contemptible than these confessions in their generalities will lead the reader to suppose.

My fall was merited. Whether poor Maria's was, it would ill become me to say. But this I ought to say in her defence, that I believe the deliberate purpose of ensnaring me into a final breach of my engagements to her former friend was foreign to her heart. If she was too regardless of consequences, it was from the influence of a blind passion like my own. I will only add that strong temptation at length concurred with fatal opportunity, and we were both undone.

The recollection of what followed in my mind at every moment of consciencious reflection is still dreadful. It is the image of a spectre which haunted all my solitary hours. Even during the delirium of gratified passion, of which reiterated indulgence was far from diminishing the force; even in the presence of the beloved object, for whom I felt a tenderness as ardent and romantic as man perhaps ever felt for woman, the sting of conscience was often poignantly severe. But it was in my solitary walks, in my hours of retirement, and on my pillow, that I had to encounter those dreadful feelings of a man "whose own heart calls him villain." The delusions of self-love were at an end. Conscience spoke out and told me with an astounding voice, that I had ruined by the indulgence of a guilty passion, three of the fellow creatures who were most dear to me; that I had repaid the fond attachment of my dear Nancy, after she had sacrificed her domestic peace, her filial duty, and a comfortable establishment in marriage for my sake, with a perfidy of the basest kind; that I had blasted forever the hopes of her Brother, my early and faithful friend; and that, after depriving poor Maria of every other friend and protector, I had myself robbed her of her innocence and her honor. As to the sin against God, which ought to have been the subject of deepest remorse, it was, tho' a painful consideration, much less so than the rest, at least for a considerable time, till his mercies redeemed me from despair and led me to true repentance. Towards Him my heart was for a while benumbed and almost hardened. For the first time in my life I could not pray. The forms, indeed, of my daily intercourse with Him were I believe preserved; but I could no longer pour out my heart before Him or confide in his favor and protection. There was even I fear, at times, a stubborn and rebellious spirit, or a repining at his holy laws, as if I had been subjected to temptation that I could not have resisted, and punished by the consequences beyond the measure of the offence. I was ready in the moments of my bitterest anguish to exclaim with the first murderer, "My punishment is greater than I can bear." Superstitious terrors also at times laid hold of me. I remember that once, on retiring to my bed, a strange black cat that had by some means got into the room presented itself suddenly before me as I was preparing to put out the candle and fixed its fiery eyes on mine with a fiend-like aspect, continuing for some time motionless and keeping me by a kind of fascination in the same state, while I thrilled with horror as if the Evil Being had taken that shape and was about to claim me for his prey. When at last I approached the ugly animal to drive it out, it disappeared in some way which my candle did not enable me to trace; and the superstitious idea seemed to be confirmed, till reason and a sense of manly duty enabled me to dispel it and with difficulty compose myself to sleep. Such phantoms of a guilty conscience, however, did not haunt me often or long. In fact I had never had much belief in the existence of a spiritual

Enemy, and my natural buoyancy of spirits always kept me from any abiding terror or depression in my religious views. God had prepared for my correction and, blessed be his mercy, for my cure, substantial miseries and such as were best fitted to torture all the sensibilities, whether moral or immoral, of my heart. The sense of guilt and shame, however, and that of having lost the favor of my Divine Friend and Benefactor, were painful enough independently of all the fear of consequences. I have never since been able to read Milton's account of the Fall of our first Parents without very strong emotions. He has seemed to paint the agonies of my own heart in describing theirs; and my tears have drop'd over his page, tho' scantily and gloomily, before my heart even was fully softened, like those of nature when

> *. . . muttering thunder some sad drops,*
> *Wept, at compleating of the fatal sin,*
> *Original . . .*[1]

Yet, like Adam, I did not, and indeed could not, forsake the fair accomplice of my guilt or decline those dear-bought enjoyments of our mutual love for which innocence was lost. To seperate myself from her was no longer possible. To myself it would have been intolerable and to her most probably destructive. Nor did duty seem at all to point that way. On the contrary, conscience seemed to concur with inclination in the resolution to make her my wife. The final and open violation of my engagement to my poor dear Nancy was, indeed, a consequence from which my heart shrunk with remorse and terror. I feared that it would be fatal, not only to her peace, but to her life, and so add murder to my other crimes. But the alternative was yet more dreadful still. When I considered the character and unprotected situation of Maria, I felt that nothing but giving her my hand could guard her against the ordinary and terrible effects of a female's lapse from virtue; and I shuddered at the fear that the criminal and shameful connection between us, however short, would debase her in her own esteem and prepare her perhaps for future licentiousness and infamy. I should have married her privately without delay if it had been in my

[1] Milton, *Paradise Lost*, Bk. IX, ll. 1002-1004. Milton has "mortal sin."

power; but, most happily as the event proved, though to the distress of my feelings at the time, the Marriage Act stood in our way. She was under-age; the consent of her guardians could neither be hoped, nor asked, nor had she any Guardian legally constituted whose consent would have sufficed. A journey to Scotland was utterly beyond any pecuniary means that I possessed or could possibly obtain and would also have been incompatible with secrecy and the preservation of her character. Of the legality of a marriage by banns in a Parish where the Parties do not reside and are unknown, and the facility of that course by the connivance of the Parish Clerks in the Metropolis, I was fortunately then ignorant or should certainly have taken it without delay. I was obliged, therefore, to be content with the resolution of making her my wife as soon as I could explore any means for the purpose. As to poor Maria, there was little or no uneasiness on her part to augment my own. Her confidence in me was as perfect as her attachment; and had a suspicion of my intentions ever suggested itself to her mind it must have been removed by that fervour and anguish of sincerity in my mind that evidenced my solicitude for our union beyond any false appearances that an impostor, however consummate, could have feigned. Above all, my remorse and my terrors in relation to the consequences that awaited my poor dear Nancy, feelings of which she was at once the confidant and the partner, proved the reality of my purpose; and it is just to poor Maria to say that in her mind as well as mine compassion and compunction towards that injured friend made delay in the consummation of the wrong more tolerable than it would otherwise have been. From her, therefore, I had no conflicts to sustain. We regarded each other as husband and wife in everything but form, gave free range to our mutual passion and should have been preeminently happy, but for the sad drawback of an accusing conscience and for the truly painful and distressing situation in which I was now placed whenever I met my still beloved and much injured Nancy. It was impossible to absent myself long from her and as impossible to hide from her affectionate anxiety the sufferings I had to sustain when in her presence. Every expression of her confidence and tenderness was a dagger plunged into my bosom; and while I feared more than death her discovery of the truth, I felt that the concealment of it was an aggravation of the cruel wrong I had committed by keeping up expectations that could never be realized and making the impending disappointment the more injurious to her character and her peace. In addition to this most painful dilemma I had the difficult and odious task of deceiving her whose open and confiding heart still trusted implicitly to my truth, and to whom the secrets of my own bosom were once familiarly known, by inventing a hundred falsehoods to account for the comparative infrequency and shortness of my visits; for all the time I could well snatch from my now laborious employments during the Parliamentary Sessions was little enough to satisfy Maria and myself in those interviews which we were continually contriving and ardent to multiply and protract. I was occasionally also embarrassed with jealousies by both these beloved women (for however strange it may appear, beloved they both at once were, tho' now in very different ways). Strangers now to each other and distant in point of residence; any absence longer than usual from the one was imputed to my having been drawn away by the society of the other; and tho' the suspicion on my dear Nancy's side was generally too well founded, I was under the odious necessity of removing it by falsehood. Sin, alas, is a prolific evil, tho' natural evil is not so: the viper is not oviparous. When a man has become the slave of Satan by unrepented and unforsaken sin, hard tasks are imposed on him by that cruel Master. To conceal and escape the consequences of one crime, he is compelled to commit many others. What a sad contrast to the "glorious liberty of the children of God"! With Maria my task was easier. I had little or nothing to conceal at this period from *her*. I had only to explain; for my attentions to my poor Nancy were no greater than Maria admitted to be necessary to avert consequences which she deprecated like myself, tho' not probably with equal alarm.

But the difficulty of satisfying both these victims of my misconduct was nothing compared to my struggles with my own heart. My situation with my dear Nancy at length became quite intolerable; and determined as I was to make

the only possible reparation to Maria, I at length felt that it
was an indispensable duty to confess to the former the in-
capacity in which I had plunged myself to fulfill my engagements to her and the necessity there was of endeavouring to
wean her affections from their unworthy object. Of all the
painful duties that I ever had to perform, of all the sufferings
that ever I was called to endure, this was by far the worst.
Many times did I make up my mind to it in her absence
and shrink from it again when I met her. My then very fertile
imagination was exhausted in contriving modes and means
by which the blow might be best softened to her feelings; but
reason on after-examination told me that all was fruitless
and that the cruel discovery, however made, must be unspeakable torture to that faithful breast whose sufferings
I would willingly have died to avert. At length I took my
resolution. It was to tell her of the perfidious crime I had
committed, to shew her all the real agonies of my remorse,
and without avowing the intended reparations to cast myself
on her compassion and advice.

It would be difficult or impossible for me to describe the
circumstances of the dreadful interview in which this purpose
was at last carried into effect. Her surprise, consternation,
and misery would be as hard to describe as my own shame,
pity, and remorse. I had no need or power to feign or to
colour. My anguish and self abhorrence were too great for
utterance and too real and conspicuous not to disarm her
resentment and turn it into sympathy. She would have bid
me at that moment an adieu forever if I had not retained
her almost by violence, till her tender feelings were alarmed
at my extreme distress, my agitation, and despair, and
induced her to stay till the storm on both sides subsided into
a pensive calm. She at length became composed enough to
consider the line of conduct which it became us on both
sides under such cruel circumstances to adopt and, calling
to her aid those sentiments of generosity and fortitude that
were natural to her character, told me that there was only
one course for me to take, which was to rescue Miss Rivers
from dishonor and perdition by making her my wife; and
she earnestly advised me to do so. No advice was ever more
adverse to its own object. The nobleness of mind that

inspired it, and made her press it with an earnestness and perseverance such as proved its sincerity, excited my admiration and made me feel at the time that it was impossible to sacrifice such a woman even for the preservation of Maria. I therefore, without dissimulation, declined to follow it and opposed to all the arguments she used to enforce it my prior engagements to herself which my heart still recognized and from which, tho' she offered to release them, I could not consent to recede. I observed that independently of this obstacle the subsisting bars to our union could not be soon removed and were equally opposed to a marriage with Maria, as I could invite her only to indigence and ruin; but that if, in prosecution of our former views, and with the expected assistance from my Brother, I should resume my profession and go to practice in the West Indies, Providence, in compassion to my distress and my remorse, might relieve us from the dilemma we stood in before the period at which I could by success in my profession have hoped to make her my wife. One of the three might die; or Maria, if her character could be preserved, might be weaned from her attachment to me and accept some eligible offer of a far better settlement in life. Such hopes had in fact before suggested themselves to my mind and been balanced against the considerations which pleaded for a marriage with Maria, when I contemplated the dreadful consequences of that measure to my poor Nancy; and now her generous conduct made me sincerely revert to them as the plan least painful to my heart. She did not, however, acquiesce but persisted in her advice and would have peremptorily declined to see me any more if the violence of my distress had not at length compelled her in compassion at least to suspend that purpose and promise me a further interview before she should carry it into effect. I not only held her to this promise but almost compelled her to see me again repeatedly and even oftener than before. Having no more reserve or deceit to practice with her, I saw her with less pain, and her simpathy however reproachful to me was a relief to my much oppressed feelings. Besides, tho' she persisted in her advice, and I was almost secretly resolved to follow it, I saw progressively a dejection in her spirits that alarmed me, and even her apparent calmness rather tended to increase that alarm.

Here I have paused much and long whether to relate or suppress one most painful incident in this tragedy of sinful passion. On the one hand, I would spare my beloved and injured Nancy's memory as to an intended crime; on the other I ought not to withhold one of the greatest and most affecting instances of God's gracious and compassionate interposition both on her behalf and mine, and which shews more than all the rest the extremity of those fatal consequences from which I was mercifully rescued. I conceived at last the dreadful thought that she was cherishing, and concealing from me, a purpose of self-destruction. I can recollect nothing that inspired the fear except that her calmness appeared to me unnatural and that her generous advice seemed to cost her nothing. So it was, however, that I was led to entertain this apprehension so much as to resolve to put it to the proof. Therefore, having engaged her to meet me once more and walk with me that we might discourse with freedom on our painful situation, I prepared myself with the strongest thoughts I could collect on the guilt of suicide and the duty of bearing with patience and submission to God's will the heaviest calamities of life. I introduced the subject, if I remember right, as connected with my own misery and remorse and perhaps not untruly said that, but for the impious and horrid nature of such an act and its dreadful consequences in the state we were to pass into, I should be tempted to resort to that relief. At that time of my life, at least when my mind was roused and deeply interested, I was not ineloquent; and I enlarged with all my powers on the terrible character of that inexpiable crime as direct rebellion against that awful Being into whose presence the offender at the same moment rushed, in defiance of his vengeance. I was long, and she heard me with a deep and progressively anxious attention that augmented my alarm and led me to persevere. At length she suddenly burst into a violent agitation and a flood of tears, and exclaiming that she was now completely wretched and her last hope destroyed, drew from her pocket a large phial of laudanum and dashed it on the ground.

It cannot be necessary to say what were my emotions. The Searcher of hearts knows that they were bitter and agonizing to excess, tho' mixed with feelings of gratitude for his mercy that encouraged the hope of final deliverance by his hand.

Of course my expostulations and reprehensions were of the most awakening kind. Guilty cause tho' I was of the criminal purpose, I was not the less gratified to display its horrors; and I did it so effectually, engaging every feeling of her heart and among them her remaining tenderness for myself on the side of repentance, that before I left her her remorse and anguish were extreme. After weeping to exhaustion she gave me the most solemn promises that she would never again harbor such a dreadful purpose for a moment in her heart, or turn a thought that way; and I am sure she kept her word. I trust I am equally sure that the sinful purpose was forgiven.

Strange tho' it may seem, I cannot with certainty recollect whether it was with Maria's previous permission that I had disclosed the secret to my poor injured Nancy; but I think it was. She had no will but mine and dissented from nothing that I proposed. Sure I am that she was not uninformed of this shocking incident and shared my own feelings upon it. Had marriage been then in our power I believe she would like myself have shrunk from it, for fear of such dreadful effects on the mind of her poor injured friend. But alas, her romantic attachment to me made her abstinence from pressing that reparation a matter not of generosity only, but of ill-directed passion. She, like too many others, had imbibed from that pestilent epistle of Eloisa to Abelard the baneful sentiments and feelings which the Poet's eloquence has embalmed; and more than once at this period did she repeat to me with ardour those seducing lines ending with, "O make me Mistress to the man I love."[1] Shame to me, that my love and vanity were more gratified than my right feelings for her alarmed by their quotation.

Still this dangerous enthusiasm was propitious to the course that I was happily led to take. Had Maria's feelings demanded from me the immediately making her my wife, I

[1] Pope, *Epistle of Eloisa to Abelard.*

could hardly have satisfied my own even with temporizing on that subject, however fearful the consequences to her rival were now found to be. My poor Nancy, indeed, soon relieved me from the worst of my apprehensions. She renewed her generous advice, and with it such assurances of her never again giving way to any dangerous feelings that I believed, and still believe, she had armed herself with patience and resignation enough to sustain the blow, and would have found consolation in the consciousness of having acted well. But this generosity of conduct raised her so much in my esteem and my best affections that I could not bear the thought of putting her to the trial; and as the romantic feelings of Maria left me at liberty on the other side, while the obstacles to a private marriage still continued, I naturally suspended a painful decision, hoping against hope for some deliverance in the course of events.

Two occurrences only were wanting to carry my embarrassments and my wretchedness to the highest possible pitch, and both those aggravations fell about this time together on my sinful head: the return of my friend Tom from his long voyage, and poor dear Maria's finding herself in a situation the natural fruit of our guilty love. Both were announced to me nearly at the same time; at least I cannot recollect which preceded the other.

It pleased God, for gracious ends known to his unerring wisdom, to embitter the former event to me in a singular and unexpected manner. My dear first friend, my deeply injured friend, had resolved to make his return as pleasing to me and to his Sister, whom he always tenderly loved, as he possibly could. He therefore hastened from Portsmouth to see his father, who was fond and proud of him to excess, and in the warmth of their mutual affection after a long seperation (in which he had encountered many dangers and greatly gained the esteem of his Captain for his gallantry in action and other professional merits) made it his earnest request that he would resume a suitable family establishment, put his Sister at the head of it, and allow her to receive my visits as her lover and intended future husband. The old Man, who had great affection for his daughter also, and thought the better of me perhaps from his Son's partial account of me, was not hard to be persuaded; and my poor Friend hastened to his Sister to communicate to her, and through her to me, whom he knew not where to find, the joyful information. His impatience no doubt was at least equally great to hear news of Miss Rivers and to learn whether his Sister's kind offices and mine, of which he had heard from her correspondence, had produced for him any favorable change in the mind of that beloved object of his early affections.

Let the compassionate reader judge what sensations were exerted in my dear Nancy's mind when her Brother, transported with joy, presented himself suddenly and unexpectedly before her with this communication! Let the compassionate, tho' at the same time indignant, reader judge also of *my* pitiable situation when through her the same communication was made to me, with the addition that I must, for she *could not*, find the resolution to undeceive my unfortunate friend. O! the humiliation, the torturing self-reproaches, the exquisite misery, that I then sustained. I then *indeed* felt the intolerable sting of a guilty conscience. I "roared", as the Psalmist says, "for the disquietness of my heart."[1] I wished for death and could have invoked the Earth to open and swallow me up alive to hide my sin and my shame together. But I had, as I have already said and shall again in the course of these memoirs have occasion to remark, a strong and sure guard against self-murder.

I went to my poor Nancy and found that she had observed a total silence towards her Brother in all that regarded myself and Miss Rivers and that he had not been alarmed, or in any way prepared, for the dreadful blow that awaited him. I found, also, to my dismay, that his feelings towards Maria were as warm as ever and that he was impatiently desirous of being allowed to see her. It was in vain that I implored my dear Nancy to spare me the torture of the explanations which I could not deny were indispensably necessary, by giving them herself. She never before or after inflexibly resisted any solicitation of mine, but now she was inexorably resolved not to be my accuser. Perhaps she foresaw that my habitual influence over his mind and my

[1] *Psalms*, 38 : 8, Book of Common Prayer.

genuine remorse, of which she could not doubt, would best soften the shock and avert any fatal consequence. For my part, I felt that it would be the greatest relief I could hope for if he should resent my conduct violently and call for what is usually termed among gentlemen *satisfaction* in such cases. If he had, my conduct would have been to expose myself to his vengeance, but of course not to take any risk of hurting him in return. While tormented with the most painful anticipations, the hour of trial speedily arrived; I had a note of the most affectionate import from him requesting me to meet him at a certain Coffee House where we might spend some hours alone. I could have gone with less sense of shame, and less of misery, to be publickly executed as a malefactor; but stern necessity commanded and I made up my mind to the dreadful interview as an unfortunate patient does to a cruel operation by his Surgeon, with less concern as to the event than the painful process.

I cannot attempt to describe what passed between us. At this hour I shudder to reflect upon it. The manner in which I received his affectionate greetings and joyous communication scarcely prepared him for the shock, and when it was given he did not relieve me by indignation or reproach. He hid his face from me, was silent, and wept bitterly; bitterly *indeed* to *me*, as well as to himself. Then, *then*, I felt pangs such as virtuous misery can never know. After an hour or more, for which the vicious pleasures of a long life would ill compensate, it was necessary to consider on both sides what was to be done. He had brought me a kind invitation to dine with his Father at their new residence at an early day, when I was to find my dear Nancy at the head of the table, and how to accept or decline it was equally difficult. I preferred the latter; but my poor friend, after his anguish had a little subsided, said to me, "Jem" (that was his accustomed appellation) "you *must* come. This unhappy affair must of course come out; but spare me, I beseech you, the mortification and misery of witnessing my dear Father's and Sister's disappointment and distress. I have been long absent from my Country and friends and hoped to have a happy, tho' short, enjoyment of them. I am now to pass immediately at the Admiralty as a Lieutt. and will endeavor to get appointed to some distant station, with a resolution if possible to return to England no more. Keep this dreadful secret from my Father, I entreat you, till it comes out in my absence, and let me have peace at least in the family while I stay, and leave my poor Sister under her Father's roof." It was easy to point out objections to this course but not so easy to combat my injured friend's feelings and entreaties. He took on himself all responsibility for the further wrong that I felt it would be doing to his Father and Sister and he was confident that her wishes would point the same way with his own, in which I soon after found he was not mistaken. In short, I was obliged, however reluctantly, to comply, feeling that they had a right in this instance to dictate to me whatever line of conduct would best end to mitigate their present and suspend their future sufferings.

The visit was to me a new source of bitter compunction and unavoidable regret. Mr. Stent was a man of a meek, gentle, kindly disposition and warm parental affections, one of the last men whom a generous mind could bear the thought of treating with injustice or disrespect. We had never before even spoke to each other, and he had entertained towards me a natural dislike. But his heart was warm, and his satisfaction in having his children again domesticated with him made his benignity at this time overflow. He was much pleased with my manners and conversation, took a great liking to me, and cordially invited me to be often a guest at his house. Nor did he omit early and frequent, particular invitations, which I found it impossible to decline. My poor Nancy always loved her Father most affectionately; and now to find him cordially reconciled to and pleased with her was such a visible source of delight to her mind, notwithstanding the secret sting which I had planted in it, that I could less than ever bear the thought of that sad reverse I had prepared for them. I felt somewhat like the remorse of the Fiend in Paradise at the sight of the happiness of our first Parents, except that the approaching ruin of it was my sad destiny, not my choice. My poor Friend was generally at home when I was expected, but it was only to keep up appearances with his Father and gratify his Sister. I saw with regret, tho' not with surprise, that I had justly lost my hold

on his affections, and with still deeper regret that he was
diverting his painful thoughts by such dissipations as Seamen
are too generally addicted to when ashore. It was a relief to
me when, after spending his pay and his prize money, he
went again to sea on a distant voyage as Lieutt. to his former
Captain and Friend, who was intent on his further promotion. My friendship for him was far from impaired, but on
his part I fear it was never cordially renewed. May it be so
in that happier world, of which I hope in the infinite mercy
of God he has long been an inhabitant.

It will be naturally supposed that this reception in the
family of Mr. Stent, with that other aggravation of my
embarrassments to which I have alluded, the deeply interesting and alarming situation of my beloved Maria, powerfully
affected her mind and made the delay of the reparation that
was due to her more painful than before, to her feelings as
well as my own. Such certainly was the case, and yet not
in so strong a degree as may well be supposed. Apprised as
she was of the cruel circumstances and irresistable motives
that led to my conduct, the occasional uneasiness that she
felt was in general easily quieted by assurances that were not
more solemn than sincere. I made her in great measure the
adviser or arbitress of my conduct. My wishes and intention
were like her own; and I had therefore no motive for reserve
towards her, except in concealing from her at times the
frequency with which I found it necessary to repeat my visits
at Mr. S's to save her from causeless apprehensions. Her
natural cheerfulness and gaiety and, let me add, her thoughtless confidence made my part much easier with her than it
would have been with most other women in the same circumstances; but the best explanation is to be found perhaps in the
unfeigned warmth of my tender attachment to her and the
irresistable energy of truth. Her new situation added all the
increase to my fond affection for her and anxiety for her
welfare of which they were before susceptible, and it would
have been impossible for dissimulation to assume such
demonstrations of them as I continually gave. Besides, great
as the sins were into which the fascination of her beauty and
her love had betrayed me, she well knew that I was not in
other respects insensible to moral or religious obligation and

that I was anxious to form and strengthen in her those principles of piety which a man wishes for, not in a Mistress, but a Wife. My standard indeed was low and my conduct, towards herself at least, still lower; but she knew that I feared God and hated injustice, even in my own heart and actions. She was not, therefore, on the whole too credulous in believing that I sincerely desired to make her my wife as soon as I should have power to do so. It must always be remembered that we both believed I had no such power while she was under age without going to Scotland; and the objection to this in point of expense was insuperable, independently of the discovery by her absence and mine of a union which compassion for my dear Nancy as well as the most urgent considerations of prudence demanded from us to make clandestine. It is but justice to Maria to say that feelings in this respect for her injured friend were hardly less powerful in her mind than my own. But the time of her majority was not far distant, and then we thought the obstacles to a private marriage would be removed. Let me again notice the singularity of that circumstance, which I now gratefully regard as Providential, my entire ignorance and hers that banns might be published in a Parish in which we had only a nominal residence and legalize a marriage of which none who knew us would hear. To explain the impossibility of our going to Scotland, and for other reasons, it is proper I should now return to some notice of our situations in regard to our means of support and my prospects in life.

I left those subjects if I remember right in the first volume of these Memoirs, not at present within my reach, at the point of my engagement as a Parliamentary Reporter for the *Morning Post*. I continued my labours in that line satisfactorily to my employers, tho' often painfully enough to myself, my very frequent interviews with the two objects of my affections at parts very distant from the seats of my labours and from my chambers, keeping me constantly in distress for time. But perhaps even this was made by a gracious over-ruling Providence beneficial in its consequences. I believe that without the vigorous bodily exercise in which those circumstances kept me I could not well have sustained my late nights at the House of Commons and long continued sedentary labours. But my constitution was rather strengthened than impaired during that period. I remember only once having been obliged by indisposition to be absent from my duties, and that was after four and twenty hours of fatigue under which most men would have sunk. It was on the occasion of the much [*sic*] interesting trial of Lord George Gordon for High Treason[1] in the matter of the riots and burnings of 1780, which it fell to my sole province to report. I was obliged to be at Westminster Hall by 3 or 4 in the morning and to stand on the floor of the Court of King's Bench, the only situation attainable, wedged so closely in the crowd of auditors that I could not take notes or even raise my arms or change my posture till about the same hour in the morning following, without any sustenance except some cakes that I took in my pocket, and afterwards to sit up and write the report while the press was at work for the same day's publication. I had the improvidence to have got in nothing to appease my hunger at my chambers and all the public Houses were shut, and in consequence before my labours were finished was so much disordered as to be obliged to desist, but was able notwithstanding to resume and finish my long Report in time for the following day. Erskine's Speech was quite irresistible. It made his fortune and saved his Client's neck, nor can a stronger proof of its merit perhaps be given than its effect on myself. Tho' exhausted nearly to fainting when he rose and tho' adverse in my feelings to his cause, I felt no weariness while he was speaking and thought, tho' it was I think two hours and more, that he finished too soon. It was a perfect masterpiece of eloquence, and my praises perhaps tended in some degree to increase his fame. The Prisoner sat between his two brothers, the Duke of Gordon and Lord William, with whose great apparent sensi-

---

[1] The trial lasted from 8 a.m. on Monday, February 5, to 5.15 a.m. on Tuesday, February 6, 1781. Stephen's report of the trial appeared in four instalments, Tuesday to Friday, February 6 to 9, in the *Morning Post*. It is a dramatic account and a remarkable feat of memory. In the third instalment, just as Stephen got well started on his admiring report of Erskine's two-hour speech, he broke off with a note: "A sudden indisposition in the Gentleman who has favoured us with our previous Narrative of this interesting trial, has compelled us to suspend the further account of Mr. Erskine's excellent and celebrated speech till to-morrow." He resumed and completed the report the next day.

bility, especially that of the latter, I was much pleased. As to Lord George himself he was perhaps the only indifferent person in Court. I must not disgress; otherwise the scene on the delivery of the verdict would be worth describing.

For these arduous labours my reward, as I probably before stated, was only two guineas a week. Reporters for Newspapers, tho' then far more respectable men and much harder worked than now, were far worse paid. We had, however, advantages which some of us valued in a gratuitous supply of tickets for the theatres, masquerades, and all other public exhibitions, the Managers, Actors, &c., being all desirous of courting our notice and favor. But it was another incidental good effect of my love engagements that I was very rarely at leisure and inclined, like my brethren, to partake of such amusements and thereby escaped perhaps habits of dissipation of a dangerous kind into which I might otherwise have fallen. It will be easily believed that my weekly salary did not more than suffice for my support, especially as my almost daily visits to the ladies made me observant of genteel appearance in point of dress, &c. In fact, I had rarely a guinea in reserve and was often obliged to anticipate my weekly income, in which cases my common resource was to pawn my watch and redeem it again when the day of payment arrived. I remember a cruel fraud once practised upon me on such an occasion. To conceal my entry into a Pawn-broker's shop, or for some necessary course, I had called a hackney and stop'd at the door of the shop; and perhaps the coachman saw by the haste with which I passed into the door that I was a novice and fit for his dupe. So it was that, on putting my just received guinea into his hand, he gave me eighteen or nineteen bad shillings in change and drove off before I discovered the cheat. Poor Maria's finances were rarely in a better condition than mine. Her Father's Executors from the time she left Mrs. Hamilton, whose friend and partizan in the quarrel the only acting Executor was, kept her as bare as possible, enabling her only to pay her quarterly bills with a small reserve for dress and other necessary expences. They alleged it was the whole income of her moiety of the residue of her Father's Estate that they so allowed her, whether truly or not I do not know, for I had

left England and she, if I remember right, was married
before they accounted to her or her husband for the property. I think it consisted of a small real estate which they
sold afterwards, probably with her and her husband's concurrence. So it was that she felt herself much straightened,
at the time referred to, in her allowance and often applied
to them in vain to increase it. The rich Uncle whom I mentioned acted very unfeelingly. He was, I think, a co-executor
of his Brother's will but always on her applications referred
her to the other and would not interfere to controul him. I
hope, and am inclined to believe, that she was not prejudiced
with him by her known attachment to me. I never heard that
such was the case or that he found any fault with her on that
account. In fact, he was quite in his dotage and governed by
a mercenary inmate, to whom, and another brother's
family, he ultimately left all his fortune. Yet Maria was
always received by him when she called with great cordiality
and kindness. Unless his mind was deranged, which I rather
believe, he must have been a man of grossly indelicate and
immoral feelings, for when she was with him one day he
mentioned to her his neighbour, who lived with Lord
Thurlow[1] as his wife, and spoke of her in terms of high com-
mendation for the prudence and address with which she had
raised herself from being bar-maid at Nando's Coffee House
to what he regarded as a splendid and enviable situation.
After hearing of this, I despaired of her ever deriving any
good from that once affectionate Brother of her deceased
Parent and advised her to desist from visiting him, which I
believe she did in great measure, if not entirely, during the
short remainder of his life. Such being our situations and
prospects, my embarrassment and alarm when I found my
poor Maria likely to become a Mother before I could make
her my wife were pitiably great; and it was I think about the
same time that letters from my dear Brother William cut off
my best remaining hope by shewing me that no early
pecuniary help was to be expected from him. He most

---

[1] Edward Thurlow, first Baron Thurlow (1731–1806), lord chancellor
1778–1792. The writer in the *Dictionary of National Biography* says of him that
"his political principles were merely a high view of royal prerogative and an
aversion to change." He was never married, but he had three natural daughters,
to whom he left a good part of his property.

affectionately renewed his expression of deep concern for my necessities, and the deviation from my professional path into which I had been forced, and his anxiety to enable me to resume it, but he had solicitated his Uncle in vain for the means of making me a small remittance. He was himself absolutely dependent on the latter who, though kind to him, was a penurious man and very sparingly, I believe, supplied him with the means of defraying his own personal expenses, thinking it enough to give him his board and lodging and other necessaries for acting as his assistant. As to me, he was inexorably angry with me on account of my breach with my Uncle Milner, not being liberal enough in his feelings to make any allowance for the honorary necessity under which I had acted.

The appalling prospect of ruin to my dear Maria's character, and probable danger to her life even, from my inability to provide for a temporary retirement and accouchement was an addition to my wretchedness that my mind could ill sustain. My best human consolation under it was the tender simpathy of her whom I had most injured, my kind and generous Nancy who, tho' she saw in this consequence of my infidelity a ground for its consummation that more effectually put an end to all her hopes, sincerely pitied my distress and felt also for her former friend. She more strongly than ever declared her opinion that I was bound in honour and justice to marry her rival the first moment that it should be in my power, and if she had possessed the means of enabling me to do so and I had been capable of accepting her assistance for such a purpose I verily believe she would have given it. But she could not make the offer. Her own finances were not less scanty than Maria's or mine, for now that she lived with her Father a small allowance for her dress and pocket money was all that she received or would have consented to receive from him; his income was small and barely sufficed for the support of their frugal family establishments. Tho' no extremity would have compelled me to accept assistance from her or him for such a purpose, I mention this inability in justice to her kind and generous feelings, which otherwise would, I dare say, have led her to make the offer.

I had, however, it should be observed, by no means professed my design to follow her disinterested advice. My heart, indeed, told me that I must inevitably do so when possible, but I could less than ever bear the thought of planting a dagger in her feeling heart and wounding deeply her kind old Father's too by such a measure. My poor friend Tom, indeed, was gone and I might, therefore, consistently with his injunctions have made the discovery; but there were new obstacles which he did not foresee and to which I had wilfully shut my eyes under the cruel dilemma in which I was placed by his distress and his earnest solicitations to save him from a dreaded scene. I must now have appeared to the old man a most unfeeling and wanton villain for having accepted his hospitalities and won his affections as a future son-in-law and disgraced him in his private circle, after I had formed a connection preclusive of ever fulfilling my engagements to his daughter. Nor could I mitigate the guilt by shewing by what means I had been reluctantly driven to such conduct without involving both the Son and daughter in his too just resentment. Such are the sad labyrinths in which vice involves us! Thus does the Enemy of Souls ensnare and inslave those who have fallen into his power, obliging them to add sin to sin in their vain efforts for deliverance. What then, it may be asked, did I really intend at this sad juncture? My answer is—nothing definitively, nothing even for a day together; my agonized mind vacillated between opposite and incompatible purposes. When I thought of the consequences to poor Maria, I was resolved to give her my hand, whatsoever miseries might follow, and regretted that it was not at the moment in my power; when I thought on my poor Nancy and her Father I shrunk from the fatal purpose and was sincere at the moment in telling the former that I would not follow her generous advice, if it were in my power to do so. My least unsteady resolution, and that which I was providentially cast upon, was to temporize, to postpone the tremendous day while I possibly could and take the chance of what death or some other occurrence might do for my ultimate deliverance.

I have said that my dear Nancy's confidence and compassion were my best human resource, but I had occasional ones of a more efficacious kind. It is long since I have said anything of the state of my heart towards God, and to that awful subject let me now return.

It may be supposed that during all these painful and guilty conflicts, and while I yet maintained (it was, I think, quite impossible to do otherwise) a sinful intercourse with Maria, I had turned my back on the Great and Holy Being whom I had offended and who is of purer eyes than to behold iniquity. I have been ever quite exempt from Antinomian heresy. Yet such was not my conduct. I prayed to God daily and often with greater earnestness and fervency than in my purer days. Sometimes, indeed, I could not venture to raise my thoughts towards him. Such was generally the case when hastening to an interivew with Maria, or under the fascination of her presence and her endearments, or when meditating some of those violations of truth into which my difficulties drove me. Sometimes even in the severity of my sufferings I indulged for a while a murmuring and rebellious spirit, feeling as if God were unkind to me and punished me more than I deserved. But rarely or never did I retire to sleep without humbling myself and disburthening my weary heart before him. Often in the paroxysms of my grief and my alarms did I pour out at his footstool floods of penitential tears and implore with reiterated supplications pardon and deliverance by his infinite power and mercy. Often did I resolve and vow before him that if he would avert the consequences of my sins from their two beloved victims, and rescue me from the cruel bonds in which my soul was bound, I would never more offend him. Nor were these prayers in vain, blessed be his goodness! nor was a soothing sense of their acceptance always wanting. Often have I risen from my knees when nearly exhausted with a nameless, powerful conviction that my penitance was accepted and that God certainly would deliver me and avert the mischiefs that I feared, tho' in what specific manner I could scarcely form an idea or a clearly directed wish.

When the state of poor, dear Maria became such as to affect her outward appearance, it was necessary without delay to concert means for the preservation of her character; and they could only be found, alas, in much elaborate falsehood. Of this, however, I hardly felt the guilt, so clear and urgent was the necessity of the case and so fearful the alternative. That she should be for some months kept out of the view of all who knew her but myself was not more obvious than that her retreat must be in or near London, for *there* I must remain to preserve the only slender means I had for her support; and a seperation from me was out of the question. Neither her feelings nor mine could have borne it. To hide her in such a place as the Metropolis, or its environs, was not difficult except that it required confinement, lest she should meet with some who knew her; and tho' I had some anxiety as to the probable effects on her health, her excellent constitution furnished tolerable security in that respect, with which we were obliged to be content. The main difficulty, poverty excepted, was how to find a pretext for her long disappearance with so much probability as might prevent suspicion; and here I had not only to tax my invention but to find proper instruments, and that from among persons who not only were, but would continue, strangers to her person. The plan that I conceived was this: to give out among her Friends at Kensington, &c., that she had formed an acquaintance with a supposed Lady, of character and fortune, to whom we gave a Scotch name, and who was progressively represented as becoming much attached to her and desirous of her company on her approaching return to her residence in Scotland. In due time the invitation was accepted and announced to the acting Executor, who consented to advance the next half-year's allowance for the expenses of the journey and return. She was next to take leave of her Friends and set out on the journey, promising to keep up a correspondence with one or two of the most intimate of them during her absence; and that promise was to be punctually performed. But to accomplish this scheme it was necessary to have two accomplices, one in Scotland and the other in London, and both females of character, the one to receive and convey to us through the London Friend the letters we had to answer, the other to personate also the Friend of the Scotch Lady here, so as to satisfy all enquiries; and the difficulty was how to find such accomplices without letting them into the secret. As to the former, my dear Sister

Sibella was my obvious resource, except that as our Uncle and Aunt, with whom she lived, saw all her letters, it was necessary to find some means of secret correspondence with her; and this was obtained by means of a Miss Scott, sister of a particular friend of mine, with whom she was in habits of intimacy and confidence, a channel thro' which I had before corresponded with her on subjects or with feelings not fit to be disclosed to her Aunt. The Friend in London was difficult and apparently impossible to find. At length I recollected that Felix McCarthy, still my humble, devoted Friend and follower, was extremely intimate with an elderly widow Lady, Mrs. S., of very respectable family and connections, her Son-in-Law being a Colonel in the Guards and she being, as I understood from Felix, a distant relation of his own family in Ireland. He visited her so often, and was by his own account so great a favorite with her, that I had already begun to suspect, what afterwards proved to be the case, that her attachment to him was of an immoral kind. But if so, as her character was respectable she was not the less fit for my purpose, which was through his influence over her to make her act the part I wanted. To this end, however, it was indispensably necessary that I should not trust him by halves. Indeed, he had already, from his continual intercourse with me, unavoidably discovered so much of my situation and habits that it was impossible to ask his assistance in the scheme without enabling him with certainty to determine who the Lady in question was and what were my motives for concealment; and it might have been dangerous not to give him such guards and lay on him such strong obligations of caution and secresy as a knowledge of the extreme delicacy and importance of the case only could create. I was unhappily constrained, therefore, to repose an entire confidence in him. As this was without Maria's consent or knowledge it may seem not to have been justifiable, but the necessities and urgent nature of the case left me no alternative. Not only had I the most perfect and well-founded reliance at that time on his honor, integrity, and faithful attachment to me, but as I disclosed to him that she was to be my future wife, it was committing *my own* honor as well as *hers* to his keeping; and he knew well that perfidy to *me* would ruin him with every friend he had in the world, his own brother included. He entered into my plan with his accustomed warmth of feeling and engaged, as he well might, for the faithful cooperation of Mrs. S., whose promise of it he readily obtained, revealing to her no more than that it was a love affair between un-named friends of his own. My dear sister also, I think, learned no more than that it was to favor me in some affair of virtuous and honorable love with a young Lady I was much attached to. I cannot, indeed, distinctly recollect what the colours held out to her were, or whether, relying on her affection and confidence, I merely instructed her what to do without giving her any reason for my request. The latter is most probable.

I may spare myself the pain and shame of stating, and the trouble of recollecting, how the plan worked as to the ostensible correspondence with Scotland. I remember only that we did not interchange many letters, finding it unnecessary, to prevent suspicion; and I believe no doubt of the reality of her journey to that country was ever entertained by any of her friends in this.

Previous to her supposed departure I found means to provide for her reception under a feigned name in a creditable family as a Boarder, in a part of the town where she had no acquaintance and where she passed as a single Lady, her appearance not yet indicating, except to those familiar with her person, the state she was in. But this was only to postpone the hazards of detection in placing her in lodgings as my wife, which was our ulterior plan, my own person and name being much more likely to be known. To this we resorted when appearances became such as to be inconsistent with her credit as a single woman. I took a frugal, ready-furnished lodging in a retired, airy situation in the suburbs of Westminster for myself and my wife, changing my name by inverting it from James Stephen to Stephen James, which I did because as her accustomed appellation for me when by ourselves was Stephen I thought it would better prevent discovery by inadvertency on her part; and it proved a very useful precaution in more respects than one. References to Mrs. S., were, I think, necessary in this part, also, of the plot.

As the strictest economy was virtually necessary to all our hopes, our lodgings were mean enough, but clean and airy. We had only two rooms, a sitting and bedroom on the same floor, and the attendance of a servant besides, for ten or twelve shillings a week. The Landlady was a widow, with no family and no other lodger; and there was a back way into fields where there was a walk so little frequented that Maria could take the air there without danger of being seen by anyone who had ever known her, all of which were most important and splendid recommendations. Hither, then, I removed my poor, dear Maria and took up my abode with her as her husband; and so romantically tender was her affection for me that I doubt not she was better contented with our humble apartments and her imprisonment on this account than she would have been in a Palace without me. Our meals were necessarily as frugal as our lodgings; but I was generally able to breakfast and dine with her at an early hour before I went to the gallery of the House of Commons, and return to sleep, and to provide her with entertaining reading in my absence; and I think she was contented and happy. I, myself, was as much so in her beloved company as conscience and apprehensions for the future would permit; and gladly, indeed, would I have compounded for the same mean situation and circumstances to the end of my days had she been indeed my wife, and my kind, generous, injured Nancy no longer in existence. I was relieved in good measure from what I had hitherto suffered by the feelings of the latter, especially as the time of accouchement drew nigh; for she was kind and compassionate enough to feel that I was bound to give as much of my company as possible to her unfortunate rival in her secluded and perilous situation. Late nights in the House of Commons were peculiarly trying to us. Poor Maria would then sit up in momentary expectation of me till her strength was quite exhausted; and I sometimes did not arrive till 2, 3, 4 or a later hour in the morning, then to awaken her from her sleep, unless I could contrive to avoid it. Often did I traverse some of the worst parts of Westminster at the worst hours rather than be absent from her, which I think I never was for a single night; and O, what joy on her part waited my arrival when I was happily able to come at an early hour in the evening. Our Landlady was at first uneasy at my habits; but, it being explained to her that I had some Parliamentary office or employment that obliged me to stay till the rising of the Houses, she was prevailed on to give me a key of the outer door, by which I let myself in without disturbing her or her Servant. She had become, I believe, attached to Maria, whose manners were always condescending and pleasant.

During this period an incident occurred which I must digress a little to relate, for it cost me great anxiety and alarm; and the event was one of those striking deliverances for which I have ever been grateful to Divine Providence. The well-known case that blasted the character of the Honble Edward, son of Lord O.,[1] and drove him from Society is one of which delicacy forbids a full account. He was a man generally esteemed and regarded, both in public and private life; the more so because his manners and conduct formed a contrast with those of his Father and elder Brother, who were deservedly disliked and despised. It was commonly said in Parliament, of which he was a Member, that he was the only respectable Member of that noble Family. But he was secretly tainted with a detestable and unaccountable vice, which the feelings of mankind in this Country justly punish with uneffaceable infamy and the law as justly punishes with death. With an infatuation not uncommon in such cases and which seems strikingly to indicate the agency of that Evil Being who holds them captive at his will, this man chose for the scene of infamous advances to the perpetration or excitement of the crime he meditated, the public rooms of the exhibition of paintings in Somerset House, at mid-day and in a crowded company of both sexes, where the object of his unnatural and detestable attempt was a perfect stranger to him, and that Stranger no other than Felix McCarthy. I cannot describe what he did, but McCarthy at first thought it an accident and moved from him

---

[1] Stephen generally uses only "O." for the family name; occasionally he slips and gives it in full. The Honourable Edward, who was only two months older than Stephen, married a French lady of aristocratic family about a year after the incident which Stephen relates and himself became the head of a respected and influential family in France.

to another part of the room. While he was there with his eyes fixed on a painting, O., whom he did not know, approached him again and the same thing was repeated. McCarthy, astonished and confounded, now thought it must have been intentional and hastening to some Friends he had in the room, one of whom was Mr. Dennis O'Brien, a Surgeon (afterwards well-known as a political writer and violent Foxite) and told them of the extraordinary occurrence, pointing out the Gentleman, whom some of them knew to be Edward O. These Friends, three in number, all said, "Go to the place again; we will observe and if the villain repeats it, disgrace him as he deserves." M. took their advice; and O., who was then talking with two or three beautiful young women, the honourable Miss Keppel's, immediately left them, went up to the object of his unnatural passion again, and repeated the same act. M. instantly struck him a blow in the face, upon which he rushed through the rooms and made his escape. A general uproar ensued, for the blow and flight had been seen by many, tho' the provocation had been so managed as to be perceived only by M. and his three friends. Many friends of O. came up, among them his intimate friend the present Lord Essex, then Lord Malden,[1] and demanded the name of the assailant, with the reason of such an outrage. M. was not slow to give them both; and O'Brien, with the two others, came up and confirmed him. Lord Malden and O.'s other Friends, of course, professed not only astonishment but incredulity and observing that the matter could not possibly end there, demanded an appointment for the same afternoon that Mr. O. might meet and confront them. As the tone was one of honorary defiance, the Irishman did not hesitate to consent; and an appointment was accordingly made to meet at the Salopian Coffee House, Charing Cross, at 3 o'clock, it being then, I think, about one.

I had just taken my seat in the gallery of the House of Commons among my brother Reporters, waiting for an

---

[1] George Capel-Coningsby, Earl of Essex (1757–1838); styled Viscount Malden till 1799; Tory M.P. 1779–1799; a friend of the Prince of Wales who became George IV and known as one of "the men of fashion of that period" (i.e., 1780–1799).

expected debate (we were obliged at that time to go down
early to get seats) when McCarthy came and called me out,
telling me of the strange event that had occurred, and of
the appointment, and entreating my advice and direction. I
was naturally much shocked and alarmed at the idea of his
meeting to confer with the Friends of the accused in such a
case, foreseeing the construction that might be put upon it;
and as to turning the matter into an affair of honor, I saw
at once its inconsistency with the nature of the charge, and
that it would on M.'s part be a virtual abandonment of
his right to treat the case as one of open and notorious
infamy and degradation, fit only for the cognizance of the
Civil Magistrate. I was still more alarmed when M. told me
that O'Brien was bent upon the meeting and would attend
the appointment whether he did or not; for I knew the man
to be a vain, conceited creature, not gifted with discretion,
and with all that, having been lately a Bankrupt, his
character perhaps was none of the purest. I asked anxiously
who and what the other *witnesses* on his side were and found
that he knew nothing of them beyond their names, and that
they were friends to whom O'Brien had introduced him. He
thought himself bound to attend the meeting at all events,
having promised to do so, and earnestly solicited me to go
with him as his legal adviser and friend. I felt extreme repugnance to mixing myself with such a transaction in any way
but on the other hand felt that it would be ungenerous and
unmanly to suffer a poor fellow whose right feelings had
brought him into it, who was so faithfully attached to myself,
and looked to me as his surest friend and counsellor, to
expose himself to such guidance as O'Brien's, or that of his
own warm and impetuous feelings, in so delicate and difficult
a case. I called out some of my Brother Reporters, who also
well knew McCarthy, among them Perry[1] and James
Sherridan, who was a very sensible and honorable man, and
consulted with them. They were unanimous that M. *must*
attend the appointment, having promised, lest he should be

[1] James Perry (1756–1821), journalist; for some time a provincial actor; came
to London in 1777 and was writer for the *General Advertiser* and the *London
Evening Post;* first editor of the *European Magazine* 1782; one of the proprietors of
the *Morning Chronicle* from 1789; several times prosecuted for political
radicalism.

thought to shrink from the charge; but that he ought not to make it an affair of honor; and above all that poor M. must not be left in the rash hands of O'Brien; and that I as his friend ought in kindness to go with and direct him. They offered among them to do my duty for the Newspaper; and I was obliged, in short, to comply, after exacting a promise from M. that he would conform himself in all points to my advice.

When we came to the Coffee House we were shewn into an upper room which Lord Malden had bespoke and were told that his Lordship, with Lord O. and others and, to my great alarm, Mr. O'Brien, were in a room below. I immediately desired that Mr. O'Brien might be requested to come up, and finding after a considerable interval that he did not come (he was, as we afterwards found, telling his story in a crowd of enemies and taking on himself to act for M. in the business) I made M. send down a note to Lord Malden, saying that he was there pursuant to his Lordship's request but should immediately depart unless his Lordship now desired to see him. This brought up Colonel, since Lord, Whitworth,[1] and one or two other gentlemen, one of whom I think was the present Sergeant O. and Coll. Whitworth, advancing to us with great politeness, immediately began to treat the affair as "an unfortunate mistake" but which, having produced a public assault from M., unavoidably obliged Mr. O. to demand honorary satisfaction, which he was authorized to claim. M. referred for his answer to me; and I clearly declared my opinion that M. was neither bound to, nor could, without dishonor meet Mr. O. as a gentleman in such a quarrel. The Colonel argued the point out with me civilly, but earnestly; but I kept to my ground and declared that tho' no man living would be more prompt to accept a challenge than M., yet as he had put his conduct in my hands I would do violence if necessary to his feelings on this occasion and not suffer him to degrade himself by meeting on equal terms one who had forfeited his title, not only to

---

[1] Charles Whitworth, Earl Whitworth (1752–1825), diplomatist; minister and ambassador at Warsaw, St. Petersburg, Copenhagen, and Paris 1785–1802; lord-lieutenant of Ireland, 1813–1817. At the time of the incident above he was a young army officer.

the gentleman, but the man. I added that, in my opinion, any conference or meeting on the subject was improper and that tho' I had suffered M. to come there it was only because he had hastily at Lord Malden's request promised to do so. That the only question with M. could be whether he ought to prosecute for the public offence, but it seemed to me that having inflicted a proper chastisement he might leave the matter where it stood. That at all events it was not a case for compromise or for discussion with Mr. O. or his friends, and whatever might be passing between them and Mr. O'Brien below, the latter was acting in opposition to M's opinion and mine in holding any conference with them; and for my own part I was determined immediately to quit the house. Coll. Whitworth, I am satisfied, in his heart applauded these sentiments and saw in them, adhered to as they were by M., the perdition of the cause in which he had reluctantly as a warm friend of the O. family been persuaded to engage. But he was, therefore, the more alarmed when he found us determined to go and was detaining us by appeals to my compassion for the family, on the assumption that the odious appearances might *possibly* have arisen from accident, when on a sudden the door opened and in came Sir Sampson Wright, the presiding Magistrate at Bow Street, and with him several constables, whom he immediately placed at the door; and said he was come to "examine into the extraordinary case which had been brought by Lord O. to his notice."

I never saw more striking exhibitions of virtuous and honorary indignation than Coll. Whitworth displayed at this occurrence. He came up to me with uplifted hands and said to me, "Sir, I hope you will do me the justice to believe that I was wholly ignorant of any intention on the part of Lord O. to adopt a proceeding like this; he has ruined his son and the consequences must fall on his and his Father's head. Be assured that if I had had any suspicion of such a purpose, I would never have consented to take any part in this most unhappy affair." It was impossible to doubt his sincerity; and I frankly told him I did not, upon which, with an indignant look at the O's, who had followed the Magistrate, he left the room.

I now summoned up that fortitude, not without secret prayer, which I bless God, weak and irresolute tho' I have often been, has on sudden emergencies rarely or never been suffered by *Him* who holds the reins of my spirit, to forsake me when needed on important occasions.

I saw at once that we had fallen into a snare; that the criminal was determined to stand at bay; and that all the influence of a powerful Family, aided by a corrupt Magistrate and, as I then believed, a Government equally corrupt and unprincipled, would be exerted to rescue O. from infamy, by retorting it if possible on McCarthy and his Friends. I resolved, therefore, to be cool and circumspect and (with one doubtful exception, to be noticed in its place) acted up to that resolution in a way that on the retrospect left me nothing to regret. I first firmly admonished Sir S. Wright that tho' he was called there by Lord O. it was under circumstances that made Mr. O. not the accusing but the accused Party, and therefore demanded that if present he should be detained and M.'s charge against him in the first place examined. He assented to this and made profession, which his looks and manner belied, that he should hear both Parties with impartiality. He then proceeded to say that he must examine the witnesses out of each other's presence, McCarthy first, and that all but he must depart the room while he heard the charge, and remain in the custody of his officers below. He thought, perhaps, thus to get rid of *me* and to examine M. in the midst of his enemies alone; but I declared "that *I* was no witness, that I was only M.'s friend and professional adviser," and demanded to be present, which he with evident reluctance allowed. O'Brien and the two others, who I think had all come, or been brought in custody into the room, were sent down with some of the officers; two other officers were placed at the door with orders to let nobody come in or depart; and M. and I were left alone, surrounded by Lord O., his sons and relatives, among whom was Serjeant O., and many others whom I did not know. The Magistrate then began to take McCarthy's account of the transaction; and it was plain from the commencement that the only object was by putting him out of temper, and by artful cross questions, to catch him in contradictions if they could. I, therefore, called for paper and pens and began to take an accurate note of the questions and answers, stopping M. continually when he began to be warm and hasty that he might answer with deliberation, and often appealing to the Magistrate in strong terms when Lord O.'s abusive exclamations, in which he was suffered to deal freely, were of a kind to put M. out of temper. The scene was trying in the extreme, everyone around us, Mr., now Serjeant O. alone I think excepted, but especially Sir S. Wright himself, receiving all that was said with affected incredulity and indignation. But I was enabled to keep my temper throughout and, what was harder, to make M. keep *his*; and by my free rebukes and expostulations at length frightened the Magistrate into more decent, tho' not less insidious, conduct. It was a late hour in the evening before M.'s examination was finished. O'Brien was then brought up; and to my great relief some of my Brother Reporters, one of them a lawyer by education, arrived from the House of Commons, the debate being over, and insisted on being let into the room. Wright would have refused; but on their protesting strongly against such a private and partially exclusive administration of public justice, he was alarmed; and it being high time that I should go to the printing office to give such a report of the debate as the concurrent help of my brethren might afford, I rose to quit the room. The officers stop'd me at the door, when I indignantly asked whether his worship meant to treat me as a Prisoner. He faultered and said something of the danger of my communicating with the witnesses below. I replied, "Send an officer to see me out of the house if you please, but detain me at your peril." He had not the courage to do so. As I was passing, some one of Lord O.'s Party said, "Sir, I beg your pardon, but I think you are connected with one of the Newspapers?" My answer (the exception to my prudent deportment to which I before alluded) was, "Certainly, Sir, I employ my pen sometimes that way; and you may depend on it that this foul business shall be as public as I have power to make it." I saw their general consternation and left the room. What afterwards passed, I heard from M. and others before I slept. The other witnesses were examined in the same unjust and partial way; but my

Brethren of the Press well supplied my place and the corrupt Magistrate, finding their relations too clearly concurrent with each others and M.'s, finally folded up his notes, saying to Lord O. before them all, "My Lord, these will be proper to be laid before your Lordship's Counsel." M. and his friends then called upon him to commit or bind over Mr. O., but he positively refused to do so and did not even put him on his defence. They protested loudly and threatened him with the King's Bench; but he took it very coolly, went away with Lord O. and his friends, and left them to go where they pleased.

Meantime I was at the *Morning Post* office, giving to the Public a very brief account of the debate in the Commons, but making our readers ample amends by a very full and pungent account of the strange occurrences of the day at the Exhibition and the Salopian Coffee House.

The Town rang with it the next Morning; and we who had been actors in the scene had many enquiries and many plaudits, from curiosity, and from approbation of our manly conduct. O.'s running away on receiving the blow, a fact attested by hundreds of Spectators, secured to us the opinion of the Public; and besides all the Newspapers were on our side, tho' they were obliged to assert specious articles sent by the O. family, cautioning the Public to suspend its opinion, hinting at a conspiracy, and ascribing the flight to an overwhelming sense of shame arising from the nature of the charge. The fact was that he knew not its nature, except from his own consciousness of the provocation. He fled at once without asking why he received the blow. But plain tho' the case was from these open and indispensable circumstances, we were in some real and more imaginary danger. We soon heard that Counsel was retained by Lord O. and that it was determined to prosecute for a conspiracy; and we well knew that all that wealth and Court influence could effect would be most indefatigably employed against us, together perhaps with all the tricks and all the perjuries that Bow Street energies could prepare. To *us*, on the contrary, even the ordinary means of legal defence were difficult. The only resource we had was in Charles McCarthy's influence with a reputable Solicitor, to whom he was clerk, and in the scanty savings of his Salary, by means of which Dunning[1] and Erskine were retained. The latter entered with great zeal, tho' perhaps little judgment, into the case. Dunning, at least, afterwards found fault with his advice, which we had followed: *viz.*, to apply to Sir S. Wright the next day in the Public office for a warrant against O. on the ground that his bad conduct at the Salopian Coffee House, on which Dunning thought we should have relied, might be excused on account of the privacy, suddenness, and irregularity of the proceeding. But he adhered to the same conduct on the Bench and the Warrant was refused.

My first and great anxiety was to learn the characters of our Witnesses; and it was with consternation that I found they were such as would not bear enquiry. The two Friends of O'Brien, whose names I forget, turned out to be like himself, or more than himself, liable to great suspicion. They dressed like gentlemen but had no known occupation or means of subsistence and probably were sharpers, or what is usually called Men of the Town. To these grounds of uneasiness others were rapidly added. It became soon unequivocal, not only that the criminal was determined to stand his ground, but that he had persuaded his Friends in the upper circles to believe and treat him as innocent. I saw him the next day, to my terror, come into the House of Commons and be received there with marked and solicitous attention and respect. He took his seat on the Treasury Bench; and Lord North immediately placed himself beside him, shook him cordially by the hand, put his arm even round his waist, and continued long in close conference with him, doubtless on the subject of "the foul conspiracy by which he had been beset." Many respectable men also of both Parties came up to him and shook him cordially by the hand.

Many intelligent persons, who saw the case in its true light, added greatly to our apprehensions by bringing to M. and to me reports of what they heard and cautioning us to be on

---

[1] John Dunning, first Baron Ashburton (1731–1783), barrister and politician; M.P. who in 1780 carried a resolution that "the influence of the crown has increased, is increasing, and ought to be diminished", counsel for the crown in trial of Lord George Gordon.

our guard; and our Newspaper Friends and others gave us many appalling anecdotes of men who had been sacrificed in similar cases, by perjurious and other foul means, to save the guilty Great and their families from infamy. If half of their relations were true, the case of the Bishop of Clogher[1] was neither a solitary nor a strong one of the kind. We heard also so many tales, true or false, of the prevalence of the same detestable vice among the nobility that I really began to believe it was pretty general among them and that their countenance and cordiality to O. was less founded on the belief of his innocence than simpathy with his guilt. Then Lord Mansfield was, however unjustly, supposed to have the same taint; and yet it was before *him* that the case was to be investigated. But what I chiefly feared was the villainous devotion of the Bow Street Squadron to the accused, in which the character and official situation of their Chief was inextricably involved. I knew much, and suspected more, of their powers by foul practices to crush the innocent and screen the guilty.

It is true that my own particular case stood on much safer ground than that of M. and his witnesses since I had had nothing to do with the transaction beyond attending the Meeting at his request and afterwards publishing the case; but of the latter I had imprudently furnished proof by my declaration; and Bond, then called the Thief taker, afterwards Mr. Justice Bond, had come into the Editor's room at the office of the *Morning Post* the day after the Meeting and found me writing there. Besides, in prosecuting for a conspiracy they would naturally cast the net of accusation as comprehensively as possible; and it is a case in which

---

[1] Rt. Rev. Percy Jocelyn (1764–1843), third son of the first Earl of Roden; Bishop of Ferns and Leighlin 1809–1820; Bishop of Clogher 1820–1822; deprived and deposed of his bishopric, October 21, 1822. The Bishop was arrested July 20, 1822, in the company of a private soldier in a Westminster Ale House; and the circumstances were such that there could be little doubt about his homosexual crime. He forfeited heavy bail and fled to Ireland, sold all the moveable chattels from the episcopal palace, and did not appear at the proceedings in which he was deprived. The poor soldier was found guilty and heavily sentenced. There had been a previous episode of this kind in the Bishop's life, when he successfully brought suit for criminal libel against his accuser, who underwent several floggings and served a prison sentence. For details see the *Annual Register* for 1822.

indirect and circumstantial evidence is much allowed and favoured. Even the being acccused of, and tried for, such a crime was inexpressibly dreadful to my feelings; and as to convictions for it, I even cherished the guilty thought that if such a calamity should fall upon me I would commit suicide in the face of the Court to prove my sense of honor at least by my desperation.

When the Motion was to be made in the King's Bench for an Information against Sir S. Wright (the course that our Counsel recommended) affidavits of all the witnesses were to be prepared, and I was requested to attend a Meeting with O'Brien and his Friends for the purpose. I was so afraid of being traced by the Bow Street people to their company that I applied to Richardson and another of my more reputable Friends to go with me and had the further alarm to find them afraid of complying, on which I myself refused to go. But my anxiety was increased beyond bounds when a few days after on returning from an early dinner with Maria to my usual avocations I found that I had been dog'd thither by Bond, whom I saw following me near the door. I reasonably concluded that he had discovered my living there, with a reputed wife, under a false name; and that this secret would, ruinously not only to my character but Maria's probably also, be brought to public notice in the course of the expected prosecutions. The employment of a Bow Street Officer to track me to my secret residence seemed also to prove that I was one of the intended victims of their machinations.

Never, I believe, was my mind under such extreme agitation and alarm as during the week (for I think it was so long) of these anxieties. My resource of prayer was by no means neglected. I supplicated the Most High earnestly and incessantly to avert from me the dreadful calamity that I feared, and at times with some hope in his mercy, but a hope checked and flattened by the sense of my sins; and the last incident above all disheartened me because it seemed as if Providence designed to visit my offences upon me by making them the immediate tho' indirect source of my disgrace and ruin. But this thought only made my penitence and devout importunity with Heaven more earnest. About the end of that dreadful period I was passing on a Wednesday or Friday by St. John's Chapel in the Broadway, Westminster, in my passage from my private lodgings, in the forenoon when the Bell was ringing for prayers, or else I perceived that some people were entering the chapel for that purpose. It occurred to me that I would humble myself before man as well as before God by attending those weekday devotions, and the rather because I felt abashed at what in the eyes of those who might see a young man dressed as a gentleman there would seem singular and ultra-devout. I followed this self-humbling purpose and found myself as I expected, stared at by a few old women and an aged man or two, who formed the whole congregation, as well as by the clergyman himself. I forget what in particular there was in the psalms and lessons, but this I well remember, that never in my life did I feel a greater fervour of humble and penitential devotion. My urgent secret prayers, indeed, made a large deviation from the service. I entreated, I importuned, the Divine Mercy to deliver me from the consequences of my sins, especially from that disgrace and infamy with which I was so nearly threatened, and added prayers not less earnest that the deliverance might be speedy or immediate; for I felt that I could not well longer sustain my dreadful apprehensions. I have mentioned before the internal convictions I have sometimes felt that my prayers were effectual, and in no instance was the impression more powerful than now. I left the chapel in tranquility, and a few hours after on my entering the gallery of the House of Commons the congratulations of my friends there told me that my troubles were at an end. It had just been announced there that Edward O. had confessed his guilt and gone off. This striking answer to prayer made a deep and indelible impression on my mind. Never have I since sat in, or passed, that chapel without a lively, devout recollection of it with heartfelt gratitude to God. It helped mightily and critically to fortify those hopes in His further delivering mercy, and those self-denying resolutions, to which I owe all the subsequent comfort and well-being of my life.

Nothing could be less probable as matters then stood than that I should be released fully and finally from my intolerable anxieties and fears for Months to come, or without much intervening care and wretchedness; and the way in which it was brought about was of a highly Providential character. In the midst of great confidence in the Onslow family, the result no doubt partly of the plots concerted by their Bow Street Friends and the warm countenance of their great connections, a report was brought to them that Coll. Michael Cox of the Guards had declared himself the friend and protector of McCarthy. This gentleman, son of an Irish Archbishop and highly esteemed in the fashionable circles, was the Son-in-law of the Mrs. S. I have mentioned; and having heard from her a highly favorable account of M., whom she acknowledged as her relation, he generously resolved to give him his countenance against his powerful enemies and declared it at one of the political clubs of which he was a Member, I think at Brook's. Startled at the news, a friend of the family, I believe it was Lord Malden, was dispatched by them to Coll. Cox to learn whether it was true. He decidedly avowed it, saying "he knew and esteemed the young man, believed him to be innocent and meritorious in the transaction, and would do all in his power to prevent his being run down and oppressed." The intelligence was a thunderclap to the O. family, at least to the guilty member of it. He desired an interview with his Father in private, confessed his crime (and as we heard also, that it was not the first of the kind), and in consequence was sent off to the Continent and has since been heard of by the Public no more.

The triumph of McCarthy and his Friends was now immediate and complete. All who had countenanced the guilty fugitive were eager, for their own reputation's sake, to be foremost in the heaping infamy upon him and applause on his manly antagonist. Lord North himself, I think, moved the same day for a new Writ for the place O. represented, he having accepted the Chiltern Hundreds as the alternative to his immediate expulsion; and Mr. Fox, as we understood, took the lead in expelling him from the fashionable Clubs they both belonged to, the ground which they thought it best to express being "that he had received a blow from a gentleman in a public room without resenting it." A hun-

dred congratulations from strangers as well as friends were
addressed to us, not without warm applause, for the manly
and intrepid part we were considered as having acted. One
of the first steps that M. was advised to take by every friend
but me was to demand honorary explanations from Lord
Malden, advice which he was sufficiently prompt to take. I
opposed it, as I have the satisfaction to reflect I have always
done every measure of that kind that was to bring *others* into
danger; tho', alas, in my own case I have too often been
ready on the call of fancied honorary necessity to involve
myself in such perils and have been saved from blood-
guiltiness only by the wonderful care of an offended, long-
suffering Providence. I thought it unnecessary in this case
and therefore protested against it and resolutely refused to
be the bearer of the Message. But I was overruled, and
another friend of M., I think it was James Sherridan,
waited on his Lordship with a demand of explanation and
apology for the part he had acted. Lord Malden acted very
properly on the occasion. He pleaded his long intimacy and
friendship with Mr. O., and the firm opinion into which he
had been deluded of his innocence, and professed his sorrow
for having in consequence acted and spoken in a manner
disparaging to the accuser, for whose conduct he now declared his perfect approbation and respect. This was accepted
on M.'s part as satisfactory and so that part of the business
ended. Very different was his resolution and mine in regard
to the corrupt Magistrate whom we were determined to
bring to merited disgrace and punishment. Accordingly a
rule for an Information against him for a corrupt breach of
duty in his Office was moved for in the Court of King's
Bench; a rule to shew cause was obtained and, after argument, made absolute by the unanimous opinion of the
Judges. Lord Mansfield at first shewed some apparent hesitation and reluctance on the ground of possible mis-judgment,
consistent with pure intention on the part of the Magistrate;
but Sir S. Wright, in the prudent view of appeasing the
Prosecutor, not only in his affidavit admitted his conviction
of the truth of the charge and of M.'s honorable intentions
but went so much further as to add that "*he had never doubted
of either.*" On the reading of this latter admission, Lord

Mansfield immediately declared there was an end of every excuse and that the Information must be granted. Beyond doubt if it had been prosecuted, a conviction, a heavy sentence, and dismission from Office, would have followed. But there remains a sequel of this extraordinary case which cost me much mortification and regret. Sir S. Wright on his part also moved for informations for libellous accounts of the transaction in different Newspapers, tending to prejudice him in the event of his being brought to trial; and the Courts at that time very properly held it an offence against public justice so to influence the public mind in respect of depending proceedings and were very ready to grant informations for such offences irrespectively of the merits of the case. Rules to shew cause therefore were granted, and among others one against the Proprietors of the *Morning Post* for articles which I myself had written. This was unpleasant enough to me, especially as I found that in shewing cause, my affidavit as to the proceedings at the Salopian Coffee House, the main subject of the articles in question, would be necessary, and as I dreaded the probable consequence, that an attack on my character for my change of name, &c., would be made by our Bow Street antagonists, either in support of their informations or their defence against ours. It was a grievous reflection, also, that in prosecuting the latter all poor Charles McCarthy's savings had been already exhausted and a large debt incurred with his employers. Still, however, we were resolute, hoping for support and finding popular feeling strongly in our favor, and resisted many solicitations from the friends of the O. family on the specious pretext that their misery from the dreadful occurrence was deeply aggravated by those impending public investigations which would keep long before the public eye their misfortune and disgrace. Our answer was that we regretted but could not help it, that M. had willingly drop'd the information against Mr. O. (for which we had also obtained a rule) without proceeding to outlawry against him as he was beyond the reach of justice, but that it was a duty to the Public to bring to punishment a Magistrate who had so foully prostituted his official authority. At length McCarthy informed me of a mediation which I saw at once

it would be extremely difficult for him to resist. His generous
Protector and human deliverer, Coll. Cox, had sent for him,
told him of the bitter anguish of Lord O. and his family, and
requested that in compassion to them and to oblige himself,
who was actuated by pity towards them, he would consent
that the proceedings on all sides should be dropped, adding
as his own suggestion that it should be on terms of ample
compensation being made for all his, M.'s, expenses and
sufferings in the business, which Lord O. was willing to
engage for in the most liberal way. Against this latter part
of the advice, when I understood that it meant more than
the mere costs at law, I decidedly protested. I could not
firmly persuade him to deny the request of a Patron to whom
he owed so large a debt of gratitude, and from whom he
expected help to raise him into a more creditable situation in
life, so far as a mere amnesty went, the mediation itself being
a sanction for it to that extent and such a termination being
a great deliverance to himself and his Brother and even to
my own anxious feelings. But I felt that to receive more than
the mere costs at law in such a case would not only be
indelicate but reproachful. M. was, or seemed to be, disposed to act on my judgment, but Coll. Cox persisted in his
advice and solicitation; other friends were consulted and
concurred; and Sherridan suggested as an expedient that
would solve all difficulties and at the same time raise M.
happily in station and credit that the mode of compensation
might be Lord O.'s using his influence with the Government
to get him a commission in the Army. When M. had made up
his mind to follow this plan he pressed me very hard and
long to aid him in the execution of it. Coll. Cox had proposed that two Friends on his part should meet two friends
of Lord O. to confer on the terms of accomodation, but
here I was happily resolute and absolutely refused to take
any part in the treaty. Sherridan and Perry in consequence
were deputed by him and, if I remember right, Lord Malden
and some other respectable character by Lord O. They met
and the plan of procuring a Commission in the Army as a
compensation was proposed and stickled for by M's referees;
but Lord O.'s, after some discussions, convinced them that
it was impossible for his Lordship under the circumstances

of the case to ask such a favor from Government; and it was
at length agreed as the substitute for it that a sum of money
should be paid sufficient to enable M. to buy a commission
for himself, which was adjusted at £500, leaving him to pay
his own costs and expenses; and so ended the whole affair.
M. was afterwards publicly attacked for dropping the
prosecution; and tho' he resented it with such violence as to
silence his assailants, or most of them, I had abundant reason
to be thankful that my name was not at all implicated in that
part of the case. To say the truth, I was not afterwards satisfied with myself for not having with more perseverance and
decision opposed myself to the compensation in any form.
It would not, I believe, have been effectual; but had I broke
with him upon it it would have been an escape, perhaps, from
much of the evils subsequently entailed upon me by that
ill-placed confidence and friendship. From what I afterwards
discovered to my cost of the baseness of his character, I have
been sometimes led to suspect that he deceived me as to the
extent and the warmth of Coll. C.'s mediation. That he
used his influence on the side of pacification I do not, indeed,
doubt; but it seems strange to me that he should have been
an advocate for, and suggested, the mercenary terms. To
McCarthy they proved not an advantage but a curse. I
believe that, except reimbursement to his Brother, no part
of it was properly used and that the command of so much
money led him deeper into vice than he had plunged before.
It was in vain that Sherridan and I anxiously advised him
to make the use of it designed, by buying into the Army.
Elated by the popularity he had acquired and the flattery of
some new associates, he gave for some time a loose to dissipation and barely reserved enough ultimately to convey himself to France, where he got a commission or cadetship in
Dillon's Brigade of Irish Catholics.[1]

I shall have too much to say of his subsequent history here-

---

[1] The Dillon Regiment was one of the most famous of the foreign units in the
French army. It entered the service of Louis XIV in 1690 under the command
of the Irish-born Arthur, Comte de Dillon (1670–1733). At the time of which
Stephen was writing the proprietor of the regiment was a later Arthur, Comte de
Dillon, (1750–1794) who was made a brigadier in 1780 and field marshal in
1784. As brigadier he commanded not only the Dillon regiment but also other
Irish regiments which went to make up the Irish Brigade.

after. Meantime for the sake of giving this episode entire I
have gone chronologically far beyond that point in my own
narrative from which I digressed, for I think there was an
interval of six months or more between the commencement
of O.'s affair and its final termination.

Chapter Ten

[*1781–1782*]

WHEN my poor Maria's time of accouchement drew nigh, my anxiety and my difficulties naturally increased and but for the growing confidence that I had in the Divine mercy would have been quite intolerable. This confidence was greatly strengthened by the deliverance I have last recorded and its being so strikingly an answer to prayer. It was strengthened also by the firm resolution that, if that dear Woman's life was spared, I would offend no more with her or any other but mortify that sin which so easily beset me and live a life of purity and self-denial till it should please Heaven to extricate me from the dreadful sin-born and sin-producing dilemma in which I stood. This, of course, could not be avowed to her in her then situation; but reason and conscience more and more convinced me that I could not make her my wife without new injustice to my dear Nancy and ruin to them both. The best or least injurious course, I progressively convinced myself, was to continue single while they both lived, unless either of them should become the wife of another man, doing the utmost that I could in the meantime for the welfare of both and being prepared joyfully to give my hand to either when it could be done without injustice and cruelty to the other. As this was the path of greatest self-denial, I was confirmed by that consideration that it was most probably the path of duty and of reconciliation with God. My plan at length steadfastly formed, and I bless God adhered to, was that as soon as dear Maria's health should be restored after her confinement I would disclose this purpose to her, or rather obtain her leave to form it; and so much were her judgment and her feelings always under my sway that I hoped to satisfy her mind, and even to persuade her heart, to concur in it, since I could with perfect sincerity convince her that it was dictated on my part not only by the purest attachment but unabated love. My part, I foresaw, would be highly difficult and painful; but I trusted in

12*

Almighty Grace to enable me to perform it. It was not long after this right resolution was formed that it pleased a gracious Providence not only to confirm me in it but to give me means for its execution by a most unexpected event, one of the many occurrences in my life which have happened so critically to extricate me from evil, moral and physical, and to lead me towards temporal and, I hope, eternal good that I cannot doubt such were among the ends for which they were appointed. At a moment when my mind was oppressed by a sense of the almost insuperable difficulties which my narrow circumstances would oppose to the completion of my plan for poor Maria's safe and comfortable accouchement and recovery, for the restitution of her personal appearance, and other means necessary for the preservation of her character, and for the nutrition and support of the infant she was soon to give me, a letter was put into my hands which seemed like a Messenger from the skies to tell me my prayers were heard, my penitence accepted, and the hand of the Most High stretched forth for my deliverance. It was from my dear Brother William announcing to me the death of our Uncle, and his having by a Will made on his deathbed left to him all his fortune, and adding an assurance of which I well knew the sincerity that the chief gratification the writer felt in this sudden and unlooked for transition from dependence to easy if not wealthy circumstances was the power it gave him of relieving my necessities and enabling me to resume my professional path, which he requested me without delay to do.

I remember that I was in company with Perry, since Editor of the *Morning Chronicle*, at or immediately after the receipt of this important and heart-stirring letter and that on communicating its contents to him I could not help bursting into tears which he, not unnaturally tho' widely, mistook the source of. He supposed me to have been cruelly disappointed in finding myself excluded by the will from any share of my Uncle's fortune and therefore began to condole with me till I stop'd him by assurances, which perhaps he did not perfectly credit, that my tears were not those of grief but joy, or rather proceeded from an over-powering sensation of the sudden and extreme reverse that this intelligence

James Stephen, 1758–1832
the author of the Memoirs

had made in my own situation and prospects. I could not tell him of the most or, I might say, only interesting effects of it on my before much depressed and anxious feelings. I think my dear Brother did not in that first letter enclose me a remittance, not being immediately able to obtain a bill of exchange, but promised to send me one by the next conveyance, a promise he punctually performed; and it came just in time to enable me under the circumstances soon to be narrated to save the character of my dear Maria and the life of our child. It has generally been a trait in the conduct of Divine Providence towards me, on which I have frequently had to look back with wonder as well as gratitude, that the deliverances I have met with in answer to prayer have not arrived till they were absolutely necessary to avert fatal or remediless evils; so that either at the moment, or afterwards retrospectively, I have seen the extremity of the dangers from which I was rescued and that further delay of providential interpositions would have been as ruinous to my hopes as its refusal. And I have derived from such observations, tho' not from them alone, a conviction that it is God's gracious purpose to make very often the hand of his Providence clearly discernable by those who trust in it and watch its operations, in the incidents of their own lives at least. The final cause of such revelations is easily to be found in the Divine condescension and goodness. They strongly confirm faith and attract confidence and love. Woe be to them (I say it with conscious awe and alarm) who do not profit in their souls by such discoveries as they ought! But with those who humbly and diligently improve them, they are likely to abound more and more. "The secret of the Lord is with them that fear him and put their trust in his mercy."

Nothing could be more unlikely to human eyes than that I should have found deliverance from the chain of my sins and from their most fearful effects at that juncture, by such or any means. My Uncle was a very few days before his death in his usual health, a strong man and long seasoned to the climate. He was also intestate, not only till attacked by his fatal disease but till he was near his end and still nearer to the loss of his faculties. He was a man whom few ventured to advise or admonish: and yet one friend who had con-

ceived a regard for my Brother, knowing that if he died
without a will the young man would be left wholly unpro-
vided for, spontaneously for his sake suggested to the dying
man the duty of making one; and, contrary to his usual
character, the suggestion was taken humbly and kindly.
He directed a short will, leaving to his Nephew all he had
and appointing him sole executor, to be prepared, and lived
long enough in sane mind to give it the forms of law.

As this early attainment of independency and easy circumstances by my dear Brother was in its effects not only a most
critical temporal deliverance for me, but the source of all my
subsequent prosperity in life and of all that has been happily
in the lot of my fellow orphans, let me gratefully look back
on the various concurrent means by which it was produced.
Nothing a few years before was more unlikely to human eyes
than that the property of my Uncle William should become
the basis of our common welfare. A younger Brother, John,
whom he had adopted, was apparently his destined heir and
was the Manager of his real estate, which lay in Dominica;
but he was suddenly cut off, a single man, by one of the
diseases of the climate just before or soon after the death of
my dear Mother. An elder Brother, Alexander, who would
have been heir-at-law, was still living in Scotland and long
survived my Uncle William. They were on good terms and
it was not probable that the latter would make a will to
disinherit him, still less that he would do so in favor of my
Father, with whom he was at irreconcilable variance, or any
of his children. He had also two Sisters living for whom he
had much regard, and the younger of whom till her marriage depended on him for her support. I have related the
providential incident of my dear Mother's letter to him in
her last illness, which led him to receive my Brother so
kindly on his uninvited visit to him in St. Kitts, and to
provide for his education and qualification for the medical
profession, and the critically happy effect of his sending him
back to Europe for those purposes, on my own destiny in life.
I have related also the circumstances which happily led to
my Brother's being called again to St. Kitts before his professional course was completed; "happily" for had he stayed
to take his degree regularly at Edinburgh he would not have

returned soon enough, I think, to find his Uncle alive, certainly would not have had time to engage his affection and confidence, and still less to gain, as he did, so much of the good opinion and good will of his Patients and the Planters whose Estates he attended as to secure the succession to his business. Our Uncle scarcely lived a day longer than was necessary to these ends and, in consequence of them, to the welfare of my dear Mother's children. When I add the very unlikely event of his making a will on his death bed after a long life of intestacy, it is impossible not to recognize in so many concurrent courses out of the line of probability, producing such beneficent effects, the hand of a disposing Providence. Our Uncle Alexander was naturally disappointed and dissatisfied, but had the inheritance fallen to *him* it would have done little or no good to himself or others. He was a sensible, but an imprudent, self-indulgent and intemperate man, whose ruined circumstances and bad habits in his later years would have made such an improvement in his situation useless if not pernicious. Had my Uncle William lived a few years longer, the inheritance would have been of little or no value to anyone. He had, like most men who raise a capital by professional industry in the West Indies, at last taken the common and fatal bait of Sugar-planting speculation, buying an Estate at Dominica, the newly settled lands in which were then, like the Demerara lands at present, the favorite fields of enterprise; and he had already found, in the usual mortality among the unfortunate slaves and the failure of the soil, the ordinary fruits of such adventures, yet from the common motives and delusive hopes was resolved to persevere; and had he come to England, as he meant the next year to do, leaving that sinking property to the care of Attorneys, the savings of a long life would in a very few years have been submerged with it in one unrefunding gulf. He had an old and very intelligent and faithful friend at Dominica who had counselled him in vain to sell the Estate at a heavy loss; but my Brother, to whom the advice was kindly renewed after his death, was wise enough to follow it and look for the further improvement of his fortune to his profession alone.

I think it was just before the interesting event of my poor

Maria's confinement that I received the promised remittance, and the water from the rock in the wilderness was not
a more welcome or hardly a more wonderful relief. It
enabled me to provide for her safety and comfort in a way
that I should otherwise have hardly found it possible to do.
Dreadful was my suspense and anxiety during the painful
crisis. Of course I was not absent, and from the small dimensions of our apartments the dear Patient's sufferings were
almost as well known to me as to her attendants in the
adjoining room. My prayers were incessant, and they were
graciously heard. An infant cry at length met my ears; and
I was soon informed that a son was born to me,[1] as fine a
child as the female accoucheur, or nurse, had ever received.
Profuse were my tears of joy and ardent my gratitude to
Heaven. And O! what was the mixture of tenderness and
self-reproach, of joy and pain, comfort and anxiety, satisfaction and remorse when, on admission to the room of the
dear, exhausted sufferer, I whispered in her ear the keen
sensations of my heart. The first feelings of a Father, when
unmixed with a sense of guilt and shame, must be truly
delightful; for even with that bad drawback mine were of a
joyous and elevating kind. I willingly believed, what comparison has since confirmed to me, that the infant was uncommonly large and with the best indications of health and

[1] This illegitimate child of "Maria Rivers" was Stephen's acknowledged
eldest son, William Stephen (1781–1867), a country clergyman, for nearly
sixty years vicar of Bledlow, Bucks, and of Great Stagsden, Beds. So far as the
outside world knew, he was the legitimate son of Stephen's marriage, which
took place in 1783 (see Chapter XII). But whether from his father's telling him,
or from the reading of these *Memoirs*, he pretty certainly knew the facts of his
own parentage. He died January 8, 1867; the death certificate in Somerset
House gives his age at death as 85; that is, he was born between January 8,
1781, and January 8, 1782. The accounts of William Stephen in the *Dictionary
of National Biography* and in the *Life of Sir James Fitzjames Stephen* are the only
instances I have ever discovered in which Leslie Stephen intentionally obscured
a significant, though certainly unimportant, fact. In both places Leslie Stephen
speaks of his uncle William as though he were the legitimate son of James
Stephen, omits to give date of birth, gives the date of death, and follows with
accurate dating of both birth and death of William's brothers and sisters. Leslie
Stephen knew the fact, for he had read and used these *Memoirs*. His motive for
the omission was probably not so much a desire for concealment as a feeling
that an adequate explanation would require more space than it deserved in
the context in which he was writing. The skill with which the omission is made
is a thing to be admired.

strength and beauty. My heart overflowed with a sense of the Divine goodness and mercy, and I resolved to evince my gratitude through all my future days. New anxiety, however, and new distress, were at hand. I have omitted, and must go back to mention, my plan for the child's nutrition. It was, of course, to engage a wet nurse, since my poor Maria's character was incompatible with her performing the most interesting duties of a Mother. I had, therefore, assiduously enquired for a proper nurse of that description and after great difficulties and many disappointments had found one whom I deemed satisfactory. But now, to my dismay, she declined the engagement. The midwife and the nurse allayed my consternation by declaring it was so fine and strong an infant that they had no doubt it could be raised as they call it *by hand*! My poor Maria was satisfied also by their assurances, and it was decided to take that course. The experiment accordingly was tried and seemed to answer wonderfully well for a considerable time, I think to the end of the month, certainly till there was no longer any possibility of recourse to the poor infant's natural sustenance by the Mother; for otherwise, with all the formidable objections to that expedient, it would certainly have been adopted. If memory serves me the dry nursing succeeded for several weeks; but *then* the child became very ill and on calling in Dr. Thynne, then the most eminent childbed physician and accoucheur, he pronounced decisively that a breast of milk must be procured or his little patient would perish. The intelligence was terrible to my feelings; but I posted away in all directions to the different women of whom I got information and found successively at least three or four who were willing to undertake the charge at their own houses, on terms to which I readily subscribed, and whom on enquiry I believed to be eligible persons. I say "successively" for to my equal surprise and distress first one of them, then another, and afterwards a third or fourth, instead of coming at the time appointed sent an excuse, either that the husband disagreed, or that some other impediment had arisen. Meantime the poor Infant progressively declined, and the danger became daily more and more imminent that he would become the speedy victim of my sin-born policy. The anguish of my feelings is not to be described. Poor Maria's, of course, were equally poignant, except that I concealed from her much perhaps of the real danger. I thought myself the murderer of my child; and nothing but the hope I still cherished, tho' with fainter and fainter confidence, from the compassion of that God to whom I earnestly and incessantly prayed could have enabled me to sustain the trial. Matters approached the last extremity; and the women, I think, had told me that unless a breast could be found within a day for the child it would be too late; when, upon reviewing as usual an excuse from the last Nurse I had agreed with and having no information of any other, I rushed out resolved to get one if possible, of whatever description, before I returned. I took my way in a solitary path across the fields that lie between Westminster and Chelsea and never in my life prayed more earnestly than I did in my progress that it would please God to rescue me from that calamity which my sins deserved but which would be a barbed arrow in my heart forever, that he would save me from blood guiltiness and spare the life of my poor injured Baby by guiding me to some person such as I sought to find. My prayers and my distress moved the compassionate Being whom I had so deeply offended. I had scarcely quitted the private path, all along which my prayers were poured forth, than I saw before me a fruit and greenshop; and a thought was thrown into my mind that I would enter it and buy some fruit in order to propitiate the Woman I saw in it towards assisting my enquiries. When I told her that I would be obliged to her to tell me of any healthy young woman in her neighbour-hood for my purpose, she replied that she knew of no such person; but on my proceeding to mention, which of course I did feelingly enough, the danger my child's life was in and the distressing disappointments I had met with, the woman, after some hesitation, said, "I myself, Sir, am nursing my youngest child: but as it is near six Months old you will no doubt think my milk will not be new enough, for your baby; otherwise I would rather take it to nurse with my own, whom I could soon wean, than your child should perish." I did not much like the woman's appearance, or that of her house, in point of cleanliness, nor her age, as she seemed

near forty; but she spoke so feelingly and had such an air
of good nature that, in the urgency of my distressing case,
I did not hesitate to close with her offer. I engaged her at
once; and my poor, dear Infant's life was unquestionably
saved by it. As soon as it got the breast the alarming
symptoms ceased, and instead of wasting further it quickly
increased in flesh and strength till my mind was set at ease
and I had to bless God with gratitude and joy for a new
deliverance.

It was strange enough that neither Maria nor I at all suspected the cause of the difficulties and disappointments we
had met with in this distressing case. They seemed to us in
their number and coincidence quite inexplicable, and yet
were natural enough. Our appearance and manners, our
seclusion in a neighbourhood in which we were entire
strangers, and being unvisited there, added to the apparent
object of all, Maria's secret accouchement, had excited
suspicions that as soon as she was able to remove we should
be heard of no more and that the child might be left on the
hands of whatever Woman took him to nurse. Our landlady
was unable, perhaps also unwilling, to repel these suspicions.
Every Nurse, therefore, with whom I successively treated,
as soon as she or her husband had enquired about us, became
alarmed and found some pretext for declining to engage with
us. Mrs. F., the woman I at last so critically found, explained
the case thus to me afterwards, adding that she herself had
been cautioned on the same grounds and would not have
taken the child had she not seen in my anxiety and distress
about him sufficient reason to be assured that I should never
abandon him. A gracious Providence, therefore, in directing
my steps to her, made the previous sufferings of mind, with
which I was so justly visited, means of averting the calamity
I dreaded and deserved.

Maria's excellent constitution, which had resisted the bad
tendency of her long imprisonment and inaction prior to her
delivery, conduced also to her speedy recovery and saved me
from the distress I should have felt had she been attacked
with any of the ordinary childbed diseases. Yet when the time
of her confinement drew towards its close, I saw too plainly
that there was a change in her personal appearance since the

time of her departure from the view of her friends that would make it dangerous for her to be seen by them again till air and exercise should have replaced the roses in her cheeks and given back to her frame its former vigour and elasticity. It would have been perceived that her health had materially suffered, which might have led to dangerous surmises and made it difficult to invent explanations reconcilable with the facts, before ostensibly stated and confirmed by her correspondence. It was necessary, therefore, to place her for some weeks at least in a retired and healthful part of the Country; and I felt anew the wonderful kindness of Providence in sending me the unexpected pecuniary resource that enabled me at once to accomplish this object and to sustain the new expense of keeping our dear Infant at nurse in an adequate and liberal way. The character of the one, and the life of the other, could hardly have been otherwise preserved. But poor Maria's spirits were also to be sustained, as the speedy recovery of her strength and blooming health would have been precluded by their depression; and this I reasonably feared would prove a very difficult work, for her feelings were about to sustain a great tho' necessary shock by the discovery of the purpose I had formed; and if a seperation from me was to be added, it was more than her mind was likely well to bear; yet without such a seperation, during her retirement at least, adherence to my penitent and self-denying resolution would require a greater degree of firmness than I was likely to command. I nevertheless determined in reliance on Divine aid to persevere. I prayed earnestly to be enabled to do so. The sense of God's wonderful mercies to me in the recent occurrences, especially the preservation of my child, added strength to my resolves, and nourished the hope that He would finally deliver me from the cruel thraldom in which sin had bound me, and rescue not only myself but the two objects of my fatal affections from the dreadful effects that I feared. Blessed be his name, the hope was not unfounded! But much was to be done and suffered in order to its accomplishment. His mercy was the greater in shewing me that the evils of sin were not to be soon or easily repaired.

My poor, dear Maria, did not first discover, I think, from

my tongue, but from my conduct, the reformation on which
I had resolved; but I was soon obliged to disclose to her my
whole plan and the irresistable reasons on which it was
founded, to relieve her from the natural and dreadful apprehensions that satiety had succeeded to passion, that I no
longer admired her person and had transferred my love to her
rival. To convince her of the contrary was not easy, but my
self-denial was too painful and my tenderness for her too
sincere to be long misunderstood. I possessed at that time
some eloquence and some powers of persuasion, at least when
my feelings were strongly excited; and it was no difficult
thing to shew that regard to her preservation and that of
my poor Nancy, as well as duty towards God, indispensably
prescribed to us both the adoption of the plan I had formed,
however painful to both our hearts. It was now a part of that
plan, by the advice of my dear Brother, that I should go in
a few Months to the West Indies, which tended at once to
allay her jealous apprehensions and to make more manifest
the ruinous and fearful consequences that would result from
any renewal of our past imprudence.

It was necessary before we gave up our lodging and retired
into the Country to tranquilize Mrs. F.'s mind as to the risk
of the child being deserted and left on her hands; for of
course we could not tell her whither we removed or where
we might be afterwards found without a discovery of our
real names and, in consequence perhaps, of all we wished
to conceal. On the other hand, the fictitious name made it
impossible to refer her to any Person who would answer for
me without placing a dangerous confidence in the person
referred to. But here again I found a resource in Felix
McCarthy's influence over Mrs. S., the old Lady mentioned
before. On some pretence, the nature of which I forget, she
was induced to allow a reference to be made to her and to
answer for Mr. James in a quite satisfactory way. What
excuse I made to Mrs. F. for not leaving my own address
with her, I have also forgot; but she was satisfied and promised me all the anxious attention to the health of my poor
Infant that its own Mother could possibly pay. I had treated
her with so much liberality, and she had seen so much of my
strong affection for the child, that she had no reason to doubt

the assurances I gave of my gratefully rewarding her for fidelity to that engagement. Having settled this interesting preliminary and given up our lodgings, I handed my poor, dear Maria into a post chaise and, closing the blinds enough to prevent her being recognized by any passing acquaintance, took a final leave of the place where she had been so long a Prisoner and drove to Godstone, as the most retired road I recollected, intending to pass from thence into some sequestered part of Sussex and search there for some suitable lodgings. Happily for her feelings and mine, Parliament had just been prorogued; and I was therefore at liberty to be absent from London, tho' bound to assist the Editor of the *Morning Post* with occasional contributions of paragraphs and essays during the recess. My company was always enough to make her happy in all circumstances, and it was not her disposition to be anxious for the future. She was, therefore, much exhilarated by the fine weather and beautiful country scenes we passed through and soon relieved me by her spirits and animation from all fear of her well sustaining as long a journey as might be expedient to take. For my part, I had deep anxieties, tho' earnest prayer and recollection of the much that Providence had hitherto done for our preservation inspired me with hopes of our finally escaping the dangers we had yet to encounter. The greatest of these, I foresaw, would be from our own passions. Much, therefore, did I pray in secret for the aid of Divine grace to fortify the resolutions I had formed; and blessed be God I did not pray in vain, tho' my steadfastness was, as I foresaw it would be, often severely tried. While relying on the goodness of the Most High, I was, alas, obliged to offend him by further breaches of truth (such is the cruel bondage into which the enemy of our Souls betrays us, and so does one sin irresistably lead to others). It was absolutely necessary, in finding a new residence for us both, to drop the assumed characters of husband and wife and to assume the equally false ones of Brother and Sister. Nothing else could at once have made appearances decorous and prevented obvious dangers; and it enabled me to pass by my real name and refer to friends in case of need, as they knew I had Sisters and might naturally believe one of them to be with me.

When we arrived at Godstone, we resolved to proceed to
East Grinstead; but while the chaise was getting ready Maria
and I were tempted by the fineness of the day to stroll across
the adjoining common, or green, and into a crossroad beyond
it and had not advanced far when a Village of inviting
appearance presented itself to our view on an eminence about
a mile before us. It struck me that this perhaps might furnish
such a retreat as we wished to find, and Maria willingly
agreed to prolong our walk to it. In this, as in a thousand
other cases, the hand of Providence wonderfully led me,
without my own foresight, and beyond all calculation, to the
best means of attaining the objects graciously conceded to
my prayers. We entered Bletchingly (for that was the
pleasantly placed Village that had enticed us from our road)
and immediately found exactly the very thing we were in
quest of, a place and a family so well adapted to our purpose
that I verily believe we might have searched over half the
Kingdom without finding either of them equally so, and
which not only furnished us with a cheap, safe and agreeable
retirement but were afterwards, as will be seen, a source of
preservation and of more, I trust, than temporal blessings to
our child. It pleased God, also, to unite with those gracious
objects, by means of our apparently most fortuitous choice,
provision for the support and comfort of an aged Servant of
his for the remainder of her days. To make his merciful
guidance the more striking, he led me at once to the very
door of the only house in the village, as I afterwards found,
in which we could have found a lodging, and directed my
application to the only individual in that house to whom I
could have applied with success. We found no bill up for
lodgings to let in any part of the village, but as we passed a
decent tho' ancient looking house an old woman of a prepossessing countenance shewed herself near the open gate in
passing from the House towards her yard or garden, and it
was at once suggested to my mind to make enquiries of her.
Accosting her in the most courteous way, I beg'd the favor
of her to tell me whether there was any house in that
pleasant village where strangers might be accomodated
with furnished lodgings. She answered in as courteous a
manner that she knew not of any, but after some conversa-

tion said that if her own house had been good enough she should have had no objection to give us such accomodations as she could. On further enquiry I found that a widow gentlewoman, who had long occupied some of her rooms as a lodger and boarder, had recently married one of her Sons and that in consequence those rooms were vacant and might be immediately had, together with the accomodation of dining with the family, if desired. On looking at the rooms we found them clean and comfortable and the terms extremely moderate. In short, the place was exactly the thing we wanted; and in less than half an hour everything was settled between the good old Widow and us, with leave for us to return in two days and take possession of the lodgings. I gave her a reference for my character; but she was so prepossessed by our appearance that, if I remember right, she declined to use it.

Now, when I add that this apparently most casual occurrence proved in its consequences most auspicious both to the poor Widow and us, that it led not only to the end immediately in my view, the preservation of Maria's character, but the saving the life of my child and the forming his infant mind to virtuous and pious habits, that our hostess was a humble and devout servant of God, and that her connection with me was a stay and comfort to her during the many years that she afterwards lived, it surely is not too much to say that the finger of Providence plainly guided me to her door.

Maria and I returned with much exhilaration to our Inn and finding the chaise ready resolved to execute our purpose of proceeding to East Grinstead to pass there the two days during which Mrs. T. was to prepare for our reception. I have much cause to remember with a particular interest the Inn at which we put up at that place. It was at that time a scene to me of no small agitation and distress and of trial which earnest prayer alone enabled me to sustain; for here began what may be called my painful seperation from Maria. Hitherto her confinement had naturally led to the division of our chambers, but now when I ordered a seperate room for her and when she had to retire to it alone, the most painful ideas naturally agitated both our minds. Tho' she

had assented to that plan of reformation to which it would
have been not only criminal but insane to object, this
necessary but marked conformity to it spoke strongly to her
heart that there was an end to that dream of conjugal union
and happiness in which we had long indulged; and a strain
of afflictive feelings followed that I could not very easily
compose. Sorrow, however, with her was always a passing
cloud. Self-enjoyment and hilarity were the native fruits of
her happy constitution, and few persons that I have ever
known were so little addicted to anxious reflection or care
about the future. My own character has always been rather
different. I *think* a great deal—to, however, little purpose—
and am not unapt to look forward with anxiety, especially
under the consciousness of sin. At this time my prospects
were bad enough to dishearten even a careless and light-
hearted man. I could not conceal from myself that the self-
denying plan, on adherence to which my every hope
depended, would be formed of very difficult and painful
practice and that the government of my own passions, tho'
hard enough, would not be my one, nor perhaps my most
painful, task. But supposing the whole arduous penitential
work accomplished, my prospects were still extremely dark
and cheerless. A long exile from my native land, an adieu
likely to be final to those I most fondly loved, probable
orphanage and destitution to my poor infant, the reasonable
apprehension of consequences worse than death to the dear
woman whose innocence I had ruined when I should cease
to be her present monitor and guardian, a most arduous part
in the meantime to be acted for the preservation of my dear
Nancy's credit with her family and her peace; such at best
was the promise of my life for many tedious years to come.
Slender, also, was my chance of ever emerging from poverty
and at the same time from a dependence which was odious
and irksome to my mind, even when a beloved brother was
the patron. These reflections pressed heavily on my mind and
were, I doubt not, transferred into my private prayers in a
strain of earnest supplication during the Evening I spent at
East Grinstead, or rather during the two days which I think
we spent there. The recollection of them was strongly
associated in my room with local ideas, not only of the town

and the Inn, but the very room, the principal one in the house, which I occupied with Maria and in which she left me at night to my solitary contemplations. My next visit to East Grinstead, thirty years afterwards, was on my election as Member of Parliament for that place,[1] when I gave a dinner at the same Inn and in the same room, to my constituents and several of the neighbouring gentry. The contrast was striking indeed! My sin-born fears and anxieties had given place to pious gratitude and peace. My contrition had been accepted, my penitent resolutions accomplished, and "my feet plucked out of the net and out of the snare" in which the enemy of my Soul had cruelly caught and entangled me. Of the two dear objects of my former solicitude one had long passed, I trust, into a far happier world, but not till after I had been able to repair my offences against her by conjugal fidelity and love; and the other had escaped all the evils that I feared for her and had become a respected Matron, happy as a wife and Mother. I myself was blessed with a numerous family, the offspring of my dear Nancy, and with a second Partner of my heart, one of the most excellent of women. The poor necessitous Reporter for the *Morning Post*, the emigrant for bread, the dependant on a Brother's purse, had become a man of property, a Master in Chancery, a Member of Parliament, and in so much consideration with the Government for the support of his tongue and his pen that if he had aspired to much higher professional preferment he might have attained it, and indeed had it then in his choice.[2] Great must have been my insensibility if, while presiding at my Parliamentary dinner, my thoughts had not dwelt much on these strange reverses, and if I had not repeatedly said to myself with humble gratitude and admiration, "*This hath God done.*"

We returned to Bletchingly, took up our abode there, and found our situation there sufficiently comfortable and

---

[1] Stephen was elected M.P. for East Grinstead in 1812; from 1808 to 1812 he had been member for Tralee.

[2] Stephen probably means here that he was offered a place in the cabinet by Spencer Perceval, prime minister from 1809 to the time of his assassination, May 11, 1812. Actually he exerted more influence upon Perceval, who had great confidence in him, from outside the cabinet than he could have from within.

pleasant. The old Widow more than verified my favourable
prepossessions. She was humble, courteous, and assiduous to
please, as were also her Sons and her newly acquired
daughter-in-law; and we found not only the latter, but the
unmarried daughter, by no means vulgar or so much below
us in manners as to be at all disgusting. They might both be
fairly rustically well-bred and little if at all inferior to gentle-
women, in the middle ranks of life, such as are usually found
in the Country, either in their conversation or deportment.
Miss T., who was in the bloom of youth and handsome, had
a natural gentility about her, the effect of good nature and
good sense united, and had captivated a City Manufacturer
in prosperous circumstances, whose wife she afterwards
became. She evidently took a strong liking to Maria and paid
to her the kindest and most respectful attentions. The Males
of the family were of a much coarser kind but not less
desirous to oblige us, and I was soon able to ingratiate myself
with them pretty strongly by conversing with them when we
met (which was only at the dinner table) on the subjects
they best understood. Condescension to inferiors in education
and rank is a duty that I have never found it hard to practise,
and of which I have rarely missed the reward in the feelings
it naturally excites. The whole family felt themselves much
honor'd by having such inmates as Maria and me, and we
soon perceived that the old woman and her daughter were
much attached to us and earnest to prolong our stay with
them independently of self-interested views. They treated us,
in fact, with a liberality that must have precluded any
pecuniary advantages by the terms agreed on.

No situation could have been chosen better calculated to
sustain Maria's spirits and speedily to restore her health and
strength than this into which we had been so happily, and by
apparent accident, thrown. The air was most salubrious, the
country beautiful; and we were attracted by numerous
pleasant walks where there was no danger of meeting any
eyes to which we were known. In the evenings I amused her
with reading; and tho' there were naturally occasional fits of
depression or agitation, I was able on the whole to soothe
and satisfy her mind without any improper indulgence of
those tender feelings which were dangerous and might have

been fatal to us both. The family saw nothing particular in our conduct, tho' they thought from our attentions to each other that we had as a Brother and Sister a more than ordinary share of fraternal affection. Even in this secluded situation, Maria's personal attractions gave her a new admirer. There was an old Scotch Doctor in the Village who had long possessed an extensive practice in the various surgical and medical branches in that and the surrounding Country; and he had recently been joined by his Nephew, a young Surgeon from Edinburgh whom he designed for his Successor. This young man, who was pleasing enough in his person and manners, availed himself of some professional intercourse with Mrs. T.'s family to form an acquaintance with us and was apparently not insensible to Maria's beauty. He paid us much attention while we stayed there; but whether from perceiving that she had no eyes for him, or from fear of his Uncle's displeasure, or both, he did not venture to express those feelings which I thought he plainly entertained for her. In no very long space of time, I think about two months, Maria had so nearly if not fully regained her former blooming and healthy appearance that I thought she might safely return, as from her sojourn in Scotland, to meet again the eyes of her friends in Kensington and London. New artifices, alas, were therefore put in practice to prepare for that reappearance and give verisimilitude to the tales with which her absence had been coloured. Deep was my anxiety for the event and, incongruous and even impious tho' it may appear, very earnest and frequent were my prayers for the success of those precautions and contrivances of which falsehood was the basis. It is one of the most painful consequences of sin that it often imposes an almost irresistable necessity of further transgressions and makes even the path of penitence impure. I cannot, even in the most impartial retrospect, perceive what course I could have taken to save the character of one injured woman and the peace of two without means in their nature offensive to the Most High, on whose mercy nevertheless I placed my main or sole reliance. His compassion and long suffering allowed for the sad dilemma and as my aims were right permitted the bad means to have the desired effect. Poor, dear

Maria was probably less anxious on the occasion than myself; but a short time before we took leave of Bletchingly feelings of a different kind from the apprehension of suspicion or disgrace agitated her very strongly. The final divorce, so to call it, from one for whom she had the feelings of the fondest wife became the more distressing as its consummation more nearly approached; and the effect for a short time was such that I conceived a new fear, more dreadful than all the rest. I had serious alarm for her understanding. But my earnest prayers again were heard. This tremendous evil also was averted. Soothed by my tenderness she became again composed, and at length I brought her back in health and tolerable spirits to London and sent her to those friends from whom she had been so long divided.

It must have been a deep, tho' necessary, humiliation to her, as well as to me, that I was obliged on this occasion to have recourse to my dear injured Nancy's assistance. To her she first went, stayed with her, if I remember right, a short time, and went with her to Kensington to call on her friends there and place herself in a new boarding house in that place, which had I think been provided through my dear Nancy's previous assistance. No other mediation could have so strongly tended to prevent or remove any suspicion of the true case, because all her Friends well knew of my engagements to Miss Stent and must therefore have regarded her countenance and friendship as the best proof that there was no cause of rivalship between them. That my dear Nancy should enact the part she kindly did might be sufficiently explained by the consideration that the ruin of Maria's character would have greatly aggravated the difficulties and distresses of our common situation, but justice to that kind and generous woman demands of me to say that she was actuated by more disinterested feelings. She felt for poor Maria pity instead of resentment and deeply simpathised with *my* sufferings and anxieties, the severity of which she well knew. I must add, however, that by this time she had probably ceased to fear that Maria would rob her permanently of my affections, for in fact my heart had in great measure returned to its first allegiance; and she had too much discernment and knowledge of my character not to perceive that truth. I have before, I believe, expressed my dissent to the notion that a man cannot sincerely and passionately love two women at the same time. I certainly experienced the contrary. But tho' both these young Ladies were truly and fondly beloved by me, there was a difference in the nature of my affections between the one and the other, which I cannot better describe than by saying that the one was dearest to me as a *woman*, the other as a *friend*, and yet in both those characters I had love enough for each to have been quite content with her as a wife and ardently desirous to make her such, if my engagements to the other had not opposed it. She who was the object of my first affections had, however, been progressively gaining ground in my heart upon her rival during that long period of remorse, distress, and anxiety in which my sins had involved me. The kindness and generosity of her conduct could not but attract my esteem, gratitude and admiration. Instead of reproaches or resentment, I met from her in general the tenderest simpathy; and it was in her faithful bosom alone that I could repose my cares with a confidence that had no reserve. It was impossible, also, not to be deeply interested in her amiable feelings and conduct as a daughter and a sister, which now that I was become a frequent guest in her Father's house were brought to my familiar notice. She loved her Father, and her Brothers, my old Friend Tom especially, with the strongest and most disinterested affection, was beloved by them in return, and in her new character of Mistress of a Family which she enlivened by her animation and good sense shewed me the happiness which I might have enjoyed in the married state if my infidelity had not forfeited that blessing. Her Father, also, had become much attached to me and treated me with such kind hospitality that I conceived a kind of filial attachment to him, which naturally tended to strengthen my affection for the daughter, She had also a great advantage over poor Maria in her understanding and the superior cultivation of her mind, in the liveliness of her conversation, and in a keen sensibility to all intellectual and rational enjoyments. After Maria's return to the social circle when, from my dear Nancy's generous resolution to countenance and protect her, I saw them often

together and oftener at short intervals apart, the disparity
in these respects became more striking to me than before;
and while in my private interviews with the one I had to
practise a painful self-denial and to encounter many fears
and anxieties in meeting her oftener than was safe for her
character, tho' not often enough to satisfy her feelings and
keep down jealous alarms, I could enjoy the company of the
other without inconvenience or disquietude. It is not strange,
therefore, that I progressively became more gratified with
the society of the latter than with that of her rival, tho' my
love for Maria was still powerful enough, independently of
a sense of justice and compassion, to make me give her as
much of my company as necessary regard to appearances
would permit. But if I should stop here, it would place my
feelings and my conduct in a more advantageous light than
truth will warrant. The progressive change in that great
preponderance of my amorous attachment towards Maria
which had once existed was assisted by other and more vulgar
causes. I still admired her beauty, which was unimpaired;
nor had possession of her person, I think, much if at all
diminished that feeling. Yet so it was that my dear Nancy's
personal attractions became much stronger with me than
before. They were, in fact, a good deal improved by an
increased share of health, in consequence of which some
eruptions of a scorbutic kind by which her naturally good
skin had been deformed were removed; and being enabled
by the liberality of her Father to dress as she pleased, her
person was set off to greater advantage. In this respect she
had, I think, been too negligent before, partly no doubt
from necessary economy and partly perhaps from the influence of what I should then have called the methodistical
strictness of her Guardian, the good old Mrs. T. with whom
she lived. Her person tho' slight was pretty, and tho' her
features were by no means good in general her eyes had
uncommon softness and vivacity of expression, and her
auburn hair was greatly to my taste. After all, she was far
from a pretty woman, even in *my* partial eyes, and would
have been generally thought a plain one: But tho' there was
no comparison in this respect between her and Maria, I
certainly began to be less sensible of that inferiority and to

think her person, as well as her mind, more than sufficiently attractive. The great charm, however, was that exquisite sensibility and ardent affection, of which I knew myself to be the object. In this respect, indeed, Maria had equal attractions, a difference in temperament excepted. She loved me as fondly as she was capable of loving any man, but that capacity was not equal to my dear Nancy's; her sensibility, like her understanding, was not so great.

There was, on the other hand, one very interesting bond of attachment to Maria to which my narrative must now return, the beloved infant to whom we had mutually given life. I had repeatedly gone from Bletchingly to London to see him and was tolerably well satisfied with his nurse, Mrs. F., who professed and perhaps felt a Mother's affection for him, tho' he was no longer a fine looking child but on the contrary had a feeble and sickly appearance. Of course Maria was impatient after her return to see him; and I could not deny her that gratification, tho' its possible dangers to her character were obvious enough. I used all possible precautions, going in a closed hackney coach and taking care not to be taken up or set down where we were known or likely to be seen or tracked. Many other visits ensued in the same way, tho' at the longest intervals that I could persuade her to admit; and she, like myself, was tolerably satisfied with the woman, tho' uneasy at the child's appearance. In a few months symptoms of teething began; and the effects were so severe that we had great fears of the event, when our alarms were much enhanced by both the infants (for Mrs. F. still suckled her own, also) being attacked with the smallpox. Putting a necessary confidence in Dr. Thynne, except of course as to the Mother, and desiring him to conceal my name, I sent him to attend the children and put up anxious prayers to Heaven many times a day that my poor dear Infant might not be taken from me as the merited chastisement of my sins. The nurse's own child had the disease with shocking severity, in the confluent form, and fell a victim to it; but mine, in consequence of what had chiefly alarmed me, his previous debilitated state, had it in as mild a degree as inoculation ever produced and happily recovered, a mercy for which I was truly thankful. That the dealings of a gracious

Providence towards me in the same line may appear more clearly in a connected view, I will carry on the history of my poor, dear infant for a year or two further in this place instead of pursuing my narrative in a chronological order as to intermediate events. Tho' the child continued in a feeble and sickly state there was little question of his remaining with Mrs. F., at least till he should be of an age to be weaned; and the weaker he grew the more I shrunk from the risk of that important change. The woman, who found me a punctual and liberal paymaster, probably contrived to enhance the apprehensions which the nearly fatal effects of the first attempt to dispense with the natural sustenance had excited; and his teething, or other causes, were always explanations at hand to quiet me as to his frequent ailments and backward state. He was at length weaned, I think from a necessary cause, and escaped any immediate ill consequence; but his strength did not increase and long after the time at which he ought to have taken to his feet he had no propensity or power to do so, nor did the medical assistance I obtained for him from time to time produce any effectual improvement. Both Maria and I became very apprehensive that we should not long preserve him. At length the visible enlargement of his head, the sutures of which had made scarce any approach towards closing, together with the impotence and crookedness of his lower limbs and the dimness of his eyes, &c., inspired me with a fear of something worse than losing him. I conceived the shocking apprehension that he would grow up an idiot and a cripple. I think he was about twenty months old when I was led by accidental observation of circumstances overlooked before, and by my own anxious reflections and enquiries, to suspect and progressively to ascertain the true cause of all the mischief. The woman whom I thought so fond and careful of him was in fact a most indolent and unfaithful nurse. Having a shop and a young family of her own to attend to, she had been in the habit of committing him to the charge of a daughter of her own scarcely old and strong enough to hold and carry him about; and the poor child had received no tossing or exercise and scarcely had there been any attempt to make him stand alone or walk. It may seem strange that Maria or I had not sooner discovered this, but the woman was very plausible; and then it should be considered that we had none of that advice from experienced old friends by which Parents are usually directed in such cases. She had also a great advantage in those fears of observation which prevented our calling at her house and taking her by surprise. It was a very public thoroughfare; and after one or two visits I perceived there was so much risk of being seen by some who knew us that my habit was to go to a neighbouring tavern or tea garden, in a retired situation, and which in the forenoons was quite unfrequented, to take a private room there and send for Mrs. F. and the child. Of course, therefore, she had time to dress him and herself, and to deceive us with the best appearances. When, by some deviations from this habit and other means, I began to suspect the truth and take advice with that clue to it, my suspicions were soon decidedly confirmed. I was informed that the child had rickets, and probably water in the head, and that better nursing alone could save him from deformity or early death. It was now that I found the further kindness of a compassionate Providence in having directed me to the Family at Bletchingly. In the midst of my deep anxiety and embarrassment it was happily suggested to my mind that old Mrs. T., and her daughter, with whom I had still kept up a little acquaintance, might possibly be induced to undertake the important charge of nursing and restoring, in that healthful situation of theirs, my poor, injured and unfortunate child; for besides the pecuniary compensations that might be an object to them, they had a visible regard for and a great desire to oblige me; and I knew from the religious and conscientious character of the kind old woman that if she undertook the trust it would be faithfully discharged. Having communicated the project to Maria, who entirely approved it, I hastened to Bletchingly and after obtaining a promise of secrecy from Mrs. T. told her my object, concealing of course who was the Mother of the child and leaving her to suppose that it was the offspring of some ordinary illicit amour, but giving at the same time the rein to my genuine feelings, so as to shew her how dear the poor infant was to me and how much my happiness was involved in its preservation. It was not hard to engage her good nature on the side of my wishes; but it was a case in which she felt it necessary to pause and consult with her children, especially her daughter, on whom a great share of the trouble would fall. I myself also felt that the cordial concurrence of the latter was indispensable. It was on *her* good health, spirits, and activity in giving exercise to the child that much of my hopes were founded. But she was a very kind-hearted young woman, and the desire to ease my anxious and distressed feelings proved as powerful with her as her Mother. I saw, indeed, that there were doubts and apprehensions with both; but my heart prompted my tongue with the best topics of persuasion, and I was at length successful. It was no doubt one prevailing consideration that my supposed Sister, whom they were much attached to, knew of the case, approved of my application, and would occasionally come and see the child. It was a further inducement that if the child should be preserved he would probably remain under their care for several years during my absence in the West Indies, where I expected to go in a few Months. That prospect was, in fact, one of my chief reasons for being anxious to place him in more respectable hands than those of an ordinary hired nurse and with persons of whose kindness and integrity I was well assured. Having attained this important object, not without earnest and penitential prayer, I felt a confidence such as I have often felt in similar cases, and which has rarely if ever deceived me, that a gracious Providence had ordered the matter for me and that the event would be happy, as it actually and greatly proved, both to the dear infant and myself. I soon after removed him from Mrs. F.'s, leaving her curiosity unsatisfied and to the utmost of my power without any means of future gratification as to where he was going and who his Parents were. To prevent any resentment that might properly be unconvenient or dangerous, I made no complaint of her conduct but left her to regard the removal as chiefly designed for the benefit of a change of air, closed accounts with her in a liberal way, and promised, I think, that she should hear of the child's health. If I remember right, I not only kept that promise but gave her afterwards some small further douceur to secure if possible that she should not have the inclination to, if she found the power of, mischief. Maria accompanied me in the execution of this important parental office. With our usual precautions we called for the child in a hackney coach, the driver of which knew not whence we came or whither we went but set us down in some place where we discharged him, before a post chaise was ordered to take us on to Croydon. In our way to Bletchingly we saw more than we had before done of the wretched state to which our poor infant was reduced. It was one of listless apathy rather than suffering. He was not fractious, but dull and sleepy. He neither cried nor smiled nor noticed the new objects around him but was content to sit or lie, as he had shamefully been used to do, in an inactive and torpid state. Mrs. T. and her daughter, when they saw him, were alarmed at the charge they had undertaken; but their compassion was engaged in his favour, and the interest they saw my supposed Sister to take in his recovery, as well as my parental anxiety, assisted to prevent their drawing back and decided them to rear him if they could. They did not conceal from us, however, their fears that the case was nearly hopeless. Maria, of course, was obliged soon to return and could see him afterwards only by short occasional visits; but I, being released from my connection with the *Morning Post*, went often to Bletchingly and made long stays there, to encourage by my presence and aid by my exertions the persevering efforts that were made to save my unfortunate infant. Many times a day when there did I act the part of a nurse to him, giving him till I was tired that motion which had been so cruelly neglected and carrying him into the fields for the air in favourable weather, which in that retired place I could do without much observation. Nor were these human means unaccompanied with frequent and ardent prayers. Well can I recollect a little rivulet on the margin of which, unseen by mortal eyes, I put down my poor, feeble, sickly child and kneeling on the grass beside him invoked with streaming eyes the Father of mercies to deliver him and me from the effects and the just chastisement of my sins. My last much loved and venerated wife once told me that she thought my character much resembled that of David. In this instance it certainly did; and in reading the account of his anxious penitential supplications when his child by Bathsheba was stricken, I have often called to mind my own feelings and my own prayers at this distressing period. But blessed be God, my prayers were not, as his on that occasion were, rejected. It was long, very long indeed, before I was assured of their acceptance. The child's health, indeed, seemed slowly to improve; but as he advanced in age the continuing impotency of his limbs became rather more alarming, and I could but doubtfully perceive that the morbid enlargement of his head and the deadness of his aspect were diminished. It pleased God to shew me by the narrowness and difficulty of the escape its providential character; for had he been the child of a Monarch greater pains could not have been taken for his recovery than were taken by the worthy family into whose hands I had been so singularly guided to commit him. If his nursery had been of an ordinary kind he would unquestionably have perished or, what I dreaded more, grown up a cripple and perhaps an idiot; but the good old woman, who soon conceived and always retained for him a truly maternal affection, was indefatigable and so was her daughter, in repairing by extraordinary care the sad consequences of the previous ill treatment. Her sons and her daughter-in-law in some degree also assisted. Each occasionally took a turn in tossing the child about and trying to enliven him. Happily there was no other child in the family; they were all active lively people, and the poor infant was so quiet and tractable that there was no drawback from trouble or noise on the compassion he excited. Before I went to the West Indies the effects of these advantages and the fine healthful air of the place, were seen in the gradual diminution of those morbid symptoms which had most alarmed me; the head was reduced to nearly its right proportions and he had learnt to walk alone, tho' not with vigour and activity, so as to inspire a confident hope that he would not grow up impotent or deformed; the fear of intellectual defect also had in great measure subsided, but an extreme timidity and nervous irritability remained, with so very narrow a chest and so slight and feeble a form that my hope of his living to manhood was still but faint. When I recollected how very fine an infant he was at his birth, and that the sad reverse was the fruits of those sins that had robbed him of maternal nutrition and a parent's constant care and placed him in mercenary, unfaithful hands, my self-reproaches were truly painful; but my prayers ascended every Morning and Evening to the throne of Grace with earnest supplications that any sins might not be thus permanently visited on my poor child, and after many years of perseverance the boon was graciously confer'd.

There were dangers of another kind, with the apprehension of which my mind was often and reasonably disturbed. The preservation of poor, dear Maria's character was essential to the hope of our ultimate deliverance and yet the danger of detection and exposure was often visible and great. Those visits to Bletchingly, which it was impossible not occasionally to indulge her with, were in several instances sources of alarm. In one instance we narrowly escaped meeting in the family a gentleman who well knew me and could have told them she was not my Sister. On two other occasions a gentleman and a lady successively came among her friends at Kensington, from a family near Guildford, a pretended visit to which had been the screen for a long visit to the child and would have unavoidably exposed the falsehood of the project if the subject had been noticed in their presence. Again, when she was walking with some female friends in Kensington Gardens, the young Surgeon of Bletchingly whom I have mentioned met them and, I think, saluted her when passing but happily did not stop to address her as Miss Stephen and ask for me. A more serious and lasting source of danger was that a girl, the daughter of Mrs. F., the former nurse, came to live as a servant in her immediate neighbourhood and in a house which she often passed; but happily we noticed her at the door without her noticing us, so that Maria was put upon her guard not to walk that way. But it would be too tedious to mention the numerous perils and narrow escapes that occurred to us. They were abundantly sufficient to shew us how continually dependent we were on the arm of a merciful Providence for our reputation and our peace, as well as the preservation of our child.

Chapter Eleven

[1782]

THE sense of that dependence was not unnecessary to save me from further gross offences, alas! against my Divine and ineffably gracious Benefactor. I have hesitated whether to record or to suppress that opprobrious truth. I have not engaged, let it be remembered, that my confession in this private history of my heart and conduct shall be complete and without reserve. Many incidents and circumstances, therefore, have been and will be suppressed, without insincerity, if on the whole my narrative does not give a more favorable picture of myself than the fullest discovery of all my actions, with all the motives that led to them and all the circumstances attending them, would present. Let me be understood rather as saying nothing that is false, than everything that is true, in what concerns my own credit and estimation. But it would, I think, be withholding a material and instructive passage in the history of my life, very illustrative of the progress of my moral character, if I were not here to notice an incident of a very guilty and reproachful kind.

While my dear Nancy boarded, as I have mentioned, with a Widow Lady whose name was Heath, or after her departure to her Father's house (I am not certain which), a Lady from Scotland, elegant and highly interesting in her person and manners, a Mrs. B., came with the most respectable introductions to Mrs. Heath and took lodgings in the house. On recollection it must have been after my dear Nancy's removal, for she succeeded to her apartments; but perceiving an intimacy with Mrs. H., who had treated her with the greatest kindness, she became acquainted with her successor and was struck with admiration of her beauty and accomplishments. So were all our friends in that neighbourhood; and I for a long time heard of nothing more frequently than the beautiful and fascinating Mrs. B., especially of her remarkable delicacy and propriety of deportment. Tho' accustomed to move in the higher circles of society, as sufficiently appeared from the figure of persons who called on her, she led a very retired life, her husband, an officer of rank, being in the East Indies and she having been left behind him on account of her family situation, for she was on the point of confinement with a first child. She took a liking to my dear Nancy, who visited her both before and after her lying in, and continued to regard her with increasing esteem and admiration. Her good sense and powers of conversation were on a par with her personal attractions. Tho' I had heard much of this paragon and was curious to see her, I had never done so till a good while after her confinement, when I accidentally met her one day walking in a party with my dear Nancy and was introduced to her. Her personal appearance justified the accounts I heard of her. She was a tall, graceful woman, with a good face and elegant person; and the Scotch accent, in which she spoke, made her soft voice rather more pleasing and the *tout ensemble* more attractive. Soon after she removed from Mrs. H.'s to a house near Vauxhall; and I saw no more of her till the period to which my narrative has arrived, when meeting her again by accident I beg'd leave to escort her home and the offer was not declined. In my walk with her, which was a long one, my penetration discovered, or my vanity surmised, that she was much pleased with my conversation and would be gratified with my further attentions. It seemed to me, indeed, so visible as to be hardly congruous with that exemplary correctness and delicacy of manners which my poor Nancy had ascribed to her. I began to conceive some little doubt whether her history, situation and character were such as were supposed and made enquiries respecting her visitors while in Mrs. Heath's family, the result of which rather tended to confirm than allay my suspicions; for I found that, with the exception I think of a Sister-in-law, no *Lady* had called upon her. A friend of her husband, a Coll. W., had been more than once there in his carriage; but his calls were ceremonious and short, and the respectfulness of his deportment towards her had fortified the opinion that she was a Lady of great respectability. Her Brother alone, a gentlemanlike man, had been a frequent guest. I found no reason to suppose that the Brother and Sister-in-law were not really such, and the Colonel's intercourse was too rare and too distantly respectful to make it probable that there was any improper connection between them; but still the want of female friends by a Lady so attractive, and during the whole interesting period of her confinement, was a circumstance of suspicion in my mind not wholly removed by the suggestion that she had come from a remote part of the Kingdom, knowing as I did how abundantly Scotch families were usually possessed of connections or friends in London. My dear Nancy had strongly condemned my doubts on their first intimation and, I blush to say, had piqued me into a kind of resentful curiosity by contrasting this new friend's delicacy with the too open manners of Maria and saying that if I should attempt to flirt with *her* she would treat me as I deserved. For a good while I was neither imprudent nor sinful enough to put this to the test. Bad as I had been, the idea of an intrigue with a married woman would always have been rejected by me with horror; and supposing her not to be such, my penitential resolutions while smarting under the rod of past offences, and trembling for their future consequences, would have made me shrink with terror from the project of my sinful connection with another woman. But I had not yet learnt the danger of approaching the confines of what is wrong and the necessity, or rather the moral duty, of avoiding temptation. It was, therefore, a floating purpose, alternately formed and rejected, that I would one day call on Mrs. B. and ascertain by a little further acquaintance whether she was indeed the character supposed.

Unluckily the opportunity of executing that purpose occurred, at a time when temptation was powerful and reason and conscience more than usually off their guard. I had agreed to make one at a dinner party at Alice's Coffee House in Palace yard, with Perry, Sherridan, Woodfall, and my other brethren the Reporters, to celebrate the close of the Session and make some further compensation to the House for the accomodations we always received there. The same object led us to dine sumptuously and drink rather freely of the best wines; and when we were a good deal elated, tho' not intoxicated, a proposal to adjourn to Vauxhall Gardens met with general consent. We accordingly took boat and with great hilarity proceeded to that place of entertainment, where the music and illuminations did not tend to lower my spirits. Recollecting that I was very near Mrs. B.'s new abode, I hastily determined to give her a call, tho' the hour, if my understanding had been cool, might have deterred me from such a freedom. I gave my Party the slip, called on her, sent in my name, and was very courteously received. I found her alone, in a very graceful undress, with the very lovely infant whom she was then nursing on her lap. She might have sat for the picture of a Madonna, and a beautiful one the likeness would have been. There was a chastity and purity in her appearance that, coupled with the associated ideas of a virtuous matron distant from her natural protector, over-awed me for a moment and tended to put to flight every injurious doubt, and still more every sinful purpose; but my reception was so very gracious, and her eyes told me so plainly that she was pleased with my visit, that I was soon placed at my ease and I willingly accepted her offer to make tea for me. I exerted myself to the utmost to please her with lively and amusing conversation in which my gay spirits assisted; and before I left her to rejoin my companions in the Gardens, we were so much pleased with each other that she cordially gave, and I readily accepted, an invitation to repeat my visit, for which I think an early day was ap-pointed. On a retrospect of this interview, I found cause enough for self-condemnation, but my suspicion of her not being a strictly virtuous woman was in no small degree confirmed; for she had permitted me, with a slight if any opposition, not only to press her hand repeatedly but to salute her lips at parting; and there was enough besides in her eyes and manner to persuade a man less vain that she was not indifferent towards me. Had I been satisfied that she was really the wife of another man, I should have resolved to see her no more; and suspecting the contrary as I did, con-science still suggests that such ought to be my conduct. It may seem strange as well as reproachful that, smarting as I was severely from the consequences of my past sins, and trembling from the danger of still heavier chastisements, and trusting for ultimate deliverance only to the great mercy of

God, I could resist the admonitions of conscience on this
occasion. In fact, I did not steadily resist them. In my
seasons of prayer and those of sober reflection I resolved
aright, but at other times a deceitful heart betrayed me into
doubt and casuistry on the subject. My passions, naturally
ardent, and a highly amorous temperament, inflamed by the
self-denial I was practising, after having long indulged in
opposite habits, made the temptation extremely strong; and
at times I worked myself into a persuasion that the great
violence I was doing to nature could not seriously be required
of me by Him, who had formed me what I was, except when
justice and regard to the happiness of my fellow creatures
commanded to abstain. If this beautiful woman had in fact
no husband, she was probably the Mistress of one who had
no right to her fidelity; and there would be no seduction in
the case, nor probably any deterioration of her morals. As
to the two beloved and injured women who had such strong
claims on my heart, the painful dilemma in which I stood
towards them would not be made worse, nor my power of
future reparation to them more hopeless, by a connection
that would neither be permanent nor of an honorary kind.
They would be ignorant of it. Adherence to a plan which had
their welfare and future happiness for its objects would
become of easier practice, and therefore more certain. As
nobody would be injured, why should I do violence to my
own feelings and those perhaps of a woman who had really
conceived (so vanity whispered) a personal attachment
towards me? Flimsy and unprincipled tho' such reasoning
was, it was strong enough when aided by the impulse of
passion to silence the still small voice of conscience, tho' only
at intervals, and thereby to keep me in an irresolute, vacillat-
ing state, or rather I fear in a secret purpose, secret even to
my own heart, of not withdrawing from temptation and
trusting to the strength of it for my excuse in falling or my
merit in escape; I had not yet been taught (even by my
sufferings) that to cherish sinful imaginations was substantive
guilt, and that God's laws were to be observed irrespectively
of their apparent consequences to our neighbours or ourselves. In other words I had imbibed, tho' Paley had not
then written, the pestilent heresy which resolves into

13*

expediency our religious and moral obligations. After many right tho' short-lived resolutions, and as many vibrations on the opposite side, the natural consequence followed that temptation at length and opportunity together found me during the prevalence of my false views; and I paid another evening visit to Mrs. B., but with a full determination to ascertain whether she was, indeed, a married woman and if so, to abstain from any further intercourse. Either then, or on some subsequent visit, I found a way, which I had indeed preconcerted, to the *ecclaircissement* I desired. Finding her disposed to let me take liberties with her person beyond what a wife or a virtuous woman should have permitted, I paused after some trespasses of that kind, professed not insincerely my compunction for having so offended, and, proceeding to avow my inviolable respect for the marriage tie, declared that if she was really a wife I would not only abstain from taking such liberties in future but shun the irresistable temptation to do so by denying myself the pleasure of any more private interviews with her. The sincerity with which I spoke made its way to her conviction, and before we parted she did not scruple to confess to me that she was not a married woman.

Such a confidence, reposed in me from such obliging motives, was of course not coldly returned: and if the consequences were not such as may be naturally surmised, it was not, alas, from any virtue or prudence on my part in that or several subsequent interviews between us nor from any right feelings on hers. Her language and her conduct were of a kind not to be mistaken. I mean that it clearly implied feelings and desires too commonly dignified with the name of love, and a wish to become to me an object of serious attachment. Yet, to my surprise and perplexity, she would not permit the full gratification of the passion she excited. She allowed me freely and fondly to take every liberty with her person but the very last; but at that point her resistance was obstinate and inflexible. She seemed to take a pleasure in inflaming my desires to the highest pitch and then disappointing them. After treatment of that kind several times repeated, and hardly to be longer endured, she told me that if I would have patience for two or three months I should not afterwards have cause to complain of her. She would not explain her reasons for the delay, but I was satisfied they must be very important ones and could not doubt the sincerity of her promise. I afterwards had an explanation of the mystery, though not from herself. I guessed it, indeed, in a general way, as soon as I found her resistance was not to be affected, but sincere and invincible. I suspected that she was under the protection, as the bad phrase is, of some Gentleman whose distance from her prevented for the time any personal intercourse, and that he was a man of rank or affluence, facts which all the known circumstances seemed to indicate, and that having just weaned her child she was afraid of a natural consequence of my gratification that would betray to him her infidelity, and that she was resolved therefore to postpone it till his return. My conjecture was right; and when I afterwards discovered who was her protector, my surprise at her inflexibility was removed. She had not told me that secret, and I thought it wrong to press her very closely to do so; but the violence of a certain Dutchess, of well-known eccentricity, at length brought it to light. The history of Mrs. B. was this. She was the daughter of persons in a genteel or respectable situation in the North of Scotland, who had given her a good education; and by her person and accomplishments she had so far attracted the liking of the Dutchess of G. as to be taken into her family, either as a humble companion to her Grace, or Governess to her daughters. There she was seduced by the Duke,[1] whose

---

[1] Unless Stephen is misleading with his initial "G" in "the Dutchess of G," this is pretty certainly Alexander Gordon, fourth Duke of Gordon (1743–1827), who at the time of his marriage was reputed to be one of the three handsomest men of his day and who was described by Lord Kames as the greatest subject in Britain, in regard not only to the extent of his rent roll but also of the number of persons depending on his rule and protection. The only other dukes of "G" at the time were the royal Duke of Gloucester and the Duke of Grafton, neither of whom can be fitted into the picture here. The Duke of Gordon's rakish amours were notorious; so, too, were his violent quarrels with his wife, Jane (Maxwell) Duchess of Gordon (1749?–1812), who, in the many years of her bitter estrangement from the Duke—dating from about this time—was celebrated as a beauty and hostess and as a successful matchmaker for her five daughters, three of whom she married to dukes and one to a marquess. If we may believe a story told of her, she paid the Duke in kind for his extramarital misbehaviour. When the second Marquess Cornwallis made a tentative proposal of marriage to her daughter Louisa and expressed some hesitation about marrying her on account of supposed insanity in the Gordon family—

propensities to such crimes were notorious; and when she
became pregnant she was secretly withdrawn from the
family and sent to, or left in, London and by the good
management of Coll. W., his Grace's confidential friend and
I think his relation, was placed with respectable credentials
in the house of Mrs. Heath, as I have already mentioned,
under a feigned name and character, where it was designed
she should remain during her confinement and until the
Duke's return to London. Her Brother-in-law and Sister
were concurrent in the plan; and his reward, I believe, for
acquiescing in the dishonor of his family was a comfortable
place under Government. She was, I doubt not, aware that
she had other rivals than the Dutchess and therefore probably thought herself not very strictly bound to be faithful
to him; but her own interest and her child's, of whom she was
doatingly fond, and that perhaps of her family too, made the
forfeiture of his favor too great an evil to be risked. When my
visits to her commenced, he had returned again for the
Parliamentary recess to his residence in the North, leaving
her in London, and was not to see her again till the commencement of the next Session should call him to the Metropolis. A pregnancy, therefore, in his absence would have
betrayed her infidelity and made of course a decisive breach
between them. The Dutchess, who had discovered both the
intrigue and its fruits, was enraged with jealousy and by the
restless activity of her character found out in the following
winter, some months after the period of time my narrative is
brought to, the retreat of the Mistress and her child. She
had heard, no doubt, how very fine a child it was and
regarded it justly as a bond on the feelings of his Grace which
it was necessary to remove before she could hope to dissolve
the connection. She determined, therefore, on the violent
measure of taking away the child by force, came in a rage to
Mrs. B.'s residence for that purpose, and tho' foiled by her
resistance or flight (for I think she had timely notice of the
intended visit) made an uproar in the house, let out the whole
secret, and ruined the assumed character of the Mother in

the mad Lord George Gordon was a younger brother of the Duke—the Duchess
assured him that she could say positively there was not a drop of Gordon blood
in Louisa.

the neighbourhood, so that she was obliged to change her abode and hide herself anew on the other side of London.

In the meantime my visits to her had been continued; and I must acknowledge, with the guilt of my criminal designs on her person, the egregious folly of thinking I had inspired her with a sincere, lively, and sentimental attachment. Among the means which she found for this purpose was one of a very alarming kind. Looking at me with a fixed and fond regard one day, she surprised me by exclaiming, "O Mr. S., what a pity it is that a Man like you, with your talents &c., should have got himself into such a foolish scrape as you have done with two young women, a union with either of whom would be throwing yourself away and ruining your prospects in life!" On my affecting ignorance of her meaning and demanding explanations, she did not scruple to tell me that she knew the whole secret of my connection with Miss Rivers, as well as my prior engagements to Miss Stent, and gave me the alarming proof of it by asking with an air of affectionate anxiety for the health of my poor child. It was in vain to persist in affecting not to comprehend her or to suppose her in jest. She added circumstances which plainly shewed that the whole case was known to her and convinced me at length that further dissimulation was useless and that to quarrel with her for the imputation on poor Maria would only expose us both to a dangerous resentment. She took care at the same time not only to allay my terrors but to disarm my angry feelings by the strongest assurances that my secret was perfectly safe in her keeping and by putting her mention of the subject on the kind and obliging ground of her wish to ease my distressed feelings in regard to the child by aiding me in its preservation; to which end she made, and pressed upon me, the offer of herself becoming its nurse if I would place it in her hands. It is impossible for me *now* to believe that she was sincere in desiring such a charge, which must of course have soon become known to the Duke and could not have been reconciled with his feelings and his confidence in her fidelity; but I did not then know of her connection with his Grace and was not sure, tho' I suspected, that she was under any such protection. I might indeed have concluded that she could not overlook the impossibility of my reconciling the Mother's feelings to such a proposal, and this ground of distrust did in fact occur to me; but her apparent sincerity, and the vain persuasion that a strong attachment to myself had made her blind at the moment to that difficulty, inclined me to give her credit for really desiring to win me by so condescending and interesting a kindness. She knew my situation and prospects too well to have any mercenary views; and vanity, therefore, was willing to ascribe the offer to a tender sympathy for my parental sufferings, prompted by an ardent and generous affection. The discovery she had made to me produced one effect which she possibly foresaw. It gave a new excuse to my self-deceiving conscience for not renouncing acquaintance or intercourse with her. As she had the power of being a fatal enemy, it was necessary to preserve her as a friend and to have her own character at my mercy as a safeguard to Maria's; and this consideration certainly did weigh powerfully with me when in my better moments I was sometimes strongly inclined to listen to the admonitions of conscience and see her no more. By what means she had obtained her information I strove in vain to learn. It was a point on which she inflexibly resisted my most earnest solicitations, but I could pretty well collect that she knew my secret before the commencement of our acquaintance, and it is probable that the very flattering reception that I met with from her was rather favor'd then opposed by the discovery. With women of her character, a triumph over the virtue of other women, instead of inspiring dislike or distrust, is in general positive recommendation.

In this very dangerous case, as in others which I recollect with strong emotions of gratitude to God as well as with shame and self-condemnation, I was providentially rescued from the moral mischiefs into which I was rushing by the gracious interposition of obstacles between me and my sinful purpose till the voice of conscience could be deliberately heard and meet my too powerful passions in an equal field, such as strong temptations did not afford to them. Often has been verified to me that scriptural promise, that He who has appointed for us this state of trial "will not suffer us to be tempted beyond what we are able to bear, but will with the temptation make a way for our escape that we may be able to bear it." The temptation would probably at this time have been beyond my moral strength, certainly beyond my resistance, if the same fellow sinner who excited my passions had not invincibly opposed that full gratification of them which I have much reason to think would have sealed my ruin and perdition. When I reflect on its natural effects, I am almost sure that it would have turned me out of that path of prudence and reformation on the pursuit of which my temporal, and probably my eternal, salvation depended. The Enemy of my Soul would have bound me with new and indissoluble chains. I should have forfeited all my salutary influence with poor Maria and all the means of rescuing her from the dreadful consequences of my sins, perhaps also the determined will to repair to her and to my dear Nancy when possible the wrongs I had done to them both. My principles might have become thoroughly perverted and my heart incurably hardened. Happy, therefore, was it for me that Mrs. B. continued to act the same extraordinary part till the violent conduct of the Dutchess, and I presume some consequent measures of the Duke, removed her out of my reach and left me for months ignorant of the place of her abode. Meantime my consciencious feelings, or rather let me say my love and fear of God, had been strongly reinforced by his own conspicuous mercies in the preservation of my child and by my sense of continual dependance on his compassion and favor in that and the other anxious interests of my heart. My power of self-command, also, in respect of the sin that most easily beset me progressively gained strength by exercise, and my penitential resolutions by prayer, and by the peace and hope with which adherence to them was followed. But after being thus prepared for new trials, it pleased God that I should meet them. Mrs. B. returned to, or appeared again, under the same feigned character, in London and took care that I should not be ignorant where she might be found. It was clear to me that there would now no longer be any obstacle to the immediate gratification of my desires if I could prevail on my own mind to allow of it. Again there was a war within me in which, tho' conscience was in the main victorious, it was often on the point of yielding. Sinful views and self-delusive reasonings recurred. "Why should I practise a self-denial extremely painful in itself, and, as I often thought, injurious to my health when no bad consequences were likely to follow from giving way to the propensities of Nature?" True, I had resolved on such abstinence and prayed earnestly for strength to persevere. But might not this be superstition? What reason had I to believe that God really required a line of conduct so opposite to the dictation of those desires and passions which he, as the author of my Nature, had implanted within me? And then, what dangers might redound to poor Maria's character if I acted in a way to make an enraged enemy of Mrs. B. by the affront of slighting the promise she had made me! I knew enough of female character to think it not too strongly marked by the Poet (Rowe, I think, in his tragedy of *Jane Shore*),

> *Earth has no spite, like love to hatred turned,*
> *Nor Hell a Fury, like a woman scorned.*[1]

In my better frames of mind I saw the fallacy and the impiety of such views, retracted them with renewed penitence, and resolved aright; but I had not yet learnt and habitually impressed on my mind that the indulgence of sinful imaginations is a substantive crime, tho' they lead to no guilty action. I did not, therefore, sufficiently put the rein on my thoughts and desires. I did not purify the fountain. I did not enough consider either that sin was in its essence, independently of its consequence to others, an offence against the Divine Lawgiver. My primary objection was not like Joseph's, "How can I do this great wickedness & sin against God!" Sometimes, indeed, such right principles occurred to my reflections but not steadily and with sufficient force. The revealed law, in fact, had too little weight with me when its correspondence with the law of nature written on the heart was not distinctly visible. To say, like our Saviour when under temptation, "*It is written*," was a higher degree of reverence for Scripture than I had attained. And here let

---

[1] Stephen, quoting from memory, is not completely accurate, and is wrong in the attribution to Rowe. The lines are from Congreve's *The Mourning Bride*, Act III, Scene 8, where they read:

> *Heaven has no rage like love to hatred turned,*
> *Nor hell a fury like a woman scorned.*

me remark how miserably defective and erroneous are such narrow views as I then entertained, *even on their own principles.* I cannot recollect that it once occurred to me to consider that I was responsible for the immoral conduct of her who was to be the accomplice of the meditated sin, that it would involve her in deceit and perfidy towards the Duke who, notwithstanding the criminal nature of their intercourse, had claims upon *her*, while it lasted, for fidelity. I considered only that he had no claim on *my* forbearance, and I fear was rather invited than deterred by the idea of rivalling and supplanting *him* who, as a married man, well deserved such treatment. I think, indeed, the fear of consequences to *her* in the possible loss of his favor, and her becoming thereby a completely abandoned woman, had with me no inconsiderable influence; but then I remembered that she had shewn herself to have, in this regard, much prudence and circumspection, by which such consequences I thought might be easily avoided.

It may seem difficult to reconcile such parleys with temptation, and such deliberate reasonings on the side of sin, with the fact that I was at the same period under the influence of strong devotional and penitential feelings. Yet, certain it is that I was thus strongly inconsistent, or to speak more accurately thus fluctuating between piety and guilt. The same day, nay the same hour perhaps, I was on my knees before God, acknowledging with no unfeigned emotions of gratitude and love his great goodness in averting from me the just punishment of my past sins, and deprecating earnestly their future very probable consequences to myself and those I most loved, and yet soon after equivocating with conscience and conceiving, if not actually contriving, a new offence of the same kind. I did not, indeed, say to myself, "I will dare to offend God again in the same way," but fancied, when imagination and passion seized the loosened reins, that God would not really be offended, because my duties to my fellow creatures would not be equally, or in any degree perhaps, transgressed and because he would make allowances for the strong and almost irresistable propensities by which I was impelled. I am the rather led to disclose these bosom secrets, opprobrious tho' they are, because they will be found

to support, or at least to elucidate, a moral theory of great
importance, suggested to me by long experience, and of the
truth of which I am fully persuaded. It is that the decadency
or advance of our moral characters depends mainly, if not
wholly, on our practical decision of *apparently doubtful cases of
conduct*, when the pleadings of passion or inclination are
strong on the one hand, and the admonitions of conscience
so powerful on the other, that the mind is placed in a nearly
equal balance between them and our free will is barely able
to determine which scale shall descend. So far I am probably
only adopting theories already current; but I further believe
that this power of free will to decide apparently doubtful
cases is in truth all the power that it possesses, that the
doctrine of moral necessity is well founded when the preponderance of the impelling or of the restraining motives is
clear, and that the power of the will to give *a casting vote* is
enough for all the purposes of moral culture and enough to
render us justly responsible as free agents for all the sins
that we commit in this our state of trial. To explain fully this
theory, to prove its truth, and to obviate apparent objections
in this place, would be to suspend my narrative too long;
and should I find room for such a dissertation in these
memoirs it will be better understood in the sequel, when I
shall have developed many cases in my own history illustrative of the views I hold.

The internal conflict from the relation of which I have
digressed is one of those cases. It was a balance, or rather an
equal oscillation of purpose, between opposite and powerful
motives. The line of moral duty, indeed, was plain enough.
In that respect the case certainly was not doubtful in its
nature; but the strength of the temptation and the casuistry
which passion suggested made it *apparently* so to me at the
time and this is enough to bring it within my theory. The
struggle between conscience and sinful desire in this instance
was highly critical to my moral character. If I had formed a
criminal connection with Mrs. B. the effects would probably
have been fatal to my soul, and more surely to my temporal
welfare and peace. I should hardly have again resumed the
thorny path of self-denial by which I had escaped, and by
which alone I could possibly have escaped, from the toils

in which sin had involved me. I should probably have
become hardened in vice and regardless of its consequences
to myself and others; or, to express all and far worse than
all this in other words, the strivings of the Spirit, the work-
ings of Divine Grace in my heart, might have been finally
suppressed. My escape was a very difficult and narrow one.
In the conscious power of gratifying without delay a powerful
passion, the Tempter had great vantage ground of me. The
grand danger of temptation with all men I suppose, certainly
with *me*, is the presence of nearness of its object. I knew and
felt that if I renewed my private visits to Mrs. B. my fall was
certain. In my prayers, therefore, and in all my seasons of
right moral feelings and reflection, my resolution was to
avoid her; but sometimes different views prevailed and they
once carried me so far as to call on her at her new abode,
when my reception was such as sufficed to prove to me that
she was not forgetful of her promise, nor indisposed to fulfill
it. But happily opportunity did not then coincide with
temptation. Further time, therefore, was given for the admonitions of conscience and the influence of prayer. I felt
new and deep contrition for having violated my penitential
resolves by the interview itself. It was a presumption which
I felt deserved and, if repeated, would draw down on me
Divine indignation. If I rightly remember, also, my penitence was reinforced by the then condition of my dear, unfortunate child, when the hopes I had begun to conceive of
his recovery increased my sense of the great mercy of God,
and at the same time of my dependency on his kind providence, in that very anxious concern of my heart.

Without further attempting to delineate these bosom
conflicts let me with humble gratitude record the ultimate
event. It pleased God to give me the victory over this
dangerous temptation. I was enabled at length to adhere to
the resolution that I would call on Mrs. B. no more. I still
felt the danger of her resentment but trusted, and not in
vain, that my prayers for poor, dear Maria's exemption from
its consequences would be answered. Mrs. B. was, no doubt,
indignant at my conduct; but I never found reason to suspect
that she had attempted to revenge herself by promulging
what she had discovered. Indeed, she had no longer any

intercourse with those who knew us. The Dutchess's conduct had exposed her in their neighbourhood; and tho' she had the confidence afterwards to call on my dear Nancy at her Father's house, her reception was such as prevented any repetition of the visit. To Maria, fortunately, she had never been personally known. So it was that I found in right conduct exemption from a dreaded evil, which the sinful means that seemed to give the best promise of averting it would probably not have prevented, but justly drawn down upon me. Many such instances of a righteous and benignant course of Providence have occurred in my eventful life. I never afterwards heard, or sought to learn, what were the subsequent fortunes of Mrs. B. About seven years after this period when I returned from the West Indies to spend a winter in England, I saw her, not much altered in appearance, walking on the opposite side of a road to that on which I was passing in the same direction and perceived her to enter a creditable looking house in a way that seemed to indicate that it was her home; but she did not see me and, tho' curiosity suggested a wish to know her then situation and character, stronger and better motives prevented my accosting her or making enquiries, as from my knowledge of the neighbourhood I could easily have done with effect. May penitence and reformation have characterized her after life! Often has that wish been turned into a prayer when I have thought of her, accompanied with thanksgiving for my narrow escape from a connection that would probably have been fatal to us both.

I will now return from the history of my sins and temptations to that of my exterior fortunes in life.

My dear Brother not only relieved me by his remittance from all present pecuniary difficulties but assured me of being regularly supplied with an adequate income to enable me to resume and prosecute advantageously my plan of professional life. He kindly insisted on my immediately giving up my employment as a Reporter and allowing him to supply all my expences till I should be called to the Bar and able to support myself by practice. From his partial views of my talents he doubted not of my progressively rising to independence and affluence as a Counsel in this Country; but if not, he thought it would be a sure *dernier resort* to follow his own migration, and that at the bar of St. Kitts I should be sure of making a fortune, for he was in the common error of greatly over-rating the profits of West India Lawyers. I was not slow to accept his affectionate offers and follow his advice so far as to give up my connection with the Newspaper, of which I was sufficiently weary, to resume my termkeeping at Lincoln's Inn, and to attend the Courts and read law again with as much industry as I could well reconcile with the secret concerns here developed, and with necessary attentions to my dear Nancy on the one hand and Miss Rivers on the other, which unavoidably diverted no small portion of my time. But I knew better than my dear Bill did, how difficult and doubtful would be my success at the English bar and how long at best the experiment would make me an incumbrance upon his purse. I, therefore, and from the desire of being with him, resolved at once that the West India bar should be my field and was confirmed in the resolution by that unfortunate entanglement which he had yet to learn, and from which an early migration afforded the most probable means of escape. The delay was not to be long, for I think at the time of adopting this plan I had only three or four Terms to keep before I could be called to the bar. I did not conceal from my dear Brother the history of my sins since our seperation and of their very embarrassing consequences. I knew that the secret was safe in his faithful breast; and besides that I could not bear to treat him with reserve and thought it would be wrong to do so in a case so likely to affect my future fortunes in life and the weight of my dependency on him. I felt the more deciding consideration that the only hope of my poor Infant for support and protection in the event of my early death rested on my dear Bill's warm and generous affections. I therefore, wrote to him the whole truth and requested an assurance from him that if my child should become an orphan before I found means to provide for him he would act towards him a Father's part. In reply he kindly acceded to that request and said all that was best calculated to soothe and tranquilize my mind under the sufferings I had divulged to him. He admitted that the painful predicament I was placed in was a powerful argument for migration and acquiesced in my purpose of going to St. Christopher as soon as I could be called to the bar.

An unexpected public event soon after occurred to delay the execution of that plan and to threaten it with entire frustration. The French, having gained a naval superiority in the West Indies, made a sudden descent on St. Christopher and, after a pretty long resistance by the Fortress of Brimstone Hill, made an entire conquest of the Island.[1] The first intelligence of the invasion was to me alarming enough, but I had soon the satisfaction to learn by letters from my dear Brother that he was not in any personal danger. The division of the Militia to which he belonged (for in the West Indies every white man, or rather every *free* man, who has no other military character is a militia man) was not, I believe, marched in good time into that only defensible Fortress; or else my Brother was by some accident too late, for he was in the Town of Sandy Point where he resided when the enemy, by a rapid movement at midnight, seized on that Town almost as soon as their first landing was heard of by its inhabitants. They were treated with liberality, but disarmed of course and obliged to engage under pain of death not to serve against the invaders pending the contest. As the Town was immediately occupied by a large detachment and the Army, under the Marquis de Boullie, which formed the Siege of Brimstone Hill, soon opened trenches in the neighbourhood, most of the inhabitants of Sandy Point who could find any Asylum in parts of the Island more distant from the seat of military operations did so; and my Brother thought himself fortunate in finding a comfortable retreat on the Estate of Sir Ralph Payne, afterwards Lord Lewington, on the North side of the Island, the Manager of which was his friend. It was an incident very important to him in his after life. The Somersall Family, also refugees from Sandy Point, took shelter in the same house; and they all continued there during the very interesting period of the Siege of Brimstone Hill, which lasted, I think, six weeks. The family, in addition to Mr. Somersall, Senior, and his Wife, a venerable looking couple far advanced in age, and their Son,

[1] Admiral de Grasse conquered St. Christopher in a decisive victory over Admiral Hood in January and February, 1782.

then the most eminent Merchant of the Island, comprised Mr. and Mrs. Forbes and the daughter of the old People and their children, the eldest of whom was a very pretty young woman then about fifteen. Whether there had previously been anything particular in my brother's feelings towards that young Lady, I forget; but thrown together as they were under such interesting circumstances, and with no employment but that of entertaining each other, a mutual attachment naturally enough ensued; and before Brimston Hill surrendered to the French my Brother had made an absolute surrender of his heart to the pretty Miss Polly Forbes and in return for my more guilty secrets wrote to me that he was deeply in love with her and was resolved if possible to make her his Wife, tho' he feared he should be obliged to do so without obtaining her Father's consent. Apparently the attachment was liable to no objection in point of prudence on either side. My Brother, in addition to his Uncle's fortune, the amount of which was as usual greatly magnified by report, had succeeded to all his medical practice and was, as he deserved to be, a great favorite both in his professional and private character, and withal a very handsome young man. As to the Lady, it was supposed she would have a good portion and her prospects of future patrimony were thought to be very considerable, for her Father was not only regarded as a prosperous Merchant but had Estates in Demerara. She had, indeed, three Brothers, then all yet boys; but she was an only daughter and a prime favorite, not only with the Grandfather but the Uncle, Mr. William Somersall, who were both supposed to be very wealthy men. The latter, who had passed the prime of life, was a bachelor and likely always to remain so, having from his youth been attached to a mulatto, or Indian woman, by whom he had several children; but these, according to the manners and morals of the Country, were not likely to be his, much less his Father's, Heirs or to stand materially in the way of white, tho' collateral, kindred. The firm of Somersall & Son was the oldest and most eminent in the Leeward Islands, and part of their supposed wealth was already realized in the purchase of a valuable sugar Plantation. In short, Polly Forbes was thought the most desirable match the Island afforded and, among other reasons, because her Mother, whose character stood high for prudence and all other moral qualities valued in that Society, was understood to have taken great pains with her education and to have made her rival in accomplishments, the young Ladies brought up in Europe. All this my Brother had heard, even from his cautious Uncle; and all this, with the garnishments of a lover's fancy, he related to me.

I loved him too well not to simpathise with his good fortune cordially, since it was plain from his statements that this well-placed attachment was by no means discouraged by the young Lady herself; and yet I could not but feel that if he was soon to become a married man the weight of necessary obligation to him in pecuniary matters would not sit so light upon me as it had hitherto done. This feeling fortified my purpose of migrating in search of independence as soon as possible and made me regard with impatience the obstacle cast in my way by the French conquest. But it was an obstacle which I could not surmount consistently with my dear Brother's advice, for tho' by the capitulation the English laws were retained, law business was put nearly to a stand, the war between English Creditors and West India Debtors being suspended in great measure while the former were alien enemies to the foreign Government, under which the latter and their mortgaged Estates were placed. We justly anticipated that the War was drawing to a close, that the captured Islands would probably be restored at the Peace, and that I should then find the St. Christopher bar as good or a better field of practice than it had ever been. Meantime, the delay gave me an opportunity of increasing my small stock of professional knowledge by reading and attending the Courts; and tho' I did not improve it as I ought to have done, I learned a good deal that was essential perhaps to my subsequent success. No small portion of my time, indeed, was unavoidably diverted from study by engagements with the two dear Women to whose satisfaction and peace my society was not less necessary than ever. They resided at a considerable distance from each other and my attentions of course were seperately paid to each; and tho' they both felt and admitted the necessity of my persevering an intercourse with

their rival in my affections, it was not easy to satisfy either
that she had her fair portion of my time, or that a larger
was not given to the other. I loved them both too well not
to be much gratified with their company, and as to Maria
the anxious interest I felt in directing her conduct would have
made me solicitous for her society even if her hold on my
affections had been lost. Yet when fear of censorious observation, or attention to my professional studies, or any other
cause, occasioned any considerable interval between my
visits, jealousies and discontents and gusts of passion would
arise which cost me no small uneasiness. My influence over
both their minds was irresistable when put forth with the
ardour of persuasion or expostulation that I could then when
necessary command. But the exertion was painful; and I felt
in this respect, as well as others, the slavery to which sin had
reduced me. My tenderest affections, tho' cordially returned,
were sources of pain rather than joy to me and to their
unfortunate objects. I might probably have sought for relief,
and fatally found it, in dissipation (the paths of which, so
far at least as public amusements went, were very open to
me) had it not pleased a gracious Providence to make that
resort disgustful and alarming to me by certain occurrences,
when the opposition of prudence and conscience, and even
taste, was in most danger of being overcome. I was tempted,
for instance, by the facility of getting tickets through my
late newspaper connections gratuitously, to go to masquerades, which to my romantic imagination had more
attractions than any other public amusements. I went to a
grand one at Madame Corelli's rooms, which I think was
the last I ever attended, in the character of a Scotch Highland Chief, which from my knowledge of Scotch and Scotland I thought myself well qualified to support, and I was,
at least, one of the most noisy characters in the rooms. At an
advanced hour of the Morning, when I was passing from one
of the brilliant and crowded rooms into another in which
they were dancing, I heard a sudden uproar and, directing
my eyes to the quarter it came from, saw my friend Perry,
afterwards Editor of the *Morning Chronicle*, receive a blow
from a Gentleman, who immediately after was seperated
from him by a rush of the crowd and was passing towards

the apartment I came from. Yielding to the impulse of the moment I sprang towards him, caught him by the collar, and declared he should pass no further till the friend of mine whom he had struck should come up. He expostulated and struggled, but I was firm to my purpose, and, holding my Highland "Chapping stick," or bludgeon, over his head, declared I would knock him down if he did not quietly wait till my friend could make his way to us. The threat was neither needless nor ineffectual, for I found that I had a powerful man in my grasp; and so dense a crowd collected by the noise from different rooms had by this time intervened between Perry and us that many minutes elapsed before he could make way towards his antagonist; but the latter, intimidated perhaps by my threats and military appearance, no longer struggled to escape from me, tho' he loudly demanded that I should unhand him. I soon found it necessary to do so, on condition of his giving me his name and address, for the crowd around us began to be offended with my violence and to take his part, so far at least as to think that I ought to be satisfied with that condition. He gave me, accordingly, his card with his name, Mr. O'Dwyer, and his address, and I was proceeding to give him mine when Perry, having at length forced a passage through the crowd and seeing his assailant, rushed forward to take his revenge. Many who wished for a pugilistic exhibition cried for a ring, but it was impossible to make one; and I said to Perry, "Never mind; I have got his address." He replied, "What is it?" and, on my reading the card, exclaimed "The Scoundrel! He has given *me* a different name!" The Gentlemen around us on this ceased to feel for him and were desirous of making way for Perry to take his revenge on the spot, for which purpose I also exerted myself and my chapping stick, when a formidable ally of the aggressor forced himself through the throng, a man above six feet high of military appearance, who announced himself as Captn. Cashel of the Guards and a friend of Mr. O'Dwyer, declaring that such was our antagonist's real name, demanding ours in return, and intimating that the affair must be settled as became Gentlemen and in another place. This, alas, we were not disposed to decline. The event, therefore, was an interchange of addresses and an appointment by Perry and me to await the call of Captn. Cashel at Perry's lodgings at a fixed hour the next Morning. When able to learn from Perry the cause of the fracas, I found reason enough to regret my violent interference, tho' he warmly applauded it as friendly and spirited conduct. The unworthy subject of quarrel was no other than a woman of bad character with whom O'Dwyer had been dancing, but who chose afterwards to prefer P. as a partner; and the jealousy or resentment of the former led him to act with the violence I had witnessed, after much reciprocal provocation that had previously led to an exchange of addresses, in which O'Dwyer had given a fictitious one from prudent or cowardly feelings. I felt that it would have been much better to let the artifice succeed than to involve my Friend and myself in further danger from the consequences of a disreputable quarrel. When returned to my chambers and to a sober tone of spirits, my reflections were painful enough; and I felt not only dissatisfaction with myself but disgust at those scenes of dissipation that were productive of such follies and sins. Repentance and earnest prayer ensued; but however inconsistent and however impious it may justly be thought, my remorse did not prevent my rising at an hour sufficiently early (after a short and broken sleep) to keep my appointment at Perry's and with a purpose of risking my life if necessary to avoid dishonor. This necessity it was most likely I should meet, for Captn. Cashel had expressly regarded me as a principal in the quarrel on account of the violence I had offered to his friend; and all that I could bring my mind to was to avoid a duel myself and prevent Perry from fighting, if it could be done without disgrace. To incur the reproach of cowardice rather than offend God was a pitch of virtuous resolution at that time, and alas for many years after, quite above my reach. But my prayers (for strange tho' it may seem I *did* pray, on this and many similar occasions in life, to be rescued from a dilemma in which impious pride alone involved me) were heard, or at least the amazing compassion of Divine Providence saved me from willful and perhaps fatal perseverance in a sinful purpose. Captn. Cashel and his friend O'Dwyer did not keep the appointment with punctuality. They perhaps felt like ourselves (for Perry was very plainly of my own opinion, tho' I fear on different principles) that it was a business better got rid of than pursued. We waited for them a quarter of an hour or twenty minutes after the appointed hour and then went out. They some time after called and left their cards, and there the matter ended.

This incident, and the penitent reflections excited by it, were greatly, and I think decisively, instrumental to my total abandonment of those dangerous scenes of public amusement and dissipation to which, in truth, I was not very strongly inclined before.

A danger and escape of the same kind occurred not long after, which I think it right also with humiliation and gratitude to a long-suffering gracious Providence to record. I was spending an Evening at a Coffee House with the same friend, Perry, and Felix McCarthy, when the latter took violent offence at a ludicrous anecdote I told of him, not very decent in its character, or rather at the burst of laughter which it excited at his expense. He grew so angry as to forget all his usual consideration for me and at length in broad terms to give me the lie, with other offensive expressions. I left the room with a feeling that it was indispensably necessary to call him to honorary account for it and went to Richardson to engage him to carry a message from me the same evening, requesting a meeting in the Morning. But providentially Richardson was not at home. I went to my chambers in doubt whether to wait for his return or apply to some other friend and had not been long there before Perry came with an apology from McCarthy, which his friendly remonstrances had with difficulty brought M. to feel the duty of after my departure, and an offer to beg my pardon if I would return to the same place. This, of course, I cordially accepted as sufficient satisfaction; and well I might, for never, I believe, before or after, did McCarthy ever recede in any degree from the provocations he had given. It was the strongest possible proof of his regard for me, but had my message previously arrived no persuasion, I am sure, would have led him to avoid a duel.

This Man's history having a connection with some future

parts of my own, I will here mention that we soon after prevailed on him to embrace the only opportunity that opened to him of extricating himself from disreputable idleness and bad connections in London and embarking in the only occupation he seemed fit for, a military one, by going to France, where some of his Irish Catholic Friends in Count Dillon's Brigade obtained his admission into that corps as a Cadet with promises of early promotion. He continued in that situation a year or two and was well liked, I believe, by his commanding officers for a while and, I think, got a Commission; but his usual indiscretions clung to him and in two instances very nearly proved fatal to him. Happily, perhaps, for himself and many others had they been so. Being stationed in one of the fortified towns in French Flanders, he rode into the Country one day on some pleasurable excursion and did not return in due time, so that when he arrived at the Gates of the Town the Drawbridge was drawn up. It being dark, and he perhaps elevated by drinking, he did not perceive this and passing forward fell with his horse into a deep Fosse. The horse was killed and he very nearly so. A sentinel on the ramparts gave the alarm. The Gates were opened and he was taken up apparently lifeless. It was thought little short of a miracle that, tho' dreadfully bruised, the vital spark was yet perceptible. By means of copious and often repeated bleedings, and at the expense of several Months confinement, his life was saved and his strength at last restored; but violent pains in his interior, which he for years afterwards felt, proved that the escape was a most narrow one. In his debilitated state he had, I believe, strong compensations for the sins of his past life and formed resolutions of amendment. I doubt not it was a dispensation mercifully intended for his reformation, but such means when resisted are by the just judgments of God permitted to harden still more the Sinner whom they do not reclaim. Again, however, and not long after his recovery, another awful visitation was employed and doubtless to the same end. At the mess room of the officers he was mad enough to contradict one of them, a Lieutt. Mahoney, who was praising their Colonel, Count Dillon, and to reflect upon him for drawing his sword against his native land, a theme the most offensive of course to all around him and in him the most inconsistent, for I suppose the whole corps he had joined were liable to service against this Country, tho' of that I am not sure. His abuse, however, of the Commanding officer before those who looked up to him for preferment was of course an affront to be avenged. Mahoney beckoned him out and demanded that he should instantly go to a neighbouring field and give him satisfaction. McCarthy, knowing that this antagonist was the best swordsman in the Brigade, proposed that they should first get pistols, he being, as Mahoney well knew, a mere novice at fencing. The other sarcastically observed that as their quarrel was public the going back for pistols was a sure way to be put under arrest, upon which M. indignantly replied that rather than risk that he would give him the advantage he sought. They fought with their swords and M. soon received a desperate wound quite through the abdomen, the sword actually passing out on the opposite side. No doubt was entertained by the Surgeons that the wound must prove mortal, but again his Herculean constitution saved him. He was confined, however, many Months to his bed and on his recovery received a message from Count Dillon that the King had no further occasion for his services. During his confinement his sufferings, as I afterwards heard him say, were dreadful but much less from the effects of his wound than from the recurrence and aggravation of the pains produced from his former contusions. He was reduced to a state of extreme debility and doubtless was for a while again penitent. This was probably the crisis of his spiritual maladies and the termination was fatal. He relapsed into his besetting sins, returned to London, and by a rapid progress became the totally abandoned character that I shall hereafter have occasion to portray. But it is high time I should return to the narrative of my own life, and I hope with fewer digressions.

Chapter Twelve
[1782–1783]

IN 1782 I was called to the Bar[1] but made no serious attempt to get into practice, tho' my dear Brother offered to sustain me if I chose in doing so. In fact, I knew that the attempt would have been hopeless; and besides my strong repugnance to remaining an incumbrance on him, now become a married man, migration seemed the only means of delivering myself from the truly embarrassing and painful dilemma in which my sins had placed me. But to go to St. Christopher before the restitution of an English Government there would have been to throw away time to no purpose, and that event did not take place till near the close of 1783. I therefore made use of my gown and wig to increase by attendance on the Courts my little stock of professional knowledge tho', except one Motion of course in the King's Bench and one Brief at the Surrey Assizes given by an Attorney of my acquaintance, I was merely a looker-on and an auditor and employed my vacations in reading lawbooks, but by no means so diligently as I ought.

When the Summer of 1783 arrived I was at length called on to make preparations for the important change before me, as the Peace was conclusively made and the Islands conquered by the French in the West Indies were to be restored, I think, within six months after the ratification of the Treaty. The most anxious subjects of arrangement, of course, were those which regarded the two dear Women whom my absence would most importantly affect, and my helpless unfortunate infant. It was impossible to regard the probable consequences of my absence to them without the most painful apprehensions. They would no longer have the benefit of my hitherto successful management, of my strong personal influence, or of my timely advice on any emergency. I should leave them exposed to many and fearful dangers, the natural fruits of my sins, especially those frightful moral

[1] Stephen was called to the Bar January 26, 1782. See Leslie Stephen, *Life of Sir James Fitzjames Stephen*, p. 14.

evils to which Maria's beauty and imprudence might subject her. Tho' my dear Nancy was in these respects less, or not at all, an object of anxiety it was impossible to reflect upon what was likely to be her situation after my departure without pain and self-reproach. However sure I might be of her confidence in my present right feelings and intentions, my conduct had given her too much reason to distrust their stability; and in the opinions of those whose sentiments and feelings on the subject were of vast importance to her comfort and welfare my going abroad without making her my wife was likely to be construed as abandonment and disgrace. Her Brother, who knew the unhappy and guilty cause, was not likely to adopt her own confidence in my future conduct, or even in my present motives. He, indeed, was then in a distant part of the world and probably would not soon, if ever, return to England; but so much the worse for her feelings if I left her without his affectionate support and protection to the mortifications she would have to endure. As to her Father we had found much reason to surmise that he had discovered or suspected the whole alarming truth. His paternal apprehensions, therefore, were likely to be very painful and perhaps to make a distressing change in his conduct towards my poor Nancy, which ever since the reconciliation had been remarkably liberal and kind. He would probably regard her as the just victim of former disobedience. But the most alarming consideration of all was that if from these causes friendly intercourse between my dear Nancy and Maria should be cut off the latter during my absence would not have a single friend on whose principles and judgment I could rely for advising and assisting her on any emergency, still less one possessed of our secret and through whose aid therefore she might relieve her maternal feelings by occasionally seeing her child, or obtaining frequent accounts of him without danger to her character. To allay my own parental anxieties it was no less necessary that there should be some confidential friend on whose affection I could entirely rely to visit the child, to watch over his treatment and send me frequent accounts of his health. But how could I expect such offices from my dear Nancy, or rather how could she possibly perform them with safety to her character and her estima-

tion by her Father without his consent and co-operation;
and what hope could there be of his concurrence while he
might reasonably doubt whether the man on whom she
conferred such delicate and suspicious obligations would
identify her honor and happiness with his own? The final
result in my mind of these embarrassing and painful reflections was a conviction that the best or only way in which I
could guard both Maria and her child from the dangerous
and probably fatal effects of my absence was privately to
seal my engagement to Miss S. by marriage before my
departure, but by the nuptial ceremony alone, provided this
could be done without risking the terrible consequences of its
discovery by Maria, taking Mr. S. entirely into our confidence and thereby obtaining his consent that unless in the
event of Maria's marriage or death the secret should never
be disclosed. About the same time I discovered what was
providentially unknown to me before, the facility with which
a clandestine marriage could be solemnized in London
without any danger of public detection. I found Mr. S. and
my dear Nancy in deep distress and astonishment at the
discovery that his youngest Son William, then not above
18 years old, had been seduced into a private marriage with a
girl still younger, the daughter of a neighbouring tradesman.
Mr. S. hoped it could not be legal because it was solemnized
by banns in a Parish in which neither of them had ever
resided, but upon researches into the facts and law of the
case we found that the knot was effectually tied. Lodgings
had been taken for a Month preceding in their respective
names and the certificate of this, tho' they had never once
slept there or even had an hour's possession of the lodgings,
was enough to satisfy the Parish Clergyman and to get their
names inserted in such a long list of banns, the Parish being
very populous, that even if they had had friends in the congregation the matter would most probably have passed un-
noticed. I was not before aware of the extreme impotence of
that bad law, the Marriage Act, in this respect, the fact of
residence not being necessary, as I had supposed, to the
validity of the marriage. Had I known this two years sooner
Maria would in all probability have been my wife. I now
saw that the plan I had begun to meditate upon was far

14

more easily practicable than I had supposed. A license could not have been obtained, tho' we were both of age, without official means of detection; and a journey to Scotland would have opened chances of discovery still more probable.

When I had made up my mind on the subject all difficulties were easily removed. My dear Nancy loved me too fondly to have any reluctance on her part. Such also was her generosity and her feelings for her unfortunate rival that I believe she would have been less disposed to consent to an open marriage if that could have been proposed. She did not hesitate to acquiesce cordially in all my terms and among them one that was essential to my purpose tho' not yet mentioned, *viz.*, that if ever by the death or marriage of Maria she should be acknowledged as my Wife the child should be at the same time acknowledged as the first fruit of our union, an object which strengthened the necessity of forming it in a way that would make the date of it unknown. She annexed to that concession, however, a condition to which I readily agreed. I gave her my promise that if there should be children of our marriage my first born should have no benefit of primogeniture, but that in the disposition of any property I might give or bequeath, he, though reputed an eldest Son, should not be preferred to the rest. Mr. Stent, when under the most solemn engagements of secrecy he was informed of the whole case and of my proposals, acted with perfect liberality and kindness. I had obtained a strong hold on his affections, and tho' it was lessened perhaps by some doubts and suspicions that he had begun as we feared to conceive as to my intercourse with Maria and the uprightness of my intentions towards his daughter, the confidence reposed in him and my offer together removed all distrust on that score and he admited fully the rectitude on my part of the conditions on which the union was proposed. I frankly avowed to him my intentions, which were rather to die in exile than return to England in the painful dilemma in which I then stood or avow my marriage while Maria was living and single, but said that with my earliest ability I would make such remittances to him for my dear Nancy's use as should relieve him from the charge of her support. He, on the other hand, spontaneously promised that until it was perfectly convenient to me to maintain her as my wife he would make her as ample an allowance as I wished and that he would concur with her in paying the best attention to my child, and also to Maria, in my absence, promises which he faithfully performed. He was in truth a very kind-hearted, generous man and had a liberality of sentiment far beyond what his education, circumstances, and station in life gave reason to expect. As an instance of it, he had an old Aunt who had been kind to him in his earliest years; and he maintained her in return during many years and till her death in a very comfortable way, giving her an annual allowance which he could often ill afford and with such privacy that it was long unknown even to his daughter. She was a pious woman, and he owed to her, I believe, early religious impressions of which he is now I trust receiving the benefit in a happier world. I cannot defend his moral conduct in all points after that cruel injury which left him when still a young man a husband without a wife; but he did not exceed the measure of offence against an unbending law into which strong temptation led him, avoided scandal and ill example in it with all the care he could, was scrupulously correct in his general manners and conversation, and sincerely repented, I hope, of what was wrong in his secret conduct. Of the duties of the First Table no man could be more observant, so far as respects public worship, at least, and reverence for the name of God; and he was remarkable for humility and meekness, as well as for kindly affections. I can add that he was a truly sincere and honest man and, but for the unhappy exception to which I have alluded, "touching the moral law blameless," in as high a degree almost as any man I have known, from the time at least of my first intimate acquaintance with his character till his death. His religion was that of an orthodox Churchman, with a strong and rather bigoted attachment to the establishment and its rites, tho' without any asperity or ill will towards Dissenters; and I think he was rather partial than otherwise to evangelical preachers, provided they were sound Churchmen. To irreligion and disloyalty he had so strong an aversion that all his meekness could hardly restrain him from angry expressions when he heard anything tending that way;

and I heard him one day rebuke, with a boldness contrary
to his nature, a man whom he had much general respect and
deference for because he was apparently commending a
publication which he admitted to be an untrue, tho' plausible
and ingenious, attack on the administration of public justice
in a popular case.

This character of my poor old Father-in-law is not unin-
structive. A single immoral connection, tho' contracted under
circumstances that much mitigated the Sin and made it in a
common, worldly estimate scarcely a sin at all, was enough
to rob him of all the good temporal fruits of the virtues he
possessed except the affection of my dear Nancy and my
friend Tom, his elder children, who truly loved him. They
unavoidably discovered the unfortunate case, notwithstanding
all the anxiety he felt and the delicacy he used to hide it from
them; but they knew too well all the allowances that were
due to him and treated him with the utmost filial respect as
well as affection while they lived; but he was soon deprived
of them and was thrown afterwards, by the effects of that
single transgression, into the hands of worthless and selfish
connections who embittered his declining years and, I
believe, shortened his life. I was not wanting in regard for
him to the last; but his modest and ingenuous feelings
obliged him to seclude himself from me, except when I found
him at his place of business and now and then got him to
see me and his grandchildren at my home. I did not even
know where he lived till I heard that he was dying and went
to it only to find him a corpse. When he found himself in
danger he earnestly requested that I might be sent for; and
a young woman whom he believed to be his daughter
would willingly have complied with his request, but her
husband would not suffer it. A will had been made in their
favor and the sordid man feared, I believe, that I might induce
him to alter it and leave part of the little he had to his Son
William's Widow and children, then in great distress. It was
from them, and with the same view perhaps, that I heard
of his danger and where he was to be found, but too late;
and I found shocking reason to believe that if I had been in
time to call in that surgical assistance which was withheld
till it could be of no use he might have been saved from a

painful death. His features bore afflicting testimony to the sharp sufferings he had endured. Much, very much, had he previously suffered in his feelings and his circumstances for many years by the incorrigible imprudence and bad conduct of William Stent, his last surviving child whom he believed to be his own by nature as well as in law, tho' nobody I believe but himself was of that opinion, among those at least who knew the circumstances of the case. His strong affection for that unfortunate man had given poignancy to those afflictions, which I could easily trace up to the same bitter fountain if the task were not both painful and tedious. Such were the sad consequences of one allowed habitual violation of the Divine law, tho' in the origin of it my poor Father-in-law was more sinned against than sinning. The history of that bad woman, his wife, would still more forcibly illustrate the retributory providence of God. She has also gone to her account, and I wish I could hope as well of her present state as I humbly do of her much injured husband.

It was in the summer of 1783, I think in the month of June, that in pursuance of the plan founded on the urgent considerations I have mentioned I made my dear Nancy my wife. Finding that Shoreditch was the Parish fittest for my purpose, as the marriages by banns there were exceedingly numerous and I had not a single acquaintance in it or its neighbourhood, I applied to the Parish Clerk and found the matter still more easy than I had learnt before; for he told me we had only to take lodgings in his house for a Month, in other words to pay him two or three pounds for certifying that we were Parishoners to the clergyman, and the banns should be called at the end of that period. Far from ever occupying the lodgings, we did not even know where they were; and I dare say the Man had in fact no lodgings to let, tho' doubtless at all times many such nominal tenants. Accordingly, at an appointed day and at the earliest canonical hour, my dear Nancy and I, attended by her Father only, went from North-end Hampstead where they then lived to Shoreditch Church, and the indissoluble knot was tied.

It would not be easy to give a right view of my agitated feelings on this occasion. They were of a mixed nature, or rather alternately those of joy and praise, hope and fear, self-approbation and doubt whether all was right; but on the whole pleasing sensations prevailed, and a pious tho' wavering trust that God would mercifully bless our union. I could not hear the awful adjuration to discover secret impediments, &c., without emotion but was sustained by the reflection that my connection with poor, dear Maria was not a "lawful" nor, with my views and intentions, a conscientious impediment, that it was not a pre-engagement, and that in truth my only engagement to marry was that which I was now fulfilling; nor did I forget that the union was one which if the prudential time for it had come my dear Mother had expressly consented to and approved. The vow of permanent love that I was making was by no means insincere but more cordial perhaps than if my first affections had never varied, for my dear Nancy had risen much in my esteem and gratitude by her generous and amiable conduct under extreme provocations and the unequivocal proofs she had given of a self-devoted attachment to myself. I believe I have before confessed that even her person had become more attractive to me than it was before my infidelity, so that higher considerations apart, I should have preferred her as a woman to any other choice. In one very interesting view my feelings were those of unmixed satisfaction. I had given peace and happiness to her who was so dear to me and who deserved everything good at my hands; and her Father, also, was delivered from his parental anxieties and rejoiced to embrace me as his Son-in-law. His affectionate heart overflowed upon us, and his joy gave the purest satisfaction to hers.

The greatest drawback on every pleasurable emotion was the fear of an accidental discovery of the marriage and its probably fatal consequences to poor Maria. But against this we had taken such precautions as I hoped would preclude all danger. To prevent suspicion in the family we had taken a glass coach for the day, having to return to meet some friends whom Mr. S. had invited to dinner; we went to a place in Town and there dismissed it for an hour or two to call for us there again, meantime walked out and when at some distance took a hackney coach from the stand, dismissing that again at a convenient distance from the Church. No clue was left, therefore, by which even suspicion if excited could take us. The only risk was the highly improbable one that some Person who knew us might be examining for another purpose a Parish Register of marriages lengthened by hundreds of new entries every Month, and accidentally recognize the names and hand writings of our own.

Still the terrible magnitude of the evil gave exaggerated views of the little risk that remained and inspired me often with painful apprehensions; but after a while they grew less from the experience of security, and my mind became more composed and satisfied than it had been since the commencement of my sinborn trials. The pain of irresolution was no more. The step was taken and irrevocable. I had acted, as I hoped, on right principles; and I trusted in the mercy of a compassionate Providence that evil consequences would be averted and happiness at length be the result of perseverance in the self-denying plan I had determined to pursue. Earnest and innumerable were the prayers I put up to that effect; and blessed be the Divine goodness, I did not pray in vain. The only painful emotions that did not soon subside were those which I felt in the presence of Maria, with whom it was of course as necessary as ever that my intercourse should be kept up, and my tender feelings for whom were rather increased than diminished by sentiments of compassion and half-formed remorse which occasionally took their place in my mind. Hitherto I had practised no falsehood or dissimulation with her as to my situation, conduct, or intentions; some necessary reserve both towards her and my dear Nancy as to the time I spent with the other and the feelings I had for her led me unavoidably into verbal insincerities and, I fear, not rarely express verbal misrepresentations or direct falsehoods to them both; but in the main I had nothing substantial to hide from either incompatible with the plan of conduct I had avowed and in which Maria herself had acquiesced. There was a secret, the discovery of which would have made her regard me as a perfidious man, unworthy of her future confidence, and driven her perhaps to despair. Every expression of her tenderness, every testimony of her reliance on my fidelity and honor, was felt by me as a tacit reproach: and there were times when it seemed to me even base and treacherous to allow her to open her heart to me with all the confidence of a fond and faithful wife when I was become the husband of another woman. Reflection, indeed, when I had parted from her, soon restored me in great measure to a more favorable and more equitable judgment of myself. What I had done was with a view to her welfare and happiness much more than my own, and so also was its concealment. Besides, my marriage coupled with the self-denying resolution I had formed with my Wife's and her Father's solemn concurrence was not *in effect* any departure from that line of conduct in which Maria herself had expressly acquiesced and did not prejudice her prospect of being one day my Wife except by precluding a chance which she herself had always regarded as hopeless, and which I had firmly believed to be so, that of my poor Nancy meeting with and accepting the hand of another lover. Should she die in my lifetime my power of making reparation to Maria would be as little impaired as if I had remained a single man, and our union would not be embittered by the self-accusations to which we should both perhaps in that case be exposed. But in the more probable event, a highly probable one considering the climate I was going to, that of their both surviving me, I should leave her a simpathising and faithful friend, of which had I acted otherwise she would have been destitute and who would in the meantime supply my place to her in my absence as well as it could be supplied, a friend whose interest as well as wish it now was to perform towards her essential offices of friendship of which no woman could be more likely to stand in need : that in particular of enabling her to gratify in some degree her maternal feelings without danger to her character. It is true that Maria expected, and afterwards supposed herself to receive, this kindness from my dear Nancy without the foundation I had laid for it ; but it was from the want of sufficient judgment and reflection. Mr. Stent was a necessary party to the means by which alone the object could be accomplished ; and it was too much to expect from the Father if not from the daughter, unless her character had become my charge and was identified with my own honor in future life, that they should both perform in my absence offices towards an illegitimate child of mine which, considering the notoriety of a long attachment between us, might be perilous to her own reputation.

Such considerations, but above all the consciousness of right and self-denying intentions, reasonably allayed the painful feelings I have mentioned and saved me from abiding self-reproaches; but still my new situation made my intercourse with Maria and her fond, unsuspecting confidence hard to reconcile with ingenuous and honorary feelings in my language and deportment towards her. I wished more than ever to escape from such painful embarrassments by a speedy migration. This, however, could not be accomplished so soon as at the time of my marriage I expected. We soon after learned that difficulties had arisen between the British and French Commanders in the West Indies respecting the terms on which the captured Islands were to be mutually evacuated by the respective Garrisons and restored to their former Owners pursuant to the Treaty of Peace, which threatened to delay, and I think eventually did delay, the restitution of St. Christopher to the utmost day of the prescribed period, or some time beyond it. It was expected, if I remember right, early in October; but did not take place till the very end of that, or the beginning of the following, year. It was my Brother's advice to me to be there at the change of Flags, because much law business suspended in expectation of that event would immediately afterwards be prosecuted and make a good harvest for the lawyers. Accordingly, I resolved to go out with one of the earliest Ships of the Season, which were expected, I think, to sail early in September but from the above or other causes were detained till near the end of the following Month. My preparations for my departure, however, began soon after my marriage; and as I had among other things an entire law library to provide, which I endeavoured to do progressively on the cheapest terms, they were not soon completed.

The delay enabled me to witness some happy effects of the measure I had taken, and such as gave the pleasing promise that my best hopes from it would not be disappointed. Tho' my dear Nancy's conduct towards Maria had always been forbearant and generous and kind also, considering the trying circumstances of the case, and they occasionally visited each other, I could not flatter myself that there was much cordiality or friendship on either side; and perhaps the suspicions which Mr. Stent had certainly conceived made his manners towards Maria not such as favor'd her being a frequent guest at his house. But now the daughter cultivated her society assiduously, and she met at North End the kindest hospitalities on every visit there. Maria on her part was not slow to meet their advances. She had once, as I have mentioned, been much attached to my dear Nancy, as much I believe as she ever was to any human being, myself excepted, and strange tho' it may seem had never lost a regard for her and relish for her company. It was the ordinary influence of a superior understanding over an inferior, for my dear Nancy was a very sensible woman and had more acquired knowledge, being always very fond of reading, than well educated young women of that day usually possessed. She was also, from a native liveliness, good nature and susceptibility of feeling, a pleasing and interesting companion; and Maria found charms in her conversation beyond that of any other female with whom she had ever been acquainted. It is due to her to say that she always did justice with me to these attractions of her rival, even while they were at variance; and I believe it would have been more difficult than it was to obtain her acquiescence in the line of conduct and the mutual sacrifices which justice, penitence, and prudence dictated so strongly to us both if personal feelings for the friend she had injured had not seconded the suggestions of compassion and remorse. I was much less surprised, therefore, than pleased to find that my dear Nancy's increased attentions were very willingly and cordially received and to perceive before my departure that mutual intimacy and confidence were perfectly restored between them.

I had, also, reason to be satisfied with the first fruits of my plan in relation to the child. My dear Nancy was introduced at Bletchingly by Maria, my still supposed Sister, as her friend and a lady to whom I was engaged and whose Father had engaged to concur with Maria in the charge or superintendance of him during my absence from England. I think that his kind old Nurse and her family were also informed that if my union with Miss S. took place the child was to be adopted by her and pass for our own, and their affection for him had become so strong that they on this account felt themselves the more strongly bound to secrecy as to all they knew or might accidentally discover or suspect. Mr. Stent likewise was brought forward as the friend and future Father-in-law who would be responsible for all expenses and through whom my correspondence with them was to be carried on and my remittances made, and the kind old Man then and afterwards acted up to the part he had undertaken as cordially as if in the origin of this delicate charge there had been nothing which he had a right to complain of. I had the further satisfaction to perceive on every successive visit to Bletchingly a progressive tho' slow improvement in the health of my poor, dear child, tho' his frame was still very delicate and his nervous system so much injured by the bad treatment he had been rescued from as to make him extremely timid and subject to agitation of spirits from every trifling cause of apprehension and surprise. He was still extremely backward for his age, and the morbid enlargement of his head, tho' a good deal diminished, was still sufficiently alarming. The sutures were as open and wide almost as those of a new-born infant. I should still, in short, have had slender ground to hope for his preservation to manhood, but for reliance on that bountiful Providence which in answer to my prayers had thus far rescued and preserved him. This reliance was greatly strengthened by reflection on the singular means by which I had been led to place him in a situation so propitious and by the unequivocal proofs that I had of the truly maternal tenderness with which he was treated by the worthy old woman and her daughter. His great fondness for them was one of the pleasing proofs of it. I was much gratified also to find that such intellectual and moral culture as his age admitted was carefully, judiciously, and piously given by them and, aided no doubt by natural disposition, had produced the effects of meekness, quietness, and gentleness of temper and made him a remarkably amiable child.

Tho' it pleased a compassionate Providence thus far to mitigate the ill consequences of my sins and to encourage the hope of their final termination, much of bosom suffering and much of deep anxiety remained; and they naturally

increased to a very painful degree as the time of my departure from England drew nigh. During the last month that preceded it my sufferings were exquisite and such as the daily,
I might almost say hourly, resource of earnest prayer alone
could have enabled me to sustain. The Ship in which I had
engaged my passage, the Lady Alleyne, Captn. Goodwin,
was detained as usual in the River long after the first
appointed time for her sailing; and the Passengers for some
weeks were kept in almost daily expectation of a Summons to
set off to meet at Ramsgate to embark on board her in the
Downs. The dreaded separation from the dear objects of my
affection and anxiety was, therefore, constantly before my
eyes and theirs as an event not above a day or two distant,
and every preparation being made I had no longer anything
to divert my thoughts from the anticipation of its pangs. One
of them, indeed, I had sustained before the first appointment
was broken. I went to Bletchingly, fondled my dear Baby
for an hour or two and then, giving him what was most likely
to prove a last embrace, resigned him to his good old Nurse,
whose tears were hardly less copious than my own. For the
greater freedom both in grief and prayer I returned by my
oft-trodden solitary walk over the hills and wild commons
that lie between that place and Croydon; and rarely I
believe has pitying Heaven been addressed with prayers
more earnest, or from a more afflicted heart, than those
which I offered up all the way for blessings upon my poor
child, and especially that I might meet him again in this life
nor did I cease till a strong conviction was impressed upon
my mind that my prayers were heard and granted. This
pang, therefore, was over; but I had two more to sustain, in
which my own feelings were to be aggravated by those of
others, and my heart shrunk from the prospect of them.[1]

[1] At this point, some time in the last six years of his life—I make a guess,
from the rate of composition in other parts of the *Memoirs*, that it was as late
as 1829—Stephen left off. The absence of end punctuation leaves doubt
whether he had completed the pre-emigration phase of his history, or whether
he was interrupted in a compound sentence to which he never returned. It is
to be regretted that Stephen's strength, or interest, did not allow him to
complete his plan. Not only should we have known more than we do about
an intrinsically interesting personality; we should also have had a substantial
contribution to the history of England, and indeed of the British Empire, in
the turbulent years from 1783 to 1832.

Genealogical Tree

DESCENDANTS OF JAMES STEPHEN OF ARDENBRAUGHT, GREAT-GRANDFATHER OF THE WRITER OF THE *Memoirs*, WHO FLOURISHED IN THE SEVENTEENTH CENTURY

(The numeral preceding a name indicates the number of generations after James Stephen of Ardenbraught. Indentation under the name of a person indicates descent from that person. This table does not pretend to completeness.)

1. James Stephen (*d.c.* 1750), grandfather of the writer of the *Memoirs*, farmer of Aberdeenshire, *m.* Mary Brown.

   2. Mary Stephen (1724–1816), *m.* Mr. Nuccoll.

   2. Anne Stephen, *m.* Mr. Calder.

   2. Alexander Stephen (*c.* 1729–1800).

   2. William Stephen (1731–1781), West Indies planter.

   2. James Stephen (*c.* 1733–1779), father of the writer of the *Memoirs*, writer on Imprisonment for Debt, *m.* Sibella Milner (*d.* 1775).

      3. William Stephen (1756–1807), West Indies planter, *m.* Mary Forbes.

         4. Mary Stephen, *m.* Rev. George Hodson, archdeacon of Stafford.

            5. Rev. G. H. Hodson, author of *Hodson of Hodson's Horse*.

            5. William Stephen Raikes Hodson (1821–1858), commander of "Hodson's Horse," *m.* Mrs. Mitford.

         4. There were other children of William Stephen.

3. JAMES STEPHEN (1758–1832), writer of the *Memoirs*, master in chancery, *m.* (1) Anna Stent (1758–1796), (2) Mrs. Sarah Wilberforce Clarke (*d.* 1816).

4. William Stephen (1781–1867), vicar of Bledlow and of Great Stagsden, *m.* Miss Grace. He was James Stephen's illegitimate child by "Maria Rivers."

4. Henry John Stephen (1787–1864), serjeant-at-law, author of *A Treatise on Pleading* and of *New Commentaries on the Laws of England*, *m.* Mary Morison.

    5. Sarah Stephen (1816–1895), author of *Anna; or, the Daughter at Home.*

    5. James Stephen (1820–1894), judge of county court at Lincoln, editor of several editions of his father's *New Commentaries*.

        6. H. St. James Stephen, editor of later editions of his grandfather's *New Commentaries*.

        6. Guy Neville Stephen (1858–1932), physiologist.

4. Sir James Stephen (1789–1859), colonial under-secretary, historian, and *Edinburgh* reviewer, *m.* Jane Catherine Venn.

    5. Herbert Venn Stephen (1822–1846), army officer.

    5. Frances Wilberforce Stephen (1824–1824).

    5. Sir James Fitzjames Stephen, Bart. (1829–1894), judge of the High Court of Justice, *m.* Mary Richenda Cunningham.

        6. Katherine Stephen (1856–1924), principal of Newnham College, Cambridge.

        6. Sir Herbert Stephen, Bart. (1857–1932), clerk of assizes for the northern circuit and writer on legal subjects, *m.* Mary Hermione Cunningham.

6. James Kenneth Stephen (1859–1892), barrister, author of *Lapsus Calami and Other Verses.*

6. Sir Harry Lushington Stephen, Bart. (1860–1945), judge of the High Court of Justice, Calcutta, and later alderman of the County of London, *m.* Barbara Nightingale.

   7. Sir James Alexander Stephen, Bart. (1908——).

6. Margaret Emily Stephen (1861–1862).

6. Helen Margaret Stephen (1862–1908).

6. Frances Cunningham Stephen (1863–1880).

6. Leslie Henry Stephen (1867–1867).

6. Rosamond Emily Stephen (1868–1951), church worker in Ireland, particularly for the Guild of Witness.

6. Dorothea Jane Stephen (1871 ——), religious teacher in India, author of Studies in *Early Indian Thought* and other works.

5. Sir Leslie Stephen (1832–1904), editor, man of letters, philosopher, *m.* (1) Harriet Thackeray (*d.* 1875), (2) Julia Jackson Duckworth (*d.* 1895).

6. Laura Makepeace Stephen (1870–1946).

6. Vanessa Stephen (1879 ——), painter, *m.* Clive Bell.

   7. Julian Bell (1908–1937), poet and university teacher.

   7. Quentin Stephen Bell (1910 ——), author of *On Human Finery*, *m.* Anne Olivier Popham.

   7. Angelica Bell (1918 ——), *m.* David Garnett.

8. Amaryllis Virginia Garnett (1943 ——).

8. Henrietta Catherine Vanessa Garnett (1945 ——).

8. Frances Olivia Garnett (1946 ——).

8. Nerissa Stephen Garnett (1946 ——).

6. Julian Thoby Prinsep Stephen (1880–1906).

6. Virginia Stephen (1882–1941), novelist and essayist, *m*. Leonard Woolf.

6. Adrian Leslie Stephen (1883–1948), doctor and psycho-analyst, *m*. Karen Costelloe.

7. Ann Stephen (1915 ——), *m*. Richard Laurence Millington Synge.

8. Jane Synge (1943 ——).

8. Elizabeth Synge (1944 ——).

8. Thomas Millington Synge (1945 ——).

8. Matthew Millington Synge (1948 ——).

8. Patrick Millington Synge (1951 ——).

8. Alexander Millington Synge (1953 ——).

7. Judith Stephen (1918 ——), *m*. Nigel Henderson.

8. Clement Drusilla Henderson (1944 ——).

8. Justin Henderson (1946 ——) .

5. Caroline Emilia Stephen (1834–1909), author of *Quaker Strongholds* and other works.

4. Two children of JAMES STEPHEN died in infancy.

4. Sibella Stephen (1792–1869), *m*. W. A. Garrett.

4. Sir George Stephen (1794–1879), author of *Adventures of a Gentleman in Search of a Horse* and other miscellaneous works, solicitor and barrister in England and Australia, *m.* Miss Ravenscroft.

    5. Alfred Stephen, churchman in Australia.

    5. James Wilberforce Stephen, judge in Australia.

    5. There were five other children of Sir George Stephen.

4. Anne Mary Stephen (1796–1878), *m.* Thomas Edward Dicey (*d.* 1858).

    5. Henry Dicey.

    5. Frank Dicey.

    5. Edward Dicey (1832–1911), author and journalist.

    5. Albert Venn Dicey (1835–1922), Vinerian Professor of English Law.

3. Mary Stephen (*b.c.* 1762), died in infancy.

3. Sibella Stephen (*b.c.* 1765), *m.* W. M. Morison, editor of *Decisions of Court of Sessions*.

3. Hannah Stephen (*b.c.* 1767), *m.* William Farish (1759–1837), Jacksonian Professor at Cambridge.

3. Elizabeth Stephen (*b.c.* 1769), *m.* William Milner.

3. John Stephen (1771–1834), judge of Supreme Court of New South Wales, *m.* Miss Passmore.

    4. Sir Alfred Stephen (1802–1894), chief justice of Supreme Court of New South Wales.

        5. Sir Matthew Henry Stephen (1828–1920), senior puisne judge of Supreme Court of New South Wales.

        5. Sir Alfred Stephen was twice married and had five sons and four daughters by one marriage and four sons and five daughters by the other. At the time of his death he had more than a hundred living descendants.

15

2. Robert Stephen (*d.c.* 1760).

2. Thomas Stephen (*d.c.* 1775), *m.* Miss Coker.

2. John Stephen (*d.c.* 1770).

2. David Stephen (*c.* 1742–1762).

1. John Stephen (*d.c.* 1750), son of James Stephen of Arden-braught.

    4. A great-grandson of this John Stephen was Oscar Leslie Stephen (1819–1898), railway director.

        5. James Young Stephen.

           6. Albert Alexander Leslie Stephen (1879–1914), officer in Scots Guards.

        5. Oscar Leslie Stephen, Jr.

        5. Sir Alexander Condie Stephen (1850–1908), diplomat.

INDEX

Where necessary to distinguish persons of the same name, I have indicated relationship to "J.S.", the author of the Memoirs.

PRINTED IN GREAT BRITAIN BY
EBENEZER BAYLIS AND SON, LTD., THE
TRINITY PRESS, WORCESTER, AND LONDON